The Lost State of Franklin

JOHN SEVIER
From portrait in Lobby of Hotel John Sevier,
Johnson City, Tennessee.

HISTORY
of the
LOST STATE
of FRANKLIN

—REVISED EDITION—

Samuel Cole Williams
Former Justice of the Supreme Court of Tennessee

"The most famous movement for the establishment of a separate State was made by the settlers near the head-waters of the Tennessee shortly after the Revolution was ended."
—*McLaughlin in "The Confederation and the Constitution."*

HERITAGE BOOKS
2020

HERITAGE BOOKS
AN IMPRINT OF HERITAGE BOOKS, INC.

Books, CDs, and more—Worldwide

For our listing of thousands of titles see our website
at
www.HeritageBooks.com

A Facsimile Reprint
Published 2020 by
HERITAGE BOOKS, INC.
Publishing Division
5810 Ruatan Street
Berwyn Heights, Md. 20740

Originally published 1933 New York

— Publisher's Notice —
The first page of this facsimile reprint is page iii rather than page i. Apparently, some blank pages were ommitted, but no text has been lost. In reprints such as this, it is often not possible to remove blemishes from the original. We feel the contents of this book warrant its reissue despite these blemishes and hope you will agree and read it with pleasure.

International Standard Book Numbers
Paperbound: 978-0-7884-2066-5
Clothbound: 978-0-7884-8416-2

TO

MATTHEW MARSHALL NEIL

Formerly Chief Justice of the Supreme Court of Tennessee

In recognition of his large and valuable contribution to the jurisprudence of Tennessee, and in appreciation of the comradeship of years spent in joint service

PREFACE TO FIRST EDITION

The author has had his home for more than a generation in Washington County, Tennessee, which was the midland and capital county of the State of Franklin. The romantic history of that Commonwealth, unique in American history, and the history of the decades that preceded its rise and fall, have always appealed to Tennesseans, and peculiarly so to one who lives in the immediate region where the early history of the Tennessee country was made.

The collection of Tennesseana was deliberately chosen by the author as his hobby, and this in turn led to research in the leading archives and libraries of America, in intervals of leisure, and to the making of notes on the early history of his native State. On retiring from public service in 1918, an opportunity was presented to carry out an earlier conception and plan—to avail of these materials in writing three or more volumes on the early history of Tennessee; and, in so doing, to treat of that history by eras or periods.

The Franklin State epoch was chosen for development first, though the plan covers the discussion of an anterior era, under the title of *The Dawn of Tennessee History*. Another work of the series is *Early Travels in the Tennessee Country*.

It is conceived that this plan will the better permit of a detailed and definitive treatment of each period. There can be no excuse for an historical work which merely revamps and repeats what Haywood and Ramsey wrote, though the histories of those writers are now out of print. Any one who attempts to write of the early history of Tennessee will find himself debtor to both. Ramsey borrowed heavily from Haywood; but he had access to materials that his predecessor had not—documents handed down by his father, Francis A. Ramsey, Sevier, and other Franklin leaders. However, Ramsey wrote long before valuable source materials had been made accessible, in the archives of Virginia, North Carolina, and Georgia. Coming later into the field, Roosevelt in preparing his *Winning of the West* was enabled to draw in a measure upon such ampler stores of information which had then been assembled, and arranged for consultation by historical students.

The purpose of the author has been to extend the research, to correct errors and supplement the work of these earlier writers, and to amplify even to the point of risking the lodgement of a valid criticism of over-elaboration. If explanation is necessary, it is to be found in the fact that source materials relating to Tennessee history, in the archives of that and other States, have never been collected and published. This seemed to warrant the bringing forward in text, notes or appendices of many documents which otherwise might have been summarized. The documents have been edited, in disregard of rules laid down for historical writing. This was almost compelled since Ramsey modernized the documents he set out in his text and notes; and these, having been destroyed by fire since he wrote, cannot be given in their original form. Many of these constituted essential parts of the story of The Lost State. To incorporate them as edited by Ramsey, leaving others unchanged as to spelling and syntax, would be unfair to some of the pioneers who wrote the documents and would detract from the symmetry of the volume.

It has been in purpose to treat of the State of Franklin not merely as a local movement, but to give it a broader setting: to discuss the effort to establish a new State, as the fourteenth in the Union, as a part of the movement for separation that was at that time rife on all frontiers, eastern as well as western. Franklin was without doubt the most pronounced and significant manifestation of the spirit of separation which gave deep concern to the national leaders. No other movement for separate statehood reached, even approximately, the stage attained by Franklin—that of a *de facto* government, waging war, negotiating treaties and functioning for a term of years in the three great departments that mark an American State, the legislative, executive, and judicial.

The author has endeavored to make the volume one of value to those interested in genealogical research. He has put on the printed page the names of minor participants in the struggle, for or against separate statehood. Of the leaders, a fuller account is given. For some of these, even, this is a rescue of their names and deeds from near-oblivion. Aid in this effort has been received from contributions made from time to time to local newspapers by such writers as Doctor George F. Mellen and Selden Nelson, of Knoxville, A. B. Wilson, of Greeneville, and the late John S. Mathes, of Jonesborough. The author's thanks are due also to Dr. Edmund C. Burnett, of the department of historical research of the Carnegie Institution, and to Mr. W. W. DeRenne, of "Wormsloe," Savannah, Georgia, owner of the invaluable DeRenne Collection, for kindnesses shown while the volume was in preparation.

SAMUEL C. WILLIAMS

Emory University
Atlanta, Georgia
January 15, 1924

CONTENTS

PREFACE vii
INTRODUCTION xv
CHAPTER
    I. THE CONTROL OF THE WEST. 1
    II. GENESIS OF THE FRANKLIN MOVEMENT . . . 5
    III. THE GREAT BEND OF THE TENNESSEE 13
    IV. THE FIRST CESSION ACT—1784. 19
    V. MOVEMENT FOR A SEPARATE GOVERNMENT IN THE WEST—1784 27
    VI. REPEAL OF THE CESSION ACT 35
    VII. THE FIRST CONSTITUTIONAL CONVENTION—1784. 39
    VIII. THE FRANKLIN MOVEMENT IN VIRGINIA . . . 45
    IX. THE FIRST GENERAL ASSEMBLY—1785. . . . 56
    X. MANIFESTO AND COUNTER MANIFESTO—1785. . 67
    XI. FRANKLIN'S CAUSE BEFORE CONGRESS—1785. . 82
    XII. SECOND SESSION OF THE ASSEMBLY—1785. . . 90
    XIII. THE SECOND CONSTITUTIONAL CONVENTION—1785 94
    XIV. CLEAR SAILING—1786 99
    XV. STORM CLOUDS GATHER—1786 106
    XVI. FRANKLIN SENDS A COMMISSION TO CAROLINA—1786. 114
    XVII. SPAIN AND CLOSURE OF THE MISSISSIPPI—1786 . 123
    XVIII. FACTORS THAT WORKED FOR CONTINUED SEPARATION—1787. 126
    XIX. EFFORTS TO COMPROMISE FUTILE—1787 . . . 140
    XX. A HIGH DEBATE—1787 149
    XXI. DEFEAT OF COMPROMISE AND RESULTING VIOLENCE 161
    XXII. A CRY FOR HELP FROM THE CUMBERLAND—1787 . 170
    XXIII. FRANKLIN AND GEORGIA—1787. 177
    XXIV. FRANKLIN AND THE WEST IN THE CONSTITUTIONAL CONVENTION—1787 183
    XXV. CLOSE OF THE CRUCIAL YEAR—1787 189
    XXVI. THE SEVIER-TIPTON SKIRMISH—1788 198

XXVII.	Occurrences on the Border—1788	210
XXVIII.	The Lesser Franklin	218
XXIX.	The Arrest of Sevier—1788	231
XXX.	The Spanish Intrigue—1788	235
XXXI.	North Carolina Convention and Assembly—1788	245
XXXII.	The Second Cession and Afterwards	249
XXXIII.	Modes of Life	255
XXXIV.	Travelers in Franklin	259
XXXV.	Religion in Franklin	270
XXXVI.	The People of Franklin	275
XXXVII.	Survival of the Conception and Spirit	282

THE FRANKLINITES

John Sevier	289
Arthur Campbell	291
William Cocke	294
Judge David Campbell	298
Landon Carter	299
James White	301
Gilbert Christian	303
Joseph Hardin	304
Charles Robertson	306
Daniel Kennedy	307
George Elholm	309
Henry Conway	310
Francis A. Ramsey	311
William Cage	313
Stockley Donelson	313
Joshua Gist	314
John Anderson	315
John Menefee	315
Thomas Amis	315
David Campbell	316
Samuel Doak	317
George Doherty	317
Nathaniel Evans	319
Samuel Handley	319
Samuel Houston	320
Moses and David Looney	322

WILLIAM MURPHEY	323
SAMUEL NEWELL	323
ALEXANDER OUTLAW	324
JAMES REESE	325
CHARLES ROBERTSON, OF GREENE	325
JAMES RODDY	326
VALENTINE SEVIER, II	326
ANDREW TAYLOR	327
PETER TURNEY	327
GEORGE VINCENT	328
SAMUEL WEAR	328

THE ANTIS

EVAN SHELBY	330
JOSEPH MARTIN	331
JOHN TIPTON	334
THOMAS HUTCHINGS	335
ROBERT LOVE	336
THOMAS LOVE	336
GEORGE MAXWELL	337
PETER PARKINSON	337
JAMES STUART	337

APPENDIX A
   THE CONSTITUTION OF THE STATE OF FRANKLIN . . . 339

APPENDIX B
   PETITION OF THE INHABITANTS OF THE WESTERN COUNTRY 348

APPENDIX C
   PROCEEDINGS OF THE CONVENTION OF 1789 356

BIBLIOGRAPHY 359
INDEX 363

INTRODUCTION

The reward of the historian lies in the unearthing of facts important in the past life of his people and in interpreting these findings in their proper proportions and settings. Judge Samuel C. Williams enjoys the satisfaction of having drawn from the mists of the past the dim and barely distinct outlines of a Commonwealth which flourished in the western part of the State of North Carolina in pioneer days. He has exercised his careful judgment and mature consideration of material to draw from little known sources the many details which make up a clear picture of the community of settlers who aspired to establish the fourteenth state of the Union.

With the patience and thoroughness which belong alone to the competent scholar, he has pieced together bits of material collected during years of searching through forgotten records. He has utilized his intimate knowledge of the men and the events connected with the life of the Southwest and of Tennessee to interpret these facts clearly and impartially. The student of the period and the section looks to this work with complete confidence in its thoroughness, integrity, and accuracy. These qualitites make another edition of this book highly gratifying.

The State of Franklin presented the most striking example of those separatist movements common on the frontier in the early days of the nation. The sectionalism which existed between the East and the West has never been thoroughly studied or sufficiently presented by the interpreters of American history. The spirit of independence displayed by the frontiersmen asserted itself in this movement by the men on the western waters. Their grievances against the mother State, their fear of continued domination, the subordination of their interests to those of the eastern part of North Carolina, their apparent abandonment by that government, and their resentment against real and fancied wrongs led them to embark upon a new experiment in self-government. They believed it to be the only hope of maintaining their liberty. Jealousy and discord among its citizens contributed to its decline and failure, but in its inception it had given great promise of success and had expressed the independence of the West against political and economic subserviency. Judge Williams has given to those interested in a study of the period a clear picture of this State. In reality, he has discovered again the Lost State of Franklin.

CARL S. DRIVER

Vanderbilt University
March 30, 1933

The Lost State of Franklin

CHAPTER I

THE CONTROL OF THE WEST

Years before the Declaration of Independence was proclaimed, spontaneous migrations of restless pioneers of the western parts of Virginia and North Carolina had formed a nucleus of civilization in the secluded valley interposed between the Great Smoky mountains on the east and the Cumberland mountains on the west, through which flowed the Watauga and the Nolachucky rivers. This community was destined to play a most important part in the successful termination of the Revolutionary War, and in the winning of the West. It was the germ-cell of the colonization and civilization of the Upper Southwest.

The earliest settlers supposed themselves to be within the jurisdiction of Virginia, but too far removed to have the benefit of the protection of her government. The Watauga pioneers were equal to the emergency. They saw that in their isolation they must depend upon themselves. Accordingly, in the spring of 1772, they formed an Association and promulgated articles for the government of the settlement. This agreement is known as the "Articles of the Watauga Association," and notable in that it was the first written constitution adopted by a community of American-born freemen.[1] Lord Dunmore, in reporting to Lord Dartmouth (May 16, 1774) said that they had "to all intents and purposes erected themselves into, though an inconsiderable, yet a separate State."

From this infant settlement, Captain Evan Shelby led a company of fifty volunteers to participate in the battle of Point Pleasant in Lord Dunmore's War of 1774. The following year, by the aid of the settlers on the Watauga, the Cherokee Indians' claim to large portions of the Kentucky and Cumberland regions was pur-

---

[1] "One can find no more striking fact in American history, nor one more typical, than the simple ease with which these frontiersmen on the banks of the western waters, on the threshold of the central valley of the continent, finding themselves beyond the reach of eastern law, formed an association and exercised the rights and privileges of self-government."—McLaughlin, *The Confederation and the Constitution*, 132.

in one hundred miles of the Atlantic ocean. It was not conceived that they extended three thousand miles. Lord Camden considers the claims to the south sea as what can never be reduced to practice. Pennsylvania has no right to interfere in those claims, but she has a right to say that she will not confederate unless those claims are cut off. I wish the colonies themselves would cut off those claims."

Harrison, of Virginia, boldly asserted: "By its charter Virginia owns to the south sea. Gentlemen shall not pare away the Colony of Virginia."[6]

Congress hesitated to bring the issue to a decision. Maryland formally instructed her delegates that "policy and justice require that a country unsettled at the commencement of this war, claimed by the British crown and ceded to it by the Treaty of Paris, if wrested from the common enemy by the blood and treasure of the thirteen States, should be considered as common property, subject to be parceled out with free governments."

North Carolina stood firmly by the side of Virginia in the struggle which well-nigh imperiled the formation of the Union of the Confederation. The weight of these and other claimant States was so great that when the Articles of Confederation were adopted the ownership and control of the West was left unsolved. That instrument incorporated the following provision in relation to the admission into the Union of new States: "No other Colony shall be admitted into the same, unless such admission be agreed to by nine States." The crucial question of sovereign power and jurisdiction was left open to vex and distract Congress and people alike in after years.

---

[6] John Adams's *Works*, II, 492–502.

CHAPTER II

Genesis of the Franklin Movement

In the uncertainty as to whether the Union had succeeded to the rights exercised by the British crown, the endeavors of the national legislature took the direction of bringing pressure to bear on the claimant States to cede their back lands to the general government.

Congress, on September 6, 1780, on motion of Joseph Jones, of Virginia, seconded by James Madison, resolved "that in case the recommendations to the States of Virginia, North Carolina and Georgia to cede to the United States a portion of their unappropriated western territory shall be complied with, the territory so ceded shall be laid out in separate States at such times and in such manner as Congress shall hereafter direct."[1]

By a resolution of October 10, 1780, it was more explicitly set forth by Congress, that such new States should be republican in form, and "members of the federal union and have the same rights of sovereignty, freedom and independence as the other States."

This is the first action of Congress in reference to new States on the western waters, and the first hint that a State in the hinterland, such as the State of Franklin, might come into existence in the near future.

The assertion of a purpose on the part of Congress to create new States was construed, it seems, in some quarters, to have been a declaration of sovereignty in the United States over the western country.[2] Information of these resolutions, in time, reached the settlements on the Holston and Watauga rivers.

A leading spirit on the upper reaches of the Holston, in Virginia, was Colonel Arthur Campbell. His progenitors emigrated from Northern Ireland to Pennsylvania, and thence to Augusta county

---

[1] *Journal Cont. Congress*, XVII, 808.

[2] *Journal of Congress*, III, 235. A report of a committee of Congress to examine the claims of Virginia, (filed November 3, 1781) proceeded on the theory that the western lands had, as crown lands, passed in devolution to the United States as an entity; but Congress itself did not so resolve.

in the Valley of Virginia, where Arthur Campbell was born in
1742. A few years before the Revolutionary War, he removed to
the Holston river section, then a wilderness; and there along with
his cousin, General William Campbell, he was active in the leadership of his people, serving as county lieutenant, legislator and Indian campaigner.

In the brain of this virile and strong-willed man, possessed of
Scotch-Irish initiative, courage and tenacity, was formed the first
conception of a separate State for the sturdy population which was
then flowing into the valleys of the Holston and its tributaries, in
South-western Virginia and the close-lying settlements to the
south in North Carolina.

What may be called the genesis of the State of Franklin was this
document circulated (evidently early in January, 1782) by Colonel
Campbell among the settlers on the border:

A Scheme for obtaining the sense of the inhabitants of the Western Country on the subject of the late Resolves of Congress declaring the sovereignty over the same to be in the United States.

1st. That Selectmen or Deputies be chosen for the five southwestern counties of Virginia and the counties of Washington and
Sullivan in North Carolina to meet at Abingdon the third Wednesday in April, 1782.

2nd. That in order that the representation be adequate, let the
Deputies be in number proportionate to the number of farmers
above eighteen years of age, allowing one Deputy for every hundred such farmers.

3rd. That the election be held at the respective Court Houses
on the third Tuesday in the month of March next, by the same officers and under the same regulations as elections for delegates are
held.

4th. The business and power of Deputies when convened to be
the consideration of the late Resolves of Congress respecting the
Western Country, and to adopt such measures as may be adjudged
proper by a majority for the interest and safety of their constituents as members of the American Union.

5th. The representation to continue one year, in which time the
Deputies may adjourn from time to time and to such places within
the Western Counties as may be found most convenient.

A search has not disclosed whether an election was held in
March, 1782. If, so it was not one of such official character as to
lead to certification and preservation.

On May 1, 1782, Congress, which in the preceding year had
declined to accept a cession from Virginia of her western lands be-

cause of conditions attached, earnestly recommended to the State of Virginia that, by a proper act of cession, her claims be surrendered to all lands "beyond a reasonable western boundary" and free of all conditions and restrictions.

That Arthur Campbell continued in earnest efforts to establish a new State at that time appears from a letter which he wrote to Arthur Lee, of Virginia, June 9, 1782:

Resolving in my mind the substance of the papers lately transmitted from Congress, I shall now take this opportunity of troubling you with a few sentiments.

I suppose it will be the policy of the Assembly to instruct their delegates to claim to the Ohio as the western bounds of the State. I could wish that Congress would admit that as our boundary for the present; because when a new State is laid off, I trust we will be more competent to fix its limits and prescribe conditions than men perhaps under an improper bias and very little acquainted with our municipal regulations.

Should not this claim succeed, I would call it a reasonable western boundary, and an ample cession, to give up the lands on the Ohio, below the mouth of the Great Kanawha and west of the Auscioto Mountains; because the Auscioto is an Indian descriptive. A line run S.W. from the mouth of Green Briar to the Carolina line would be near the thing. It should be the last retreat, the ridge and the mountains that divide the Eastern and Western Waters. Because in that case the people in the two southwestern counties, Montgomery and Washington (which contains an extent of 150 miles by 40 or 50) would necessarily be obliged to associate with the inhabitants of North Carolina situated on the heads of the Cherokee [Tennessee] river, and have in contemplation a new State in that beautiful valley of which the Cherokees are yet the principal possessors. It will be more inconvenient for that valley to be connected with Kentucky, than remain an appendage to the eastern parts.

It to me appears a very unwise temper to talk of force, spilling of blood, or persecution, to retain more dominion under the fallacious idea it will give us weight in the continental scale, and in the eye of Europe. I would rather conjecture that abolishing slavery, or sending away the blacks, introducing artists and other emigrants from Europe, wise laws, pure manners, and a predominance of virtue, would make us truly respectable and powerful. Truly weighty is the consideration that when a separation takes place, it may be like good friends, promoting reciprocal interests, and happy in seeing each other so well. I think such an event might be brought about by the same temper as the division of a county. The Chesapeake may long be the mart of the Western Country, except for exports. This will be a channel for intercourse;

and might not wise men or rather wise legislators improve it to be a very beneficial one?

It was some entertainment to me to be frequently told of the sentiments of individuals respecting my conduct lately in the Western Country; some considered that I was aiming at public good, others private aggrandizement. To an enlightened and unbiased mind, I will always take pleasure to give an explication. I have hitherto endeavoured by my political conduct to be guided by two principal landmarks: the Constitution and the *voice of the people*. Whilst I persevere under this description, I shall hope to be approved of by wise republicans and good men. [Marked "confidential."][3]

This letter discloses that Colonel Campbell's efforts in behalf of the new State had caused no inconsiderable stir in Virginia. His conduct was criticized and resented by a faction in Southwest Virginia which was in opposition to Campbell and his friends, on this and other questions of the day. For years the Campbells had been in practically undisputed leadership in that section. General William Campbell, one of the heroes of the King's Mountain campaign, had but recently died (August 22, 1781) while in military service against Lord Cornwallis near Williamsburg and Yorktown; and his coöperation was lost to his kinsman.

About the same year, 1781, a forceful character, General William Russell, moved into the Campbell neighborhood. He had been educated at William and Mary College, and, serving as a captain in the French and Indian War, had risen to the rank of colonel and brigadier-general in the Revolutionary War. He had long been engaged as a soldier in the exploration and protection of this part of the frontier. Of commanding presence and cultured, General Russell paid court to Mrs. Elizabeth Campbell, the widow of General William Campbell, who was a sister of Patrick Henry, and to whom Russell was married in 1783. Colonel Arthur Campbell's wife was a sister of General Campbell. The stage was thus set for a close alliance of Arthur Campbell with Russell, or for disagreements engendered by resentment, jealousy and rivalry. "Beneath Russell's polished exterior there was a proud and stern nature, and imperious temper."[4] He was by no means disposed to act as a subordinate of

---
[3] *Calendar Virginia State Papers*, III, 414.
[4] Preston, *Sketch of Mrs. Elizabeth Russell*, 21. It seems that General Russell's temperament led to something like a family feud. "The discipline in his family was austere, and so harshly did it press upon his step-daughter, Sarah B. Campbell, that

Colonel Campbell, and a breach between the two was the outcome.

The two men had served, in 1776, as commissioners to take evidence in behalf of Virginia in respect to the claims of Richard Henderson and his associates to the Transylvania Country[5] and they had also served together as delegates in the House of Burgesses, but they were not suited to be yoke-fellows in the changed conditions. At least budding hostility is manifested in a letter written by Russell to Governor Harrison from Aspenville, on September 25, 1783, complaining of Campbell's official conduct, and concluding: "I fear Colonel Campbell's present close attention to effect a new State in this part of the country will engage his time to the neglect of any individual among us."

Campbell was yet pertinacious in his advocacy of separate statehood. To what extent he had enlisted in the movement the men of the settlement on the Watauga and the Nolachucky rivers, we are left to surmise. He had but recently (December, 1780) led three hundred of these men of the lower settlements in a campaign against the Cherokees. John Sevier served as a lieutenant-colonel under him[6] and it is not improbable that Sevier and his friends were not lacking in sympathy with Campbell's scheme. It is plain that Campbell felt assured that this was true. But little of actual negotiations in these early days went to written record (much that did has not escaped loss) to speak of motives, purposes and plans to the historian today.

There trickled to Congress, however, enough to arouse the fears of the North Carolina delegates.

In August, 1782, there was presented to Congress a petition from the inhabitants of a "tract of country called Kentucky," setting forth that the petitioners deemed themselves subjects of the United States, and not of Virginia; and that by virtue of the Revolution the right of the British crown to that country had devolved on the United States. They, therefore, prayed the Congress to erect them into a new State. Arthur Lee boldly asserted that to countenance the petition would be to insult Virginia, and that the document should be referred to Virginia as the only authority competent to act. Madison denounced the claim of the petitioners as extravagant.

her uncle (by marriage) Arthur Campbell, applied to the court of Washington county to have her taken under his guardianship. This was done in 1789."—*Ib.*

[5] *Calendar Virginia State Papers*, I, 272.
[6] *Calendar Virginia State Papers*, I, 434.

Williamson, of North Carolina, expressed the opinion that the question was of such serious import that the sword alone could decide it, and the wish that it might be put off and not be renewed in the time of their children or grandchildren. He about the same time wrote from Congress to Governor Martin, of his State, expressing the hope that the Assembly of that State would turn its "attention to the Western Country; those lands are certainly in a critical situation. The spirit of migration prevails to a high degree in these Middle States, and the spirit of making new States is becoming epidemic. It is certain that many of the small States, or at least many of the inhabitants of those States, encourage that spirit. They look with envious eyes on the large States and wish to make us all of pygmy breed. The Assembly of this State [Pennsylvania] have just received accounts that the inhabitants in general over the Alleghany Mountains are disposed to declare themselves independent. There is the utmost reason to believe that the people of Vermont and their abettors in the minor States are endeavoring to persuade the people in general on the western waters to revolt."

Respecting the petition sent to Congress by Arthur Campbell and his associates early in 1782, or to the Kentucky petition, Williamson was particularly concerned:

"A petition was some time ago handed to Congress, said to be from some people back of Virginia, praying to be erected into a State . . . Utmost attention is required by our State to prevent, if possible, any bad impressions from being made on the citizens of the State on the western water. The spirit of our government is so moderate and the general disposition of the western inhabitants is so good that our subjects will be among the last to run riot."[7]

The passage of six months did not leave Williamson so confident. He now (June 19, 1783) sought to further clinch the hold of the claimant States on the West by moving to recommend to the States to amend the Articles of Confederation so that the affirmative vote of ten (instead of nine) States should be requisite to the admission of a fourteenth State into the Confederation. Bland, of Virginia, seconded the motion. Madison in his notes of the proceedings, made at the time, explains: "The motion had reference to the fore-

---

[7] *North Carolina State Records*, XVI, 459. In January 1783, Campbell was endeavoring to interest John Rhea, of Sullivan in the movement: "The talk about a New State is far from being husht either in Philadelphia or Richmond. Great schemes require time to arrive at maturity." Hyde MSS.

seen creation of the western part of North Carolina into a separate State."⁸ North Carolina leaders were alert to the situation and desired to forestall consummation.

The earlier plan of Campbell and his associates for a new State included five of the Virginia counties. The suggestion in the letter of Campbell to Lee, nearly six months later, was that the counties of Montgomery and Washington be so incorporated. It may have been thought wise to lop off counties in which Colonel Campbell's influence was not so dominant.

Turner says: "There is evidence that Arthur Campbell continued in correspondence with congressional leaders. In the summer of 1783, Jefferson reported that Patrick Henry was ready to restrict Virginia to reasonable boundaries, but that instead of ceding the parts lopped off, he was for laying them off into small republics."⁹

The movement for statehood was renewed in Kentucky in 1783. A petition of the inhabitants of the Kentucky Country was now laid before the Virginia Assembly asking for a new State beyond the mountains. In that document it was quaintly said: "Some of our fellow citizens may think we are not able to conduct our affairs and consult our interests; but if our society is rude, much wisdom is not necessary to supply our wants, and a fool can put on his clothes better than a wise man can do it for him. We are not against hearing counsel, but we attend more to our feelings than to the arguments of others."

It is not beyond suspicion that Arthur Campbell was at this time influential in the separatist movement in Kentucky. A number of his old neighbors were leaders in that district. Jefferson in a letter written to Madison about this time showed that there was danger that the movement would, if allowed to run unchecked, take away from the Old Dominion several of the counties west of the Alleghanies and east of the Cumberland mountains, named by Campbell to be parts of a new State. He urged that it was for the welfare of Virginia to cede the Kentucky region immediately because the settlers there would "separate themselves and be joined by all our settlements beyond the Alleghany, if they are the first movers... I am afraid that Congress would wish them well."¹⁰

---

⁸ *Madison Papers*, I, 401.
⁹ Turner, *Western State-making*, citing Jefferson's *Writings*, III, 334.
¹⁰ Jefferson, *Writings*, IV, 244.

As will be disclosed in a subsequent chapter, Campbell was an adviser of the Kentucky separatists at a later date.[11]

Colonel William Christian, who had also led Virginia and Carolina troops in a campaign against the Cherokee Indians down the valley of the Holston and Tennessee rivers and had noted the beauty and fertility of the country, was a co-worker with Campbell in his statehood scheme. Referring to the uncertainty produced by the refusal of Congress to accept Virginia's tender of cession, he wrote: "In the general confusion and disturbance we ought to take care of ourselves."[12]

---

[11] *Post*, p. 236.

[12] Turner, *Western State-making, supra*, 256. Christian also observed a decided drift of emigration to the Watauga-Nolachucky district. He informed Governor Harrison of Virginia (September 28, 1782) that "Indian troubles in Kentucky tended to turn the tide of migration into Carolina towards the Cherokees where they may live in safety." *Calendar Virginia State Papers*, III, 331.

CHAPTER III

THE GREAT BEND OF THE TENNESSEE

The settlements in the Holston-Watauga region suffered a serious loss in the removal to the Cumberland Country of an increasing number of settlers of the better class. A main reason for their removal was the lack of room for expansion in the valleys to the southward. The Avery Treaty of 1777 with the Cherokees (at Long Island of Holston) fixed the Indian line about twenty miles south of Jonesborough. All entries and surveys of land which had been made below this line were declared utterly void by legislative act.[1] North Carolina did not move to remedy this situation until 1783, when her General Assembly undertook to fix the upper line of the hunting grounds of the Cherokees at the French Broad river, without having obtained the consent of the Indians.[2] By a later act of the same session, the governor was empowered to appoint commissioners to treat with the Cherokees for a further cession of territory and the sum of twenty-five hundred pounds was appropriated to be laid out in goods to be delivered as a consideration.[3]

At the time there was grave danger of another exodus that would drain entirely away from trans-Alleghany Carolina more of that region's most energetic and enterprising citizens. In the Great Bend of the Tennessee river was a fine body of land, to which there were rival claims by Georgia and South Carolina. For a time, North Carolinians were hazy as to the true southern boundary line of that State and thought that the territory in the Bend was within the limits of their State. The investigations and report of North Carolina commissioners, appointed by the act of 1782, to locate lands for a reservation for the continental line of the State, demonstrated that this was an erroneous conception. Immediately a plan was formulated by East Carolinian leaders, General Richard Cas-

---

[1] *North Carolina Act 1777*, ch. 3; Scott's *Revisal*, I, 275; *North Carolina State Records*, XXIV, 160.
[2] *North Carolina Act 1783*, ch. 2; *North Carolina State Records*, XXIV, 479.
[3] *Ib.*, ch. 21.

well,[4] James Glasgow and William Blount, to exploit the region and settle it with men then residing on the western waters of Carolina. Joseph Martin, at the time Virginia's Indian agent to the Cherokee and Chickasaw nations, was now caused to be chosen North Carolina's agent to the Cherokee and Chickamauga Indians. Martin was at the Assembly at Hillsborough when the report of the locating commission was made. Writing to Patrick Henry on May 21, 1783, he said of the report:

"They find all the Bent of Tennessee in Georgia, and several Indian nations between. General Caswell and three other gentlemen have agreed to join with Colonel [John] Donelson and myself in said purchase. They promise the goods; Donelson and myself are to make the purchase; the whole jointly concerned and intend to take possession immediately, letting the same out on such reasonable terms as will make that part so strong in a short time that they cannot be ousted. If you should, after consideration, incline to be an adventurer in that scheme, you will please let me hear from you as soon as possible."[5]

There is much of record to lead to the belief that Patrick Henry did become interested under cover of Colonel Martin, who was his confidential agent and friend. In fact, Martin was, at the time this letter was written, on his way to the Holston region of Carolina to purchase lands for Henry.[6]

By the summer following, Stockley Donelson, son of Colonel Donelson, and Martin had consummated a contract with the Indians—by what means, it would be interesting to know.

Blount wrote to Martin from Hillsborough, North Carolina, October 26, 1783:

I am very glad to find that you have made the purchase of the

---

[4] Caswell was also preparing to locate lands on the French Broad river, in partnership with Donelson, under the act of 1783, opening the western country to entry and grant. He wrote his son, from Hillsborough, May 4, 1783: "Col. Donelson is here; by him I have a message from his son who was engaged to explore the country about the French Broad and fix on proper locations for Col. Glasgow and myself. This he has done, and when the office is opened will be ready to enter.... Stockley Donelson is now surveyor of Sullivan and the Colonel, his father, I find here in expectation of obtaining the appointment in Greene; if this should be the case, the advantages will be still greater in interesting ourselves with them." *N. C. Rec.*, XVI, 960.

[5] Henry, *Patrick Henry*, II, 243.

[6] *Ib.*

Indians of the Bent of Tennessee, and I think cheap enough. The most of the goods to make the payment with were purchased in Philadelphia early in September. . . .

I am told that a dispute has arisen between the States of Georgia and South Carolina by the latter claiming a right to the back lands as far west as the Mississippi.[7] Now if South Carolina has any back lands, the Bent of Tennessee must be a part of it. This dispute between the two States, will in my opinion, be very favorable to our designs of obtaining the Georgia title or the South Carolina title, and either will answer our purpose equally well, for we shall surely settle the country before the dispute can be determined; and, in order to procure a title from one or both of these States, I will certainly attend both their next Assemblies; and I have not the least doubt I shall succeed.

General Rutherford has agreed to become a joint adventurer with us in the purchase, and I have this day given him an instrument of writing interesting him as much as either of the original adventurers. It was good policy to do so, and General Caswell advised it to be done, and I hope it will be agreeable to you and Colonel Donelson. I am glad to find that Colonel Sevier has also joined the Company. . . .

It now seems that every person I have seen envies us the purchase and wished to own a part of the Bent of Tennessee.[8]

On February 9, 1784, "petitions of William Blount, Richard Caswell, Griffith Rutherford, with sundry others from North Carolina" (doubtless including Stockley Donelson, one of the boldest and most persistent promoters in the West, Joseph Martin and John Sevier, all of the western territory of North Carolina) were presented to the Assembly of Georgia. A bill was passed for the laying out of a county to the westward and pointing out the mode of laying out and settling the lands.[9]

Blount evidently had complied with his promise to attend this session of the Georgia Assembly. The next action was the report of the committee (February 20) and in it the petition was referred to as that of "Mr. Blount in behalf of himself and other citizens of North Carolina, respecting the expediency of laying out a new county" to include all that tract of territory in the Bend of Tennessee river. The report recited that in the opinion of the committee, it would be necessary in order to prevent future contests to settle

---

[7] The dispute arose because of the uncertainty of the source of the Savannah river referred to in the charter of Georgia.

[8] *Draper MSS*, II, vol. 4; no. 17; also *Gulf States Magazine*, II, 417.

[9] *Georgia Revolutionary Records*, III, 492.

that tract of country, and it was recommended that seven commissioners be vested with the powers necessary to ascertain the quantity, quality and circumstances of the lands and report their findings to the legislature. The commission or board of seven was empowered, however, to grant warrants of survey, provided that grants based thereon should be limited to one thousand acres to any one person, issuable on payment of one-eighth of a dollar per acre into the State treasury. The board was authorized to appoint militia officers for the district, who were to be commissioned by the governor.[10]

The board of commissioners was composed of Lachlan McIntosh, Jr., William Downes, Stephen Heard, John Moore, John Donelson, Joseph Martin and John Sevier.[11]

The board visited the Bend Country and appointed as officers of a battalion of militia, three residents of the West Carolina region: John Sevier, colonel; John Donelson, lieutenant-colonel, and Valentine Sevier, Jr., major. Commissions for captains and subalterns were issued in blank.[12] It was recognized that a collision with the Indians must be avoided, if possible, and the surveyor-general of Georgia was authorized to have surveyed and marked "the line that is to circumscribe the Indian hunting grounds."[13]

Valentine Sevier, Junior, a brother of John Sevier, was chosen to represent the Bend Country in the General Assembly, but he was denied a seat. John Donelson was made surveyor and John Sevier was appointed to receive locations and entries of land.[14] Donelson, Charles Robertson, Joseph Martin and Valentine Sevier, Jr., were appointed justices of the peace; and Martin was recommended for appointment as Indian agent.

Manifestly the push was to come from the Holston Country with cheap and abundant land as lure. The Board of Commissioners provided for the opening of a land-office at Long Island of Holston in March, 1785, on learning of which Blount wrote in behalf of Caswell and himself to Sevier and Martin: "Should you open the entry-office before you see one or both of us, we wish you to secure as much of the Bent as may be in your power."

[10] *Georgia Revolutionary Records*, III, 525.
[11] *Ib.*, 536, 564.
[12] *Ib.*, II, 739.
[13] *Ib.*, III, 565.
[14] Land warrants were signed by Sevier and Donelson, some bearing date as late as December 21, 1785.

This Board also assembled at Jonesborough in fall of 1785, and advertised for adventurers who should rendezvous at the confluence of the Holston and French Broad Rivers and from there proceed to the old Chickamauga towns. The Commissioners and their escort of adventurers went to the Bend Country by water, and there laid off Houston County, Georgia—including all the land of that State north of the Tennessee. Warrants of survey for one thousand acres were issued to each adventurer, signed by Donelson, Sevier and Wm. Downs, as entry-takers. The scheme was defeated by the hostile attitude of the Indians,[15] and by North Carolina's first cession of her western domain to the general government. The restless Westerners found vent for their enterprise and ambition in forming a new state government for the ceded territory.

The Spaniards at the South were alert to the danger from an American penetration. The *South Carolina Gazette*, of February 17, 1785, stated "on the authority of a gentleman from the western parts of North Carolina that a body of Spaniards have taken post at the Muscle Shoals and are building a fort. The Chicamauga tribe have abandoned and burnt their towns and moved off to some distant part, greatly disgusted with the attempts of individuals to get their country without a purchase." It is likely, however, that, if any post was in contemplation, it was not to be a military fort, but a trading post.

However the lands in the Great Bend continued to attract and engage attention of the West Carolinians for two decades. Phases of the history of the States of Franklin and Tennessee can only be understood in the light of this fact.[16]

---

[15] Haywood, 159. The noted chief, Bloody Fellow, put a stop to the operations.

[16] The project was so enticing to Caswell that he, in the spring of 1784, proposed giving up his candidacy for the governorship of his State in order that he might visit the Bend. "I think to visit the Western Waters. Commissioners from Georgia are to be at the Long Island the 15th of June, to proceed down the Tennessee and settle the claims of Wm. Blount and Company to that territory. I should be willing, if able, to attend them, and visit the Bend." *N. C. State Rec.*, XVII, 138.

Martin became uneasy respecting the part he took in the scheme. He was conscious that the purchase from the Indians made while he occupied the fiduciary relationship of agent was subject to just censure. In reporting to Col. William Christian (June 6, 1784) the danger incident to efforts of Spanish commissioners sent out from Pensacola to draw the Cherokees to the support of that power, he said that he would have sent an express to Richmond, but thinks the governor (Harrison) is offended and might suppose he, Martin, "wanted to answer some private end about the Tennessee purchase." *Cal. Va. St. Papers*, III, 590.

Indeed, the contact between the inhabitants of the Tennessee Country with those in the Great Bend was so close that Gilbert Imlay, writing about 1790-91, predicted that the latter would join the former "in their separation from North Carolina."[17]

For later events, see Whitaker, "*The Muscle Shoals Speculation*", *Miss. Valley Hist. Review*, XIII, 365; and *The Spanish-American Frontier, passim.*

[17] *Topographical Description of the Western Territory*, 80.

CHAPTER IV

The First Cession Act—1784

Little or no heed was given by North Carolina to the earlier calls of the Continental Congress for a cession of her western territory.

Hugh Williamson had written Governor Martin from Congress, in August, 1782, that the public prints were holding up to shame the States that were backward; and that North Carolina had long been viewed in an unfavorable light.[1]

During the debate in Congress (October, 1782) on the status of the transmontane territory, Hugh Williamson and William Blount had written to Governor Martin from Philadelphia a long letter in which were expressed their views as to the policy the state should pursue: It was to the interest of North Carolina to retain the provision of article 8 of the Articles of Confederation, which was to the effect that in the payment of expenses of the war, the quota of each State should be fixed according to the value of all lands in the several States "granted to, or surveyed for any person together with the buildings and improvements thereon." The provision was more favorable to their State than to most any other in the Union. Other States must pay for their cities and highly improved lands, while North Carolina had few towns and much land. The retention by the State of her western lands would swell her quota to nearly double what it would be otherwise. Since the valuation would probably be made by impartial officials, "we may be assured that the western lands, located but not improved, will be rated at their full value since land jobbers are not a very popular set of men in any country."

The delegates then ventured the suggestions that, if North Carolina could be induced to cede her western territory at all, she should at least impose as parts of the conditions, the following:

(a) The whole expense of the State's Indian expeditions should pass to her account in the quota of the Continental expenses.

---

[1] *North Carolina State Records*, XVI, 288.

(b) Actual valuation of all lands and improvements claimed by any State should be made before the cession should be confirmed.

(c) If any separate State should ever be erected on any of those lands, part of the public debt should be transferred to such State according to the value of the lands therein.[2]

The sentiment of the leading men of the State was distinctly in opposition to a cession; and, again, the method adopted was that of postponement. Governor Alexander Martin, as early as January, 1783, wrote to the delegates in Congress expressing opposition and asking them to influence a postponement of the discussion of the subject as long as possible. "It will not be our interest or policy to make a cession of our western lands on any terms yet proposed by Congress . . . To insist that the State should cede her vacant lands which are daily settling up with numerous inhabitants and from which she expects to derive considerable advantage . . . is the same as to urge an individual to give up to a stranger without compensation part of his land he is daily improving with husbandmen and husbandry to his own enrichment and that of his family. This is, in short, endeavoring to carry into effect, a vile agrarian law the Romans anciently made in vain respecting their conquered lands."[3]

One of the purposes of the delay is disclosed in a letter of Martin to the delegation in Congress, of date December 8, 1783:

"Perhaps Congress may be dissatisfied with the mode of our land office being opened, as we have made no cession of any part of our western lands. We have made provision for our continental line on Cumberland,[4] and a territory reserved for the purpose is erected into a county by the name of Davidson; the residue of the lands to the northward [southward] and westward is opened for entry of any citizen of this or the United States, who will pay to the entry taker ten pounds per hundred in specie, specie certificate of this State, or currency at 800 for one, restricted however to 5,000 acres . . . No doubt we are railed at for want of generosity, but I know not for what reason . . . I can venture to say there will be no cession of

---

[2] *North Carolina State Records*, XVI, 434. (October 22, 1782)

[3] *North Carolina State Records*, XVI, 733.

[4] By *North Carolina Act 1783*, ch. 186, the following boundary of lands was reserved for the soldiers and officers of the continental line: Beginning on the Virginia line where the Cumberland river intersects the same; thence south fifty-five miles; thence west to the Tennessee river; thence down the Tennessee river to the Virginia line; thence with the Virginia line east to the beginning.

any land worthy of acceptance, as the principal lands will be entered before this reaches you."[5]

In this correspondence of the chief executive of North Carolina there is no hint of any equities of the national government or of the western settlers. The western domain was to be looted of the best lands by the land jobbers of the State. Thereafter a cession might be made. As a part of this plan, not merely lands cleared of Indian title, but also the Chickasaw country, west of the Tennessee river, was, by act of 1783, ch. 185, opened for settlement. Thereunder there became subject to entry the immense domain south of the Virginia line and west of the Tennessee river to the Mississippi, then down the latter stream to the 35th parallel of north latitude; thence due east to the Appalachian mountains; thence with them to the ridge between the French Broad and the Nolachucky rivers; thence with the same until it strikes the line of the Indian hunting ground as set forth in act of 1778.[6] The full meaning of this step, and the cupidity it evidenced, more clearly appears from the fact that it disregarded and was in violation of the unquestionable rights of the friendly Chickasaw Indians, and preceded by a generation the acquisition on purchase by the general government of the title of the Chickasaws in the Jackson-Shelby treaty of 1818.

A rush to the entry taker's office followed. It may be instanced, by way of example, that the site of the present city of Memphis, on one of the Chickasaw Bluffs, was entered by John Rice and John Ramsey on October 23, 1783, (5,000 acres each) and Isaac Roberts was sent to survey it in 1786, the land later passing to grant. The State of North Carolina received ten pounds per hundred acres for

---

[5] *North Carolina State Records*, XVI, 919. The same thought was expressed by the North Carolina delegation in Congress to Gov. Martin: "The eyes of every State to the northward are now turned towards the Carolinas and Georgia and expecting from them liberal cessions.... We are necessitated to declare that the blame lies on Congress for having so long neglected to take up and determine on the Virginia cession.... It is probable our State may have gone so far by opening the land office as to put it out of their power, however well inclined they may be, to make a cession worth the acceptance of Congress.... You may readily imagine that we are not a little embarrassed." *Ib.*, 888.

[6] Potter's *North Carolina Revisal*, 435; *North Carolina State Records*, XXIV, 478. This rash step gave to the Spanish authorities an argument in their attempt to wean to Spanish support the Chickasaws in a conference held with their tribe in May, 1784. Haywood says that with regrets the Chickasaws felt compelled to show the sting of displeasure by attacking the Cumberland Settlements. Haywood, 130.

lands which were, in substance and in fact, paid for and made vendible by the national government—denominated by Governor Martin "a stranger" to whom no cession should be made "without compensation."

Other surveyors were sent into the same section to locate entries of 1783-4. Colonel James Robertson was called upon to go from the Cumberland settlement to aid in locating the entries; he and E. Harris going to the Wolf and Loosahatchee waters, while Henry Rutherford went to the Forked Deer, Obion and Reelfoot rivers.[7]

One of the surveyors located three hundred and sixty-five thousand acres of land; the total of choice lands put under entry in West Tennessee must have been a staggering one. The statement of Governor Martin, that the principal lands would be entered before any cession would be made, was not an idle one. Surveys for speculators and leading politicians of North Carolina were being hastened in 1783 from the French Broad to the Mississippi. General Caswell, who succeeded Martin as governor, with Colonel John Donelson was feverishly locating desirable lands on the French Broad.[8]

North Carolina had, as seen, delayed a response to the repeated requests by Congress that her western lands be ceded to the general government, but the views of the Virginia leaders and the steps

---

[7] Glass, "Sketch of Henry Rutherford," 5 *American Historical Magazine*, 225: Some of the lands surveyed at this time on Reelfoot river, for George Doherty were submerged by the waters of Reelfoot Lake following the earthquake of 1811. *Reelfoot Lake Cases*, 127 Tennessee, 575.

[8] *North Carolina State Records*, XVI, 958. In the Recollections of Memucan Hunt Howard, the amount of lands entered in Armstrong's office in 1783-4 is placed at 3,000,000 acres. *American Historical Magazine*, VII, 58.

Promptly after the Jackson-Shelby treaty of purchase of the Chickasaws in 1818, North Carolinians sent agents into "the Purchase" to relocate lands. Calvin Jones writing from Raleigh in November 1818, of his visit to West Tennessee (*Raleigh Register* of December 12, 1818) says: "By this cession many individuals are at once made rich. One gentleman in the lower part of this State owns 123,000 acres, worth at a moderate calculation more than a million dollars."

One of the first Carolina settlers in the Chickasaw Purchase stated "from the most authentic source" that of the 6,000,000 acres purchased from the Indians, after all the Carolina entries and warrants were satisfied, there would remain only 2,000,000 acres of land fit for cultivation. Hoyt, *Papers of Archibald D. Murphrey*, I, 176-7. "The truth is, the rich spoil has been divided among a few, *very few*. It is all a mystery even to the people of Nashville." *Ib.*, 248. The mystery was in the frauds perpetrated in Armstrong's Entry Office, and later on in the inclusion in surveys and grants of larger acreages than were paid and called for.

taken by that State were soon to affect sentiment and action in the neighbor State to the south.

Jefferson wrote to Madison from Annapolis (February 20, 1784) "We hope that North Carolina will cede all beyond the meridian of Kanawha, and Virginia also. For God's sake push this at the next session of Assembly."

On the 29th of April Congress voted to urge again the States which had made no cessions to do so.[9] Williamson, from Annapolis, on March 19th wrote Governor Martin that Virginia had completed her cession of territory to Congress, and in the letter he insisted that a large national debt was a chain of slavery and he "presumed it is North Carolina's duty to leave no honest measure unattempted by which we may pay off that debt."[10]

Spaight, the other delegate in Congress, had written in February approving a cession as the best means of paying the State's quota of the national debt.[11]

The attitude of Virginia and her delegates had no inconsiderable influence on the North Carolina delegates in Congress.

The General Assembly of North Carolina met at Hillsborough on April 19, 1784. General, and former Governor, Richard Caswell was speaker of the senate and Thomas Banbury presided over the house of commons. The ablest men of the Commonwealth had seats in the legislature. Among those with previous experience in public life were: Samuel Johnston, afterward governor; William Hooper, who had signed the Declaration of Independence and served in the Continental Congress; William Blount, who had served in Congress; Nathaniel Macon; A. Maclaine; Alexander Mebane; and William Lenoir and Thomas Person, both of whom had been officers in the Revolutionary War.

A number of new members of unusual ability appeared in the legislature for the first time—William R. Davie,[12] John Hay, John Baptist Ashe and Stephen Cabarrus among them.

---

[9] *Journals of Congress* (W. & G. ed.) IV, 392.

[10] Bancroft's *History Constitution U. S.* II, 343.

[11] *North Carolina State Records*, XVI, 21.

[12] Of these leaders in the Assembly, Caswell and Davie were the only ones perhaps who had visited the Western Country. As a young lawyer Davie had been admitted to practice in the court at Jonesborough as early as 1779. Records of Washington County, *American Historical Magazine*, VI, 54. And Caswell before 1782 had entered lands on Big Limestone Creek in Washington county. *Ib.*, 90. Visited the Western Country in June, 1781. *The Portfolio*, of Nashville, I, 218.

An act to cede the western lands was introduced by William Blount, but the Kanawha meridian was not even proposed for adoption. The watershed of the mountains, which had been fixed as the eastern boundary of Washington county, was wisely chosen, instead. The bill in the house of commons met with stubborn opposition, led by William R. Davie and General Thomas Person. The first defensive step was a motion to postpone consideration to the succeeding session of Assembly, and it failed by only one vote—forty-six to forty-seven. The act was then passed by a vote of fifty-two ayes and forty-three nays. Ramsey, followed by Phelan, says that the "members from the four western counties were present at Hillsborough, and voted for the act of cession." This is an error. The western members were divided in opinion. Charles Robertson, of Washington county, Joshua Gist, of Greene, and David Looney, of Sullivan, voted in favor; and Landon Carter, of Washington, and William Cage, of Sullivan, cast their votes in opposition. Elijah Robertson, the only member present from Davidson county, voted against the measure. The delegates of the transmontane counties were, therefore, evenly divided on the question.[13]

The cession act[14] contained a preamble which referred to the resolutions of Congress of September 6–October 10, 1780[15] in which the States which asserted claims to western lands were urged to cede same "as a further means of extinguishing the debt and establishing the harmony of the United States."

Among the stipulations and conditions of the cession act were the following:

(a) After the cession should be accepted, neither the lands nor the inhabitants of the ceded territory should be estimated in ascertaining North Carolina's proportion of the expenses of the late war.

(b) The lands provided for North Carolina officers and soldiers should inure to their benefit.

(c) The ceded lands should be deemed a common fund, for the benefit of all existing and future States of the Union.

---

[13] *North Carolina State Records*, XIX, 642, 683. James White, who afterwards removed to the West and founded the city of Knoxville, was a member from one of the eastern counties, and voted against the cession act.

[14] *North Carolina State Records*, XIX, 642.

[15] *Ante*, p. 18. An able and comprehensive treatment of the North Carolina Cession Act by St. George L. Sioussat appears in *Proceedings of Mississippi Valley Historical Association* (1908), II, 35, *et seq*.

(d) "The territory so ceded shall be laid out and formed into a State or States, containing a suitable and convenient extent of territory; and that the State or States so formed shall be a distinct State or States and admitted as members of the Federal Union, having the same right of sovereignty as other States; and that the State or States which shall thereafter be erected in the territory now ceded shall have the most full and absolute right to establish and enjoy, in the fullest latitude, the same constitution and the same bill of rights which are now established in the State of North Carolina, subject to such alterations as may be made by the inhabitants at large or a majority of them, not inconsistent with the Confederation of the United States. Provided always, that no regulation made or to be made by Congress shall tend to emancipate slaves, otherwise than shall be directed by the Assembly or legislature of such State or States."[16]

(e) If Congress should not accept the cession and give due notice within twelve months, the act should be of no force and the lands should revert to the State.[17]

At a later day of the same session another act was passed, declaring: "That the sovereignty and jurisdiction of this State in and over the territory aforesaid, and all and every inhabitants thereof, shall be and remain the same in all respects, until the United States in Congress shall accept the cession, as if the act aforesaid had never been passed," and in the same statute the land office for western entries was ordered closed, with minor exceptions having relation to the reservation for the military.[18]

Not content with opposing this cession in debate and by vote, thirty-seven members of the house of commons, led by Davie, placed of record their protest. They dissented on several grounds. They conceived (erroneously of course) that two-thirds of the soil of the State was being yielded up to the Confederacy, and thought it too much so long as Virginia and Georgia retained an immense territory. North Carolina, they urged, had been forced to aid South

---

[16] Jefferson, a few months before, barely failed of success in imposing prohibition of slavery in the territory "ceded and to be ceded" to the United States in the enactment of the Ordinance of 1784. The effort failed only by the vote of Spaight of North Carolina. The irritation of Jefferson was expressed in a letter to Madison. *Jefferson's Writings* (Ford ed.) IV, 329.

[17] Act 1784, April session, ch. XII; *North Carolina St. Records.*

[18] *North Carolina State Record*, XIX, 712.

Carolina and Georgia, when those States had been sorely pressed and weakened in the revolutionary struggle, and allowance of credit for her expenses had been opposed by the Eastern States. It should have been stipulated as a condition of cession that these expenses, and also the whole expense of expeditions against the Indians in aid of the same States should pass to the account of North Carolina along with Continental expenses. Moreover, the western territory was solemnly pledged, by legislative action, as security for the domestic creditors of the State; that debt, due in large part to her own citizens, should be paid first. "They could never consent that the public faith should be violated and the general interest sacrificed to the aggrandizement of a few land-jobbers, who have preyed on the depreciated currency of their country ... A just regard for the rights of the people have induced us to suspend the passage of the bill until the sense of our constituents could have been collected on this *irrevocable step*."[19]

Among the signers of the protest were Landon Carter and Elijah Robertson from the western counties.

Governor Martin promptly notified the North Carolina delegation in Congress of the passage of the act; and added: "Whether the cession will be accepted is with some a doubt, as our land office hath been open for some time for entries of these lands, and large quantities have been taken up; but still there remain great tracts undisposed of beyond the Tennessee to the Mississippi claimed by the Chickasaws."[20]

---

[19] *North Carolina State Records*, XVII, 78.

[20] As the Revolution drew to a close North Carolina was in a desperate condition. There was a lack of specie and the State was honeycombed with debts. The members of the Assembly of 1782 were paid in corn, and in January following the call for a session failed. "The poverty of some of the members is urged as the excuse, which perhaps is true." The citizens were in debt to the State, the State to the citizens, and the latter to one another. Issue of paper currency was resumed as an expedient. "The assertion is made that the first call for it came from very respectable citizens who were all greatly in debt." Schoepf, *Travels in the Confederation*, II, 131-2. The temptation to retrieve by exploiting the western lands was too great to be resisted. *N. C. St. Rec.*, XIX, 712; *ib.*, XVII, 78.

CHAPTER V

Movement for a Separate Government in the West—1784

The North Carolina Assembly adjourned a day or two after passing the cession acts, and the news was carried to the western counties by their returning delegates. The minds of the people there had not been prepared for the information by any discussion of probable action at that session of Assembly; and in this respect they were taken by surprise. They were not, however, unprepared for separation by lack of previous consideration of the subject. They, of course, knew of Arthur Campbell's movement for a separate government in 1782. Kept in close touch with the Kentucky Country, as they were by the tide of travel which flowed forward and backward along Boone's trail through Cumberland Gap, the West Carolinians were not unaware of the repeated efforts to bring about a separation of Kentucky from Virginia. As early as 1780, the settlers in that district had appealed to the Continental Congress for separate statehood.[1] As great a celebrity as Thomas Paine, in a widely published attack on Virginia's claim to territory lying westward to the south seas, had foreseen the difficulties and championed the cause of the western people: "The situation of the settlers on those lands will be hazarded and distressing; and they will feel themselves aliens to the commonwealth ... The distance the settlers will be from her (Virginia) will immediately put them out of all government and protection ... and they will appear to her as revolters, and she to them as oppressors." It was in the same year (1780) that Congress resolved that western lands on being ceded should be "formed into distinct republican States, which shall become members of the federal Union."[2]

The movement in Kentucky for separation appeared above the surface again in December, 1783, when a memorial was sent to Congress asking for autonomy in which the view-point of the western people was quaintly expressed: "Much wisdom is not required

---
[1] Roosevelt, *Winning of the West*, II, 398, and appendix.
[2] Paine's *Public Good*, 6-38.

to supply our wants. A fool can put on his clothes better than a wise man can do it for him."[3]

Washington wrote to Hamilton that such a concession should be made by Virginia;[4] and Jefferson wrote to Madison (February 20, 1784): "We have transmitted a copy of a petition from the people of Kentucky to Congress praying to be separated from Virginia. . . . It is for the interest of Virginia to cede so far (Kanawha meridian) because the people beyond that will separate themselves, and be joined by other settlements beyond the Alleghany."[5]

The inhabitants of the western territory of North Carolina in circumstances and aspirations were not different from those of their neighbors in Kentucky.

The passage of Jefferson's Ordinance of March, 1784, had not gone unnoticed by them, as affecting territory "to be ceded" by the States, and as evidencing congressional encouragement of self-government.

The attitude of the people on the waters of Holston and Nolachucky was not one of resentment because of the cession. In all probability a large majority would have favored it, in a plebiscite. The Virginian element of the population, strong in number and influence, had never felt a warm attachment to Carolina, and the feeling of alienation from the mother State was general. But they did deeply resent the motives that prompted some members of the Assembly to vote for the act; and as well the disposition manifested by many North Carolinians to exploit the Western Country before ceding it.

Particular offense was taken at language used in the debate over the cession act by some of the most eminent members of the Assembly. "When the members from the western country were supplicating to be continued a part of your State, were not these their epithets: 'The inhabitants of the western country are the off-scourings of the earth, fugitives from justice and we will be rid of them at any rate'."[6]

The spirit of independence that had projected and won the War of the Revolution was fanned into flame when the details of the passage of the cession act were passed by word of mouth from house

---

[3] *Maryland Journal*, December 9 and 20, 1783.
[4] Bancroft, *Hist. Constitution U. S.*, II, 343.
[5] Jefferson, *Writings*, III, 401.
[6] *Address* of Franklin Assembly to Gov. Martin, March 22, 1785, *post*, p. 61.

to house on the frontier. The people were not without experience in independent government, gained in the years of the existence of the Watauga Association. There was at the time no precedent afforded of a people forming a territorial government under congressional authority and control; nor was one made until after the adoption of the Ordinance of 1787 creating the Territory Northwest of the Ohio. A crisis was at hand and the initiative of the Wataugans served again in the solutions of the problem. If they were a separate people, why should they not provide for their own government? The period of one year, allowed for acceptance of the cession by Congress would probably be followed by further delays, and in the meantime nothing in the way of governmental protection or advantages could be expected from the parent State. Indian attacks were a constant menace to the borderers; the population was fast increasing, and there was all the more need of the orderly enforcement of civil, criminal and military law.

The North Carolina Constitution adopted by the Provincial Congress of 1776, of which John Sevier was a member from Washington District, contained a provision that looked to the "establishment of one or more governments westward of this State by consent of the legislature"; and in one of the stipulations of the Ordinance of 1784 was a virtual invitation to the western people to form separate governments in ceded territory, on their own initiative: "The settlers either on their own petition, or on the orders of Congress ... to meet together for the purpose of establishing a temporary government."[7]

In this situation there was formulated a plan to call a convention to consider what trend should be given to public affairs. Here there was resort to the same convenient machinery that had been used by Arthur Campbell and his followers in Southwest Virginia in 1782—that of the militia organization. Two men from each captain's company were elected delegates to a primary convention in their respective counties, to deliberate upon a general plan of action. The county conventions named delegates to a general convention to be

---

[7] One of the rectangular States provided for in this Ordinance of Jefferson included most of the territory occupied by Holston-Watauga settlers. However, the astronomical lines did not accord with the demands of physical geography or the convenience of the settlers. A part of the trans-Alleghany country, that now known as Johnson county, Tennessee, would have been, by Jefferson's scheme, left detached, east of the Kanawha meridian.

held at Jonesborough empowered to adopt such a course as should appear wise.

The elections of delegates to the general convention resulted as follows, according to Haywood: Washington county: Charles Robertson, William Purphey [Murphey], John Sevier, Joseph Wilson, John Irwin, Samuel Houston, William Trimble, William Cox, Landon Carter, Hugh Henry, Christopher Taylor, John Chisholm, Samuel Doak, William Campbell, Benjamin Holland, John Bean, Samuel Williams and Richard White.

Sullivan county: Joseph Martin, Gilbert Christian, William Cocke, John Manifee, William Wallace, John Hall, Samuel Wilson, Stockley Donelson and William Evans.

Greene county: Daniel Kennedy, Alexander Outlaw, Joseph Gist, Samuel Weir, Asahel Rawlings, Joseph Bullard, John Maughan, John Murphey, David Campbell, Archibald Stone, Abraham Denton, Charles Robinson [Robertson] and Elisha Baker.

On the appointed day, August 23, 1784, the convention was held. John Sevier was made president, and Landon Carter secretary. No formal record of the proceedings of this convention has been preserved; but Samuel Houston, one of its members, left a memorandum which shows:

"A member arose and made some remarks on the variety of opinions offered, for and against separation, and taking from his pocket a volume containing the Declaration of Independence by the Colonies in 1776, commented upon the reasons which induced their separation from England, on account of their local situation, etc., and attempted to show that a number of the reasons *they* had for declaring independence applied to the counties here represented by their deputies. After this member had taken his seat, another arose and moved to declare the three western counties independent of North Carolina, which was unanimously adopted."[8]

It was, in all likelihood, William Cocke who made the speech above referred to. He was a man of great eloquence, and he headed the committee which was appointed by the convention to take under consideration and report upon the state of affairs as they had been affected by the cession of the Western Country. The Committee, composed of Cocke, Outlaw, Carter, Campbell, Man-

---

[8] MSS. Reverend Samuel Houston, quoted by Ramsey, *Annals of Tennessee*, 287.

ifee, Martin, Robertson, Houston, Christian, Kennedy, and Wilson, brought in a report which was adopted:

"Your committee are of the opinion and judge it expedient, that the counties of Washington, Sullivan and Greene, which the cession bill particularly respects, form themselves into an Association and combine themselves together, in order to support the present laws of North Carolina, which may not be incompatible with the modes and forms of laying out a new State. It is the opinion of your committee, that we have a just and undeniable right to petition Congress to accept the cession made by North Carolina, and for that body to countenance us in forming ourselves into a separate government, and either to frame a permanent or a temporary constitution, agreeable to a resolve of Congress, in such case made and provided, as nearly as circumstances will admit. We have a right to keep and hold a convention from time to time, by meeting and convening at such times and places as said convention shall adjourn to. When any contiguous part of Virginia shall make application to join the Association, after they are legally permitted, either by the State of Virginia, or other power having cognizance thereof, it is our opinion that they should receive and enjoy the same privileges that we do, may, or shall enjoy. This convention has a right to adopt and prescribe such regulations as the particular exigencies of the time and the public good may require; that one or more persons ought to be sent to represent our situation in the Congress of the United States, and this convention has a just right and authority to prescribe a regular mode for his support."

The following "articles" were also adopted:

FIRST. We agree to entrust the consideration of public affairs, and the prescribing of rules necessary, to a convention to the chosen by each [military] company as follows: That if any company should not exceed thirty, there be one representative; and where it contains fifty, there will be two; and so in proportion, as near as may be, and that their regulation be reviewed by the Association.

SECONDLY. As the welfare of our common country depends much on the friendly disposition of Congress, and their rightful understanding of our situation, we do therefore unanimously agree, speedily to furnish a person with a reasonable support, to present our memorial, and negotiate our business in Congress.

In the action thus taken, the western folks were feeling their way, as indeed they must have done in the absence of any precedent to guide them in the creation of a separate state government. The natural thing for them to do was temporarily to fall back upon the once-tried association form of government; and, until broader plans could be matured, "either to frame a permanent or temporary constitution, agreeable to a resolve of Congress"—the Ordinance of April, 1784.

They stood ready, moreover, to proceed in disregard of that Ordinance in respect to a rectangular State, so that "when any contiguous part of Virginia shall make application to join this Association, after they are legally permitted," they should be received into the body politic. There were doubts as to whether such permission, in respect of legal power, should come from Virginia or the Congress as the "other power having cognizance thereof."

It seems certain that Colonel Arthur Campbell, about this time, made visits to the Western Carolina counties concerned in the movement, and with the purpose of bringing about concert of action in combining Southwestern Virginia counties with those south of the state line in a new government, thus reviving his scheme of 1782.[9]

---

[9] Letter from a gentleman, living in the territory ceded by North Carolina to his friend in Virginia (Colonel Arthur Campbell) dated December 20, 1784, refers to "the reasons you gave when last here," thus indicating that more than one such visit was made by Campbell. *Pennsylvania Journal*, of February 5, 1785; *Gazette of the State of South Carolina*, of February 24, 1785. The writer of this letter corresponded with Campbell at intervals during the years of 1784-89. Several of his communications are to be found in the Draper Collection of Manuscripts at Madison, Wisconsin; but all are unsigned. The handwriting is far above the average for the times, and a reading of the whole leaves the impression that the writer was a clergyman of the Presbyterian church, and the impractical Reverend Samuel Houston. The writer started out an advocate of separation, but later he took an attitude of unrelenting bitterness and antagonism toward Sevier and his party. His last letter to Campbell may shed light on the latter's design in corresponding with him:

Cedar Spring, October 28, 1789.

"...That perfidious wretch Sevier has publicly asserted to the people of this quarter that letters from you have informed him that a criminal correspondence was carried on between myself, Russell, Martin and from them on to the Governor of Virginia, and so on to Congress; and that you give it as your opinion that this country would be ruined unless the inhabitants would join and drive me from amongst them." The writer, in the same letter says that he had "ever preserved the idea of a separate government and am fond of it," but he ventures the prediction that "another century would not bring the time when 60,000 free inhabitants would be found between the Appalachian and the Cumberland mountains, and, in short, it is a doubt with me whether the bounds above would contain that number of inhabitants, suppose it to be settled as fully as it could possibly bear."

MOVEMENT FOR SEPARATE GOVERNMENT 33

The reference in the report of the committee to an indefinite "contiguous part of Virginia," may be ascribed, in part at least to Campbell.[10]

The August Convention felt concern as to the status, after the cession, of the former fiscal agents of the State of North Carolina. On motion of William Cocke, it was

"Resolved, That the clerks of the county courts who have bonds and recognizances of any, officers, sheriffs and collectors, who have collected any of the public monies, or are about now to collect any of the same, are hereby specially commanded and required to hold said bonds in their possession and custody until some mode be adopted and prescribed to have our accounts fairly and properly liquidated with the State of North Carolina. And, moreover, that all the sheriffs and collectors, who have before collected any of the public monies, shall be called on, and render due account of the monies that they have collected and have in their hands, or may collect by virtue of their office.

"Messrs. White and Doak moved, and were permitted to enter their dissent against both of those resolutions, because, in their opinion, it was contrary to the law to retain the bonds."[11]

Having made provision for delegates to a second assembly or convention of the Association, as above noted, it was resolved that the next session be held at Jonesborough, on September 16, 1784.

Ramsey states that for some reason not distinctly known, the delegates did not meet in convention until November, and then broke up in great confusion. There was not unanimity on the details of the plan for a new government. The Assembly of North Carolina was in session in November, and one element desired to wait until the attitude and further action of that body was known.

The county of Davidson, which was laid out on the Cumberland river in 1783, did not send delegates to this or any later convention. That county steadfastly stood aloof from association with their brethren of the three counties on the upper waters of the Tennessee river. The reasons for this are not far to seek.

North Carolina had chosen the Cumberland district as one in which to make reservations for the officers and soldiers of the Revolution; and in 1784, a tide of North Carolinians was flowing to

---

[10] See *post*, p. 45 for further evidence of Campbell's interest and participation.
[11] Haywood, 139; Ramsey, 289.

that country to make their homes. This tended to allign the inhabitants of Davidson county with the mother State. The members of the Carolina Assembly from Davidson county "on account of the good offices they could do for those who wished to become owners of land on the Cumberland, and to have military warrants they had purchased well located and attended to, were regarded and treated with great attention."[12] James Robertson, the acknowledged leader on the Cumberland, and other influential men in Davidson county had further interested themselves in behalf of North Carolina warrant-holders in the location of choice lands in the domain of the Chickasaws.

Certificates of preëmption rights were liberally granted by the North Carolina Assembly to the earlier settlers on the Cumberland.[13] Furthermore, the Constitution of 1776 and the Cession Act of 1784 alike looked to the possible creation of more than one State in the back territory of Carolina, and the Ordinance of 1784 provided for a future rectangular State on the Cumberland, distinct from that on the Holston and Watauga. The Cumberland mountains separated the two regions, and the seat of government would, in all likelihood, be in the East where the bulk of the population was. If coalition with the people of another district were to become necessary, that to be sought by the Cumberland settlers was one with the people of central Kentucky rather than with those of the Tennessee Valley, separated from them by a mountain wilderness.

---

[12] Haywood, 211. Haywood was in public life in North Carolina at the time, and later lived in the Cumberland Country, so his statement carries weight.
[13] *Ib.*

CHAPTER VI

Repeal of the Cession Act

On July 5, 1784, Hugh Williamson, a delegate in Congress, having returned to North Carolina on the adjournment of that body, wrote to Governor Martin, saying that while he had not seen the act of cession he was surprised to hear that it contained no provision for passing the expenses of the State's Indian expeditions to her credit in account with the Federal Government. He presumed that the Assembly when it reconsidered this matter, would suspend the cession; and he called attention to the fact that certain of the New England States were advancing extraordinary claims for credit; and he also suggested that North Carolina should do likewise.[1]

In the political campaign of the summer of 1784, those who had opposed cession at the spring meeting of the Assembly made it an issue, and created much sentiment against the act. William Hooper confided his troubles to James Iredell, in a letter of July 8th: "I have absolutely refused to serve in the Assembly again. Butler doubts. At the close of the session his and my conduct were severely animadverted upon by a few fools in the county for having patronized the cession bill—wretches stimulated to it by that prince of fops and fools, A. M. [Alexander Mebane] whose conduct, Mr. Johnston will inform you, was highly singular and unbecoming while the bill was in agitation.... All clamor here is at an end. Butler and I may go if we like. The people only want information to do right."[2]

Williamson, finding his own views supported, addressed another letter to the governor on September 30th, in which he discussed at length state and federal relations, and asked consideration of the points developed in his earlier communication. He urged that the State of Georgia, which had rendered comparatively little service in the war, had obtained by the peace a very extensive territory,

---
[1] *N. C. St. Rec.*, XVII, 81; also Sioussat, *The North Carolina Cession*, 53.
[2] McRee's *James Iredell*, II, 107.

and should cede a part of it. "If we should immediately complete the cession we shall give up the power of making advantageous terms, and shall lose the argument which may bring others to adopt federal measures. . . . The situation is critical. Perhaps it is most consistent with prudence and sound policy to make a pause. Whatever shall finally appear to be for the honor and true interest of the State may be done twelve months hence as well as now."[3]

This letter was evidently intended to be used in influencing the action of the Assembly which was soon to convene. How far, if at all, Williamson was prompted to write so insistently by the fact that he was interested in land grants within the rich Chickasaw domain (the present West Tennessee) one may only surmise. The fact is he held large surveys in that faraway region which could be more advantageously perfected and preserved should North Carolina retain jurisdiction over the West.[4]

Although Virginia and other States had ceded western lands, Georgia had not. Georgia could of course retort on North Carolina in kind. The possible loss of making more advantageous terms for North Carolina was, at any rate, the major incentive for a repeal of the cession act.

In August, an election was held for assemblymen, and in October, the Assembly met at New Bern. The people did not approve the cession act, and the new Assembly was in sympathy with Davie and his followers. An act of repeal[5] was passed by a vote of 37 to 22 in the House of Commons, and by a vote of 19 to 11 in the Senate. There was, of course, not a full delegation in the Assembly from the three western counties which had joined in the forming of an independent governmental Association. At a comparatively late date, Alexander Outlaw did appear as a representative from Greene county.[6]

The action did not fail to call out vigorous dissent. In the Senate Gen. Allen Jones entered a protest on the journal signed by himself and seven others, stating:

(a) "The act of the former Assembly evidently vested an optional right in Congress, and the repeal is attempted before that body could accede."

(b) "Political and moral honesty are unvariable and immutable.

---

[3] *N. C. St. Rec.*, XVII, 94.
[4] *American Historical Magazine*, I, 181.
[5] *Acts 1784*, October Session, Chapter 16; *N. C. St. Rec.*, XXIV, 678.
[6] *N. C. St. Rec.*, XIX, 761.

We cannot agree in a political capacity to do that which would dishonor us in a private action."[7]

In the House of Commons, a protest, drafted by John Hay, presented by A. Maclaine and signed by twenty members, recited:

(a) The grant by the act of cession is irrevocable on the part of the State, and therefore the repeal is disgraceful.

(b) We prove ourselves unworthy to receive for North Carolina any benefits resulting from the liberal cessions by other individual States.

(c) "During the confusion which must naturally spring from such situation, the numerous inhabitants resident in the country contended for may from necessity erect themselves into a distinct government" and the repeal "may produce confusion and distress, to our brethren westward of the Alleghany mountain."

The champions of repeal were in an unenviable plight on the first ground, since Davie and his followers had themselves in the protest filed at the previous cession, taken the position that the cession as made, was an irrevocable step.[8]

Both factions were thus in agreement, and of record, on that construction.

Maclaine further manifested the depth of his resentment by writing to his friend, George Hooper: "The Assembly have very rapidly and very disgracefully passed an act to repeal the cession of the western territory to Congress, which they certainly had no power do."[9]

---

[7] *N. C. St. Rec.*, XIX, 460.

[8] *Ante*, page 26. The soundness of this view has been demonstrated by many later judicial decisions. If it be premised that the offer of North Carolina to Congress was either under seal or based upon a valuable consideration (and that there was a concurrence of both seems certain) then it was not within the power of the offerer to withdraw within the period of one year allowed to Congress for consideration and acceptance. The offer was irrevocable within that period. Nor was the right of Congress lost by reason of the fact that North Carolina repealed the cession act or refused to perform before Congress could accept and demand performance. If there had been in existence a court with jurisdiction to pass upon the rights of the two sovereigns involved, a specific performance would have been grantable on the prayer of the National Government. *O'Brien vs. Boland*, 166 Mass. 481; Pomeroy, *Specific Performance*, sec. 169; *Waterman on Specific Performance*, sec. 200. The courts of the three jurisdictions concerned have since concurred in holding to this doctrine.—*Richardson vs. Hardwick*, 106 U. S. 252; *Bryant Timber Co. vs. Wilson*, 151 N. C. 154, and *Bradford vs. Foster*, 87 Tenn. 9.

[9] *N. C. St. Rec.*, XVII, 185.

A member of the Senate, and Alexander Outlaw in the House of Commons, pending the repeal, introduced a bill to authorize the creation of a third Carolina by empowering "the inhabitants of the Western Territory, by and with the consent of this State, to form themselves into a separate State to be known by the name of West Carolina, which is reserved to them by the cession of 1784, and to open a land office to sink the North Carolina specie tickets occasioned by the late war, and to explain how far that reservation extends." The bill was rejected. Its introduction was an effort to make the State the beneficiary of the proceeds of the back lands; with a new sovereign State created by the State itself. This would have conformed to Patrick Henry's original contention as to Virginia's proper action in regard to her western lands—"instead of ceding the parts lopped off, he is for laying them off into small republics."[10]

Documents of that time[11] show that the distance between the frontier settlements and the seat of government in Eastern Carolina could be covered by a traveller in twelve or fifteen days; so it is not improbable that news of the action taken in the August Convention at Jonesborough had reached the General Assembly and may account for the phraseology of the Maclaine protest. At any rate, it was thought wise to enact laws that might tend to quiet discontent and conciliate the over-mountain people. The judicial district of Morgan was divided and the four western counties "declared to be a distinct and separate district by the name of Washington."[12] An assistant-judge, David Campbell, was appointed to preside over a superior court in the District, and the militia was formed into a brigade with John Sevier as brigadier-general.

---

[10] Jefferson to Madison, June 17, 1783, Jefferson, *Writings*.

[11] See letter Joseph Martin to Sevier, Dec. 31, 1784, *Draper Coll.*, Shelby MSS. XI, 76, later quoted.

[12] *Acts N. C. 1784, October Session*, Chapter 28.

CHAPTER VII

THE FIRST CONSTITUTIONAL CONVENTION—1784

Before information reached the Western Country of the repealing act of the North Carolina Assembly, an important and fateful step had been taken. The delegates elected to the second convention met at Jonesborough, December 14, 1784. Among those representing Washington county were John Sevier, William Cocke, John Tipton, Thomas Stewart and Rev. Samuel Houston; from Sullivan county, David Looney, Richard Gammon, Moses Looney, William Cage and John Long; and from Greene county, James Reese, Daniel Kennedy, John Newman, James Roddy and Joseph Hardin. It is believed that Haywood, followed by Ramsey, gives an incomplete list as above, and that Tirril, Samms, North, Christopher Taylor, Thomas Talbot, Joseph Wilson, William Cox, John Manifee, Gilbert Christian, Carnes, Andrew Taylor, Garrett Fitzgerald, Alexander Cavet, Joshua Gist, Benjamin Gist, Ahahel Rawlings, Joseph Bullard, Valentine Sevier, Charles Robertson, Williams Evans, John Maughan, George Maxwell, Vincent, Provincer, William Davis, Samuel Wear, James Wilson, Joseph Tipton, and Captain David Campbell were also delegates.

William Cocke and Joseph Hardin, as a committee to outline a plan of action, brought in the following report:

To remove the doubts of the scrupulous; to encourage the timid, and to induce all, harmoniously and speedily, to enter into a firm association, let the following particulars be maturely considered: If we should be so happy as to have a separate government, vast numbers from different quarters, with a little encouragement from the public, would fill up our frontier, which would strengthen us, improve agriculture, perfect manufactures, encourage literature and every thing truly laudable. The seat of government being among ourselves, would evidently tend, not only to keep a circulating medium in gold and silver among us, but draw it from many individuals living in other states, who claim large quantities of lands that would lie in the bounds of the new state. Add to the foregoing reasons, the many schemes as a body, we could execute to draw it among us, and the sums which many travellers out of curiosity, and men in public business, would expend among us.

But all these advantages, acquired and accidental, together with many more that might be mentioned, whilst we are connected with the old counties, may not only be nearly useless to us, but many of them prove injurious; and this will always be the case during a connexion with them, because they are the most numerous, and consequently will always be able to make us subservient to them; that our interest must be generally neglected, and sometimes sacrificed, to promote theirs, as was instanced in a late taxation act, in which, notwithstanding our local situation and improvement being so evidently inferior, that it is unjust to tax our lands equally, yet they have expressly done it; and our lands, at the same time, not of one fourth of the same value. And to make it still more apparent that we should associate the whole councils of the state, the Continental Congress, by their resolves, invite us to it. The assembly of North Carolina by their late cession bill opened the door, and by their prudent measures invite to it; and as a closing reason to induce to a speedy association, our late convention chosen to consider public affairs, and concert measures, as appears from their resolves, have unanimously agreed that we should do it, by signing the following articles:

First. That we agree to entrust the consideration of public affairs, and the prescribing rules necessary to a convention to be chosen by each company as follows: That if any company should not exceed thirty, there be one representative; and there it contains fifty, there be two; and so in proportion, as near as may be, and that their regulations be reviewed by the association.

Secondly. As the welfare of our common country depends much on the friendly disposition of Congress, and their rightly understanding our situation, we do therefore unanimously agree, speedily to furnish a person with a reasonable support, to present our memorial, and negotiate our business in Congress.

Thirdly. As the welfare of the community also depends much on public spirit, benevolence and regard to virtue, we therefore unanimously agree to improve and cultivate these, and to discountenance every thing of a contradictory and repugnant nature.

Fourthly. We unanimously agree to protect this association with our lives and fortunes, to which we pledge our faith and reputation.

An advance step was to be considered—the formation of a separate State to take the place of the Association, and its importance was such as to call for a larger representation in the convention than fifteen. John Sevier was president and Francis A. Ramsey was secretary.

The convention, being organized and ready for business, the Rev. Samuel Houston, one of the deputies from Washington county, arose and addressed the convention on the importance of their meeting, showing that they were about to lay the foundation upon which was to be placed, not only their own welfare and interests, but, perhaps, those of their posterity for ages to come; and adding that, under such interesting and solemn circumstances, they should look to Heaven, and offer prayer for counsel and direction from Infinite Wisdom. The president immediately designated Mr. Houston, and he offered up a solemn and appropriate prayer, in which all seemed to unite.[1]

Ramsey, making use of the papers left by General Daniel Kennedy, who was a member of the convention, records the following action, but attributes it to the August convention, expressing doubt, however, whether the action was taken then or at a later session:

"On motion of Mr. Cocke, whether for or against forming ourselves into a separate and distinct State, independent of the State of North Carolina, *at this time*, it was carried in the affirmative.

"On motion of Mr. Kennedy, the yeas and nays[2] were taken on the above question:

"*Yeas.*—Mr. Tirrill, Samms, North, Taylor, Anderson, Houston, Cox, Talbot, Joseph Wilson, Trimble, Reese, John Anderson, Manifee, Christian, Carnes, A. Taylor, Fitzgerald, Cavit, Looney, Cocke, B. Gist, Rawlings, Bullard, Joshua Gist, Valentine Sevier, Robinson, Evans, and Maughan. (28)

"*Nays.*—John Tipton, Joseph Tipton, Stuart, Maxfield [Maxwell], D. Looney, Vincent, Cage, Provincer, Gammon, Davis, Kennedy, Newman, Wear, James Wilson, and Campbell. (15)"

A member of the convention from the door of the rude courthouse announced the result to the large crowd that had been drawn to Jonesborough, and the proclamation was received with joyful acclaim.[3]

That the declaration for a "separate and distinct State, *at this time*" was made at the December convention, appears from contemporary communications, to which Haywood and Ramsey did not have access.

---

[1] Ramsey, 292.

[2] Influential members of the first convention are not recorded as voting—Doak, Donelson, Outlaw and Carter. Leaders such as Hardin, Talbot, John Tipton, Valentine Sevier and Reese, who were not delegates to the August convention, are here recorded as voting.

[3] Ramsey, 288.

Arthur Campbell's correspondent, writing December 20, 1784, said: "Last week in convention we ventured to declare ourselves independent. I confess it was contrary to my opinion."[4]

Haywood states that on the day when the people were collected in Washington county to elect deputies to the approaching convention, of December 14th, Sevier at Jonesborough ascended the steps of an elevated door and took from his pocket a letter which he had received from Colonel Joseph Martin, who had just returned from the Assembly of North Carolina, giving an account of the repeal of the cession act and of the enactment of conciliatory measures.

The letter itself, not before the historian Haywood when he wrote, discloses that it was written after the adjournment of the December convention. Addressing Sevier, December 31, 1784, Martin wrote:

"I left Governor Martin's the 19th instant. He informed me that Outlaw was sent forward nearly four weeks ago with some dispatches to you, enclosing your general's commission with a number of other papers. He likewise charged me with a letter to you with many others to the different gentlemen in the District. He informed me the first business that the Assembly did was to repeal the cession bill before Congress could meet to accept it. David Campbell is appointed one of the circuit judges. But as Mr. Outlaw has been so long on his way home, I have no doubt but that you have the particulars; and as you have formed a government here, I must beg that you will inform me whether you will persist or let it lay over until you can be better informed, as the governor has sent me on to purchase a large quantity of beef, pork and corn, for the use of a treaty to be held with the Cherokees in April next, which treaty he is to attend in person; also many gentlemen from below, in particular General Caswell, who is to succeed the present governor, and Colo. Blount. But if you are determined to oppose the measure, I shall not proceed to purchase. The letters from the governor to the other gentlemen, together with all my own, I left in Mr. Hardin's wagon as I landed with him two nights and when I pushed on forgot them, but expect him down by Monday. Thus shall forward on your letter."[5]

---

[4] *Gazette of the State of South Carolina*, Charleston, of February 24th, 1785. The writer had heard the debate.

[5] *Draper Collection*, Shelby MSS, vol. II, 76. Allison in *Dropped Stitches in Tennessee History* (p. 28) is yet more confused. He states that delegates met at Jones-

THE FIRST CONSTITUTIONAL CONVENTION   43

Evidently it was on the first Monday of January, 1785, county court day, that Sevier made public announcement of the news brought by Martin. The latter had been an active participant in the August convention, and he had learned through Joseph Hardin as he passed through Greene county, that an important and more decisive step had been taken, during his absence, in the formation of a separate government.

Martin, since May, 1783, had been in the employ of North Carolina as agent to the Cherokee and Chickamauga Indians; and the result of his visit to the State's Assembly was the chilling of his enthusiasm for separation. He was not prepared to hazard his place by coming to a breach with the State's authorities. He also knew that Sevier's heart, as well as his own, was fixed on the speculation in lands in the Bend of the Tennessee, which enterprise was calling their associates Caswell and Blount to the West.

Sevier himself was on the point of veering. He promptly wrote his confidential friend, Colonel Daniel Kennedy, of Greene county, under date of January 2, 1785:

"I have just received certain information from Colonel Martin that the first thing the Assembly of North Carolina did, was to repeal the cession bill, and to form this part of the country into a separate District, by name of Washington District, which I have the honor to command. I conclude this step will satisfy the people with the old State, and we shall pursue no further measures as to a new State. David Campbell, Esq'r. is appointed one of our judges. I could write to you officially, but my commission is not yet come to hand."[6]

Sevier later issued an official address to the people of Greene county, giving information of what had been done by the Assembly of North Carolina for the relief of the people west of the mountains; and, with a view to composing controversy and confusion, urged that they decline to take further action toward establishing a new government.[7]

The December convention largely devoted itself to the work of preparing a temporary constitution for the new State, which, from the outset, was called the State of Franklin, and not Frankland, as

---

borough in November, "but broke up in confusion because of the repeal of the cession, John Sevier having received official information."
[6] Ramsey, 292.
[7] *Ib.*

is sometimes stated.[8] The document was unique in form in that it was prefaced by a Declaration of Independence, in which was set forth the "reason which impels us to declare ourselves independent of North Carolina,"—"a decent respect to the opinions of mankind" making it proper.

There follows the usual bill of rights, under the title "Declaration of the State of Franklin"; and next in order is the governmental scheme, the latter closely modeled after the North Carolina Constitution of 1776.[9]

The closing paragraphs declare that the instrument was not intended to preclude the convention then in session from making temporary laws for the well ordering of the State until the General Assembly, organized under the Constitution "shall establish government agreeable to the mode herein described." It is believed, however, that the convention did not undertake to legislate under this power.

It recommended the temporary Constitution "for the serious consideration of the people during six months," after which period and before the expiration of a year, another constitutional convention should be held to pass upon its adoption as the permanent fundamental law, or to amend it to conform to the popular will.

William Cocke and David Campbell probably collaborated in the preparation of this document.

Nowhere, in any document discovered, are the boundaries of Franklin formally defined. By implication jurisdiction was assumed over all of the ceded territory. Thus, the boundaries were coincident with those of the present Tennessee, though for practical purposes the Indians had possession and ruled over large portions of the domain.

---

[8] The news reached Charleston, S. C., in May and was communicated from there to England "The new State is named Franklin." *London Chronicle*, Aug. 20, 1785. Arthur Campbell consistently wrote the name "Frankland"—his preference.

[9] This document escaped the search of Haywood and Ramsey. A certified copy of it was transmitted to the State authorities of North Carolina; and was found, in 1904, in a small paper box in the office of the Insurance Commissioner of North Carolina, and not in the State Archives. The complete instrument appears in Appendix, *infra*. See also *American Historical Magazine*, IX, 399. "The form of government established is under a constitution similar to that of North Carolina." *London Chronicle*, Aug. 20, 1785.

CHAPTER VIII

THE FRANKLIN MOVEMENT IN VIRGINIA

It cannot be a matter of doubt that Colonel Arthur Campbell took an active part in encouraging and aiding the people living in the territory ceded by North Carolina in June, 1784, to form a separate and independent government. He saw in the act of cession an opportunity to carry into execution his favorite plan for a new State including the Southwest Virginia and East Tennessee counties. Campbell attended one or both of the conventions held at Jonesborough, in furtherance of his scheme. "It is notoriously known that Col. Campbell did, in a convention of the North Carolina people, publicly propose to separate himself with the citizens of Washington and Montgomery in Virginia; and, joining them, declare themselves independent of the States of Virginia and North Carolina; moreover to stand in the front of battle between these people and Virginia when necessary . . . The charges herein contained can be supported by General Russell, Captain Andrew Kincannon, and Captain Wm. Cocke of the Franklin Settlement."[1]

Martin wrote to Henry: "Col. Campbell made use of many arguments to draw me over to that [the Franklin] party . . . as it would be much to my interest, as I had a body of valuable lands in Powell's Valley; that as soon as the new State would take place, I might have a county laid off and the court-house on my land and convenient to the seat of government. My reply to him was that as long as I appeared in public character, I did not look altogether at private interest; that I was in every sense of the word against a new State."[2]

On his return from Franklin to his home, Campbell began an agitation in favor of joining the fortunes of the contiguous part of

---

[1] Charges preferred against Campbell by James Montgomery and others, July 25, 1785. *Va. Cal. State Papers*, IV, 45.

[2] Martin to Governor Henry (*Va. Cal. St. Papers*, 53). Martin must have assumed that Campbell was in ignorance of the former's Tennessee Bend purchase of the Cherokees while he was under the trust relation of agent to those Indians.

Virginia with those of the promoters of Franklin. A large element of the people in Southwest Virginia was ripe for action. General Russell and his friends at this time had the ear of the governor in respect to State appointments, rather than the Campbell faction.

One of the complaints of the Western Virginians, not dissimilar to that put forward by the Western Carolinians, was that they were excessively taxed and received no adequate governmental benefits in return. Campbell contended that two million dollars more than was justly due had been collected from the inhabitants of his county; and he urged resistance to further payments on days when, as chief judge in his county, he held county court. Rev. Charles Cummings, who had been a member of the committee of safety organized in his county in revolutionary days and who was a leader among the Presbyterians of his section, appealed to his people to stand for their rights; and he presided at meetings held to advance separation. At one of these gatherings there was set on foot a memorial to Congress asking for the establishment of an independent government. This must have been some time before January 1, 1785, since the document was read in Congress January 13, 1785. It was signed by many leading Virginians on the Holston waters; and, it is interesting to note, by Gilbert Christian, John Anderson, David Looney and John Adair, residents of Sullivan county, across the state line. Concert of action on the part of the two peoples is evident. The connecting link was Arthur Campbell. His was the master mind that moulded the

MEMORIAL
To the Honorable Congress
of the
United States of America.

The Memorial of the freemen inhabiting the county westward of the Alleghany or Appalachian mountain, and southward of the Ouasioto, humbly showeth:

That having been made acquainted with the several Resolves and other Acts of Congress respecting the Western Territory, and having considered maturely the contents of the same, we are highly pleased with that equal respect to the liberties of the people which seems to induce the councils of Congress. That nothing but a firm adherence to the principles of the Confederation, and a sacred regard for the rights of mankind could produce the late resolves for laying off independent States, thereby pointing out such effectual measures to prevent the encroachment of arbitrary power in the asylums of freedom.

Next we are happy to find so large a part of territory already ceded to the United States for national purposes, and trust that every obstacle will speedily be removed for the completion of that business by the individual States effected thereby. That we are too much elated at the prospect before us not to wish that we very speedily enjoy the advantages of such government as will be exercised over a convenient territory, not too small for the support of authority, nor too large for the security of freedom.

That our situation is such, inhabiting valleys intermixed with and environed by vast wilds of barren and inaccessible mountains, that the same compensation of latitude allotted to the new States northwest of the Ohio might prevent us from ever being on an equal footing with our neighbors, blessed with so many natural advantages, navigable waters, and a level, fertile country.

That a State bounded by a meridian line that will touch the confluence of Little River near Ingles Ferry, thence down Kanawha to the Roncovert or Green Briar River, thence southwest to latitude 37 degrees north, thence along the same to the meridian of the Rapids of the Ohio, south along the meridian until it reaches the Tennessee or Cherokee River, down the same to the part nearest latitude 34 degrees, south to the same, and eastwardly on that parallel to the top of the Appalachian mountains, and along the heights that divide the sources of the waters that fall into the Mississippi from those that empty into the Atlantic to the beginning. This, though not equal in quantity of habitable lands with the adjoining States, yet may be sufficient territory for a society that wishes to encourage industry and temperance as cardinal virtues.

That in our present settlement we have maintained our ground during the late perilous war, and frequently gave effectual aid to our brethren to the south and eastward; that we are first occupants and aborigines of this country; freemen claiming natural rights, and the privileges of American citizens.

Our prayer, therefore, is, that your Honourable Body, with a generous regard to the rights of mankind, would speedily erect the aforesaid described Territory into a free and Independent State, subject to the federal bond, and likewise confirm and guarantee to the inhabitants all their equitable rights and privileges acquired under the laws of the States lately claiming this territory; that the disposition of the vacant lands be under the power of the Legislature of the new State, in as full a manner as that exercised by such Eastern States having unappropriated lands, with this reservation, that the monies arising from the sale of vacant lands shall be faithfully paid to the order of Congress, towards the payment of the national debt.

And your memorialists shall ever pray, &c.

Approved and subscribed by us, in behalf of ourselves and the freemen of our respective districts, who we represent.

Charles Cummins,
Chairman,

John Campbell	John Kincaid,
John Jameson,	Arthur Campbell,
Robt. Buchanan,	Thos. Woolsey,
Alexander Wiley,	John Campbell, S'n'r.,
William Tate,	Richard Brownlow,
George Finley	John Davis,
Mathew Willoughby,	
Gilbert Christian,	
John Anderson,	
David Looney,	
John Adair.	

Campbell's enthusiasm for a new government was, at this time, great. He was asked by an opponent: "If the State of North Carolina were to send a force against the Franklin people to subject them to obedience to the government of North Carolina, whether he would be willing to give them aid, meaning the Franklin people? On which he answered, by all means we ought, if we expect to share with them the benefits of government."[3]

Turner says:[4] "Again, in the spring of 1785, another petition went to Congress from the deputies of the same county. They proposed modifications in the rigid rectangles that Jefferson had laid down for the western States in the Ordinance of 1784. The eastern meridian lines, they complained, passed across a great number of the most inaccessible and craggy mountains in America; and severed communities naturally one. The western meridian divided the Kentucky settlers. They proposed two States with natural boundary lines: the Kentucky settlements bounded by the Great Kanawha were to make one, and the upper waters of the Tennessee, including the Muscle Shoals of that river, another. The Cumberland settlers would have been left as a nucleus of another State provided for by the Ordinance of 1784. As thus modified, the settlers declared the Ordinance the basis for liberal and beneficial compact. With this petition they forwarded an association which they had drawn up, resolving, among other things, that the lands cultivated by individuals belong strictly to them, and not to the government; otherwise every citizen would be a tenant and not a landlord, a

---

[3] Deposition of Andrew Kincannon, May 3, 1786, for use in the trial of Arthur Campbell for misconduct in office. *Cal. Va. St. Papers*, IV, 116.

[4] Turner, "Western State-Making in the Revolutionary Era," *American Historical Review*, I, 260; *Archives*, Continental Congress, No. 48, pp. 281, 289, 297.

vassal and not a freeman; and every government would be a usurpation, not an instrumental device for public good."⁵

Their conception of their rights differed materially from the view expressed by Governor Alex. Martin in opposing a cession by North Carolina in 1783: "For cogent is the reasoning, when we can with great truth say: our own blood was spilt in acquiring land for our own settlement, our fortunes expended in making these settlements effectual; for ourselves we fought, for ourselves we conquered, and for ourselves alone we have a right to hold."

The two peoples, on the Holston in Virginia and those of Franklin, were animated by the spirit of independence; and they sought from the beginning the guardianship of the Congress of the Confederation.⁶ Alike they refer in their resolutions to the Ordinance of 1784 for justification, though both saw the impracticability of its provision for rectangular States. They had experienced the inconvenience of being severed by an arbitrary line of latitude—that dividing Virginia and Carolina—and even that line they would disregard, if Congress could be brought to approve.

The boundaries for the new State at the South named in this petition differed somewhat from the earlier ones:

The "State to the South will include the inhabitants on the heads of Kanawha and Cherokee [Tennessee] rivers, to be bounded by a line extended due South from that part of Cumberland river where the meridian line drawn from the mouth of Salt river will touch it, until it reaches Elk river, down that river to the Tenasee, thence South [easterly] to the top of Appalachian mountain, eastwardly along same to a point from whence a north line extended would meet the Kanawha at the mouth of Little river near Ingles' Ferry; and down that river to the Ronceverte [Greenbriar], westwardly along the boundary as above described for the Kentucky Country.

"At this day, we find a new Society forming itself back of North Carolina, which, if the requisition of Congress of the twenty-ninth

---

⁵ Turner: "They are here using the language of Jefferson's Proposed Instructions to the Virginia Delegates, 1774. Ford's *Jefferson's Writings*, I, 437."

⁶ There is no basis in fact for the opinion expressed by Allison (*Dropped Stitches*, 30) that "in the beginning they [the Franklinites] did not intend to join the Union of the States, but that later they concluded they would" Here again, a stitch is dropped rather than picked up. The first resolution passed contained a reference to the resolves of Congress and to the sending of a commissioner to the national legislature.

day of April last is regarded, we of course will be annexed to; and the natural situation of the country points out the connection; but we are yet restrained from formally joining them by a deference to the opinion of those who bear rule in Virginia, and the want of an orderly accession to Independence under the auspices of Congress. These obstacles, we confide, the rulers of the Federal Government will remove. The interest of America seems urgently to call for it, and the peace and prosperity of the western inhabitants will no longer admit of delay."

This well-phrased resolution of the deputies of Washington county, Virginia, was signed by Chas. Cummings, as chairman.

A formal remonstrance[7] was lodged against Campbell with the governor and council of state, by the Russell faction; learning of which Campbell wrote Governor Henry (July 26, 1785):

"We are told (but it is only from report) that we have offended the government on account of our sentiments being favorable to a new State, and our looking forward to a separation. If such a disposition is criminal, I confess that there is not a few in this county to whom guilt may be imputed, and to many respectable characters in other counties on the Western Waters. If we wish for a separation, it is on account of grievances that daily become more and more intolerable; it is from the hope that another mode of governing will make us more useful than we now are to the general Confederacy, or ever can be, whilst so connected. But why can blame fall on us when our aim is to conduct measures in an orderly manner, and strictly consistent with the Constitution? Surely men who have bound themselves by every *holy tie* to support republican principles, cannot, on a dispassionate consideration, blame us. Our want of experience and knowledge may be a plea against us. We deplore our circumstances and situation on that account. But, sir, why may we not take courage and say we are right when adverting to our own Constitution, to the different Acts of Congress, that of different Legislatures, the opinions of the best statesmen in America, among whom we can number an illustrious Commander, a great Lawyer and Judge in this State, and a Governor of Virginia himself."[8]

---

[7] The Humble Remonstrances of the Captains of Washington county (1785) charging that Campbell was "artful in having a majority of the court favorers of his proceedings for a new State." *Va. Mag. Hist. and Biog.*, XVII, 165.

[8] *Cal. Va. St. Papers*, IV, 44.

Campbell's activity for a separation gave no little concern to the leading statesmen of Virginia. Richard Henry Lee wrote from Congress to Madison (May 30, 1785) favoring the grant of self-government to the Kentucky people, since they would remain for a long time "more expense than profit to the rest of the country. Washington county seems to be stimulated by a troublesome person who for self-aggrandizement appears to be willing to dismember that part also, and join with the revolters from North Carolina. This last seems to merit the *wise* and *firm* attention of the government and the legislature."[9]

Governor Henry had written an account of the Franklin proceedings to the Virginia delegates in Congress; and Col. Martin had notified Henry that a firm hand would be shown by the North Carolina government toward the Franklinites in her western counties.[10] This in reply to an inquiry from Henry: "Let me hear from you how the Overhill Carolina folks go on."[11]

Under these influences, Governor Henry issued a proclamation of warning (June 10) to the "freemen of Washington county."

By the summer of 1785, Campbell deemed it unwise to coöperate directly any longer with the other projectors of the State of Franklin.[12] Governor Sevier evidently noted his change of attitude; and thought it good diplomacy to court the favor of Virginia, with a view to changing the position of her delegation in Congress in respect to a recognition of the State of Franklin. On July 19, 1785, Sevier wrote to Henry:

"Having an opportunity to send a letter to Gen. Russell's from whence I expect it can be forwarded to your Excellency, I take the liberty of writing to you. The people of the Western Waters in No. Carolina, for many reasons too long to trouble you with, have formed themselves in a new State by the name of Franklin, and have appointed me their Governor . . . I will beg leave to mention to your Excellency that I am taking every measure in my power to prevent encroachment on the Indians' lands. This, however, is a difficult task, because North Carolina actually sold the lands up to their towns. I have fixed a temporary line as far as the people have settled, and none shall settle over it until it can be done by mutual

---

[9] *Letters* of R. H. Lee, II, 364.
[10] *Cal. Va. St. Papers*, III, 292 (April 16, 1785).
[11] *Ib.*, IV, 18 (March 26, 1785) and 25 (April 17, 1785).
[12] Henry to Martin, Feb. 4, 1785.

agreement. Although we have been forced into necessary measures for separation from North Carolina, I think it is necessary to inform you that we will, on no account, encourage any part of the people of your State to join us, nor will we receive any of them unless by consent of your State. We reverence the Virginians, and I am confident the Legislature here will, at all times, do everything to merit your esteem. Congress have again called upon No. Carolina to confirm the cession which they unwisely withdrew, and I believe a majority of the people in Carolina are in our favor. I do not expect your Excellency to correspond with us until our government is recognized by Congress; but in the meanwhile you may rely we shall do everything in our power to contribute to the welfare of all our neighboring States as well as our own cause. And we hope to convince them all that we are not banditti, but people who mean to do right, as far as our knowledge will lead us."[13]

Governor Henry on the convening of the Assembly of Virginia, sent in the following message on the subject:

"I transmit herewith a letter from the Honorable Mr. Hardy, covering a memorial to Congress from sundry inhabitants of Washington county, praying the establishment of an independent State to be bounded as therein expressed. The proposed limits include a vast extent of country, in which we have numerous and very respectable settlements, which, in their growth, will form an invaluable barrier between this country and those, who, in the course of events, may occupy the vast places westward of the mountains, some of whom have views incompatable with our safety. Already the militia of that part of the country is the most respectable we have, and by their means it is that the neighboring Indians are awed into professions of friendship. But a circumstance has lately happened which renders the possession of the territory at the present time indispensable to the peace and safety of Virginia. I mean the assumption of sovereign power by the western inhabitants of North Carolina. If the people who, without consulting their own safety, or any other authority known in the American Constitution, have assumed government, and while unallied to us, and under no engagements to pursue the objects of the federal government, shall be strengthened by the accession of so great a part of our country, consequences fatal to our repose will probably

---

[13] Roosevelt erroneously states that Campbell acknowledged that he became a member of the privy council of the State of Franklin under Governor Sevier.

follow. It is to be observed, that the settlements of this new society stretch into a great extent in contact with ours in Washington county, and thereby expose our citizens to the contagion of the example which bids fair to destroy the peace of North Carolina. In this state of things it is, that variety of information has come to me, stating that several persons, but especially Col. Arthur Campbell, have used their utmost endeavors, and, with some success, to persuade the citizens in that quarter to break off from this Commonwealth, and attach themselves to the newly assumed government, or to erect one distinct from us. And to effect this purpose, the equality and authority of the laws have been arraigned, the collection of the taxes impeded, and our national character impeached. If this most important part of our territory be lopped off, we lose that barrier for which our people have long and often fought; that nursery of soldiers from which future armies may be levied, and through which it will be almost impossible for our enemies to penetrate. We shall aggrandize the new State, whose connections, views and designs we know not; shall cease to be formidable to our savage neighbors, or respectable to our western settlements, at present or in the future.

"Whilst these and many other matters were contemplated by the Executive, it is natural to suppose the attempt at separation was discouraged by every lawful means, the chief of which was displacing such of the field officers of the militia in Washington county as were active partizans for separation, in order to prevent the weight of office being put in the scale against Virginia. To this end a proclamation was issued, declaring the militia laws of the last session in force in that country, and appointments were made agreeable to them. I hope to be excused for expressing a wish that the Assembly, in deliberating on this affair, will prefer lenient measures, in order to reclaim our erring citizens. Their taxes have run into three years and have thereby grown into an amount beyond the ability of many to discharge; while the system of our trade has been such as to render their agriculture unproductive of money. And I cannot but suppose, that even the warmest supporters of separation had seen the mischievous consequences, they would have retraced, and considered that intemperance in their own proceedings, which opposition in sentiment is too apt to produce."[14]

The Assembly determined to adopt vigorous measures to check

---
[14] *Cal. Va. St. Papers*, IV, 34.

the separation movement in the southwestern counties, and passed an act in the fall of 1785, by which it was declared to be high treason to erect, without authority of the Assembly, an independent government within the limits of the State.[15] But conciliatory steps were also taken. Governor Henry had appointed Gen. William Russell as head of the western militia instead of Campbell, but when Edmund Randolph succeeded Henry in the governorship, Campbell was reinstated and again in ascendency. Col. Joseph Martin lost his office as Indian agent shortly after this change in administration.

Haywood states that Campbell drafted a constitution for the new State proposed by him, in which the boundaries were set forth with more particularity. Nothing but the "declaration of rights" of this instrument remains.[16]

Colonel Arthur Campbell doubtless felt that he was compelled by circumstances to give over his pet project and turn undivided attention to the defense of himself against his enemies before the Virginia Assembly. He was there deprived of his office; but he grimly fought on. The succeeding administration and General Assembly (1787) were favorable to him, and an act was passed[17] de-

---

[15] *Cal. Va. St. Papers*, IV, 42.

[16] Haywood, 320. See Summers, *History of Southwest Virginia*, 400, for the declaration of rights. Haywood gives the boundaries as follows:

"Beginning at a point on the top of the Alleghany or Appalachian mountains, so as a line drawn due north from there will touch the bank of New River, otherwise called Kanawha, at the confluence of Little river, which is about one mile above Ingle's ferry; down the said river Kanawha to the mouth of Rencovert, or Green Briar river; a direct line thence to the nearest summit of Laurel mountain, and along the highest part of same to the point where it is intersected by the parallel of thirty-seven degrees of north latitude; west along that latitude to a point where it is met by a meridian line that passes through the lower part of the rapid of Ohio; south along the meridian to Elk river, a branch of the Tennessee; down said river to its mouth, and down the Tennessee to the most southwardly part or bend in said river; a direct line from thence to that branch of the Mobile river called Donbigbee, to its junction with the Coosawatee river, to the mouth of that branch of it called the Hightower; thence south to the top of the Appalachian mountain, or the highest land that divides the sources of the eastern from the western waters; northwardly, along the middle of said heights, and the top of the Appalachian mountain, to the beginning." The name of the commonwealth was to be Franklin, or Frankland. This grand project reached out for the much-sought territory in the Great Bend of Tennessee river, and also included lands lower down on which Colonel Joseph Martin had fixed his heart.

[17] Hening's *Statutes*, XII, 41.

claring the former legislative action to be void because unconstitutional, in that it trenched on judicial power. Campbell resumed the performance of the duties of the office, and William Edmiston prosecuted a *qui tam* action against him, but lost.[18]

---

[18] Edmiston vs. Campbell, *1 Va. Cases*, 16. The constitutional question was of so much importance that the case was abstracted in Tucker's *Blackstone's Commentaries*, I, 125.

CHAPTER IX

The First General Assembly—1785

An interesting situation was now presented for the play and interplay of influences, tending on the one hand to anchor leaders to the cause of the old State, or, on the other, to attach them to the fortunes of the fledgling Commonwealth. Later researches, it is to be regretted, fail to disclose anything that adds to the bare statement of Haywood that Cocke in an interview with Sevier "erased the favorable impressions he had received towards the government of North Carolina." Cocke, more than any other man, Sevier excepted, had shaped the course of recent events. He was a lawyer and the drafting of the resolutions, articles of association and a declaration of independence naturally, in large part, fell to him; and, quite as of course, he felt the pride of parenthood. He could not easily yield assent to the wrecking of his handiwork in the construction of a new government in which his popularity and talents gave promise of raising him to high station. His must have been a persuasive appeal to Sevier, without whose coöperation headway could not be made.

Sevier felt that he owed a duty to his people. He was their recognized leader; and popular sentiment at the time ran strongly in favor of independence. By that, rather than by the influence of any leader or leaders of the frontier, Sevier was constrained to surrender his own conviction as to what was true policy. Sevier, himself, stated the case, in sum, when (in 1788) he wrote to Joseph Martin that he was "dragged with the Franklin measures by a large number of the people of this country."[1]

In reviewing the conduct of Sevier, the North Carolina Assembly of 1789 found that Sevier did in 1784 oppose efforts made to subvert North Carolina's authority "in such manner as actually to prevent elections being held under the new government in two of the counties."[2]

---
[1] *Calendar Virginia State Papers*, IV, 416.
[2] *Report*, North Carolina Senate, Nov., 1789, signed by John Rhea, Chairman.

THE FIRST GENERAL ASSEMBLY

This indicates that the first attempt to hold an election for members to an Assembly of Franklin under the Constitution was frustrated by Sevier, in efforts initiated by his Jonesborough speech and Kennedy letter; and also explains why the Assembly did not meet until March, 1785.

The Assembly met early in March and did not adjourn until near the end of the month, though it is probable that there were recesses taken in order that committees charged with the drafting of a series of legislative acts might mature the same for report and passage. The Assembly was held at Jonesborough, as Ramsey correctly states;[3] though Allison states that the meeting was at Greeneville.[4] This fact entitles the county site of Washington county to the honor of having been, in the fullest sense, the first capital of the Commonwealth.

John Sevier was elected governor, perhaps without opposition.

No roster of the members of the first Assembly of Franklin has been preserved. Landon Carter was speaker of the senate, and Thomas Talbot its clerk; and William Cage was speaker and Thomas Chapman, clerk of the house of commons. The government was organized by the election of John Sevier as governor. A judiciary was established, David Campbell becoming judge of the

---

Rhea was from Sullivan county; and in later years represented the first district of Tennessee in Congress.

[3] Ramsey, 293.

[4] Allison, *Dropped Stitches*, 28. This statement called out a newspaper controversy as to which of the two towns was the first capital of the State. Judge Allison was drawn into the discussion, and in a communication of April 5, 1916, (*Johnson City Daily Staff*, April 8, 1916) after quoting and reaffirming his statement, he says that he gathered the facts from Haywood's *History of Tennessee*, records and other official sources (without citation) and concludes: "So it appears that while there were meetings at Jonesborough, on the subject, the Constitution of Franklin was finally adopted at Greeneville, the government organized there, and state officers elected and located there, and the legislature met, first and last at Greeneville." Haywood, however, is silent on the point in issue. The Assembly's reply to Governor Martin was dated Jonesborough, March 22nd. A proclamation was issued by Governor Sevier dated "in Washington [County] this 15th day of May 1785, and in the first year of our independency:" *Pennsylvania Packet*, August 9, 1785; *State Gazette* of South Carolina, August 8, 1785. Governor Sevier wrote from "Washington Court House" to Governor Martin 1785—while the Assembly was yet in session. Not only was the March session of the Assembly held at Jonesborough; there was an August, 1785 session held at the same place, as is shown in a later chapter. Allison was a native of Washington County, and that fact might be thought to add weight to his statement.

superior court, and Joshua Gist and John Anderson assistant judges.

The records of the legislature and council of state of the State of Franklin have been lost. The laws were never printed or published save by oral proclamation at the door of Assembly. Col. Gilbert Christian, it appears, may have had possession of the records at the time of his death in 1793.[5]

Copies of the titles of the Acts passed at the March, 1785, session of the Assembly were forwarded to the North Carolina authorities, and filed. Haywood evidently drawing from that source gives a list of acts, ratified on March 31, 1785:

"An act to establish the legal claims of persons claiming any property under the laws of North Carolina, in the same manner as if the State of Franklin had never formed itself into a distinct and separate State."

"An act to appoint commissioners, and to vest them with full powers to make deeds of conveyance to such persons as have purchased lots in the town of Jonesborough."

"An act for the promotion of learning in the county of Washington."[6]

"An act to establish a militia in this State."[7]

---

[5] George Christian's statement to Draper (1842): "I can say that in father's possession at the time of his death, there were a quantity of manuscript copies of the laws of Franklin, all of which fell into the hands of others after the death of my mother which occurred in 1812. I presume my youngest sister, Margaret, who married Rev. Thomas Milligan, must have possession of the old papers, if preserved at all."

[6] By this act, Martin's Academy was reincorporated. The North Carolina Assembly of 1783 had provided for the establishment of that Academy, naming it in honor of Governor Alexander Martin. It was the institution that had been founded by Rev. Samuel Doak about 1780, near Jonesborough, at Salem church (Presbyterian) on Hominy branch of Little Limestone creek. Doak had been a member of the Franklin December convention, and doubtless asked legislative recognition of his classical school. Later the Assembly of the Territory South of the Ohio River (1795) on motion of John Sevier, granted a charter to the institution under the name of Washington College. John Sevier, Jr., was named as one of the trustees. It was the first literary institution west of the mountains, and has had a useful and honorable existence ever since. Alexander, *Historical Sketch of Washington College, Tennessee*, 4–10.

[7] Under this act, field officers for the several counties were named, as follows: For Sullivan county: Gilbert Christian, colonel; John Anderson, lieutenant-colonel; George Maxwell, first major. For the "middle county" (later at the same session created Caswell county): Alexander Outlaw, colonel; James Roddy, lieutenant-

THE FIRST GENERAL ASSEMBLY 59

"An act for dividing Sullivan county and part of Greene, into two distinct counties, and erecting a county by the name of Spencer."[8]

"An act directing the method of electing members of the General Assembly."

"An act for procuring a great seal for this State."[9]

"An act to divide Greene county into three separate and distinct counties, and to erect new counties by the name of Caswell[10] and Sevier."[11]

"An act to ascertain the value of gold and silver foreign coin, and the paper currency now in circulation in the State of North Carolina, and to declare the same to be a lawful tender in this State."[12]

"An act for laying a tax for the support of the government."
Under this caption was the following section:

"*Be it enacted*, That it shall and may be lawful for the aforesaid land tax, and all free polls, to be paid in the following manner: Good flax linen, ten hundred, at three shillings and six pence per yard; nine hundred, at three shillings; eight hundred, two shillings and nine pence; seven hundred, two shillings and six pence; six hundred, two shillings; tow linen, one shilling and nine pence; linsey, three shillings, and woollen and cotton linsey, three shillings and six pence per yard; good, clean beaver skin, six shillings; cased otter skins, six shillings; uncased ditto, five shillings; rackoon and fox skins, one shilling and three pence; woollen cloth, at ten shillings per yard; bacon, well cured, six pence per pound; good, clean tallow,

---

colonel; John McNab, first major; Nathaniel Evans, second major. For Greene county: Daniel Kennedy, colonel; George Doherty, lieutenant-colonel; James Houston, first major; Alexander Kelly, second major. For Washington county: Charles Robertson, colonel; Valentine Sevier, lieutenant-colonel; Landon Carter, first major; Jacob Brown, second major.

Haywood and Ramsey state that Daniel Kennedy and William Cocke were made brigadier-generals of the Franklin militia.

[8] Corresponding to Hawkins county, North Carolina, and Tennessee.

[9] Ramsey, 294: "This act was probably never carried into effect. More than two years afterward commissions to the officers of Franklin were issued, having upon them a common wafer as the seal of the State."

[10] In honor of General Richard Caswell, who had been elected and was soon to be inaugurated governor of North Carolina.

[11] In honor of John Sevier. In 1794 at the Assembly of the Territory South of the Ohio River, a county, covering a part of the same territory, was created and given the name of Sevier.

[12] Conveyances registered at Jonesborough in the year 1785, in recital of the consideration, say: "good and lawful money of the State of Franklin." Bonds were payable in "Franklin currency."

six pence per pound; good, clean beeswax, one shilling per pound; good distilled rye whiskey, at two shillings and six pence per gallon; good peach or apple brandy, at three shillings per gallon; good country made sugar, at one shilling per pound; deer skins, the pattern, six shillings; good, neat and well managed tobacco, fit to be prized, that may pass inspection, the hundred, fifteen shillings, and so on in proportion for a greater or less quantity."

"An act to ascertain the salaries allowed the Governor, Attorney-General, Judges of the Superior Courts, Assistant Judges, Secretary of the State, Treasurer and members of the Council of State."

The salary of the governor was fixed at two hundred pounds, per annum; the attorney-general twenty-five pounds for each court he attended; the secretary of state, twenty-five pounds, in addition to fees allowed him by the law; the judge of the superior court, one hundred and fifty pounds; the assistant judges, twenty-five pounds each for every court attended; the treasurer, forty pounds; and each member of the council of state, six shillings per day, for each day of actual service. The last section of the act was in these words:

"And all the salaries and allowances hereby made shall be paid by any treasurer, sheriff or collector of public taxes, to any person entitled to the same, to be paid in specific articles as collected, and at the rates allowed by the State for the same; or in current money of the State of Franklin."

"An act for ascertaining what property in this State shall be deemed taxable, the method of assessing the same, and collecting public taxes."

"An act to ascertain the powers and authorities of the judges of the Superior Courts, the Assistant Judges and Justices of the Peace, and of the County Courts of Pleas and Quarter Sessions, and directing the time and place of holding the same."

"An act for erecting a part of Washington county and that part of Wilkes lying west of the extreme heights of the Appalachian or Alleghany mountains, into a separate and distinct county by the name of Wayne."[13]

Haywood, who, by reason of his intimate knowledge of North Carolina legislation, could speak with authority, says that these enactments conformed closely to those which had been made on the same or similar subjects-matter in North Carolina. The enacting

---

[13] Named in honor of General Anthony Wayne. It embraced the territory now within the limits of Carter and Johnson counties.

clause was, "Be it enacted by the General Assembly of the State of Franklin."

Those named for the offices of civil government were, in large part, those who had been in the service of the old State.

Ramsey states that, as far as could be ascertained at the time he wrote, James Sevier was clerk of the Washington county court; John Rhea, of the Sullivan court;[14] Daniel Kennedy of the Greene court; Thomas Henderson, of the Spencer court;[15] Joseph Hamilton, of the Caswell court; and Samuel Wear, of the Sevier court.

Francis A. Ramsey, father of the historian, was appointed by Governor Sevier to the clerkship of the superior court for the District of Washington, which was held at Jonesborough.

Manning the state offices were: Landon Carter, secretary of state; William Cage, treasurer; and Stockley Donelson, surveyor-general. The council of state was composed of William Cocke, Landon Carter, Francis A. Ramsey, David Campbell, Daniel Kennedy, and Colonel Taylor.[16]

[14] In respect to Rhea the historian must be in error, since Rhea wrote to Governor Caswell, May 4, 1787, stating that he had been clerk of the Sullivan county court, under North Carolina, previous to the establishment of the Franklin government; but that he had been called abroad by business. "At my return lately, it appeared that during my absence there had been a change respecting a government called Franklin, that the justices of the county had let the court [North Carolina] fall, a majority if not all having joined the new-made government. When the courts were erected under the Franklin authority, the person who was deputy for me was by them made clerk of their court in Sullivan, by which proceeding all the records of this county have fallen into the hands of the people of Franklin," and "as an officer of the State of North Carolina" Rhea asked instructions from the governor how to proceed. The letter sheds much light upon the sentiment of the inhabitants of Sullivan County toward the new State at that time. Rhea had been clerk of the Sullivan county court as early as 1780.

[15] It appears that Thomas Hutchings, before his defection, was for a time clerk of the Spencer county court. *Ingram's Heirs vs. Cocke*, 1 Overton Rep. 22.

[16] Ramsey, 296. An effort was made to win Col. Joseph Martin's adherence to the Franklin government. As seen, he had been active in the earlier stages of the movement, but on visiting the seat of government of North Carolina, he had learned that the separation would meet with Governor Martin's determined resistance; whereupon he shifted his course. He was chosen as a member of the council of state of Franklin, but declined to qualify. Active in the affairs of Virginia, as well as those of North Carolina, he had incurred the displeasure of Col. Arthur Campbell of Washington county, Virginia. Campbell wrote to Governor Patrick Henry, June 3, 1785, in regard to Martin's appointment as lieutenant-colonel of Virginia militia; "since that he became a citizen of North Carolina, resided in that State and served there in different offices—no duty having been done by him in this for years;

On Cage's election as state treasurer, Joseph Hardin, of Greene, succeeded to the speakership of the house of commons, and served for a remnant of the March session, 1785.

Governor Martin determined to send to the disaffected region a personal representative to ascertain and report the true state of affairs. He selected Major Samuel Henderson, a brother of Judge Richard Henderson, who had in former years been on the western frontiers;[17] and on February 27, 1785, a letter of instructions was delivered to Henderson.[18]

---

and lately, at his own solicitation, was chosen one of the privy council for the State of Frankland (as it is called)." *Va. Cal. State Papers*, IV, 31. Martin wrote to Governor Henry a letter, in which he made no reference to his active participation in the Franklin movement and guardedly stated: "As I am informed, Colo. Arthur Campbell informed your Excellency that I was an officer in the new State. I beg to assure your Excellency that the report is vague, and that no earthly thing shall prevail on me to neglect my duty as agent for the State of Virginia so long as I have the honour to fill that office. True it is the Assembly of Franklin, as they call themselves, elected me one of their privy council, which I refused to accept." *Va. Cal. St. Papers*, 53 (Sept. 19-1785). Martin on the same day wrote the governor of North Carolina quite as "vague" a denial as the above: "I find myself under some concern ... wherein I am considered a member of the new State. I beg leave to assure your Excellency that I have no part with them." *N. C. St. Rec.*, XVII; Ramsey, 318.

[17] Henderson: *Conquest of the Old Southwest*.

[18] "You will please to repair with despatch to General Sevier and deliver him the letters herewith handed you, and request his answer. You will make yourself acquainted with the transaction of the people in the Western Country, such as holding a convention; and learn whether the same be temporary, to be exercised only during the time of the late cession act, and that since repeal thereof they mean to consider themselves citizens of North Carolina; or whether they intend the same to be perpetual; and what measures they have taken to support such government. That you procure a copy of the constitution, and the names of such officers at present exercising the powers of the new government. That you be informed whether a faction of a few leading men be at the head of this business, or whether it be the sense of a large majority of the people that the State be dismembered at this crisis of affairs, and what laws and resolutions are formed for their future government; also, where the bounds of their new State are to extend, and whether Cumberland or Kentucky, or both, are to be included therein, and whether the people of these places have taken part in these transactions. You will learn the temper and disposition of the Indians, and what is done in Hubbard's case, and how his conduct is approved or disapproved in general. Lastly, every other information you think necessary to procure, you will communicate to me as soon as possible; at the same time you will conduct yourself with that prudence you are master of, in not throwing out menaces, or making use of any language that may serve to irritate persons concerned in the above measures." Ramsey, 307, and *N. C. St. Records*.

THE FIRST GENERAL ASSEMBLY 63

When Henderson reached Jonesborough, he found the first Assembly of Franklin in session. Governor Sevier laid before the Assembly a letter brought to him from Governor Martin—addressed to him as "brigadier-general." The Assembly formulated a reply to it:

         Jonesborough, 22nd March, 1785.
Sir:

Your letter of the 27th of February, 1785, to his Excellency Governor Sevier, favored by Major Henderson, was laid before the General Assembly of the State of Franklin by the Governor.

We think it our duty to communicate to you the sense of the people of this State. We observe your Excellency's candor in informing us that the reason North Carolina repealed the cession act was because the sense of Congress was to allow the State of North Carolina nothing for the land ceded. The truth of that assertion we will not undertake to determine; but we humbly conceive the terms on which Congress was empowered to accept the cession were fully expressed in the cession act itself. Consequently every reason existed for not passing the cession act that could have existed for the repeal, except that of doing justice to the United States in general, who, upon every principle of natural justice, are equally entitled to the land that has been conquered by our own joint efforts.

We humbly thank North Carolina for every sentiment of regard she has for us; but we are sorry to observe that it is founded on principles of interest, as is apparent from the tenor of your Excellency's letter. We are therefore doubtful, when the cause ceases which is the basis of your affection, we shall consequently lose your esteem.

Sir, reflect upon the language of some of the most eminent members of the General Assembly of North Carolina at the last spring session, when the members from the Western Country were supplicating to be continued a part of your State. Were not these their epithets: "The inhabitants of the Western Country are the off-scourings of the earth, fugitives from justice, and we will be rid of them at any rate." The members of the Western Country, upon hearing these unjust reproaches and being convinced it was the sense of the General Assembly to get rid of them, consulted each other and concluded it was best to appear reconciled with the masses in order to obtain the best terms they could, and were much astonished to see North Carolina, immediately on passing the act of cession, enter into a resolve to stop the goods that they, by the act of the General Assembly, had promised to give the Indians for the lands they had taken from them and sold for the use of the State. The inadequate allowance made the judges who were appointed to attend the courts of criminal justice, and who had to travel over the mountains, amounted to prohibition as to the administration of justice in this quarter, and altho' the judge appointed on this side of the mountain might, from the regard he had to the administration of justice in the Cumberland Country, have held a court there, yet, as your Excellency failed to grant him a commission agreeable to the Act of Assembly, he could not have performed that service had he been ever so desirous of doing it. In short, the Western Country found themselves taxed to support government, while they were deprived of all the blessing of it—not to mention the injustice done them in taxing their lands, which lie five hundred miles from trade, equal to the land of the same quality of the sea shore. The frequent murders committed by the Indians on our frontiers have compelled us to think on some plan for our defense. How far North Carolina has been accessory to these murders we will not pretend to say. We only know that she took the land the Indians claimed, promised to pay them for them and again resolved not do to it; and that in consequence of the resolve, the goods were stopped.

You say it has been suggested that the Indian goods are to be seized and the commissioners arrested when they arrive on the business of the treaty. We are happy to inform you that the suggestion is false, groundless and without the least foundation; and we are certain you cannot pretend to fault us that the goods are stopped by a resolve of the Assembly of your State; and if your State are determined to evade their promise to the Indians, we entreat you not to lay the blame upon us, who are entirely innocent and determined to remain so. It is true that we have declared ourselves a free and independent State, and pledged our honors, confirmed by a solemn oath to support, maintain and defend the same. But we had not the most distant idea that we should have incurred the least displeasure from North Carolina, who compelled us to the measure; and to convince her that we still retain our affection for her, the first law we enacted was to secure and confirm all the rights granted under the laws of North Carolina in the same manner as if we had not declared ourselves an independent State; have patronized her Constitution and laws and hope for her assistance and influence in Congress to precipitate our reception into the Federal Union. Should our sanguine hopes be blasted, we are determined never to desert that independence which we are bound by every sacred tie of honor and religion to support. We are induced to think that North Carolina will not blame us for endeavoring to promote our own interest and happiness, while we do not attempt to abridge hers; and appeal to the impartial world to determine whether we have deserted North Carolina or North Carolina deserted us.

You will please to lay these our sentiments before the General Assembly, whom we beg leave to assure, that, should they ever need our assistance, we shall always be ready to render them every service in our powers, and hope to find the same sentiments prevailing in them towards us; and we hereunto annex the reasons that in-

THE FIRST GENERAL ASSEMBLY

duced the convention to a Declaration of Independence, which are as follows:

1st. That the Constitution of North Carolina declares that it shall be justifiable to erect new States westward whenever the consent of the Legislature shall countenance it; and this consent is implied, we conceive, in the cession act, which has thrown us into such a situation that the influence of the law in common cases became almost a nullity, and in criminal jurisdiction has entirely ceased; which reduced us to the verge of anarchy.

2nd. The Assembly of North Carolina have detained a certain quantity of goods which was promised to satisfy the Indians for the lands we possess, which detenure we fully conceive has so exasperated them that they have actually committed hostilities upon us, and we are alone impelled to defend ourselves from their ravages.

3rd. The resolutions of Congress held out from time to time encouraging the erection of new States have appeared to us ample encouragement.

4th. Our local situation is such that we not only apprehend we should be separated from North Carolina, but most every sensible, disinterested traveler has declared it incompatible with our interest to belong in union with the eastern parts of North Carolina. For we are not only so far removed from the eastern parts of the State, but separated from them by high and almost impassable mountains, which naturally divide us from them. Have proved to us that our interest is also in many respects distinct from the inhabitants on the other side and much injured by a union with them.

5th. We unanimously agree that our lives, liberty and property can be more secure and our happiness much better propagated by our separation; and consequently that it is our duty and inalienable right to form ourselves into a new independent State.

We beg leave to subscribe ourselves,
Your Excellency's Most Obedient Humbl. Sert's.
William Cage, S. H. C.
Landon Carter, S. S.
By order of the General Assembly.
Thomas Talbot, C. S.
Thomas Chapman, C. C.

Governor Sevier also returned a short reply by Henderson, in which only one point was reinforced—that North Carolina had granted, for a consideration inuring to herself, the lands of the Cherokees up to the mouth of Holston river, the actual settlement of which lands she was now threatening to resist.

William Cocke was elected agent or commissioner of the State of Franklin to appear before the Congress of the Confederation and present a memorial prepared by the General Assembly, praying admission to the Union.

The Assembly considered it necessary to bring the Cherokee Indians into relationship with the new Commonwealth, and Governor Sevier, Alexander Outlaw and Daniel Kennedy were appointed commissioners with authority to make a treaty with the Overhill Cherokees.

The first session of the Franklin Assembly was the longest ever held. The bulk of the legislation was large; necessarily so in the launching of a new State.

Buoyancy and hopefulness were in the hearts of the Franklin people as they faced the future. In the summer of 1785, a neighbor across the line in Washington county, Virginia, wrote that the "new society or State called Franklin has already put off its infant habit and seems to step forward with a florid, healthy constitution; it wants only the paternal guardianship of Congress for a short period to entitle it to be admitted with *eclat* as a member of the Federal Government. Here the genuine Republican! here the real Whig will find a safe asylum, a comfortable retreat among those modern Franks, the hardy mountain men."[19]

---

[19] Quoted by Turner, "Western State-making," *Am. Hist. Rec.*, I, 258. Col. Arthur Campbell was perhaps the writer.

CHAPTER X

Manifesto and Counter Manifesto—1785

While Henderson was making his investigations west of the mountains, news, coming in some way from the Cumberland Settlement, reached Newbern, the temporary seat of the Carolina government, that indicated his might prove to be a fool's errand: "The reports prevailing of the dismemberment of this State to the westward, are entirely groundless." "The political fool (Sevier) was restrained from the exertion of his own will," says the Newbern correspondent of the South Carolina *Gazette*, under date of March 24th.[1]

On the return of the special representative from Jonesborough disillusionment soon passed into pique, and Governor Martin issued a call (April 7th) for a meeting of the council of state to advise on the measures necessary in view of the declaration of independence and formation of a state government in the West. As a result of the council's session, Martin, under date of April 25th, published and sent to the Western Country, a manifesto:

STATE OF NORTH-CAROLINA:

By His Excellency ALEXANDER MARTIN, Esquire, Governor, Captain-General and Commander-in-Chief of the State aforesaid—
To the Inhabitants of the Counties of Washington, Sullivan and Greene:

A MANIFESTO.

Whereas, I have received letters from Brigadier-General Sevier, under the style and character of Governor, and from Messrs. Landon Carter and William Cage, as Speakers of the Senate and House of Commons of the State of Franklin, informing me that they, with you, the inhabitants of part of the territory lately ceded to Congress, had declared themselves independent of the State of North-Carolina, and no longer consider themselves under the sovereignty and jurisdiction of the same, stating their reason for their separation and revolt—among which it alledged, that the western country was ceded to Congress without their consent, by an act of the legislature, and the same was repealed in the like manner.

---

[1] The *South Carolina Gazette* of April 25th, 1785.

It is evident, from the journals of that Assembly, how far that assertion is supported, which held up to public view the names of those who voted on the different sides of that important question, where is found a considerable number, if not a majority, of the members—some of whom are leaders in the present *revolt*—then representing the above counties, in support of that act they now deem impolitic and pretend to reprobate—which, in all probability, would not have passed but through their influence and assiduity—whose passage at length was effected but by a small majority, and by which a cession of the vacant territory was only made and obtained with a power to the delegates to complete the same by grants, but that government should still be supported, and that anarchy prevented—which is now suggested—the western people were ready to fall into. The sovereignty and jurisdiction of the state were, by another act passed by the same assembly, reserved and asserted over the ceded territory, with all the powers and authorities as full and ample as before, until Congress should accept the same.

The last Assembly having learned what uneasiness and discontent the Cession act had occasioned throughout the state, whose inhabitants had not been previously consulted on that measure, in whom, by the constitution, the soil and territorial rights of the state are particularly vested, judging the said act impolitic at this time, more especially as it would, for a small consideration, dismember the state of one half of her territory, and in the end tear from her a respectable body of her citizens, when no one state in the Union had parted with any of their citizens, or given anything like an equivalent to Congress but vacant lands of an equivocal and disputed title and distant situation; and also considering that the said act, by its tenor and purport, was revocable at any time before the cession should have been completed by the delegates, who repealed it by a great majority; at the same time, the Assembly, to convince the people of the western country of their affection and attention to their interest, attempted to render government as easy as possible to them, by removing the only general inconvenience and grievance they might labour under, for the want of a regular administration of criminal justice, and a proper and immediate command of the militia; a new district was erected, an assistant judge and a brigadier-general were appointed.

Another reason for the revolt is assigned, that the Assembly on the Cession act stopped a quantity of goods intended for the Cherokee Indians, as a compensation for their claim to the western lands; and that the Indians had committed hostilities, in consequence thereof. The journals of the Assembly evince the contrary; that the said goods were still to be given to the Indians, but under the regulations of Congress, should the cession take place; which occasioned the delay of not immediately sending them forward; of which the Indians were immediately notified, and I am well informed that no hostilities or mischiefs have been committed on this account; but, on the other hand, that provocations have been, and are daily given, their lands trespassed upon, and even one of their chiefs has been lately murdered, with impunity.

On the repeal of the Cession act, a treaty was ordered to be held with the Indians, and the goods distributed as soon as the season would permit; which, before this, would have been carried into effect, had not the face of affairs been changed.

Under what character, but truly disgraceful, could the State of North-Carolina suffer treaties to be held with the Indians, and other business transacted in a country, where her authority and government were rejected and set at naught, her officers liable to insult, void of assistance or protection.

The particular attention the legislature have paid to the interest of the western citizens, though calculated to conciliate their affection and esteem, has not been satisfactory, it seems: but the same has been attributed to interest and lucrative designs. Whatever designs the legislature entertained in the repeal of the said act, they have made it appear that their wisdom considered that the situation of our public accounts was somewhat changed since that Assembly, and that the interest of the state should immediately be consulted and attended to, that every citizen should reap the advantage of the vacant territory, that the same should be reserved for the payment of the public debts of the state, under such regulations hereafter to be adopted; judging it ill-timed generosity at this crisis, to be too liberal of the means that would so greatly contribute to her honesty and justice.

But designs of a more dangerous nature and deeper die seem to glare in the western revolt. The power usurped over the vacant territory, the Union deriving no emolument from the same, not even the proportional part intended the old states by the cession being reserved, her jurisdiction and sovereignty over that country (which, by the consent of its representatives, were still to remain and be exercised) rejected and deposed; her public revenue in that part of her government seized by the new authority, and not suffered to be paid to the lawful Treasurer, but appropriated to different purposes, as intended by the Legislature,—are all facts, evincing that a restless ambition and a lawless thirst of power, have inspired this enterprise, by which the persons concerned, therein, may be precipitated into measures that may, at last, bring down ruin, not only on themselves, but our country at large.

In order, therefore, to reclaim such citizens, who, by specious pretences and the acts of designing men, have been seduced from their allegiance, to restrain others from following their example who are wavering, and to confirm the attachment and affection of those who adhere to the old government, and whose fidelity hath not yet been shaken, I have thought proper to issue this Manifesto, hereby warning all persons concerned in the said revolt, that they return to their duty and allegiance, and forbear paying any obedience to any self-created power and authority unknown to the constitution of the state, and not sanctified by the Legislature. That they and you consider the consequences that may attend such a dangerous and unwarrantable procedure; that far less causes have deluged states and kingdoms with blood, which, at length, have terminated their existence, either by subjecting them a prey to foreign conquerors, or erecting in their room a despotism that has bidden defiance to time to shake off;—the lowest state of misery, human nature, under such a government, can be reduced to. That they reflect there is a national pride in all kingdoms and states, that inspires every subject and citizen with a degree of importance—the grand cement and support of every government—which must not be insulted. That the honour of this State has been particularly wounded by seizing that by violence which, in time, no doubt, would have been obtained by consent, when the terms of separation would have been explained and stipulated, to the mutual satisfaction of the mother and new state. That Congress, by the confederation, cannot countenance such a separation, wherein the State of North-Carolina hath not given her full consent; and if an implied or conditional one hath been given, the same hath been rescinded by a full Legislature. Of her reasons for so doing they consider themselves the only competent judges.

That by such rash and irregular conduct a precedent is formed for every district, and even every county of the state, to claim the right of separation and independency for any supposed grievance of the inhabitants, as caprice, pride and ambition shall dictate, at pleasure, thereby exhibiting to the world a melancholy instance of a feeble or pusillanimous government, that is either unable or dares not restrain the lawless designs of its citizens, which will give ample cause of exultation to our late enemies, and raise their hopes that they may hereafter gain, by the division among ourselves, that dominion their tyranny and arms have lost, and could not maintain.

That you tarnish not the laurels you have so gloriously won at King's Mountain and elsewhere, in supporting the freedom and independence of the United States, and this state in particular, to be whose citizens were then your boast, in being concerned in a black and traitorous revolt from that government in whose defence you have so copiously bled, and which, by solemn oath, you are still bound to support. Let not Vermont be held up as an example on this occasion. Vermont, we are informed, had her claims for a separate government at the first existence of the American war, and, as such, with the other states, although not in the Union, hath exerted her powers against the late common enemy.

That you be not insulted or led away with the pageantry of a mock government without the essentials—the shadow without the substance—which always dazzles weak minds, and which will, in its present form and manner of existence, not only subject you to the ridicule and contempt of the world, but rouse the indignation of the other states in the Union at your obtruding yourselves as a power among them without their consent. Consider what a number of men of different abilities will be wanting to fill the civil list of the State of Franklin, and the expense necessary to support them suitable to their various degrees of dignity, when the District of Washington, with its present officers, might answer all the purposes of a happy government until the period arrive when a separation might take place to mutual advantage and satisfaction on an honourable footing. The Legislature will shortly meet, before whom the transactions of your leaders will be laid. Let your representatives come forward and present every grievance in a constitutional manner, that they may be redressed; and let your terms of separation be proposed with decency, your proportion of the public debts ascertained, the vacant territory appropriated to the mutual benefit of both parties, in such manner and proportion as may be just and reasonable; let your proposals be consistent with the honour of the state to accede to, which, by your allegiance as good citizens you cannot violate, and I make no doubt but her generosity, in time, will meet your wishes.

But, on the contrary, should you be hurried on by blind ambition to pursue your present unjustifiable measures, which may open afresh the wounds of this late bleeding country, and plunge it again into all the miseries of a civil war, which *God* avert, let the fatal consequences be charged upon the authors. It is only time which can reveal the event. I know with reluctance the state will be *driven to arms;* it will be the last alternative to *imbrue* her hand in the blood of her citizens; but if no other ways and means are found to save her honour, and reclaim her head-strong, refractory citizens, but this last sad expedient, her resources are not yet so exhausted or her spirits damped, but she may take satisfaction for this great injury received, regain her government over the revolted territory or render it not worth possessing. But all these effects may be prevented, at this time, by removing the causes, by those who have revolted returning to their duty, and those who have stood firm, still continue to support the government of this state, until the consent of the legislature be fully and constitutionally had for a separate sovereignty and jurisdiction. All which, by virtue of the powers and authorities which your representatives and others of the state at large have invested me with in General Assembly, I hereby will command and require, as you will be liable to answer all the pains and penalties that may ensue on the contrary.

Given under my hand and the Great Seal of the State, which I have caused to be hereunto affixed, at Hillsborough, the twenty-fifth day of April, in the year of our Lord 1785, and ninth year of the Independence of the said State.

ALEXANDER MARTIN,

By His Excellency's command.
JAMES GLASGOW, Secretary.

On April 25th, also, Governor Martin issued a call for a special session of the General Assembly in which he referred to "the revolt of the inhabitants of the counties of Washington, Sullivan and Greene" as one of the matters to be considered.

Henderson while in Franklin had feit out the situation to ascertain what individuals would be likeliest to coöperate with the authorities of the old State. John Tipton, of Washington county, was without doubt reported by him to be one of these, for a copy of the manifesto was hurried to Tipton, along with a letter of the Governor, by a special messenger. Tipton replied on May 13th, saying that he thought himself duty bound to obey the governor's commands, "both from the zeal I bear to the old State and towards your Excellency . . . I shall continue to discountenance the lawless proceedings of my neighbors."[2] It is difficult to make this square with Tipton's subsequent action in accepting election to and taking part in the constitutional convention of Franklin in November following, unless his appearance there was of purpose to subvert the cause of Franklin. Tipton sent copies of the manifesto to Evan Shelby, of Sullivan, and to Joseph Hardin, of Greene. The latter was, however, warmly attached to Sevier and the cause of independence, and it is probable that the first news of the document reached the governor of Franklin through him. Promptly—within two days—after the manifesto reached Tipton, the governor of Franklin countered in a concise but spirited proclamation:

State of Franklin
A PROCLAMATION.

WHEREAS, a manifesto is sent in and circulating through this State, in order to create sedition and stir up insurrection among the good citizens of this STATE, thinking thereby to destroy that peace and tranquility that so greatly abounds among the peaceful citizens of the new happy country.

And, notwithstanding that their own acts declare to the world that they first invited us to the separation, if in their power, would now bring down ruin and destruction on that part of their late citizens, that the world well knows saved the State out of the hands of the enemy, and saved her from impending ruin.

Notwithstanding we have the fullest confidence in the true attachment and fidelity of the good citizens of this State, I have thought it proper to issue this my Proclamation, strictly enjoining and requiring all and every the good citizens of this State, as they

---

[2] *North Carolina Records*, XXII, 648.

will answer the same at peril, to be obedient and comfortable to the laws thereof.

Witness, John Sevier, Esq., Governor, and Captain-General in and over the said State, under his hand and seal of arms, in Washington, this fifteenth day of May, one thousand seven hundred and eighty-five, and in the first year of our Independency.

JOHN SEVIER.

GOD SAVE THE STATE![3]

The issue was now joined; and, had Martin succeeded himself as governor, it seems certain that the decision would have been favorable to the State of Franklin. Martin's policy would have taken color from his personal views which were derogatory of the western folk and of any rights or equities they supposed themselves to have had; and he would have had to combat an opposition solidified thereby. He was succeeded in the executive office by General and former Governor Richard Caswell, in the spring of 1785. As has been observed, Caswell knew the West and its people better than did Martin; he had their confidence, above any other Eastern Carolinian, unless William Blount be excepted. To Caswell, soon to come into power, Governor Sevier wrote even before he issued the above proclamation:

STATE OF FRANKLIN,
Washington County, 14th May, 1785.

Sir: Governor Martin has lately sent up into our country a Manifesto, together with letters to private persons, in order to stir up sedition and insurrection, thinking, thereby, to destroy that peace and tranquility, which have so greatly subsisted among the peaceful citizens of this country.

First in the Manifesto, he charges us with a revolt from North-Carolina, by declaring ourselves independent of that state. Secondly, that designs of a more dangerous nature and deeper die seem to glare in the western revolt, the power being usurped over the western vacant territory, the Union deriving no emolument from the same, not even the part intended for North-Carolina by the cession, and that part of her revenue is seized by the new authority and appropriated to different purposes than those intended by your legislature.

His Excellency is pleased to mention that one reason we have assigned for the revolt, as he terms it, is that the goods were stopped from the Indians, that were to compensate them for the western lands, and that the Indians had committed murders in consequence

---

[3] *Pennsylvania Packet* of August 9, 1785; *South Carolina Gazette,* of August 8, 1785.

thereof. He is also pleased to say that he is well informed to the contrary, and that no hostilities have been committed on that account; but on the other hand, provocations are daily given the Indians, and one of their chiefs murdered with impunity. In answer to the charge relative to what His Excellency is pleased to call the revolt, I must beg leave to differ with him in sentiment on that occasion; for your own acts declare to the world that this country was ceded off to Congress, and one part of the express condition was, that the same should be erected into one or more states; and we believe that body was candid, and that they fully believe a new state would tend to the mutual advantage of all parties; that they were as well acquainted with our circumstances at that time, as Governor Martin can be since, and that they did not think a new government here would be led away by the pageantry of a mock government without the essentials, and leave nothing among us but a shadow, as represented by him.

But if Governor Martin is right in his suggestion, we can only say that the Assembly of North-Carolina deceived us, and were urging us on into total ruin, and laying a plan to destroy that part of her citizens she so often frankly confessed saved the parent state from ruin. But the people here, neither at that time nor the present, having the most distant idea of any such intended deception, and at the same time well knowing how pressingly Congress had requested a cession to be made of the western territory ever since the 6th of September and 10th of October, in the year 1780—these several circumstances, together with a real necessity to prevent anarchy, promote our own happiness, and provide against the common enemy, that always infest this part of the world, induced and compelled the people here to act as they have done innocently: thinking, at the same time, your acts tolerated them in the separation. Therefore, we can by no means think it can be called a revolt or known by such a name. As to the second charge, it is entirely groundless. We have by no act, whatever, laid hold of one foot of the vacant land, neither have we appropriated any of the same to any of our use or uses, but intend everything of that nature for further deliberation, and to be mutually settled according to the right and claim of each party.

As to that part of seizing the public money, it is groundless as the former. For no authority among us, whatever, has laid hold of or appropriated one farthing of the same to our uses in any shape whatever, but the same is still in the hands of the sheriff and collectors. And on the other hand, we have passed such laws as will both compel and justify them in settling and paying up to the respective claimants of the same; all which will appear in our acts, which will be laid before you and fully evince to the reverse of Governor Martin's charge in the Manifesto.

Very true, we suggest that the Indians have committed murders in consequence of the delay of the goods. Nearly forty people have been murdered since the Cession Bill passed, some of which lived in our own counties, and the remainder on the Kentucky Path; and it is evidently known to the Cherokees, and their frequent talks prove, they are exasperated at getting nothing for their lands, and in all probability had their goods been furnished, no hostilities would have been committed.

The murder committed with impunity, alluding to Major Hubbard's killing a half-breed, which Governor Martin calls a chief (but who was never any such thing among the Indians). We can't pretend to say what information His Excellency has received on this subject, more than the others, or where from. This we know, that all the proof was had against Hubbard that ever can be had, which is, the Indian first struck, and then discharged his gun at Hubbard, before the Indian was killed by Hubbard. As Governor Martin reprobates the measure in so great a degree, I can't pretend to say what he might have done, but must believe, that had any other person met with the same insult from one of those bloody savages, who have so frequently murdered the wives and children of the people of this country for many years past, I say had they been possessed of that manly and soldierly spirit that becomes an American, they must have acted like Hubbard.

I have now noticed to your Excellency the principal complaints in the Manifesto, and such as I think is worth observation, and have called forth such proofs as must evince fully the reverse of the charge and complaints set forth.

The menaces made use of in the Manifesto will by no means intimidate us. We mean to pursue our necessary measures, and with the fullest confidence believe that your legislature, when truly informed of our civil proceedings, will find no cause for resenting anything we have done.

Most certain it is, that nothing has been transacted here out of any disregard for the parent state, but we still entertain the same high opinion and have the same regard and affection for her that ever we had, and would be as ready to step forth in her defence as ever we did, should need require it.

Also our acts and resolutions will evince to the world, that we have paid all due respect to your state. First, in taking up and adopting her constitution and then her laws, together with naming several new counties and also an academy after some of the first men in your state.

The repeal of the Cession act we cannot take notice of, as we had declared our separation before the repeal. Therefore, we are bound to support it with that manly firmness that becomes freemen.

Our Assembly sits again in August, at which time it is expected commissioners will be appointed to adjust and consider on such matters of moment as will be consistent with the honour and interest of each party.

The disagreeable and sickly time of the year, together with the great distance from Newbern, as also the short notice, puts it out of the power of any person to attend from this quarter at this time.

Our agent is at Congress, and we daily expect information from that quarter, respecting our present measures, and hope to be advised thereon.

We are informed that Congress have communicated to your state respecting the repeal of the Cession act. Be that as it may, I am authorized to say nothing will be lacking in us, to forward everything that will tend to the mutual benefit of each party and conciliate all matters whatever.

Governor Caswell replied on June 17, 1785, in a tone less peremptory than Governor Martin's:

KINGSTON, N. C., 17th June, 1785.

Sir:—Your favor of the 14th of last month, I had the honour to receive by Colonel Avery.

In this, sir, you have stated the different charges mentioned in Governor Martin's Manifesto, and answered them by giving what I understand to be the sense of the people, and your own sentiments, with respect to each charge, as well as the reasons which governed in the measures he complained of.

I have not seen Governor Martin's Manifesto, nor have I derived so full and explicit information from any quarter as this you have been pleased to give me. As there was not an Assembly, owing to the members not attending at Governor Martin's request, the sense of the Legislature on this business, of course, could not be had, and as you give me assurances of the peaceable disposition of the people, and their wish to conduct themselves in the manner you mention, and also to send persons to adjust, consider and conciliate matters, I suppose, to the next Assembly, for the present, things must rest as they are with respect to the subject matter of your letter, which shall be laid before the next Assembly. In the meantime, let me entreat you not, by any means, to consider this as giving countenance, by the executive of the state, to any measures lately pursued by the people to the westward of the mountains.

With regard to the goods intended, by the state, for the Indians as a compensation for the lands, they, I believe, have been ready for many months, at Washington, and if I can procure wagons to convey them to the place destined, (the Long Island,) I mean to send them there to be disposed of according to the original intention of the Assembly, and will either attend myself or appoint commissioners to treat with the Indians; but in this, you know, it is necessary that whoever attends should be protected by the militia, and under the present situation of affairs, it is possible my orders may not be attended to in that particular; and however a man may submit to these things in a private character, he may be answerable to the people, at least they may judge it so, in a public situation.

Therefore, without your assurances of the officers and men under your command being subject to my orders in this case, as matters stand, I think it would be imprudent in me to come over or send commissioners to treat with the Indians. Of this you will be pleased to write me the first favourable opportunity. It is my wish to come over myself, and if matters turn so that I can with convenience, it is probable I may.

Governor Caswell in effect waived further action until the sense of the Assembly might be obtained; and any opponents in Franklin of the new government had little to encourage them to active obstruction in the meanwhile. In all counties the authority of Franklin was recognized and enforced, judicially and in respect to administrative functions. Deeds and wills were probated and recorded by Franklin officials,[4] and all writs ran in the name of the State of Franklin, shortly after the adjournment of the first session of the General Assembly.

John Sevier, as commissioner of the Assembly of Franklin, proceeded to exercise another attribute of sovereignty, as one inhering the new State. He, accompanied by Outlaw, Hardin, Luke Bowyer and others met a number of the chiefs of the Cherokees at the home of Major Samuel Henry (May 31, 1785) and entered into a treaty for the purpose of quieting the title to the tract of country lying south of the French Broad river and north of the watershed which divided the waters of Little river and Little Tennessee river (then called the Tennessee). The treaty, so far as preserved, is as follows:[5]

At a treaty of amity and friendship begun and held with the Cherokees at the mouth of Dumplin Creek on the French Broad river, and continued by adjournment the 31st day of May, Anno Domini, 1785, present, John Sevier, Commissioner; the King of the Cherokees; Ancoo, chief of Chota; Abraham, Chief of *Chilhowe;* the Bard, head-warrior of the Valley Towns; the Sturgeon, of Tallassee; the Leach, from Settico; the Big Man Killer, from Tallassee; and nearly thirty more warriors, &c., of the Cherokee Nation; together with Cherokee Murphy, the half-breed Indian and linguister of the treaty.

---

[4] The first deed so registered in Washington county, was one from Jesse Walton, of the State of Georgia, to James Taylor, of the State of South Carolina conveying 200 acres "lying in Washington county in the State of Franklin," May 2, 1785. Valentine Sevier and Nicholas Hall were witnesses. In Greene county the first record was of date June 25th, 1785, a marriage license, Anderson Walker to Letia Wilson.

[5] *North Carolina State Records* XXII, 649, *et seq.*

Ancoo, chief of Chota, chosen speaker on the part of the Cherokees, began and spoke as follows:

It is agreed by us, the warriors, chiefs and representatives of the Cherokee Nation, that all the lands lying and being on the south side of Holston and French Broad rivers, as far south as the ridge that divides the waters of Little river from the waters of Tennessee, may be peaceably inhabited and cultivated, resided on, enjoyed and inhabited by our elder brothers, the white people, from this time forward and always. And we do agree on our part and in behalf of our Nation, that the white people shall never be by us or any of our Nation, molested or interrupted, either in their persons or property, in no wise, or in any manner or form whatever, in consequence of their settling or inhabiting the said territory, tract of land and country aforesaid, or any part of the same whatever.

John Sevier, for and in behalf of the white people, and for and in behalf of the State or government, or the United States, as the case may hereafter be settled and concluded on with respect to the jurisdiction and sovereignty over the said tract or territory of land, agrees that there shall be a reasonable and liberal compensation made the Cherokees for the lands they have herein ceded and granted to the white people, and to the State or States that may hereafter legally possess and enjoy the country aforesaid, in good faith. That this bargain and engagement now made and entered into between us, the white people and the Cherokees, may never be broken, disannulled, or dissolved, in consequence of any claim, right or sovereignty over the soil hereby mentioned and described, as aforesaid.

Done in open treaty, the 10th of June, 1785.
     John Sevier,
     The King,
     Ancoo, chief of Chota,
     And chiefs of the different towns.

Witnessed:
  Lew Boyer,
  Alex. Outlaw,
  Joshua Gist,
  Ebenezer Alexander,
  Jos. Hardin,
  Charles Murphy, Ling't.

The engagements of the Indian chiefs are very definite as compared with those of the representatives of the white people. The Cherokees' hold on the particular territory was weak; many white families had already settled on it, and this may account in part for the vagueness of the covenanting on Sevier's part.[6]

---

[6] In a memorial to Congress from the inhabitants south of the French Broad river (September, 1794) it was stated that as a result of this treaty "The Indians

"The governor, in a speech well calculated to produce the end he had in view, deplored the sufferings of the white people; the blood which the Indians spilt on the road leading to Kentucky; lamented the uncivilized state of the Indians, and to prevent all future animosities he suggested the propriety of fixing the bounds beyond which those settlements should not be extended which had been imprudently made on the south side of French Broad and Holston, under the connivance of North Carolina, and could not be broken up; and he pledged the faith of the State of Franklin, if those bounds should be agreed upon and made known, the citizens of his State should be effectually restrained from encroaching beyond it."[7]

The treaty was in fact negotiated with only one faction of the Overhill Cherokees, who entered into it the more readily in reliance upon its repudiation by the chiefs and warriors of the towns not represented.

In a "talk" sent to the governor of North Carolina after this treaty, Tassel, the beloved man of Chota, complained of the treaty. He insisted that the Franklin authorities only sought of the Cherokees "liberty for those that were then living on the lands to remain there, till the head men of their nation were consulted on it, which our young men[8] agreed to. Since then we are told that they claim all the lands on the waters of Little river, and call it their ground."[9] The Tassel repeated the complaint of his people made at the treaty of Hopewell in November, 1785, but expressed the Cherokees' willingness to allow those who had settled in the fork of Holston and French Broad rivers to remain there until Congress could pass on the Cherokees' claim to the land.

As a result of the treaty of Dumplin Creek, settlers in great numbers crossed the French Broad and occupied lands. Many came from the Valley of Virginia, among them the Houston family, relations of Rev. Samuel Houston and of General Sam Houston; Samuel Wear, and Samuel Newell. The station of the last named be-

---

received a compensation in clothing and other articles for said lands" and, it is set forth, numbers of the petitioners had settled on lands for which North Carolina had issued warrants or grants. Ramsey, 631.

[7] Ramsey, 299, quoting Haywood.

[8] Old Abram's participation in the treaty evidences that this was not the whole truth.

[9] Ramsey, 319.

came the first seat of justice for Sevier county and he along with Wear became a leader in the Franklin movement. Here, Ramsey says, was "the nucleus of an excellent neighborhood of intelligent, worthy and patriotic citizens ... who diffused around them republicanism, religion, intelligence and thrift."[10] The settlements gradually worked southward leading to the formation of the county of Blount under Franklin authority.

The holding of the treaty was made the occasion of rumors that the Franklin leaders contemplated an incorporation of the Cherokees into the new State, getting an accession of territory, and increasing the number of inhabitants in the borders of that State to the number that was by the Ordinance of 1784 made a requisite to her admission into the Union.

Alden says: "What was at the bottom of the report we cannot say. We have it from at least three different sources, letters dated May and June, 1785. Arthur Campbell wrote to Governor Henry that Governor Sevier was then 'treating with the Cherokees with a view to an incorporation.'[11] A 'gentleman in Washington' wrote that 'the executive of the State of Franklin has lately concluded a treaty of amity and perpetual friendship with the Cherokee Indians, and a negotiation is on foot to give that nation a representation in the new legislature'."[12] The Maryland *Gazette* (October 11, 1785) published an "Extract of a letter from Caswell county, in the State of Franklin," whose author said: "A negotiation is on foot with the Cherokees, and the aim will be to incorporate them and make them useful citizens. I dare say the project will startle your rigid sectaries,—but you, we expect, will be more liberal, when it manifestly appears that the interest of humanity and of our new society will be promoted." No evidence appears to show whether the Indians declined to be made useful citizens in this way, or the Franklin leaders changed their minds about it.[13]

The suggestion was probably advanced by one of the young Presbyterian ministers, Balch or Houston, who were at the time in Franklin and ambitious to try their hands at statecraft. It is unlikely that Sevier, with his intimate knowledge of the Cherokees,

---

[10] Ramsey, 369.

[11] *Cal. Va. St. Papers*, IV, 32 (June 7, 1785). Campbell wrote that the negotiation of the treaty of Dumplin Creek "was of a neighborly and friendly kind." *Ib.*, 37.

[12] *Pennsylvania Packet*, August 6, 1785.

[13] Alden, "The State of Franklin," *American Historical Review*, VIII, 283.

gave approval to the plan, if such it may be called, or took any step in its furtherance. Houston wrote frequently for the newspapers of the day, and the idea was almost certainly his, and born of missionary zeal.

CHAPTER XI

Franklin's Cause Before Congress—1785

William Cocke proceeded promptly to New York where the Continental Congress was in session. He arrived May 15, 1785, and the next day[1] he presented to the president of Congress the memorial of the Assembly of Franklin praying Congress to accept the cession made by North Carolina and admit Franklin into the sisterhood of sovereign States. This memorial, never before published in full, was as follows:

To the Honorable Continental Congress:
This memorial of the freemen, by their representatives in General Assembly met, who were included within the limits ascertained by an act of the General Assembly of the State of North Carolina ceding certain vacant lands to Congress,
      Humbly sheweth,
That having in many instances discovered the friendly disposition of Congress, not only to guard the liberties of the States now in the Union, but also to encourage the erection of new States on the western side of the Appalachian Mountains; and finding the disposition of North Carolina to comply with the requisitions made by Congress requesting liberal cessions of vacant western territory, which requisitions being complied with by North Carolina, she immediately stopped the goods she had promised to give the Indians for the said land which so exasperated them that they began to commit hostilities on our frontiers; in this situation we were induced to a declaration of independence, not doubting but we should be excused by Congress when she came to hear the reasons that called for such a declaration and when she was assured that it was necessity rather than choice, as North Carolina seemed quite regardless of our interest; and the Indians were daily murdering our friends and relatives without distinction of age or sex. And we are sorry to inform Congress that notwithstanding the act of cession must have bound North Carolina at least in honor to have continued the act in force for the space of twelve months from the passing of the same, unless Congress should have refused to accept the cedure, yet North Carolina has repealed the cession act and claims a sovereignty over a country whose prayers she has re-

---
[1] Spaight to Governor Caswell, June 5, 1785, *N. C. State Records*, XVII, 464.

jected and whose interests she has forsaken. Impressed with every sentiment of our duty and respect, we earnestly request Congress to accept the offered cession and to receive us into the federal union that we may enjoy all the rights reserved to us in the cession act, and which freemen are entitled to. And we humbly pray that you be pleased to call upon our agent for such further information as you in your wisdom shall think proper, in whose integrity we confide, and earnestly pray that you will adopt such suitable measures as may promote the peace and prosperity of those who wish ever to be found a zealous and useful part of the people that form so dignified a union; and your memorialists shall ever pray.

       Landon Carter, S. S.
       Wm. Cage, S. C.
   By order
       Thomas Talbot, C. S.
       Tho. Chapman, C. C.

   State of Franklin, March 12th, 1785.
This is to certify that William Cocke, Esq., was chosen by the General Assembly of this State as an Agent to carry and introduce this Memorial to the Congress of the United States of America. And he is further invested with full power and authority to state and explain the local and political situation of this State, and to make such representation as he may find conducive to the interest and independence of this country.

       Landon Carter, S. S.
       Wm. Cage, S. C.
   By order
       Thomas Talbot, C. S.
       Tho. Chapman, C. C.[2]

A committee was at once appointed to examine the cession act of North Carolina. The committee consisted of King, Johnson, Grayson and McHenry, and they promptly (May 20th) reported their opinion:

"That the act of cession of the State of North Carolina, of the 2nd day of June, 1784, gives a right to the United States in Congress assembled, at any time within one year from the passing of the act, to accept the cession of western territory therein described, subject to the conditions and reservations in said act contained; and that no subsequent act or law of the State of North Carolina could so repeal and make void the said act of cession as to annul the right of the United States in Congress assembled to accept the territory therein ceded within the period, and subject to the conditions and reservations aforesaid.

---

[2] *State Department MSS.*, Library of Congress.

"That consistently with the objects of the resolution of Congress of the 6th of September and the 10th of October, 1780, and with the duty Congress owes to the federal union, they cannot decline an acceptance of the cession aforesaid; and therefore recommend:

"That the United States in Congress assembled, do accept the cession of western territory made by the State of North Carolina. . ."

An effort was made to postpone consideration of the report of the committee, but it failed by a vote of seven States in opposition to two in favor, the delegation of one State (South Carolina) being divided.

The report, after a brief debate, was brought to a test vote, and the States of New Jersey, Rhode Island, Connecticut, New York, New Hampshire, Pennsylvania and Georgia voted in favor of adoption; Maryland and Virginia in opposition. South Carolina's delegation divided—Pickney aye, and Ramsay nay. North Carolina, being interested, did not vote.

Under a rule of the Articles of Confederation, the report failed of adoption, two-third of the States not concurring.

The moral victory was with Cocke on the issue raised by the State of Franklin, that North Carolina had not the right by a repeal of the cession act to defeat acceptance by Congress; and that victory was made the more pronounced by a unanimous vote on another paragraph of the same report:

"That it be recommended to the State of North Carolina to consider the principle of magnanimity and justice that induced the passage of said act of 2nd day of June, 1784, and evince the operation of the same good sentiments by repealing their act of 20th of November, 1784, and directing their delegates in Congress to furnish a proof of their liberality in the execution of a deed to the United States of the territory ceded by the act of 2nd of June aforesaid."[3]

Cocke seems not to have pressed further the admission of Franklin into the Confederation. It would have been unwise to do so, in view of the test votes above outlined and of the specific provision in the Articles of Confederation that "No other colony shall be admitted into the same, unless such admission be agreed to by nine States."[4]

---

[3] *Journal of Continental Congress* (Way & Gideon) IV, 525, *et seq.*
[4] Art. XI.

The people of Franklin could but feel a degree of elation. The North Carolina delegates in corresponding degree were chagrined. Spaight wrote home to Governor Caswell complaining that scant courtesy and "a great degree of indelicacy" had been shown the delegation from his State. He thought that too great avidity for western territory had hurried Congress to action.[5] Williamson waited until his return to his home at Edenton before reporting to Caswell:

"On the last day of my sitting in Congress, which was two days before the arrival of Cocke in New York, it was moved by a member from Massachusetts and seconded, I believe, by one from New Jersey, that Congress should accept the cession by North Carolina. Whatever my sentiments might have been respecting the policy of the cession or the repeal, you may presume that when the honor or even the competence of the State to make good and proper laws was squinted at, I was not silent. The motion was after considerable debate withdrawn. That was on Friday. On Monday or Tuesday following the very same motion was made, and was, as you will see by the journal, very nearly carried. Cocke was then in town, but I think his presence produced no effect, *pro* nor *con*. I question whether Mr. Spaight's health permitted him to attend during the whole of their debate. I am fully informed that the question was lost by the negative of some gentlemen who wished very much for the cession but who were very unwilling to give offense to a State that is admitted on all occasions to be observant of federal measures."[6]

Thus it is made plain that the State of Franklin came within a scratch of receiving the approval of her crucial contention by the Continental Congress. Cocke's efforts came near to success notwithstanding the depreciatory remarks of Williamson.[7]

Monroe wrote (June 5, 1785) from Congress to Jefferson, expressing surprise at the strong support and the number of advocates the

---

[5] June 5, 1785, *ante*. "The report does not much credit to the gentlemen who drew it, though it convinces me that my opinion is right—that they are willing to have lands on any terms." *Ib*.

[6] Historical Society of Pennsylvania, Dreer Coll., *Members of the Old Congress*, V, 74. The quoted paragraph is, for some reason, omitted from the reprint of this letter in *N. C. State Records*, XVII, 477. "Possibly what appears in the *State Records* was an unfinished draft." (Edmund C. Burnett.)

[7] Grayson to Short, *Historical Society of Pennsylvania*, Dreer Coll., *Members of Old Congress*, II, 50; *Pennsylvania Magazine of Hist.*, XXIX, 203.

report of the committee brought out. "It is in contemplation to send a committee to North Carolina and Georgia upon the subject of western land and finance, to press their attention to those subjects."[8]

Jefferson thought that this unanimous appeal of Congress to North Carolina would result in the success of the Franklin movement. "Congress recommended to the State of North Carolina to desist from opposition, and I have no doubt they will do it. It will, therefore, result from the act of Congress laying out the Western Country into States, that these States of Kentucky and Franklin will come into the Union in the manner therein provided."[9] He was a consistent friend of the western people. In January, 1786, he wrote: "The people of Kentucky think of separating from Virginia, in which they are right."[10]

It is interesting to speculate on the fate of the new State had it been named "Jefferson" instead of "Franklin"—linked, so to speak, with a personality of abounding vigor and breadth of vision; to a rising rather than to a setting sun. Jefferson, in 1782 had joined others in a land project—the only one he was ever connected with—to purchase lands in Tennessee; but "while I was in expectation of going to Europe, and that the title to the western lands might possibly come under discussion of the ministers, I withdrew myself from the company," and the other members abandoned the enterprise.[11]

From Paris, where he was in the service of his country, following peace, as minister to France, he evinced continued concern for the western folk. He thought Vermont occupied too small a territory for a State of the Union. "I am anxious to hear what is being done with the States of Vermont and Franklin. I think that the former is the only innovation on the system of April 23, 1784, which ought possibly to be admitted. If Congress are not firm on that head, our

---

[8] Monroe's *Writings*, I, 89. At this time Monroe was opposed to the admittance of western applicants for statehood. "On the part of the Union or rather the States upon the Atlantic, it is, in my opinion, their policy to keep a prevailing influence upon the Ohio, or rather to the Westward. . . . When the Mississippi shall be open, removed at a distance, they will necessarily be but little interested in whatever respects us; besides, they will outnumber us in Congress unless we confine their number as much as possible." Monroe to Jefferson, August 25, 1785.

[9] Ford's *Jefferson's Writings*, IV, 458 (Sept. 5, 1785).

[10] *Ib.*, V, 74.

[11] Jefferson to Madison (November 1784) Ford's *Jefferson's Writings*, IV, 368.

several States will crumble to atoms by the spirit of establishing every little canton into a separate State." That this reference was not intended to have application to Kentucky or Franklin, is shown by the next sentence: "I hope that Virginia will concur in that plan as to her territory South of the Ohio and not leave the western country to withdraw themselves by force and become our worst enemies instead of best friends."[12] Indeed, he was of opinion that an "occasional rebellion," such, we may assume, as that of the separatist Western Carolinians, was "not wholly inadvisable and ought not to be too much discouraged."

Sevier, Cocke and associates in their plans had it in mind to avail of the implied invitation of Jefferson's Ordinance of April, 1784; and Arthur Campbell was tauntingly quoting Jefferson's scheme for new States to Governor Henry.

The fitting and graceful as well as politic thing to have done was to give to the new Commonwealth the name of "Jefferson" in honor of him who, beyond all other statesmen of his time, embodied in his personality the spirit of independence and friendliness toward western aspirations.

The formation of the new State did not go unnoticed by Great Britain. So pronounced an exhibition of the separation spirit was of no little interest in that quarter. The *Gentlemen's Magazine* of August, 1785,[13] announced:

"An authentic account has been received that the counties of Washington, Sullivan and Greene have declared themselves independent of the State of North Carolina, and have chosen a governor under the authority of the new government. The reason is, the people of the western counties found themselves grievously taxed for the support of government without enjoying the blessings of it."

Britons in America, and their friends, could not repress expressions of hopefulness that the separation movement might result to the advantage of the mother country. One such wrote (June 1, 1785 from Suffolk, Va.,) to a friend in Scotland respecting the organization of the State of Franklin: "We are daily in expectation of hearing of a coalition between them and the Vermonters and New Hampshire Grants, who are also disaffected; and it is a matter of doubt whether the balance of power would not be in their favour, even against the United States, if matters should come to an open

---
[12] To Richard Henry Lee (July 12, 1785) Ford's *Jefferson's Writings*, IV, 434.
[13] Volume LV, page 656.

rupture, as there are a great many over the whole continent quite tired of their independence."[13a] So far as the movement at the South was concerned, this writer misread the signs.

In forming a judgment as to the wisdom of the Franklinites in continuing their efforts for separate statehood at this time, it may be well here to make a summary of the views of other thoughtful men who were, by reason of distance and detachment, able to take a dispassionate and just view of the situation that confronted the western people in 1785.

John Marshall, in a letter to Judge Muter, of the Kentucky district (January 7, 1785) said: "I begin to think that the time for a separation is fast approaching . . . It is impossible that we can, at this distance, legislate wisely for you, and it is proper that you should legislate for yourself."[14]

Wm. Grayson as one of Virginia's delegates to Congress had not felt that he could give affront to the neighbor State of Carolina and her delegation, by voting in favor of the committee's report of May, 1785; but in a private letter to Governor Randolph, of Virginia, he was able to express his real opinion: "With respect to the State of North Carolina, it must be acknowledged that they have acted with great imprudence. After having given up the country to the United States and the government to the people, they ought not afterwards, on the resumption, to have expected a voluntary obedience."[15]

Washington in 1783 recommended the laying out of two new States in the western country; and even Monroe had not always been jealous of the rise of the West to power in the national councils. On October 19, 1783, he had written to George Rogers Clark, urging that a new State be set up with the traditions of Virginia, so that the old Commonwealth might have a needed ally in federal affairs. Of like mind was Madison.[16]

Governor Patrick Henry's view of the propriety and justness of the step taken for separation by "the Overhill Carolina folks" expressed in his message above, was colored by his sense of official responsibility and by his favoritism for William Russell and Joseph Martin. The opinion of Patrick Henry, the man, was expressed with vigor and directness after the passage (1789) of the second act

---

[13a] *London Chronicle*, Aug. 6, 1785.
[14] Tyler's *Quarterly History and General Magazine*, I, 28.
[15] *Cal. Virginia State Papers*, IV, 206.
[16] Winsor, *Westward Movement*, 207, 245, 247.

of cession by North Carolina. His position was truly an irony of circumstance. The contrast was, indeed, a strange one, and surprising too, if self-interest may not be supposed to have tinctured his later language. "I still think that great things may be done in the Tennessee Country and below. For surely the people of Franklin will never submit to be given away with the lands, like slaves, without holding a convention of their own. . . . I am apprehensive Sevier may be hushed by preferment so as to make no opposition. But really it is a pity some other person would not, as the law is destructive of the people's liberty and that right to choose a form of government which belongs to every free man. Vast injury is done these people in taxes for they have not left the means of paying them. Mr. Ross[17] sent me the act, and I do think it a most abominable instance of tyranny. . . . If Sevier has not turned tail on his former professions of zeal for the rights of the Franklin people and means to support their just contentions, it will be well to join heart and hand with him or any other person so as to bring about their just claims as Americans. . . . The right to all North Carolina west of the line mentioned in the act is, in my opinion, vested in the people of Franklin, if they will but insist upon it. . . . Being cut off from government, without holding any convention of the people there to consent to it, all rights of sovereignty over the district and laws therein belong to the people there."[18]

If this letter of Henry to Martin had been shown to John Sevier, he well might have exclaimed, in view of his vain appeal to Henry in 1785: "Where then was Roderick Dhu!"[19]

---

[17] David Ross, a wealthy Virginia merchant, planter and speculator, at the time associated with Henry in the Virginia Company which had secured a grant of a vast tract of territory in the Bend of the Tennessee from Georgia. He was the father of the celebrated Reverend Frederick Ross, of the Presbyterian church. Ross also wrote to Sevier (Feb. 20, 1790) protesting that the terms of the cession were not favorable but dangerous to the western people. And, stranger still, another letter of like trend was written to Sevier by Ex-Gov. Alexander Martin.

[18] Henry to Joseph Martin, Draper Coll., *King's Mountain MSS.*, XI. He advises Martin to locate in Franklin and secure lands there. The letter is *not* included in Henry's *Life of Henry*.

[19] The attitude of the mecurial Henry is hard to understand. Ruffner, writing in justification of the Virginian Franklinites, says: "It is sufficient to say that, four years later than the birth of the State of Franklin, in the Virginia convention of 1788, Patrick Henry threatened to form a State out of the lower western tier of counties on the North Carolina line and of those identical counties that were to compose the State of Franklin."—*Founders of Washington College* (Virginia), 25.

CHAPTER XII

SECOND SESSION OF THE ASSEMBLY—1785

The general Assembly of Franklin convened for its second session of the year 1785, on August 1st at Jonesborough. The barest mention is made of this session by Haywood in connection with the call for a constitutional convention at Greeneville in the month of November following. However, some data is given by the North Carolina State records and the newspapers of that time from which the Assembly's proceedings may be partially outlined.[1] It was, perhaps, the first occasion afforded Governor Sevier for a message, which must have treated of the Indian treaty of Dumplin Creek and the new State's relations with North Carolina.

James White was speaker of the Senate, and R. Mitchell its clerk; Stockley Donelson was speaker of the house of commons, and Francis A. Ramsey its clerk.[2]

At this session, an act was passed for the encouragement of an expedition down the Tennessee river to take possession of the Bend, under titles derived from the State of Georgia.[3]

It was deemed advisable to give the authorities of North Carolina assurance that public moneys found in the hands of fiscal agents of that State would not be withheld for the use of the new government. Accordingly it was

"*Resolved*, That where any sheriff or commissioner of confiscated property, who has failed to settle with the State of North Carolina, or who has acted under their authority and received their appointments from that State, and failed to account for collections they have made, or ought to have made, that the bonds of all such delinquents shall be given up to the order of the State of North Carolina to be recovered according to law.

"*Be it further, Resolved*, That a commissioner be appointed to

---

[1] A few acts, now irretrievably lost, were passed. *South Carolina State Gazette*, of October 21, 1785.

[2] *North Carolina State Records*, XXII, 714, 727.

[3] Ramsey, 318.

wait upon the General Assembly of the State of North Carolina, in order to convince them that it is our desire to establish a lasting and permanent union as well with North Carolina as the rest of the States on the continent; and to remove any doubts that may arise in that State respecting the goodness of our wishes towards them on the subject of our separation, and to assure them we are determined to pay most strict observance to the true intent and meaning of the act of cession passed Second day of June, 1784."[4]

Thomas Stewart was chosen as commissioner and he attended the winter session of the North Carolina Assembly. He delivered a copy of the resolutions to Governor Caswell, who on December 21st sent them to the senate and house with a message saying that Stewart was waiting on the Assembly for the purpose of giving it full information on the subject-matter of the resolutions.[5] The visit of the commissioner was unavailing. The only steps taken by the legislature was the passage of an act to pardon the inhabitants of refractory counties, for all things done in setting up an independent government. In the same act it was recited that in some of those counties the freemen might be defeated in a desire to be represented in the Assembly of North Carolina should elections be held according to law, and it was provided that it should be lawful for freemen convened on election day to choose by ballot members to represent them in Assembly, *under the inspection of three good and honest men*.[6]

This was intended to be an entering wedge, driven for the disruption of the people west of the mountains; and it could not fail to arouse deep resentment on the part of those who were faithful to the common pact for independence.

A new Franklin county, by the name of Blount, in honor of a consistent friend of the western inhabitants, William Blount, is mentioned as being in existence south of the French Broad river in this year.[7] It is unlikely, however, that a government for the new county was perfected at that time.

The Franklin Assembly reaffirmed the call for a convention to be

---

[4] *N. C. State Records*, XXII. Governor Sevier gave notice in advance of the sending of a commissioner to wait on the North Carolina Assembly, in a letter to Governor Caswell of date October 17. Ramsey, 317.

[5] *Ib*.

[6] *N. C. State Rec.*, XXIII, ch. 46 (Dec. 29, 1785).

[7] *Pennsylvania Packet*, January 5, 1786.

held at Greeneville the second Monday in November, "for the express purpose of adopting the then existing frame of government or altering it as the people may see proper—to conform to the act of Congress of April 23, 1784." The following number of delegates from the several counties of the State, it was declared, should form the convention, the election to be held on the second Monday in October: Washington, fifteen; Sullivan, twelve; Greene, twelve; Caswell, eight; Sevier, six; Spencer, five; Wayne, four; Blount, two.[8]

This representation was thought to have been in accord with the existing population of the counties. There was a great flow of settlers to Franklin and westward in 1785. A letter from Nashville (November 5, 1785) stated that "not less than one thousand families have crossed the Appalachian mountains to settle here and in Kentucky this fall."[9]

The members of the Assembly on adjournment disbanded sanguine that North Carolina would acquiesce in the separation. "We have now the most friendly assurances from North Carolina since Governor Martin's administration has expired... Why does [Virginia] seem so much out of humor at these events? Did it not originate with them, the plan of having new States 150 miles square? Was it not a celebrated genius of yours, when a delegate in Congress, who drew up the scheme last year for ten new States; and a system adopted, as matters arrived at maturity, to lay off the remaining part of the Western Country with similar jurisdictions?"[10]

Joseph Martin, however, reported (September 19) to the governor of Virginia that "the people of the new State are much divided. Several of their members refused at their last Assembly to take seats";[11] though in a letter of the same date, to Governor Caswell, of North Carolina, he made no such claim, doubtless being dubious respecting Caswell's attitude toward Sevier and his followers.[12]

In his letter to Governor Patrick Henry, Martin gave informa-

---

[8] *Pennsylvania Packet*, Feb. 17, 1786.
[9] "Extract from a letter of a gentleman in Franklin to his friend in Virginia, dated August 17, 1785." *Pennsylvania Packet*, September 30, 1785.
[10] *Cal. Va. State Papers*, IV, 53.
[11] Ramsey, 318.
[12] *North Carolina St. Rec.*, XVIII, 591.

tion that the Great Warrior of the Cherokees, Oconostota, had passed away in the summer of 1785; and that great confusion in the nation resulted from the rapid encroachment of the whites on the Indians' lands.[13]

---

[13] From Chota, Sept. 19th. Bushnell, *Native Villages East of the Mississippi*, 61.

CHAPTER XIII

THE SECOND CONSTITUTIONAL CONVENTION—1785

An election was duly held for members of the convention called to meet November 14, 1785, at Greeneville for the adoption of a permanent Constitution for the State. An amicable settlement with North Carolina seemed probable. The refractory John Tipton took part as one of the delegates of Washington county.

From an early day the Presbyterian church had been planted on the upper waters of the Tennessee by the Scotch-Irish immigrants, and it had grown to such proportions that the parent Presbytery of Hanover, in Virginia, felt that it was advisable to subdivide its territory, and in 1785 Abingdon Presbytery was organized, including in its bounds Southwest Virginia and the contiguous State of Franklin. It was felt that the time had come to make sure of the predominance of that church in the region assigned the Presbytery, and all available ministers were encouraged to lead the advance. Liberty Hall, an educational institution of the Valley of Virginia presided over by Rev. William Graham, was the source from which were to come the laborers in that moral vineyard. Thence years before had come Samuel Doak, who had deserved and won a firm hold on the frontiersmen of Watauga and Nolachucky, and joining him later were the Revs. Hezekiah Balch and Samuel Houston. The latter was awarded a bachelor's degree in 1785, the class of that year being the first to receive degrees under the privilege of a charter granted the school by the Virginia legislature.[1]

Influential laymen of Franklin had received their education at Liberty Hall under Graham, among them David Campbell and Samuel Newell.

Graham had been a leading figure of the Valley for many years; he was active in the struggle for independence in revolutionary

---

[1] Other members of this class were Revs. Samuel Carrick and James Priestly who also became pioneers in educational work in the Tennessee Country. Carrick became the president of Blount College, at Knoxville; Priestly of Cumberland College at Nashville, and Balch of Greeneville College, in Greene county.

days; and, later, in the prolonged contest in Virginia for religious freedom. To him, as friend and mentor, the Liberty Hall coterie in Franklin naturally turned for advice and assistance in the working out of the confronting problems of state. A committee, of which Graham and Arthur Campbell were probably the leading spirits, began work on the draft of a constitution for the new Commonwealth which was to be submitted for adoption by the Greeneville convention; and which should also meet the needs of Campbell's greater "Frankland." The name proposed was State of Frankland —to be changed from Franklin.

Samuel Houston who had taken charge (1783) of a congregation near the Washington-Greene county line, in North Carolina, was chosen to be the proponent and advocate of the draft in the approaching Franklin constitutional convention. Some, indeed most, of Graham's notions of government were visionary. He thought that by provisions in the fundamental law the vicious part of society could be excluded from political power. The electoral franchise should belong to the virtuous believers in God, in a future state of rewards and punishments, in the inspiration of the scriptures and the trinity of the Godhead. These ideas were carried into the draft of his Frankland Constitution. By the same section it was provided that no person should be eligible to serve in any office in the civil department "who is of an immoral character, or guilty of such flagrant enormities as drunkenness, gaming, profane swearing, lewdness, Sabbath-breaking, or such like;" and, further, that no minister of the gospel, attorney at law or doctor of physic should be a member of the Assembly.

"Ecclesiastical hierarchies and dignitaries" were prohibited, but every citizen of the Commonwealth should have full and free religious liberty. However, as Caldwell, in his *Constitutional History of Tennessee*,[2] remarks, "one condition to office holding was a perfect orthodoxy. A citizen might have held whatever opinion he pleased, but he would not have been eligible to office unless his beliefs were entirely orthodox."

Other provisions of this curious document evince suspicion of officials who might run the gauntlet of such safeguards. The governor was to be chosen annually; all bills of public nature introduced in the legislature were required to be printed and submitted to the people "for debate and amendment" before being read in the

---

[2] Caldwell, 2nd edition, 55.

Assembly the third time and enacted into law; "except on occasions of sudden necessity" bills should not be passed into laws before the next session of the Assembly. The legislature was to consist of but one body, and was to meet annually.

On the first day of the convention at Greeneville, Samuel Houston, first reading the document as a report of a committee on a draft, proposed that it be made the basis of a permanent constitution, alterations and amendments to be offered for discussion and action. A spectator, Rev. Hezekiah Balch, asked and was granted the privilege of the floor to speak in opposition. He dealt severely with the document. The convention rejected it and adopted the modified North Carolina Constitution, doubtless in the form of the provisional Constitution under which the State was being governed at the time. The only record extant of the members who composed this convention is that shown by a protest against this action signed by nineteen of the delegates: David Campbell, Samuel Houston, John Tipton, John Ward, Robert Love, William Cox, David Craig, James Montgomery, John Strain, Robert Allison, David Looney, John Blair, James White, Samuel Newell, John Gilliland, James Stuart, George Maxwell, Joseph Tipton, and Peter Parkinson.

Francis A. Ramsey was secretary of the convention, and John Sevier or William Cocke was probably the president.

Houston felt aggrieved, and smarted under the defeat of the proposed constitution; and some of the members of the convention, who did not have over-concern for orthodox religion, made its defeat the occasion for schism. Two factions arose; one to defend the merit of the Graham-Houston system and another to decry it; and the debate waxed warm and then hot. Something unknown on the border now occurred; pamphlets were printed and circulated by the disputants. The Franklin Commonwealth Society bore the expense of publishing one of these on the "Principles of Republican Government by a Citizen of Frankland."[3] Balch violently assailed the position of his adversaries, and the contest grew so bitter that strife was engendered among the people. Some were so irritated

---

[3] Ramsey, 324, where it is said that Francis Bailey of Philadelphia, was the printer. Houston was doubtless the author. Ramsey says of one of the pamphlets put out by the Houston faction: "They sent it in manuscript by express to Newbern, N. C., and had it printed and distributed extensively."—*The Magnolia Magazine* (of Charleston), IV, 312.

that an effigy of Graham was burned. Hearing of this, and attributing the blame to Balch, Graham published an open letter to Balch, in pamphlet form, which was replete with satire, keen even to bitterness. Balch called his opponent to answer before the judicatory of the church.

Graham also published a pamphlet in defense of the proposed Frankland constitution in which he declared that the article which excluded immoral persons from the legislature was one of the "wisest and best . . . whether the people of Frankland be wise enough to adopt it or not. To this article it is objected that it excludes some men of great ability and experience who might do good. The devil has great ability and long experience."[4]

Governor Sevier had experience in subduing Indians who were on the war-path, but was comparatively helpless in quelling a controversy between the two ministers and their followers. Ramsey deciphers from the minute book of the Washington County court this entry which relates to a phase of the dispute:

"On motion being made by the Attorney for the State, who at the same time exhibited a hand-bill containing an 'Address to the Inhabitants of Frankland State,' under a signature of a citizen of the same, the Court, upon the same being read publicly in open court, adjudged it to contain treasonable insinuations against the United States, and false and ungenerous reflections against persons of distinction in the ecclesiastical department, fraught with falsehood, calculated to alienate the minds of their citizens from their government and overturn the same.

"Upon mature deliberation, the Court condemned said hand-bill to be publicly burned by the High Sheriff, as a treasonable, wicked, false and seditious libel."[5]

Strange to say, the deep feeling created by this controversy operated to weld the loose-knit elements of discontent into a fac-

---

[4] For a full account of this controversy, see Ruffner, "Early History of Washington College" (*Washington and Lee Historical Papers*), 60; Grigsby, "Founders of Washington College" (*W. and L. Hist. Papers No. 2*); Foote, *Sketches of Virginia*, 457. The church trial went for review to the Synod of New York and Philadelphia, which had jurisdiction over the Southern Presbyteries. It found that Graham's attack appeared to be a very unwarrantable treatment of a brother. Balch had the testimony of William Cocke to show that he was blameless as to the burning of the effigy.

[5] Ramsey, 403. The Greene County Court took similar action. Balch resided in that county.

tion that only wanted, for one reason or another, an opportunity openly to oppose the new State's authority. The agitation continued for more than year. Samuel Houston published and circulated the "Frankland Constitution" in 1786, with a preface from which it appears that he still hoped to have the people adopt it when "the loud and bitter outcry that has been raised against the Report and its friends," should subside.[6]

---

[6] The "Frankland Constitution" appears in full in *American Historical Magazine*, I, 49–63. Graham made the provision in Section 42 of the draft: That the legislature "shall employ some person, at public expense, to draw it (the Constitution) out into a familiar catechetical form" for its being taught in schools.

The opening of the General Assembly was to be with a sermon by a minister of the Gospel.

CHAPTER XIV

CLEAR SAILING—1786

The State of Franklin continued to exercise the powers of sovereignty over her territory for the first half of the year 1786, without a schismatic outbreak of importance among the inhabitants. An event that tended to crystallize the sentiment in favor of the new State was the negotiation of the Treaty of Hopewell, in South Carolina, by commissioners appointed under the authority of the Congress of the Confederation, with the Cherokees, November 18-28, 1785.[1] This treaty was a departure. For the first time the national government assumed to exercise the power of making treaties with these Indians. For generations the colonies had, by the exercise of that function, governed the relations between the white and the red races. The Treaty of Hopewell included a formal acknowledgment by the Indians of the supremacy of the United States, and there was conceded and confirmed to the Cherokees a considerable extent of territory that was claimed to have been previously ceded by the tribe. The commissioners, as national agents, proceeded upon the principle of disregarding such pacts when the Cherokees raised objection. The Treaty of Dumplin Creek, along with others, went into the discard. The borders of Franklin were severely contracted. The treaty line on the west and south ran from a point on Campbell's[2] line near Cumberland Gap to the mouth of Cloud's Creek on Holston river (three miles west of the present town of Rogersville, in Hawkins county); thence in a northeasterly direction to Chimney Top Mountain (at the present date the corner of Greene, Sullivan and Hawkins); thence to Camp Creek on Nolachucky river (four miles southeast of Greeneville); and thence southerly six miles to the Great Smoky Mountains, in which Camp Creek has its source. The enormity in this appears when it is considered that the site of the town of Greeneville was by

---

[1] The commissioners were Benjamin Hawkins of North Carolina; Andrew Pickens of South Carolina; Lachlan McIntosh, of Georgia; and Joseph Martin.

[2] Surveyed by General William Campbell in 1777-78, marking, as it was supposed, the boundary between Virginia and the Cherokees.

the treaty placed in the domain of the Cherokees, and that in a constitutional convention, held in that town but a few days before the treaty was signed, Greeneville had been made the permanent capital of the State of Franklin.

Thus, by national action, Franklin was denied jurisdiction over a large portion of the counties of Greene and Hawkins, as they now exist; and a much larger domain as those counties stood in 1785.

By another clause of the Treaty of Hopewell, any settler south and west of the line, who refused to remove within six months after ratification, should forfeit the protection of the United States; and —particularly galling to the Franklinites—"the Cherokees may punish him or not as they please."[3]

A considerable population had settled between the line and the French Broad river; and four or five hundred families had located south of the stream, and one of those residents predicted "there will be double that this year (1786)."[4]

Situated between mountain ranges on the east and west, Franklin's thrust of population was toward the south along the valleys of the Holston, the Nolachucky, and the Tennessee rivers. Nature had so decreed.

The tide of immigration from Carolina that had mounted forbidding steeps and flowed through the gaps of two mountain ranges, the Blue Ridge and the Alleghany, into these valleys, could not be restrained by mere lines drawn by surveyors across rivers whose southward currents beckoned onward and down the rich valleys. The national authority which thus sought to hold back that tide was too anemic and nerveless to compass its purpose. The government of the confederation was itself in a state of decay and near to dissolution.

[3] *U. S. Statutes at Large*, VII, 18. There was an exception in favor of the inhabitants in the forks of the French Broad and Holston rivers, whose status was to be fixed by Congress. At Hopewell, Tassel, the beloved man of Chota, said: "If commissioners are not able to do me justice in removing the people from the fork of French Broad and Holston, I am unable to get it for myself. Are Congress, who conquered the King of Great Britain, unable to remove these people? I am satisfied with the promises of the commissioners to remove all the people from our lines except those in the fork, and I will agree to be content that the particular situation of the people settled there, and our claims to the lands should be referred to Congress, and I will abide by their decision." Congress never acted on the point submitted.

[4] Alexander Outlaw to Governor Caswell, October 8, 1786, protesting against the Treaty of Hopewell. *N. C. State Records*, XVIII, 757.

There was indignation on all the frontiers affected by the treaty, in Georgia as well as in Franklin. It was felt that, as North Carolina furnished two (Benjamin Hawkins and Joseph Martin) of the four negotiating commissioners, she had been remiss in allowing such broad concessions to be made to the Indians. Particular resentment was felt by the borderers toward Martin, who, as Carolina's agent to the Cherokees, had not availed of his influence with the tribe to discourage in advance extreme claims and demands. Martin lost in influence in Franklin; and especially in the lower settlements was public sentiment consolidated in favor of the new-state movement. That solidarity in the lower counties continued to the end. North Carolina had granted and had received compensation for lands in the territory which was now surrendered to the Cherokees. The surrender could only have been consummated by the concurrence of Hawkins and Martin.[5]

There was not lacking some basis for the view that the people of Franklin had been intentionally punished by this action. The commissioners did induce the Indians to give up their claims to lands within the bounds of Henderson's Transylvania, thus leaving all the settlers in the Cumberland region outside of Indian territory.

Many residents of North Carolina had invested in the lands excluded by the treaty, Governor Caswell among the number. William Blount, the State's agent on the treaty ground, filed a formal protest against the validity of the treaty as violative of the State's sovereign rights; and in April following Governor Caswell, with the concurrence of the Council of State, strongly urged the delegation from the State in Congress to oppose the ratification of the treaty.[6]

At the next session of the North Carolina Assembly, the senate adopted a joint resolution expressing "utmost horror and indignation." The treaty, it was said, was calculated to deprive citizens of their property; and instead of procuring the blessings of peace "will most likely produce the contrary effect and involve our citizens in the horrors of war, as the savages appear much more hostile since than before."[7] The house of commons did not give its approval to

---

[5] *Am. St. Papers*, Indian Affairs, I, 44.

[6] *N. C. State Records*, XVIII, 591.

[7] *N. C. State Records*, XXII, 105. The report of the committee embodied an argument based on the assumed validity of the cession act of 1784, and an insistence that Congress must thereunder treat the State's grants of western lahds as valid,

the resolution, which accordingly failed. The treaty was ratified by Congress April 17, 1786; but by no means did it meet with the acquiescence of the western people, but rather with a resistance that was not passive. On July 12, 1786, Governor Caswell wrote to Sevier that "Congress itself will be persuaded that the result is so repugnant to the rights of the State that they will not consider us by any means bound to abide by that treaty."

The spring session of the General Assembly of Franklin was held in March. A careful search has not been rewarded by the discovery of any of the acts of that session so signed or certified as to show who were the speakers of the senate and the house of commons.

Steps were taken to adopt a great seal of State. Martin wrote to Governor Caswell (May 11, 1786) "I am told they have a coat of arms of their own," having reference to the State of Franklin.

From the same source we learn that Colonel Charles Robertson was empowered by the Assembly to establish a mint and to coin thirty thousand dollars specie, and that "the Colonel was in such forwardness with his mint that in the course of three weeks, he could furnish their member to Congress with cash of the new coin." If coins were ever struck off at this rude mint, as seems probable, none has survived to become the veritable treasure of some numismatist.

The position of peril to the settlers on the lower fringe of Franklin, produced by the Treaty of Hopewell, compelled the attention of the Assembly. The infant State determined to act for herself. Commissioners were appointed to negotiate a second treaty with the Cherokees—William Cocke, Alexander Outlaw, Samuel Wear, Henry Conway and Thomas Ingles.

In the spring of this year, Haywood says, the Cherokees made open war upon the settlers on the waters of the Holston, in the present county of Knox. Governor Sevier raised a volunteer force and followed in pursuit. He crossed the Unaka mountains, and de-

---

"whereas the citizens to whom grants were made before the cession act have been left to the mercy of the Indians." *Ib.*, XVIII, 465.

Joseph Martin wrote to Patrick Henry that "North Carolina is about to say in the protest that the Continental commissioners have given up to the Indians lands that North Carolina purchased of said Indians, which is notoriously false. I speak with confidence." Jan. 20, 1787. Henry's *Patrick Henry*, III, 384. Martin was smarting under the stinging criticism of his work as commissioner and (Feb. 10) represented to Henry that the Cherokees were so disheartened as to be considering a removal. ". . . I incline to think they will cross the Ohio." *Cal. Va. St. Papers*, IV, 235.

stroyed the valley towns of the North Carolina Cherokees on the Hiwassee river.[8]

In April a party of Cherokees, returning from a raid on the whites with fifteen scalps, sent Sevier a letter saying they they had now taken their satisfaction for their friends who had been murdered and did not wish for war, "but if the white people wanted war, it was what they would get."[9]

On July 20th, two young men were murdered by the Chickamauga Cherokees. Colonels Cocke and Outlaw, at the head of two hundred and fifty men, marched to Chota Ford, about six miles from the Indian towns, and sent for the headmen to come to a conference. When The Tassel and Hanging Maw came in, they were charged with complicity in the murder. The Tassel denied that accusation. Learning in the conference that the guilty Indians lived in Coyatee (Coytoy) town, at the mouth of Holston, about twenty miles below Chota, the colonels marched their forces to Coyatee and "luckily killed two of the very Indians that did the murder." They again sent for the chiefs, The Tassel and Hanging Maw, and the warriors from the nearby towns, and renewed the conference begun at Chota Ford. Colonel Outlaw, in a letter to Governor Caswell,[10] after stating these facts, enclosed the treaty there negotiated, and claimed that the Indians "seemed friendly and well satisfied we should settle the country, and say they will sell us the country on the south of the Tennessee, and let us settle around them, if we will keep the Creeks from killing them; or they will leave the country entirely, if we will give them goods for it."

The treaty on its face,[11] however, gives evidence of undue pressure, amounting to duress, or of unfairness on the part of Cocke and Outlaw, backed as they were at the time by an adequate force. No act of the State of Franklin is less creditable to her than this Treaty of Coyatee.

The white settlements at the time had passed the line established by the treaty of Dumplin Creek and it was determined that all the Cherokee lands north of the Little Tennessee river should be

---

[8] Haywood, 162.

[9] Martin to Governor Caswell, May 11, 1786, *N. C. State Records*. See also *Va. Cal. State Papers*, IV, 162, 164, 256.

[10] Ramsey, 343; also *Maryland Journal*, Aug. 29, and Oct. 6, 1786, for letters from Franklin on the campaign.

[11] Given in full by Ramsey, 344-5.

opened to settlement, the treaty of Hopewell to the contrary notwithstanding. Instead of submitting to be removed from that region, the settlers advanced to possess more of it. The following spring, we shall see, an office was opened by the Franklin authorities for the entry of all the lands north of the Little Tennessee.

William Cocke was again chosen by the Assembly to attend on Congress, then in session, and continue his efforts for the recognition of Franklin. It seems that he did not, this year, undertake the long journey to New York to discharge his duties. Benjamin Franklin, who had been absent in Europe in the diplomatic service when the new State was launched, had recently returned to America. To him, Cocke wrote a letter, after the adjournment of the Assembly, outlining what had taken place, and appealing for advice:

State of Franklin, 15 June, 1786.

Sir:

I make no doubt you have heard that the good people of this country have declared themselves a separate State from North Carolina, and that, as a testimony of the high esteem they have for the many important and faithful services you have rendered to your country, they have called their State after you. I presume you have heard also the reasons on which our separation is founded, some of which are as follows: that North Carolina granted us a separation on certain well-known conditions, expressed in an act of the General Assembly of that State, which conditions, we think, she had no right to break through without our consent, as well as the consent of Congress. We therefore determine strictly to adhere to the conditions expressed in said act, and doubt not but Congress will be uniform in their just demands as well as honorable in complying with their resolve to confirm all the just claims of such persons, as have purchased lands under the laws of North Carolina, for which they have paid the State.

The confidence we have in the wisdom and justice of the United States inclines us to leave every matter of dispute to their decision, and I am expressly empowered and commanded to give the United States full assurance, that we shall act in obedience to their determination, provided North Carolina will consent that they shall become the arbiters. I had set out with the intention to wait on Congress to discharge the duties of the trust reposed in me, but I am informed that Congress will adjourn about the last of this month; and I will thank you to be so kind as to favor me with a few lines by the bearer, Mr. Rogers, to inform me when Congress will meet again, and shall be happy to have your sentiments and advice on so important a subject.[12]

---

[12] *Works of Franklin* (Sparks ed.), X, 266.

Franklin made prompt acknowledgment, expressing appreciation of the honor done him in the naming of the State, and approving the resolution of the leaders of the movement to submit the points in dispute to the decision of Congress:

Philadelphia, 12 August, 1786.

Sir:

I received yesterday the letter you did me the honor of writing me on the 15th of June past. I had never before been acquainted that the name of your new State had any relation with my name, having understood that it was called *Frankland*. It is a very great honor, indeed, that its inhabitants have done me; and I should be happy if it were in my power to show how sensible I am of it, by something more essential than my wishes for their prosperity.

Having resided some years past in Europe, and being but lately arrived thence, I have not had the opportunity of being well informed of the points in dispute between you and the State of North Carolina. I can therefore only say, that I think you are perfectly right in resolving to submit them to the discretion of Congress, and to abide by their determination. It is a wise and impartial tribunal, which can have no sinister views to warp its judgment. It is happy for us all that we have now in our own country such a council to apply to, for composing our differences, without being obliged, as formerly, to carry them across the ocean to be decided, at an immense expense, by a council which knew but little about our affairs, would hardly take any pains to understand them, and which often treated our applications with contempt, and rejected them with injurious language. Let us, therefore cherish and respect our own tribunal; for the more generally it is held in high regard, the more able it will be to answer effectually the ends of its institution, the quieting of our contentions, and thereby promoting our common peace and happiness.

I do not hear any talk of an adjournment of Congress concerning which you inquire; and I rather think it likely they may continue to sit out their year, as it is but lately they have been able to make a quorum for business that must therefore probably be in arrear. If you proceed in your intended journey, I shall be glad to see you as you pass through Philadelphia.[13]

---

[13] *Works of Franklin* (Sparks Ed.), X, 268.

CHAPTER XV

Storm Clouds Gather—1786

In likelihood the Assembly of Franklin at the spring session had under consideration a campaign against the Creek Indians in conjunction with the State of Georgia.[1]

Early in the year Governor Edward Telfair, of the latter State, had approached Governor Sevier on the subject, giving notice of the probability of vigorous operations against the Creeks in November, 1786; and in February, in accordance with resolutions of the Georgia General Assembly, he had appointed Robert Dixon and Stephen Jett commissioners to effect an alliance with the Cherokees and Chickasaws, and to visit the Franklin settlement for the purpose of explaining to the people there the plan of campaign that had been formulated.[2] In preparation for the campaign, Governor Telfair applied to Governor Henry, of Virginia, for a loan of five hundred muskets, but instead Henry arranged for Georgia's purchase of the necessary arms. Dixon was directed to go on to Virginia to receive the arms and provide for their transportation to Georgia. In doing so Dixon probably passed through Franklin and laid before Sevier the design of Georgia in detail.

Sevier kept in close touch with the authorities of Georgia because of his interest in the Great Bend enterprise, and because of a purpose on his part to induce an emigration from Franklin to found settlements there. In reply to a letter from Telfair on the subject, Sevier wrote from Franklin, May 14, 1786, summarizing the conditions in that Commonwealth:

Being appointed one of the commissioners of the Tennessee district, I beg leave to inform your Honor that it appears impracticable to proceed on that business before the fall season.

The people here are apprehensive of an Indian war. Hostilities are daily committed in the vicinities of Kentucky and Cumberland. Cols. Donelson, Christian, and several other persons, were lately wounded and are since dead.

---

[1] Sevier to Telfair, September 28, 1786, Ramsey, 383.
[2] *Georgia Historical Quarterly*, I, 145, 148.

The success of the Mussel Shoals enterprise greatly depends on the number that will go down to that place. A small force will not be adequate to the risk and danger that is to be encountered, and the people here will not venture to so dangerous a place with a few.

Your Honor will be pleased to be further informed, and, through you the different branches of your government, that no unfair advantage will be taken from this quarter; and no surveying will be attempted until a force sufficient can be had, and timely notice given to those who may intend to move down. The people in this quarter wish to proceed in the fall, but will wait your advice on the subject. Your Honor may rest assured that I shall, with pleasure, facilitate everything in my power that may tend to the welfare of this business.[3]

Telfair did not reply until August 27th in order to await the action of the legislature of his State, which was about to meet when Sevier's letter was received. He gave information that the Assembly had postponed consideration of the Tennessee District until January, 1787. "The Creek Indians have committed murders and depredations on the persons and property of the citizens of this State, which have caused the Legislature to adopt measures for further security... The General Assembly have appointed commissioners to meet the 15th day of October, next, for the purpose of negotiating a peace with the Creek Nation; on failure of which, this State will carry on immediate and vigorous operations against the said Indians. It has been suggested that you intend to march a body of men against the Creek Indians. I flatter myself it will tend greatly to the success of both armies to begin their movements at one and the same time, should it become necessary; which movements will take effect in this State about the first of November. On this subject I have to solicit your immediate answer and determination."

The provision for elections in the western counties to be held by citizen-inspectors, acting independently of the Franklin officials, proved to be what was intended—a firebrand that excited, confused, and disrupted. Malcontents, led by John Tipton, concerted plans to hold an election in Washington county for members of the North Carolina General Assembly in August following. Tipton appeared as a candidate for a seat in the senate, and James Stuart and Richard White for seats in the house of commons. The sheriff of Washington county was prevailed upon to advertise the election,

---

[3] Ramsey, 379.

which he did under date of July 19th, 1786:

"Advertisement.—I hereby give public notice that there will be an election held the Third Friday in August next, at John Rennoe's near the Sycamore Shoals, where Charles Robertson formerly lived, to choose members to represent Washington county in the General Assembly of North Carolina, agreeable to an act of Assembly in that case made and provided, where due attendance will be given by me.

George Mitchell, Sheriff."

How to meet this issue gave the Franklin adherents no little concern, though its gravity was not fully appreciated. They, however, hit upon a counter plot, which, as the event proved, was a fatal error: to make the confusion that of Carolina, and to demonstrate to her legislators the futility of their unofficial electoral machinery. They planned to have like inspectors open a poll on the same day at which the Franklinites should vote, thereby electing two of their members to the seats in the Carolina house of commons. Evidently at their prompting, Sheriff Mitchell refused to open the North Carolina polls in accordance with his advertisement. Jonesborough, the county site, was chosen as the polling place of the Franklin adherents and Landon Carter and Thomas Chapman there received a unanimous vote, according to the returns made by inspectors Robert Rogers, Samuel Williams, and Anderson Smith. The number of votes cast was 254. At Rennoe's[4] 179 ballots were cast. While the insurgents afterward claimed that the inhabitants had been warned to go to the Jonesborough polls by the militia officers for a muster, and that many were prevented from voting by threats, "both elections were conducted without violence and in an orderly manner," as the committee of the house of commons of North Carolina reported.[5]

This election furnished the basis for the fairest estimate of the relative strength of the opposing factions at the time in the central county of Franklin, the home of both Tipton and Sevier, where the rivalry of these leaders gave rise to the greatest discord and strife.

The result of the poll disproves Joseph Martin's "best calculations" that (in May) two-thirds of the people were for the old

---

[4] John Rennoe resided on Sinking Creek where Charles Robertson had formerly lived and where the county court had been held under the act of 1777, creating Washington county.

[5] *Infra*, of date March 18, 1787.

State; and equally refutes the later estimate of Judge David Campbell that perhaps nineteen-twentieths of the inhabitants favored perseverance in separation, given in a letter to Governor Caswell.

This election, brought on by the dissenters, was also according to Sevier the first interference with Franklin's exercise of jurisdiction.[6] It was the entering wedge, which when further driven brought on a reassertion by the old State of her authority in the borders of Franklin. The clash of the two rival States led to increasing bitterness and retaliation. The result is best described by Haywood,[7] who, however, erroneously attributes the conditions to the early part, rather than to the middle part of the year 1786; and the same description is applicable to the year 1787: Here

was presented the strange spectacle of two empires exercised at one and the same time, over one and the same people. County courts were held in the same counties under both governments; the militia were called out by officers appointed by both; laws were passed by both Assemblies and taxes were laid by the authority of both States. The differences in opinion in the State of Franklin between those who adhered to the government of North Carolina and those who were friends to the new government became more acrimonious every day. Every fresh provocation on the one side was surpassed in the way of retaliation by still greater provocation on the other. The judges commissioned by the State of Franklin held superior courts twice in each year, in Jonesborough. Colonel Tipton openly refused obedience to the new government. There arose a deadly hatred between him and Sevier, and each endeavored by all means in his power to strengthen his party against the other. Tipton held courts under the authority of North Carolina, ten miles above Jonesborough, which were conducted by her officers and agreeable to her laws. Courts were also held at Jonesborough in the same county under the authority of the State of Franklin.

As the process of these courts frequently required the sheriff to pass within the jurisdiction of each other to execute it, an encounter was sure to take place, hence it became necessary to appoint the stoutest men in the county to the office of sheriff. This state of things produced the appointment of A. Caldwell, of Jonesborough, and Mr. [John] Pugh, the sheriff in Tipton's court. Whilst a county court was sitting at Jonesborough in this year, for the county of Washington, Colonel John Tipton with a party of men entered the court house, took away the papers from the clerk, and turned the justices out of doors. Not long after, Sevier's party came to a house where a county court was sitting for the county of Washington, under the authority of North Carolina, and took

---

[6] Sevier to Benjamin Franklin, April 9, 1787, *infra*. [7] Haywood, 160.

away the clerk's papers and turned the court out of doors. Thomas Gourley was the clerk of this court. The like acts were several times repeated during the existence of the Franklin government. ... In these removals, many valuable papers were lost, and at later periods for want of them, some estates of great value were lost. In the county of Greene, in 1786, Tipton broke up a court sitting at Greeneville, under the Franklin authority. The clerks in all the three old counties issued marriage licenses, and many persons were married by virtue of their authority. In the courts held under the authority of the State of Franklin, many letters of administration of intestate estates were issued, and probates of wills were taken. The members of the two factions became excessively incensed against each other, and at public meetings made frequent exhibitions of their strength and prowess in boxing matches. As an elucidation of the temper of the times, an incident may be mentioned which otherwise would be too trivial for the page of history. Shortly after the election of Sevier as governor of Franklin, under the permanent Constitution, he and Tipton met in Jonesborough, where as usual a violent verbal altercation was maintained between them for some time, when Sevier, no longer able to bear the provocations which were given him, struck Tipton with a cane. Instantly the latter began to annoy him with his hands clenched. Each exchanged blows for some time in the same way with great violence and in a convulsion of rage. Those who happened to be present interfered and parted them before victory had been declared for either. But some of those who saw the conflict believe that the governor was not so well pleased with his prospects of victory as he had been with the event of the battle of King's Mountain, in which his regiment and himself had so eminently distinguished themselves... To such excess was driven by civil discord a people who, in times of tranquility, is not exceeded by any on earth for all the virtues, good sense and genuine politeness that can make mankind happy and amiable.

Only Sevier's moderation, in the face of danger threatening from a common foe, the Indians, prevented the prompt adoption of repressive measures which, while they might have provoked civil war on a small scale, could have terminated only in favor of the new government. The time for successful vigorous action on the part of Franklin was soon to pass. One cannot escape the conviction that Sevier at the time was too much concerned in the exploitation of the rich country in the Great Bend, and too hopeful of success in making a military pact (which he designed should lead to an alliance) with Georgia, advantageous to the Commonwealth over which he presided.

To this last object he again turned his attention by replying to Governor Telfair's last communication:

You will please to be informed that the deliberations of our Assembly have not, as yet, been fully had respecting the marching of a force against that [the Creek] nation of Indians. Our Assembly will be convened in a few days, at which time I make not the smallest doubt but that they will order out a respectable force to act in conjunction with an army of your State. The determinations of our Legislature I shall immediately communicate to your Honor as soon as the same can be fully obtained. The movements to begin the first of November, I fear, will be rather early for our army. Could the time be procrastinated a few days, I hope it would not obstruct the success of the expedition. Shall be much obliged by being informed of the time of marching, should the same be found necessary. Also, as near as may be, of the time and place your army may be expected to be in the Creek country.[8]

The faith that in some way effectual aid would come to Franklin from Georgia had back of it a history that abounds in pathos.

Shortly before the battle of King's Mountain, the British commander-in-chief at Charleston ordered that all men under forty years of age remaining in the States of Georgia and South Carolina, where the patriots were hard pressed, should enroll as British soldiers, and that any who refused to do so should be shot as traitors. In September, 1780, a large number of the Whigs who were determined not to yield sought safety for their families from the advancing Tory horde by flight to the north. A multitude (400) women and children, led by Colonels Elijah Clarke and William Candler, commenced an eleven-day march of two hundred miles through a mountain wilderness to the settlements on the Watauga and Nolachucky rivers. They arrived in a deplorable condition, nearly starved. Many of the adults had gone without food except nuts, for several days. During the last two days even the children subsisted on the same kind of food. After their helpless charges had been disposed of in a place of security and comparative plenty, to remain till the coming of peace among a sympathetic people, the men turned back, in October, to the borders of South Carolina to confront the British. Colonel Clarke and family were received as guests in the home of Sevier.[9]

---

[8] Date September 38, 1786; Ramsey, 383.

[9] Letter Clarke to General Sumter, October 27, 1780, cited Draper's *Heroes of King's Mountain*, 214; Candler, *William Candler*, 29, 35, 47; Williams "The Battle of King's Mountain," *Tennessee Historical Mag.*, VII, 51, 57.

Colonel William Candler, while yet on the march, learned that forces had collected on the west side of the mountains to march against Ferguson, and filed off

With many of the leading men of Georgia, Sevier and his men had come in touch in their campaigns in the South during the Revolutionary War. George Mathews, who was from Sevier's old neighborhood in the Valley of Virginia, had but recently removed to Georgia where he was soon afterward elevated to the office of governor. Upon all such Sevier felt that he and his people had a claim in the crisis that was impending.

Among the number was a young soldier of fortune, a foreigner, George Elholm[10] with whom, according to Ramsey, Sevier had become acquainted while campaigning in the South. Elholm was a German-speaking Dane, a native of the Duchy of Holstein in the dominion of Denmark,[11] and came to America in the early part of the Revolutionary War. He received a commission in the corps of Count Pulaski, and afterward one in Colonel Horry's regiment of dragoons, in both of which commands he served with great gallantry. After the war he was made adjutant-general of Georgia under the administration of Governor Telfair. It is probable that he while so serving learned from the correspondence between Telfair and Sevier of the situation in Franklin. He appears to have turned up there in 1786, perhaps the "embassy" of Georgia to Franklin, which he referred to in a letter to Governor Telfair, under date of September 30, 1786. This letter evidences the former's imperfect English, and the fact that he was, in a sense, an emissary of Georgia:

>   GOVERNOR SEVIER'S, Franklin, September 30, 1786.
> Sir:—I does myself the honour to inform your Excellency, that your Commissioners set out from this the 28th inst., by way of Kentucky and Cumberland. They were received very politely by his excellency the Governor, from whose zeal for to assist you, aided by the inclination of the Franks, I am fully convinced your embassy will meet all wished success by the Assembly of this State, which is ordered to assemble 12th next, by his Excellency's com-

---

with a force of thirty men. They joined the western forces at Gilbert Town and shared with them in the defeat of Ferguson in the fateful battle of King's Mountain. It is interesting to note that two of the descendants of Sevier and Candler, who were thus linked together by ties of hospitality and of comradeship in battle, became in the third generation afterward close friends and confreres as bishops of the Southern Methodist church—Hoss and Candler.

[10] Ramsey, 381. For sketch, see *post.* p. 301.

[11] Ramsey surmised that Elholm was a Frenchman or Pole, *Ib.* See Faust, *German Element in the United States*, I, 370; Wagener, "Frankland und Franklin," in *Der Deutsche Pioneer*, II, 268; White's *Historical Collection of Georgia*, 628.

mand, in consequence thereof. Several of the inhabitants have waited on the governor, for to be informed of the contents of the embassy from Georgia. And when being acquainted therewith, it gave me great pleasure to find no other apprehension appeared, but that of making peace with the Creeks without fighting, by which occasion they said so favourable a chance for humbling that nation would fall dormant. The Governor, in order that the Americans may reap a benefit from the dread the Cherokees and Chickasaws feels from the displeasure and power of the Franks, he has despatched letters to them, offering them protection against the Creek nation, with condition that they join him.

Cumberland, it seems, has it at this time in contemplation to join in government with the Franks. If so, so much the better, and it would surely be their interest so to do, as they are yet few in numbers, and often harassed by the Indians.

Judging from apparent circumstances, you may promise yourself one thousand riflemen and two hundred cavalry, excellently mounted and accoutred, from this state, to act in conjunction with Georgia.

P.S. Governor Sevier received letters from the principal men in Cumberland, which inform him of a convention held lately at that place, when Commissioners were chosen by the people with power for to join with the Franks in their government.

Mr. John Tipton's party, which is against the party of the new government, seems deep in decline at present, which proves very favourable to the embassy from Georgia.

Major Elholm entered the service of the State of Franklin as adjutant-general and continued faithful to the cause to the end of her existence. He organized and drilled the militia, having had the advantages of experience in foreign service and a technical skill beyond that of any of the border soldiery.

CHAPTER XVI

FRANKLIN SENDS A COMMISSION TO CAROLINA—1786

As in the preceding year, a special fall session of the General Assembly was called by Governor Sevier in 1786. The month of October was chosen for it. The officers of the senate were, Gilbert Christian, speaker, and Joseph Conway, clerk; and of the house of commons, Henry Conway, speaker, and Isaac Taylor, clerk.

One of the principal matters for consideration was a plan for a campaign against the Creek Indians. Under the governor's advice and guidance, provision was promptly made to raise in the State a force of mounted riflemen, composed of a draft of one-fourth of the militia from every county, and the light-horse regiment of the State, provisioned for twenty days.

Preparations for the expedition were halted on the receipt of a communication from Governor Telfair, under date of November 28, 1786, stating that commissioners appointed to treat with the Creek nation had concluded peace, on account of which preparations for hostile operation were suspended. One object of Sevier in projecting this campaign was thus temporarily frustrated—that of diverting the attention of the men of the region from civil feud by concentrating it on and attaching them to a movement of a kind that never failed to enlist the enthusiastic support of the fighting frontiersmen. Peace for the infant Commonwealth was sought in hostile action in another direction.

Two commissioners, William Cocke and Judge David Campbell, were appointed to attend the approaching session of the North Carolina Assembly to negotiate for a separation. Each of them was well suited for the purpose of his mission. The former was identified with the new settlements by an early participation in the privation, enterprise and danger of the pioneer life. More recently, he had taken an active part in founding the new State—had been appointed its delegate to Congress; commanded a brigade of its militia and held other positions implying confidence in his talents and address. His colleague had also a minute acquaintance with every question relating to either of the parties, held the highest judicial station in the government from which he was accredited, and by his private worth, was entitled to the respect of the one to which he was sent.[1]

The commissioners were to confront members of the Carolina Assembly who had been chosen by the old-state faction from the region, and two of these members, Stuart and White, were themselves to confront contestants for their seats in two Franklinites, Landon Carter and Thomas Chapman. The mission was, indeed, a difficult one. The governor of Franklin sent an argument and appeal to Governor Caswell in support of its object, in which he uttered words of caution. "It may occasion much confusion should your Assembly listen too much to prejudiced persons"—the reference being to Tipton in the Senate and his associates in the Assembly. The communication embodied a candid statement of Franklin's claims and attitude, and was so shaped as to put to test the willingness of Carolina to yield assent to a separation on any reasonable terms.[2]

Judge Campbell was unable, because of ill health, to make the long trip to Fayetteville, where the North Carolina Assembly convened; and he likewise stated his State's case in a written argument addressed to Governor Caswell, but to be laid before the Assembly:

STATE OF FRANKLIN,
Caswell County, Nov. 30th, 1786.

May it please your Excellency—

I have hesitated to address your Excellency on so delicate a subject as the present. I shall only state a few facts, and leave your Excellency to draw the conclusion.

Is not the continent of America one day to become one consolidated government of the United States? Is not your state, when connected with this part of the country, too extensive? Are we not, then, one day to be a separate people? Do you receive any advantage from us as now situated? or do you ever expect to receive any? I believe you do not. Suffer us, then, to pursue our own happiness in a way most agreeable to our situation and circumstances. The plans laid for a regular and systematic government in this country, are greatly frustrated by the opposition from your country. Can a people so nearly connected as yours are with ours, delight in our misfortunes? The rapid settlements that are making, and have been made out of the bounds prescribed both by your state and ours, is a matter worthy your consideration; our divisions are favourable

---

[1] Ramsey, 347.
[2] This letter was carried by Cocke, who reached Fayetteville November 16, 1786.

to those who have a mind to transgress our laws. If you were to urge us, and it were possible we should revert back to you, in what a labyrinth of difficulties would we be involved? Witness the many lawsuits, which have been decided under the sanction of the laws of Franklin, the retrial of which would involve many persons in certain ruin.

If we set out wrong, or were too hasty in our separation, this country is not altogether to blame; your state pointed out the line of conduct, which we adopted; we really thought you in earnest when you ceded us to Congress. If you then thought we ought to be separate, or if you now think we ever ought to be, permit us to complete the work that is more than half done; suffer us to give energy to our laws and force to our councils, by saying we are a separate and independent people, and we will yet be happy. I suppose it will astonish your Excellency to hear that there are many families settled within nine miles of the Cherokee nation. What will be the consequence of those emigrations? Our laws and government must include these people or they will become dangerous; it is vain to say they must be restrained. Have not all Americans extended their back settlements in opposition to laws and proclamations? The Indians are now become more pusillanimous, and consequently will be more and more encroached upon; they must, they will be circumscribed. Some of your politicians think we have not men of abilities to conduct the reins of government; this may in some measure be true, but all new states must have a beginning, and we are daily increasing in men both of political and law knowledge. It was not from a love of novelty, or the desire of title, I believe, that our leaders were induced to engage in the present revolution, but from pure necessity. We were getting into confusion, and you know any government is better than anarchy. Matters will be differently represented to you, but you may rely on it, a great majority of the people are anxious for a separation. Nature has separated us; do not oppose her in her work; by acquiescing you will bless us, and do yourself no injury; you bless us by uniting the disaffected, and do yourself no injury, because you lose nothing but people who are a clog in your government, and whom you cannot do equal justice by reason of their detached situation.

I was appointed to wait on your General Assembly, to urge a ratification of our independence, but the misfortune of losing one of my eyes, and some other occurrences, prevented me. You will therefore, pardon me for the liberties I have taken, whilst endeavouring to serve a people whose situation is truly critical.

On the opening day of the session a number of petitions from the trans-Alleghany counties were presented and referred to a select committee appointed to report on the western situation, Elisha Battle, of the senate, being its chairman.

At this juncture appeared Cocke who asked leave to be heard, at the bar of the house of commons, by both branches of the Assembly. The scene was an impressive one. Cocke was himself of an imposing presence, tall, swarthy, black-haired, black-eyed; and bold and eloquent in utterance. To some of his hearers he had been comrade in arms on battlefields of the Revolution, the principles of which he now urged in behalf of Franklin. Fortunately, John Haywood, the historian, as secretary of the senate of Carolina, was present lending an ear peculiarly attentive because upon himself had been bestowed an appointment to serve as chief judge in one of the districts of the Western Country. He thus graphically outlines Cocke's address:

In a speech of some hours, he pathetically depicted the miseries of his distressed countrymen; he traced the motives of their separation to the difficult and perilous condition in which they had been placed by the Cession act of 1784; he stated that the savages in their neighbourhood often committed upon the defenceless inhabitants the most shocking barbarities; and that they were without the means of raising or subsisting troops for their protection; without authority to levy men; without the power to lay taxes for the support of internal government; and without the hope that any of their necessary expenditures would be defrayed by the State of North-Carolina, which had then become no more interested in their safety than any other of the United States. The sovereignty retained being precarious and nominal, as it depended on the acceptance of the cession by Congress, so it was anticipated would be the concern of North-Carolina for the ceded territory. With these considerations full in view, what were the people of the ceded territory to do, to avoid the blow of the uplifted tomahawk? How were the women and children to be rescued from the impending destruction? Would Congress come to their aid? Alas! Congress had not yet accepted of them, and possibly, never would. And if accepted, Congress was to deliberate on the quantum of defence which might be afforded to them. The distant states would wish to know what profits they could respectively draw from the ceded country, and how much land would remain, after satisfying the claims upon it. The contributions from the several states were to be spontaneous. They might be too limited to do any good, too tardy for practical purposes. They might be unwilling to burthen themselves for the salvation of a people not connected with them by any endearing ties. The powers of Congress were too feeble to enforce contributions. Whatever aids should be resolved on, might not reach the objects of their bounty, till all was lost. Would common prudence justify a reliance upon such prospects? Could the lives of themselves and their families be staked upon them? Immediate and pressing necessity called for the power to concentrate the scanty means they possessed of saving themselves from destruction. A cruel and insidious foe was at their doors. Delay was but another name for death. They might supinely wait for events, but the first of them would be the yell of the savage through all their settlements. It was the well-known disposition of the savages to take every advantage of an unpreparedness to receive them, and of a sudden to raise the shrieking cry of exultation over the fallen inhabitants. The hearts of the people of North-Carolina should not be hardened against their brethren, who have stood by their sides in perilous times, and never heard their cry of distress when they did not instantly rise and march to their aid. Those brethren have bled in profusion to save you from bondage, and from the sanguinary hands of a relentless enemy, whose mildest laws for the punishment of rebellion, is beheading and quartering. When driven in the late war, by the presence of that enemy, from your homes, we gave to many of you a sanctified asylum in the bosom of our country, and gladly performed the rites of hospitality to a people we loved so dearly. Every hand was ready to be raised for the least unhallowed violation of the sanctuary in which they reposed.

The act for our dismissal was, indeed, recalled in the winter of 1784; what then was our condition? More pennyless, defenceless and unprepared, if possible, than before, and under the same necessity as ever, to meet and consult together for our common safety. The resources of the country all locked up, where is the record that shew any money or supplies sent to us?—a single soldier ordered to be stationed on the frontiers, or any plan formed for mitigating the horrors of our exposed situation? On the contrary, the savages are irritated by the stoppage of those goods on their passage, which were promised as a compensation for the lands which had been taken from them. If North-Carolina must yet hold us in subjection, it should at least be understood to what a state of distraction, suffering and poverty, her varying conduct has reduced us, and the liberal hand of generosity should be widely opened for relief, from the pressure of their present circumstances; all animosity should be laid aside and buried in deep oblivion, and our errors should be considered as the offspring of greater errors committed by yourselves. It belongs to a magnanimous people to weep over the failings of their unfortunate children, especially if prompted by the inconsiderate behaviour of the parent. Far should it be from their hearts to harbour the unnatural purpose of adding still more affliction to those who have suffered but too much already. It belongs to a magnanimous people to give an industrious attention to circumstances, in order to form a just judgment upon a subject so much deserving of their serious meditation, and when once carefully formed, to employ, with sedulous anxiety, the best efforts of their purest wisdom, in choosing a course to pursue, suitable to the dignity of their own character, consistent with their own honour, and the best calculated to allay that storm of distraction in which their hapless children have been so unexpectedly involved. If the mother shall judge the expense of adhesion too heavy to be borne, let us remain as we are, and support ourselves by our own exertions; if otherwise, let the means for the continuance of our connexion be supplied with the degree of liberality which will demonstrate seriousness on the one hand, and secure affection on the other.

North Carolina's legislative leaders were not yet willing to turn loose the State's western domain, whatever may have been their sentiments respecting the claims of the over-mountain people.

It was their firm determination that separation should not be granted but that North Carolina's sovereignty should yet be more distinctly asserted. The select committee, through its chairman, "impressed with a sense of the suffering of those people," suggested "the necessity of extending to them the benefits of government and protection, and that they be assured they will be neither neglected nor discarded by their brethren on this side of the mountains." The committee was of the opinion that the numbers and wealth of the western counties would not enable them to support a separate government. "Whenever the wealth and numbers of the citizens on the western waters so increase as to make same necessary, we are free to say a separation may take place upon friendly and reciprocal terms and under certain compacts and stipulations." The "compacts and stipulations" remained for future definition; but what was in mind to be imposed, the event showed.

General Griffith Rutherford,[3] evidently after consulting with Cocke, four days later introduced a bill to conciliate the inhabitants of the western counties that would have proved acceptable to the supporters of Franklin and brought peace to her borders. It met with short shrift. On its first reading it was rejected.

Tipton, in the senate, sought to punish the town of Jonesborough for the attitude of its citizens in the August election by introducing a bill to remove the seat of justice of Washington county. After being amended so as to name commissioners (Benjamin Ward, Robert White, Edward Williams, William Moore, John Hammer, Robert Love and William Priestly) merely *to select* a site, the bill passed. The commissioners later selected Jonesborough, the old

---

[3] *N. C. State Records*, XVIII, 112. General Rutherford later removed to the Western Country where he was honored with membership in and the presidency of the Legislative Council of Territory South of the Ohio, and by having one of Tennessee's richest counties given his name.

county seat, and Tipton's real intention was defeated. The act provided, however, that in the meantime the courts should be held in Tipton's neighborhood at the home of William Davis, near the present Johnson City.[4]

Other enactments toward the close of the session followed the recommendations of the committee. Separation was denied; tender of oblivion and pardon was offered for the offenses of all persons engaged in the Franklin movement; taxes for the years 1784 and 1785 were remitted to the inhabitants of the counties that had adhered to the new State; civil and military officers were provided for in order to the restoration of statal functioning there; a new county was carved out of the territory of Sullivan county and named in honor of Benjamin Hawkins; and an extension of two years was made for the completing of surveys of lands west of the Cumberland mountains, and for the perfecting of military grants in that region.

This grasping for a firmer hold of the western lands was coincident with the communication of a renewed appeal made by Congress (August 9, 1786) on North Carolina for a cession of those lands. The State was "once more solicited to consider with candor and liberality the expectations of sister States, and, the earnest and repeated applications made by Congress on this subject."[5]

The appeals of Congress and of Franklin were alike unheeded.

A strong side-light is thrown upon the attitude and action of the North Carolina Assembly by a letter to General James Robertson from one of the most experienced, influential and astute leaders in the legislature of Carolina, General Thomas Person, written after the adjournment of the session. Requesting that surveys of western land for himself be speeded, Person wrote further: "I fully intend to be with you in the next Assembly; we will do the best we can to open the land office once more and grant out all the western country; and leave Congress no further hopes of obtaining it from us to whom it justly belongs, that is to say, the State. . . I am clear you must soon be a separate State, for which you have my

---

[4] *N. C. State Records*, XVIII, 91; Acts 1776, ch. 79, and *N. C. State Records*, XXIV, 850. Had Tipton's design been carried through the chances are that Johnson City, at this day a thriving city of 25,000 population, would today be the site of Washington county, and that Carter county would never have been created, at least with her present territorial limits.

[5] *Journal of Continental Congress* (W. and G. ed.), IV, 680.

hearty concurrence as soon as you can act for yourselves."[6] Person had been and continued to be an opponent of all cession or separation measures. He along with others of his type was, indeed, favorable to a separate State when the western people could act for themselves—in the sense of "doing for themselves," without a public domain worthy of the name to attract settlers or to aid in the establishment of an educational system.

Major Elholm in September, 1786, expressed the view that "Cumberland was at this time in contemplation to join in government with the Franks." At least, discontent with Carolina's failure to adopt protective measures against the Indians was manifest in that quarter, to stay which the Assembly of that year deemed it good policy to make a provision for the raising of a military force of three companies for the protection of the inhabitants of that region. The force was, preliminarily, to open a road ten feet wide, at least, from the Franklin settlements to those on the Cumberland. Each man embodied in the troop was to receive for each year's service four hundred acres of land, to be allotted out of those lying west of the Cumberland mountains; and the Westerners were thought to be able to act for themselves to the extent of paying the expenses of raising and equipping the troops by way of taxes imposed by the act, "on all lands lying west of the Appalachian mountains."[7]

Joseph Martin, though not a member of the North Carolina Assembly, went to Fayetteville to lay before that body "the proceedings of the pretended State of Franklin; and their encroachment on the Indian lands"; and lent his aid to the defeat of Cocke's mission.[8]

The separation movement was by no means confined to the State of Franklin. It was in this year rife in Vermont and yet farther east. A convention was held at Portland to effect a separation of the district of Maine from the State of Massachusetts. In Kentucky the movement for a separate government, begun at Danville in December, 1784, renewed in January and May, 1785, was carried to the point of "confirming a decree of separation from Virginia," in August, 1785. An immediate erection of the district into a new State was asked of the Virginia legislature, which body, in January,

---

[6] *American Historical Mag.*, I, 78.
[7] *N. C. State Records*, XXIV, 786.
[8] *Virginia Calendar State Papers*, IV, 183.

1786, stipulated that a new convention should be held in the district in September, 1786; and that, if it declared for independence, a separate State should come into being after September 1, 1786; provided, however that Congress, before June 1, 1787, should consent, and agree to its admission into the Union.[9] Kentucky was, during the year 1786, in turmoil, produced by this action of Virginia, deemed as it was by many of the leaders of the district to be purposely and needlessly dilatory. The two movements, in Franklin and Kentucky had some phases in common. Each tended to bolster the other.

---

[9] Roosevelt, *Winning of the West*, IV, chapter V, and Brown's *Political Beginnings of Kentucky*, give an extended account of the movement in Kentucky.

CHAPTER XVII

Spain and Closure of the Mississippi—1786

In this year (1786) was revived the question of the closure, by treaty, of the Mississippi river to American commerce. In May, 1785, Gardoqui appeared as Spain's representative to negotiate a treaty of commerce with Secretary Jay, and in July the latter was authorized by Congress to carry forward parleys. Washington thought this was a mistake, and that the true policy was to wait until actual settlements were far advanced toward the Mississippi, with the western people in a strategic position to impose their will upon Spain. "I may be singular in my ideas, but they are these: to open a door to, and make easy the way for those settlers to the westward (who ought to advance regularly and compactly) before we make any stir about the navigation of the Mississippi."[1]

Henry Lee was of like mind. In a letter to Washington he said: "the moment our Western Country becomes populous and capable, they will seize by force what may have been yielded by treaty."

But the question was pressed, and at the instance of the commercial classes of the East. A severe depression was felt by them at this time as a result in part of the clogging of the channels of foreign commerce; and they turned for relief to the advocacy of a treaty that would admit of a freer trade with Spain and her possessions. Rufus King, of Massachusetts, expressed the belief that if the free navigation of the river were secured the East and West must separate, since the commerce of the West would follow the current of that stream.

Charles Pinckney, of South Carolina, saw separation threatening from another direction: "Should it [the right of navigation] be surrendered . . . can the western people be blamed for immediately throwing themselves into Spanish arms for that protection and support which you have denied them? Is it not to be clearly seen, by those who will see, that the policy of Spain in thus inducing us to

---
[1] Sparks, *Writings of Washington*, IX, 102, 172.

consent to the surrender of navigation for a time, is, that she may use it for the purpose of separating the interests of the inhabitants of the Western Country entirely from us and making it subservient to her own purposes? Will it not produce this? When once this right is ceded, no longer can the United States be viewed as the friend or parent of the New States, nor ought they to be considered in any other light than that of their oppressors."[2]

Jefferson wrote to Madison in January, 1787, of Jay's project, giving quite the true view of the situation: "I never had any interest westward of the Alleghany, and never will have any. But I have had great opportunities of knowing the character of the people who inhabit that country. And I will venture to say that the act which abandons the navigation of the Mississippi, is an act of separation between the Eastern and Western Country. It is a relinquishment of five parts out of eight of the territory of the United States; an abandonment of our fairest subject for the payment of our public debts and the chaining of those debts on our necks *in perpetuum*... If they declare themselves a separate people, we are incapable of a single effort to retain them. Our citizens can never be induced, either as militia or as soldiers, to go there to cut the throats of their own brothers and sons... They [the Westerners] are able already to rescue the navigation of the Mississippi out of the hands of Spain."

In the same letter, Jefferson expressed the opinion that a little rebellion now and then was a good thing, and as necessary in the political world as storms in the physical.[3]

Timothy Bloodworth, of North Carolina, pointed out in an official letter from Congress to Governor Caswell, that the Eastern States would receive the benefits of the commercial clauses in the sale of their fish and oil, while tobacco, a staple commodity of the South, was excluded, though the purchase price for the treaty was to be paid for by the South and West by the closing of the river. Then with his eye on Carolina's western possessions, he remarked that a pernicious consequence irreparably connected with the measure would be the alienation of the citizens, and the depreciation of the land, on the western waters.[4]

---

[2] Debate on Jay's proposal, August 16, 1786, in *American Historical Review*, IX, 825.

[3] January 30, 1787, *Jefferson's Writings* (Ford ed.) V, 256.

[4] *N. C. State Records*, XXII, 902.

To this representative of North Carolina the success of Jay's proposal would mean the consolidation of all factions in Franklin and on the Cumberland against the people of the seaboard; and the depreciation in value of the immense holdings of transmontane lands of Carolinians. The passing of political control of the West from North Carolina would imperil titles claimed by her citizens covering 3,736,493 acres of choice land; not to speak of the State's control of ungranted parts of the trans-Alleghany regions.

It is significant that just at the time that plans for the Federal Constitution were being projected, threats of secession were so freely uttered from diverse sources. No closure of the Mississippi meant separation to the East; closure justified secession on the part of the South and West. The issue took a sectional color. Otto wrote Vergennes in September, 1786, that he feared that the heat engendered between the sections would lead to yet more open advocacy of disunion. This French diplomatist saw the issue in its true light. "The fertile plains of the interior would always attract a considerable number of the inhabitants of the different States, and it would be easier to stay a torrent than the constant flow of this population. . . . This emigration doubly enfeebles New England, since on the one hand it deprives her of industrious citizens, and on the other it adds to the population of the Southern States. These new territories will gradually form themselves into separate governments."[5]

Early in 1787 a Southern newspaper advocated that separation take the form of erecting four new nations on the ruins of the Confederation—one of the four to be comprised of the Southern States; another to be founded in Trans-Alleghania.[6]

---

[5] Otto to Vergennes, Bancroft, *History of the Constitution*, II, Appendix, 389.
[6] Quoted in *Massachusetts Centinel*, of Apr. 18, 1787.

CHAPTER XVIII

Factors that Worked for Continued Separation—1787

The inhabitants of the West were by no means out of accord with Jefferson's opinion of them—that they were already able to take care of themselves, whether against the East or the Spaniards. At the Falls of Ohio, there was initiated a movement that looked to concert of action for independence along the frontiers more immediately concerned—Kentucky, Franklin and Georgia. That stalwart of stalwarts, George Rogers Clark, lent his influence to the movement, though intending himself to stand in the background. The open lead was taken by Thomas Green, a Georgian, who during the year 1785-6 had been active in promoting the organization of the territory around Natchez into a county to be called Bourbon, under the authority of the State of Georgia.

Georgia, by act of Assembly of February 7, 1785, had appointed Green and eleven others justices of the peace to organize the county, in an effort to establish her claim to the Natchez district under her colonial charter which extended her boundary westward to the Mississippi river, and under the definitive treaty of September 3, 1783, with Great Britain, which fixed the southern boundary of ceded territory at the thirty-first parallel of latitude. Spain resisted the claim and the effort of Georgia was to colonize the district. Spain contended that, by right of conquest in the capture of Natchez by Galvez from the British in 1779, she was entitled to hold as far north as latitude thirty-two and a half degrees. The efforts of Green, lieutenant-colonel of the county, and his associates, inadequately supported by the state authorities of Georgia, were abortive. A number of the inhabitants of the Watauga-Holston Settlement emigrated to the Natchez district at this time.

Baffled by Miro, Green sought safety among the friendly Chickasaws, from whose country he wrote a letter (Sept. 10, 1785) to Col. Anthony Bledsoe, of the Cumberland Settlement, stating that the Spaniards would not give up Natchez, but were reinforcing the garrison, and warning him that the encroaching tyrants were claiming "as far as the Tennessee if not farther." In July, 1786, Green was at Nashville, from which place he wrote an appealing letter to Governor Telfair, of Georgia, urging that relief be sent to the American settlers around Natchez. "If not, they wish to be given up to Congress, who are sure to relieve them."[1]

Shortly afterward, Green turned up at the Falls of Ohio (Louisville) where he learned of the Jay proposal, which he saw afforded an opportunity to unite and rally the western people to resist all Spanish schemes.[2] No doubt Green hoped and purposed that one result would be a restoration of Bourbon county. From the Falls he wrote to the Governor of Georgia a letter (dated December 23, 1786) in which he denounced the Continental Congress on account of its attitude toward the opening of the Mississippi to navigation, and threatened a revolt against national authority and hostilities against the Spaniards.

By William Wells, the bearer of this letter, there was also sent another document which was to be shown *en route* to Georgia through the State of Franklin, the purpose being to enlist the sympathy and support of Sevier and his friends. This document purported to be a "copy of a letter from a Gentleman at the Falls of Ohio to his Friends in New England" dated December 4, 1786; and patently was meant to engender and deepen resentment against the leadership of the East in Congress. What had actually occurred in Congress was magnified by the time the news reached Kentucky, and Jay's proposal was there understood to be a treaty consummate, as the document shows:

> The late commercial treaty is shutting up, as it is said, the navigation of the Mississippi for a term of twenty-five years, has given the Western Country a severe shock, and struck its inhabitants with amazement. To sell and make us vassals to the merciless Spaniards is a grievance not to be borne. . . . Shall one part of the United States be slaves while the other part is free? Human reason will shudder at the thought and free men despise those who could be so mean as to contemplate so vile a subject. . . .[3]

Our situation is as bad as it possibly can be; therefore every exer-

---

[1] For details respecting this interesting phase of western history see Burnett's Papers Relating to Bourbon County, *American Historical Review*, XV, 66, 297.

[2] *Ib.*, 334.

[3] *Dip. Corres. of U.S.A. 1783–1789*, III, 233–51; Green, *The Spanish Conspiracy*, 73, 385. Wells was engaged to make this tour by an interested group at Louisville, twelve in number. Chief contributors to his expenses were: George Rogers Clark, Thomas Green, Richard Brashears and James Patton.

tion to retrieve our circumstances must be manly, eligible and just. . . .

We can raise twenty thousand troops this side of the Alleghany and Appalachian Mountains; and the annual increase of them by emigration from . . . other parts is from two to four thousand.

We have taken all the goods belonging to the Spanish merchants of post Vincennes and the Illinois, and are determined they shall not trade up the river, provided they will not let us trade down it. Preparations are now making here (if necessary) to drive the Spaniards from their settlements at the mouth of the Mississippi. In case we are not countenanced and succored by the United States (if we need it) our allegiance will be thrown off, and some other power applied to. Great Britain stands ready with open arms to receive and support us. They have already offered to open their resources for our supplies. When once re-united to them, 'farewell, a long farewell to your boasted greatness.' The province of Canada and the inhabitants of these waters, of themselves, in time will be able to conquer you. You are as ignorant of their country as Great Britain was of America. These are hints; if rightly improved, may be of some service; if not, blame yourselves for the neglect.[4]

The acidity in the closing sentences is biting because distilled from the grains of truth, as Roosevelt shows in his treatment of New England's attitude toward the West at this time.[5]

The feeling in 1786 was so strong as to produce much talk of a separation of the Eastern and Middle States from the Southern, should the latter win the freedom of the Mississippi at the expense of the commercial interests of the East in the Spanish West Indies.[6]

This statement that Great Britain stood ready to receive and support the Westerners may not be lightly treated as whole-cloth fiction. America's representative at the court of George III, in a letter received by Congress in September, 1786, had warned Congress to guard against British influence in the Western Country.[7]

In fact Spain, Great Britain, and France, all alike, deemed it not "impossible that American settlers in the great valley of the Mississippi might be won to accept another flag than that of the United

---

[4] This part of the letter appears in *Cal. Va. St. P.*, IV, 242, and was transmitted by Arthur Campbell to Gov. Randolph, Feb. 16, 1787, with the statement that "great pains were taken to circulate copies in Franklin, giving them an air of secrecy." See also, *Secret Journals of Cont. Cong.*, IV, 323; Perkin's *Western Annals*, 282; Ford, *The United States and Spain in 1790*, 13.

[5] *Winning of the West*, IV, Chap. III.

[6] Monroe to Madison, Sept. 3, 1786.

[7] Bloodworth to N. C. Assembly, *N. C. St. Rec.*, XXII, 902; *Dip. Corr. of U.S.A. 1783-89*.

FACTORS THAT WORKED FOR SEPARATION 129

States." Gardoqui had the assurance and audacity in 1787 to suggest to Madison, that the Kentuckians would make good Spanish subjects. A British diplomatic agent, appointed in 1786, was making observations which led him to report to his government: "Nature seems to have pointed out a plain line of division between the eastern and western parts of this continent—that wonderful range of mountains [the Alleghanies] will probably one day or other be the line of partition, when the Western Country shall have attained a degree of strength and population competent to separate establishment, or be driven to the expedient of seeking support from some other Empire more capable of contributing to its progress and protection."[8]

Grayson, of Virginia, in a letter to Madison, gives one of the reasons for this persistent cupidity: "If the federal government remains much longer in its present state of imbecility, we shall be one of the most contemptible nations on the face of the earth."

Madison foresaw clearly what would be the effect of the concession to Spain, and the drift affairs would take:

"Figure to yourself the effect on the people at large on the western waters, who are impatiently waiting for a favorable result of the negotiations of Gardoqui, and who will consider themselves as sold by their Atlantic brethren. Will it be an unnatural consequence if they consider themselves absolved from every Federal tie, and court some protection for their betrayed rights? Their protection will appear more attainable from the maritime power of Great Britain than from any other quarter; and Britain will be more ready than any other nation to seize an opportunity of embroiling our affairs. . . . I should rather suppose that he [the Spanish minister] means to work a total separation of interest and affection

---

[8] Phineas Bond Report, *Am. Hist. Assn. Rep.* (1896) 649. "It is an undoubted truth that communications are held by Lord Dorchester with both the Vermonters and the insurgents of Massachusetts, and that a direct offer has been made to the latter of the protection of the government of Great Britain. . . . Here is felt the imbecility, the futility, the nothingness of the federal powers. New Hampshire has already shown herself kindred to the revolters; Connecticut is not free from infection. . . . That Great Britain will be in readiness to improve any advantage, which our disarrangements may present, for gaining her lost dominions, we are not in doubt. . . . A Mr. Bond, formerly of Philadelphia, has lately arrived as consul for the Middle States, and it is said that others are to be sent for the Eastern and Southern States, and thus the scheme of communication will be complete." *Cal. Va. St. Papers*, IV, 195.

between the eastern and western settlements, and foment the jealousy between the Eastern and Southern States."⁹

Even McGillivray, leader of the Creek Indians, appreciated the situation when he reported to the Spanish authority the flow of population into the district of Natchez: "The Americans will certainly attempt to establish a new State in that country at the risk of a war. The authority of Congress is but weak even in the heart of the States, and those that are settled at the distance of five or six hundred miles from the seat of government despise its mandates."

This disesteem of Congress was not diminished by its own attitude toward the navigation of the Mississippi. And so far as the State of Franklin was concerned, the issue injected into its politics by the appearance of the Green letter, continued to agitate the people during the whole of the after-history of the Commonwealth.

The national authority had already affronted the new-state adherents by carrying to consummation, by ratification, the treaty of Hopewell, which had been negotiated in studied disregard of the treaties that the Franklin authorities had entered into with the Cherokees. The North Carolina Assembly had just failed to register a protest against such action; and Cocke had brought back with him the details of his fruitless mission to secure the recognition of Franklin. The North Carolina legislature, on January 6, 1786, passed an act, the purpose of which was to put an end to opposition to her government in the West. In its preamble it was recited that "divers persons within the counties of Washington, Sullivan, Greene and Hawkins, who had withdrawn themselves from their allegiance to this State, have returned thereunto, and have expressed a disposition to continue peaceful subjects of the same." It was then provided that all offenses committed by any persons against the sovereignty of North Carolina, be pardoned "and buried in total oblivion," with restoration to full privileges of citizenship; "provided that where any decisions have been had [by Franklin authority] respecting property, which are incompatible with justice, the person or persons injured shall have his or their remedy at common law."¹⁰

It was further stipulated that all persons who were in office, civil or military, on April 1, 1784, should be continued therein, but that offices and appointments, the exercise of which are considered to be

---

⁹ Madison to Jefferson, Aug. 12, 1786.
¹⁰ *Acts 1786*, ch. 23; *N. C. St. Rec.*, XX, 641.

a resignation of former offices under North Carolina, should be deemed vacant.

To influence the return of the inhabitants of the western counties to allegiance to North Carolina, taxes due and unpaid since 1784 were released. But, on the other hand, steps were taken for the removal of inhabitants who had settled on the hunting grounds of the Cherokees, as North Carolina conceived them to be.

The last clause in the above act, in relation to vacant offices, was purposely shaped to exclude Sevier and other leaders of Franklin who had continued faithful to her fortunes. It produced great dissatisfaction and called for a vigorous protest from Judge David Campbell, who, in a letter to Governor Caswell, said:

The majority of the people of Franklin proclaim, with a degree of enthusiastic zeal, against a reversion to your state. Indeed I am at a loss to conjecture whether your Assembly wished us to revert; if so, why did they treat the old faithful officers of this county with such contempt—officers who have suffered in the common cause, who have been faithful in the discharge of the trust reposed in them, have been displaced without the formality of a trial. Representations by a few malcontents might have been the cause of such proceedings, but surely it was a most impolitic step. If the old officers, who were the choice of the people under whom they have long served, had been continued, I doubt not that all things would have been settled here, agreeable to the most sanguine wishes of your general Assembly; but such infringements on the liberties and privileges of a free people, will never be attended with any salutary consequence. I also blame the law which passed in your Assembly, to enable the people here to hold partial elections. If it were intended to divide us and set us to massacreing one another, it was well concerted, but an ill-planned scheme if intended for the good of all. . . .

The people here—for I have been in public assemblies, and made it my business to collect their sentiments—dread the idea of a reversion. They say if North Carolina is in earnest about granting them a separation, why not permit them to go on as they have begun, and not involve them in inextricable difficulties by undoing the work of two or three years past.

They made offers by their agents which they think were favorable to your country, but they rejected them with contempt. I mean the bill offered by General Rutherford to your assembly in behalf of this people. What conditions, say they, would North Carolina extort from us were we under their laws and immediate influence? Indeed my mind is filled with a degree of painful anxiety for this people.[11]

[11] March 18, 1787, *N. C. St. Rec.*, XX, 641.

The concurrence of all these circumstances tended only to demonstrate to Governor Sevier and his followers that the time had come for the use of force to stay the undermining influences and to establish the sovereignty of Franklin within the borders. Judge Campbell, in the same letter, did not mince words in declaring this purpose to Governor Caswell:

The sword of justice and vengeance will, I believe, be shortly drawn against those of this country, who overturn the laws and government of Franklin, and God only knows what will be the event. If any blood is spilt on this occasion, the act for partial election from your country will be the cause of it; and I am bold to say the author of that act was the author of much evil.

That your Excellency may not be in the dark about the spirit and determination of a majority of these people in supporting, maintaining, and defending their beloved Franklin, I shall give you a brief and concise detail of what has transpired here since the fate of our memorial and personal application to the legislature of North Carolina has been announced to us: Pains were taken to collect the minds of the people respecting a reversion. Many who were formerly luke-warm are now flaming patriots of Franklin; those who were real Franklinites are now burning with enthusiastic zeal. They say North Carolina has not treated us like a parent, but a step-dame. She means to sacrifice us to the Indian savages. She has broken our old officers under whom we fought and bled, and placed over us many men unskilled in military achievements, and who were none of our choice.[12]

The General Assembly has been convened and steps taken for our internal security with a degree of unanimity never before seen in a deliberative assembly.[12a] A treaty is set on foot with the Indians; the land office opened to the Tennessee from the south (Carolina) side of French Broad and Holston rivers; did not interfere with the north side where your office was opened; cautiously avoided interfering with the rights of Congress.

You may judge from the foregoing whether these people are in earnest or no. You must not conclude we are altogether unanimous; but I do assure you a very great majority, perhaps . . . nineteen-twentieths, seem determined to persevere at all hazards.

I make no doubt but your Excellency will use your influence to bring matters to a friendly and advantageous issue, for both countries.

Governor Caswell had not waited for this spur to action. Above

---

[12] The reference is to the displacement of the Franklinites in North Carolina's effort to re-establish her governmental authority.

[12a] Ramsey printed a copy of a land warrant issued by Franklin State for land in Caswell county, Apr. 20, 1787. *Annals*, 402.

all other men of North Carolina, he had the politician's instinct and had sensed that a storm of indignation would break across the Alleghanies. The cumulation of so many acts adverse to them could but irritate the people of Franklin; and he knew that North Carolina was utterly unable to send troops across the mountains to subdue Sevier and his indignant people. It cannot be doubted that Caswell stood with General Rutherford in the latter's efforts in behalf of the Westerners.

He felt that oil must be poured on the troubled waters. Fortunately again for the Commonwealth over which he presided no man in her borders was as capable as he to do the pouring.

As early as February 23, 1787, Caswell had written to Judge Campbell, respecting the defeat of the western memorial which Campbell had advocated:

Your reasoning on the necessity and propriety of establishing the independence of the people of the western waters from this government, to unprejudiced minds and those as well-informed of the situation of those people as myself, would, if persons from amongst those very people had not represented circumstances and things in a different point of view[13] I have no doubt, have had its proper weight and brought about its deserved object. But for the present, it is presumed, they will return to the laws and government under which they first settled that country. For my own part I have been perfectly satisfied from my acquaintance with that country in the year 1781, that nature never designed that settlers there to be longer under the same government with the people here, than their numbers, abilities, and opulence would enable them to support a government of their own. This, I am also satisfied, may early be effected if those can be brought to agree among themselves and make general application to the legislature hereafter, returning to the former government and agreeing to certain reasonable stipulations, somewhat similar to those held out by the State of Virginia to the Kentucky District. In full confidence that you would not hesitate in returning to the former government, the General Assembly again elected you to be judge of the Washington District, and I have the honor to enclose herewith the commission. I expected to have seen Col. Outlaw before he left Fayetteville and conversed with him further on the subject of a separate government, but he did not return . . . until he had set out.[14]

On the same day, Caswell wrote a letter of like tenor to Sevier.

---

[13] This reference is to John Tipton in the senate and White and Stuart in the house of commons of North Carolina.

[14] *North Car. St. Rec.*, XX, 616.

After expressing his belief in the feasibility of a friendly separation, he says: "I have my own satisfaction in view, as I expect, if life and strength shall last, to lay my bones on the western waters. Twelve months will bring about a release to me from public employment, and it is my intention to visit that country once more; and, if I can find a place to secure an agreeable retreat for the remainder of my time, I mean to establish it as the place of my residence."[15]

Caswell repeated the same flattering assurance of a purpose "to lay his bones on the western waters" in a letter to Evan Shelby, the new brigadier-general of Washington District under North Carolina. Shelby replied: "I would be much rejoiced if, as you mentioned, you would think in earnest to come and live among us. You might do much here."[16]

At the time Caswell was appealing so adroitly to the western folk, Colonel Joseph Martin was exhibiting a letter, the writing of which he had evidently inspired, for propaganda purposes, from Governor Patrick Henry, of Virginia.

Henry, in this communication, asked Martin to appeal to the people of Franklin to come to an understanding with North Carolina. "Strictest union is required to defeat the efforts of Spain to deprive the western people of the navigation of the Mississippi. Why are they in such a hurry to separate? I know the history of their improper treatment when they were given up to Congress. But that proceeding has been given up and atoned for. It was certainly wrong; but, as it is not persisted in, why is the resentment springing from it continued? Why do not the people imitate our Kentucky friends?[17] The people are unable to support government: for how can they do it when even Virginia finds it a burden almost too heavy to bear?"

---

[15] *North Car. St. Rec.*, XX, 617.

[16] *Ib.*, 646.

[17] *Cal. Va. St. Papers*, IV, 374. Governor Henry's reference to Kentucky was not altogether fortunate, since at this time (January 6, 1787) an influential element in a gathering at Danville "reflected the current aspiration when they voted that immediate separation from Virginia would tend to the benefit of Kentucky." Winsor, *Westward Movement*, 351; and in the fall of the same year, Samuel McDowell wrote that the "convocation of the District of Kentucky yesterday (Sept. 22) came to a solemn vote on the business of separation from Virginia, and thirty-two out of thirty-four were in favor of the separation." It is not to be doubted that Kentucky would have pursued the same course that Franklin did had Virginia passed a cession act like that of North Carolina in 1784.

FACTORS THAT WORKED FOR SEPARATION

If rival propaganda was rife in the borders of Franklin in the years' beginning, turmoil and strife soon followed in the wake.

Commissions for the newly appointed Carolina officials were sent into the territory by Governor Caswell, his son Winston being the messenger. Along with the commissions came copies of the executive proclamation ordering the settlers off the hunting-grounds of the Cherokees—as Carolina, not the Franklin, officials conceived those grounds to be. This was a mistaken step, as well as *brutum fulmen*. As has been noted, the number of settlers in that region was great. To handle them would require a force far beyond the ability of the parent State's entire militia, not to speak of her civil officers west of the mountains. The proclamation could, therefore, only do harm. It tended only to solidify and make desperate the people in Greene county and the region below it. No one could be found to accept a commission and hold office under North Carolina, in that section, General Evan Shelby confessed.[18] There, at least, the people were cemented in loyalty to the new State, and there was no conflict of jurisdictions.

The two men who stood highest in authority in the two rival governments, Governor Sevier and General Evan Shelby, were intent upon bringing peace to the distracted country, if practicable. The approach was made by Shelby, and Sevier replied in a letter (Mount Pleasant, February 11, 1787) that was tinged with deep resentment toward Tipton and the other western members of the Carolina Assembly, but marked by amiability toward Shelby, who was, however, addressed as "Esquire," and not as "General."[19]

---

[18] *N. C. St. Rec.*, XX, 646; XXII, 682; Ramsey 357-358.

[19] "I have been informed by several gentlemen that you have expressed a great desire to see me. I also assure you that I am as anxious to have the pleasure of seeing you, as I ever had to see any person. I find the country in total confusion and disorder, and the ferment so great that I hardly see where the matter may end. If you will please to take a view of the conduct of the members that were at the Assembly, I presume you see that they have done everything to disorder, and not to reconcile, the people of this country; and have calculated matters, as they expect, on purpose to set friends to cutting each other's throats. However, I trust in this they will be disappointed; and convinced, although we live on the west of the Appalachian Mountain, that we are not such dupes, or fools, that will render us void and destitute of rational understanding.

"I presume, Sir, that though we profess ourselves Franklinites, you are sensible your warmest friends are among that class. Also that those people have on all occasions distinguished themselves as men of spirit and honor. Only reflect for a moment, how disgusting it must be to be treated in the manner they have been, by

Tipton, however, was for pressing the issue and saw to it that the North Carolina court was opened in February at Davis's in pursuance of the act he had introduced and piloted through the Carolina Assembly, thus bringing conflict with the courts of Franklin held at Jonesborough, ten miles below.[20] Courts were also opened in Sullivan and Hawkins counties.

The spring session of the Franklin General Assembly met at Greeneville early in March; and a progressive and aggressive policy was adopted. Countering the removal proclamation, the Assembly passed an act to open a land office for the entry of lands south of the French Broad river, the lands to be sold at forty shillings per hundred acres, the first ten shillings to be paid in cash, two years' credit to be allowed for the remaining thirty shillings.

An act was passed to punish any person who should perform any official act under the authority of North Carolina, the first offense by a fine of five pounds, the second by a fine of ten pounds and one year's imprisonment, with power and discretion in the governor to set a guard over the offender, the cost of the guarding to be a charge upon the property of the offender.

Governor Sevier was empowered to enlist and call out a militia force, each man to receive as compensation four hundred acres of land, ostensibly for an Indian campaign, but, as the North Carolina adherents feared, to be used in case of need to put down opposition to Franklin.[21]

---

the vile reprobates at the Assembly, and in all companies wherever they have been admitted. Sound reason will dictate to you that it would be more honorable to die and hang on a gallows, than to tamely submit to such ill treatment without resentment. Permit me to inform you that your cool and candid conduct has gained you immortal honor, and your treatment of us in respect of our new government, will forever endear your real friends to you.

"I shall omit saying more on this occasion, relying that I shortly have the pleasure of seeing you, taking the liberty to inform you that I will do myself the honor to wait on you, at any time and place you will be pleased to appoint and notify me of." *MSS., Tennessee Historical Society.*

[20] Ramsey, 356. Ramsey gives an extract from the Washington county record which shows that the following were appointed justices: John Tipton, Landon Carter, Robert Love, James Montgomery, John Hammer, John Wyer, John Strain, Andrew Chamberlain, Andrew Taylor, Alex. Muffet, William Pursley, Edmond Williams, and Henry Nelson. Some of them evidently declined to serve under the appointment. Landon Carter continued in the service of Franklin as entry-taker, and afterward, in behalf of the separatists, contested an election to the Carolina Assembly against Tipton. The effort to convert him was a failure, and this is likely also true of others mentioned.

[21] *N. C. St. Rec.*, XXII, 678–9; Ramsey, 360; *Cal. Va. St. Papers*, IV, 256.

FACTORS THAT WORKED FOR SEPARATION 137

By another act, taxes were laid on polls, one shilling; and on land, six pence per hundred acres, on payment of which, for the first year, the lands were to be exempt for three years. Thus was to be parried the blow sought to be delivered by North Carolina in the release of her taxes for the years 1784-86.

The mood of the people at the spring Assembly was ugly—marked by bitterness and rancor, as their differences came to open rupture.[22] "The misunderstanding has at last teemed an open dispute," wrote a correspondent from Franklin, who continued his account:

"The people here condemn a certain Col. Tipton for being the instigator of our unhappiness. They have lately hanged him in effigy, with a will in his mouth. A very extraordinary will, indeed! It bequeathed his ignorance, his perjury, his folly, and his ambition to be divided among his friends, and a wooden sword to the most deserving of them."[23]

The onslaught on Col. Tipton by the hot-head element of the Franklinites could only have the effect to further embitter and determine him to oppose the new-state party, even though it was yet predominant. This fact, however, was over-stated by the same writer when he said: "Col. Tipton has lately attempted to hold an election for a captain by the authority of North Carolina; only three or four were found to adhere to that State."

Much of the animosity toward Tipton was based on the fact that he had undertaken to speak for the western folk in the Carolina Assembly, without their authority, and contrary to their will. On him fell the blame for "the indignity with which the Assembly

---

[22] *N. C. St. Rec.*, XXII, 681. A letter of Hugh Williamson to William S. Johnson, of Feb. 14, 1787, shows how little the North Carolina leaders knew of the true situation in the West: "I hope you have heard with pleasure that our counties who formed what is called the State of Franklin are returned to the government of their State. If measures equally lenient had been adopted, and that too at any early hour, with dissidents from other States, I think that our Union needed not have been disgraced as it is now by the *imperium in imperio*." *Johnson's Papers, Susquehannah Lands*, No. 39. *Conn. Hist. Soc.*

[23] March 2, 1787, *Georgia State Gazette*, March 24th. The attempt to win over Gen. Evan Shelby took a different trend: "North Carolina had made Col. Shelby a brigadier-general; he accepted the commission but observed that, if they did conjecture he would quarrel with his neighbors for the sake of a d—d commission, they would find themselves mistaken. A few days after he went to Sullivan, where our court of justice was then held, and got married to a young lady by one of our judges and was saluted as a friend of the State of Franklin." *Ib.*

loaded our men in office for acting in concurrence with the sense of our good citizens."[24]

The superior court of Franklin met at Jonesborough on the first Monday in April. George Middleton Clarkson was tried for murder, found guilty and hanged on the 13th at Jonesborough. This was the first legal execution in Franklin, or on what is now Tennessee soil, of which we have record.[25]

Added to the other elements of unrest were the efforts of pestiferous persons to bring the antagonism to the Spaniards to open outbreak and an attack on New Orleans. At this time, March, 1787, John Sullivan, describing himself as "late Captain Fourth Regiment American Light Dragoons," wrote from the Georgia frontiers a bombastic letter:

"Being a soldier of fortune as I profess, practical war is now my pursuit. From Natchez to Kaskaskia, from Pittsburg to St. Mary's river, they are prepared to pour forth 50,000 veterans in arms in defense of the commercial rights throughout the navigable rivers of the southern part of the empire. The States of Georgia, Franklin and Kentucky, confederated, the county of Bourbon, the settlements of Cumberland, all abound with seeds of war... The harvest is ready for the hook, and the hook for the harvest."[26]

In September the same plotter wrote to a comrade in arms urging him to come west and secure lands on the Tennessee river, as there would soon be work cut out for men of that region. "I want you much—by God, take my word for it, we will speedily be in possession of New Orleans!"[27]

In May, Sullivan, or one of his ilk, wrote from Nashville to a friend in Georgia, predicting that in the space of ten years "we shall have mustered at least 60,000 men capable of bearing arms. Is it probable that we shall suffer our lands to lie without cultivation or our produce to perish on hands from want of a river by which our products may be carried to a market? Is it probable we shall suffer a few Spanish soldiers to seize our boats? I think not!"[28]

---

[24] *Georgia State Gazette.*

[25] Letters from the State of Franklin, April 24, 1787, in *Ga. State Gazette*, May 24th.

[26] *New York Morning Post*, Aug 1.

[27] Roosevelt, *Winning of the West*, IV, 227, citing State Dept. MSS., No. 150, Vol. III, Sullivan to Major Wm. Brown, Sept 24, 1787.

[28] *Georgia Gazette*, October 20, 1787. The seaboard people were far from sympa-

FACTORS THAT WORKED FOR SEPARATION

The unrest in the West caused by agitators such as Green and Sullivan, gave the Congress no little concern. The North Carolina delegates communicated, March 30th, to that body, sundry papers tending, with other proofs, to show discontent in the Western Country at the supposed surrender of the Mississippi river, and hostile machinations against the Spaniards. The documents were referred to the committee on foreign affairs with instructions to report thereon.[29]

---

thizing with the western folk in their purpose to force an opening of the Mississippi. The same issue of the *Gazette* contained a contribution deprecatory of the efforts of people on the western waters, describing them as troublesome children of Uncle Sam:

> "He'd many children, and we've been told
> The following three were pert and bold,
> Kentucky, Cumberland and Frank
> Who played their Father many a prank."

[29] *Madison Papers*, II, 603, March 30, 1787; *Sec. Journals*, IV, 343.

CHAPTER XIX

Efforts to Compromise Futile—1787

There seems to have been a spring session of the Franklin Assembly.[1] The *Kentucke Gazette*, of September 29, 1787, published a news item, bearing date "New York, August 7" to the effect that "the General Assembly of the State of Franklin, at their last session, have divided that State into two districts and appointed Col. D. Kennedy brigadier-general of Washington District, and Col. Wm. Cocke brigadier-general of Elholm District. They have likewise appointed the Honorable Wm. Cocke and Wm. Nelson and George Elholm, Esqrs., delegates to wait on Congress for the purpose of being admitted to the federal union. From the frequent murders committed in Kentucky and Cumberland on unwary travellers to and from these countries by the Creek and Chickamauga tribes of Indians, the State of Franklin has lately resolved to place a strong garrison at the mouth of the Highawassee river, in order to give a check to the future progress of such a banditti of bloodhounds who make it their business to live by their predatory excursions, and likewise to secure the great number of emigrants that are daily settling on the frontiers of Franklin."

Ramsey could find no trace (save the bare name of one of them) of the formation of Franklin into districts, but gives a tradition, which was erroneous in that it assigned Greene county to Elholm District.[2] The distribution of counties probably was: To Washington District, Sullivan, Washington, Wayne and Greene; and to Elholm District, Caswell, Spencer, Sevier and Blount. Elholm District was named in honor of Major Elholm.

There was serious danger of Indian hostilities, and provision was made by the Assembly for the raising of a force of four hundred men. A party of about seventy-five from Lincoln county, in the Kentucky District, under the command of Col. John Logan, invaded the country of the Chickamaugas, for the purpose of destroy-

---

[1] Governor Sevier to Governor Mathews, August 30th.
[2] Ramsey, 376.

ing a small Indian town (Crow Town) on the north side of the Tennessee river, west of the Cumberland Mountains, in punishment for depredations committed by the Indians in the Kentucky country. Col. Logan's troops met a band of Cherokees, who were then in friendship with the whites; and, mistaking them for Chickamaugas, killed seven, among them a chief belonging to Chota. Joseph Martin, agent to the Cherokees, rushed to Chota from Long Island of Holston, and found the Cherokees in greater confusion than he had ever before seen. About forty of their warriors had already gone to make war on the settlers of Cumberland and Kentucky.[3]

Col. Arthur Campbell feared that Southwest Virginia would be attacked, and wrote a friendly "talk" to the Cherokees, assuring them that the Virginians east of the Cumberland mountains were not to blame, and would not molest the Cherokees unless provoked by an attack, in which event it was threatened that "we can send a great many against you and destroy you altogether."[4]

Martin reported that the Cherokees felt deep resentment toward the settlers south of the French Broad. As Martin passed through the white settlements on his way to Chota and spoke of Governor Caswell's removal proclamation, the settlers retorted that "they knew enough to judge for themselves, and that they should not ask North Carolina how they were to be governed."[5]

Only fear of the prowess of the Franklinites stayed the embittered Cherokees from an attack on the frontier settlements.

In March, a small delegation of Choctaw and Chickasaw Indians stopped to visit Governor Sevier and were entertained at his Mount Pleasant home on the Nolachucky river in Washington county. They were on their way to New York to lay before the Continental Congress the state of their tribes, and to insist upon an early compliance with a treaty agreement to establish a trading post on Tennessee river near Muscle Shoals,[6] so that the Choctaws and Chickasaws might be more readily supplied with merchandise. Toboka, a principal chief of the Choctaws, headed the delegation, which was

---

[3] Martin to Governor Randolph, March 16th and 25th, 1787, *Cal. Va. St. P.*, IV, 254, 261.

[4] March 3rd, *Ib.* 249.

[5] *Ib.*, 250.

[6] Treaty with the Chickasaws, Hopewell, Jan. 10th, 1786. 18 *N. C. St. Rec.*, 493; *U. S. Stat. at Large.* 24.

conducted by Capt. John Wood, who at one time had been continental commissioner to the Choctaws.

Piomingo sent a talk in behalf of the Chickasaws to Martin (February 17th) in which he referred to the cession by his nation of a tract of land for the trading-post, and said:

"We have had nothing of goods since, only what we got by way of the Spaniards. This makes us very uneasy, and it seems that you only meant to jockey us out of our lands. The Spaniards are often sending talks to us, but we want to have nothing to say to them if we can help it, but must have trade from some place... Necessity will oblige us to look to new friends if we cannot get friends otherwise."[7]

The program laid down by the Assembly brought the officers of the old State to a consideration of the frightfulness of an armed conflict. There can be no doubt that at this time the friends of the new State were in the majority and prepared to put the issue to crucial test. Their chosen leader, however, in some unexplained way, was led into a grievous error. Sevier had no stomach for fratricidal warfare; he had it not in his heart to resort to the shedding of the blood of men, now in opposition, whom he had led to victory time and again in warfare with the Indians, if by any peaceable means it could be avoided. Shortly after the adjournment of the Assembly, he was again approached and asked to enter into conference with General Evan Shelby; and he consented.

Shelby was a blunt, stern man, sixty-seven years of age. He deserved and had the confidence of the people of the entire section. Ramsey says that "he was remarkable for his probity, candor, good sense, and patriotism." Sevier had been induced by him to remove to the Holston-Watauga country; and the younger man had been, not unnaturally, disposed to defer to Shelby's judgment. At any rate, the older man out-witted him in the formation of a *modus vivendi*. The representatives of the two States met at Samuel Smith's, in Sullivan county, and entered into the following agreement:

Conference at Smith's

At a conference at the house of Samuel Smith, Esquire, on the 20th day of March, 1787, between the Hon. Evan Shelby, Esquire, and sundry officers of the one part, and the Hon. John Sevier, Esquire, and sundry officers on the other part.

---

[7] *Cal. Va. St. Papers*, IV, 241, 287.

Whereas disputes have arisen concerning the propriety and legality of the State of Franklin, and the sovereignty and jurisdiction of the State of North Carolina over the said State and the people residing there.

The contending parties, from the regard they have for peace, tranquility and good decorum, in the Western Country, do agree and recommend as follows:

"First, that the courts of justice do not proceed to transact any business in their judicial departments, except the trial of criminals. the proving of wills, deeds, bills of sale, and such like conveyances; the issuing of attachments, writs and legal process, so as to procure bail, but not to enter into final determination of the suits except the parties are mutually agreed thereto.

"Secondly, that the inhabitants residing within the limits of the disputed territory are at full liberty and discretion to pay their public taxes to either the State of North Carolina or the State of Franklin.

"Thirdly, that this agreement and recommendation continue until the next annual sitting of the General Assembly of North Carolina, to be held in November next, and not longer. It is further agreed that if any person, guilty of felony, be committed by any North Carolina justice of the peace, that such person or persons may and shall be received by the Franklin sheriff or jailer of Washington, and proceeded against in the same manner as if the same had been committed by and from any such authority from under the State of Franklin. It is also recommended that the aforesaid people do take such modes and regulations, and set forth their grievances, if any they have, and solicit North Carolina, at the meeting of the next general assembly, for to complete the separation, if thought necessary by the people of the Western Country, as to them may appear most expedient, and give their members and representatives such instructions as thought to be most conducive to the interest of our western world, by a majority of same, either to be separate from that of North Carolina, or be citizens of the State of North Carolina.

"Signed and agreed on behalf of each party, this day and year above written,

"Evans Shelby
"John Sevier."

Ramsey is mistaken when he states[8] that "a temporary quiet succeeded this compromise... Anywhere else, anarchy, misrule, tumult and violence would have followed." Tumult reigned, and violence was scarcely held in leash. Other Franklin leaders, Cocke among the number, on learning of the truce, declined to concur; and

---
[8] Ramsey, 259.

set about to put Sevier in the straight path, while others, such as Stockley Donelson, had their ardor cooled. Only harm to the cause dear to his heart came from this action of Governor Sevier—particularly in the decline of the morale of numerous followers.

Six days after the conference, Colonel Anthony Bledsoe, then on a visit to General Shelby on his way from Carolina to his home on the Cumberland, wrote to Governor Caswell:

"Politics in this part of the country run high. You hear in almost every collection of people frequent declarations, 'Whorah for North Carolina!' And others in the same manner for the State of Franklin... God only knows where this confusion will end. I fear it ends in blood."[9]

Thomas Hutchings, who had just been appointed colonel of the Hawkins county militia, expressed the opinion to the governor of North Carolina that it would be difficult to prevent an effusion of blood; and appealed for military aid:

"I think your excellency will readily see the necessity for the interference of government; and unless those people are entitled to exclusive and separate emoluments from the rest of the community they ought certainly to be quelled. If we are in our allegiance, protection should be reciprocal. I therefore give it as my opinion that it is highly necessary that notice should be taken of the conduct of these people, as there are many plans and matters agitated by them which seem to have a tendency to dissolve even the federal bands."[10]

A few days later, Hutchings in reporting to General Shelby from Hawkins county states that "Major Elholm advises Cromwell's policy to be adopted; Mr. Cocke is threatening confiscation and banishment. Cocke's party is getting very insolent, but success against his boasted numbers is foreseen if they have not assistance from Greene county."[11]

At the same time Shelby was sending out a cry for help to Brigadier-General Wm. Russell, of Southwest Virginia, saying that North Carolina measures were being treated with the utmost contempt.[12] "The new-State party are now falling on the civil officers of the government with men at arms wresting their property from

---

[9] March 26th, 1787. *N. C. St. Rec.*, XXII, 676.

[10] April 1st. *Ib.*, 678.

[11] *N. C. St. Rec.*, XX, 680.

[12] John Rhea (later a member of Congress from Tennessee) who was at the time county clerk of Shelby's own county, wrote the same day to Caswell, that "a majority, if not all the justices had joined the new-made government... All the

them forcibly. . . I am not certain that I may not be under the disagreeable necessity of making a very speedy application to you for assistance, should troops from our State not arrive in time to relieve us."[13]

To Governor Caswell, after a conference at his home with Cols. Tipton, Maxwell and Hutchings, Shelby wrote that the safety of government was at hazard; that the Franklinites were proceeding with the greatest vigor imprisoning, and by armed forces seizing the property of those in opposition. "I have, therefore, thought it expedient to call upon you for your immediate assistance, having the faith and honor of the legislature of North Carolina pledged to us that we shall remain secure in our liberties and properties. The matter is truly alarming, and it is beyond a doubt with me that hostilities will in a short time commence, and without the interference of government without delay an effusion of blood must take place. I, therefore, think it highly necessary that one thousand troops, at least, be sent, as that number might have a good effect, for should we have that number, under the sanction of the government, it is no doubt with me they would immediately give way, and would not appear in so unprovoked an insurrection. On the contrary, should a faint and feeble resistance be made the consequences might be fatal, and would tend to devastation, ruin and distress. Should your Excellency think it convenient to call on the Commonwealth of Virginia, I have reason to believe it might meet their aid, as they have four counties nearly bordering on us, and would be the most speedy assistance we could come at in case your troops do not reach us in time to relieve us. I think it highly necessary that a quantity of ammunition be forwarded to us as it is very scarce in this country. . . Thus, sir, you have the result of my conference with the aforementioned Colonels. . .

"Your Excellency will perceive that the people of Franklin have not assented to the agreement I entered into with their governor for the preservation of peace and good order in the country. Not many men here are engaged in vindicating the authority of North Carolina."[14]

---

records of this county have fallen into the hands of the people of Franklin," *Ib.*, 691.

[13] April 27th. *Cal. Va. St. Papers*, IV, 275. The North Carolina delegates in Congress were now undeceived: "I am sorry that the conduct of the Franklinites is likely to involve the western country in a civil war." Spaight to Iredell, July 3rd, 1787. McRee's *Iredell*, II, 162.

[14] *N. C. St. Rec.* XXII, 680.

These disclosures show that the situation was acute and that the affairs of the old State bordered on the desperate.

Sevier now took a bolder tone. He seized the opportunity to send a belated reply to Governor Caswell's letter of February 23. As to the disappointing action of the North Carolina Assembly, he said:

I had the fullest hopes and confidence that the body would have either agreed to a separation on honorable principles and stipulations, or otherwise endeavored to have reunited as upon such terms as might have been lasting and friendly, but I find myself and country entirely deceived; and if your Assembly have thought their measures would answer such an end, they are equally disappointed. But I firmly believe had proper measures been adopted, a union, in some measure or perhaps fully, would have taken place. We shall continue to act as independent, and would rather suffer death in all its various and frightful shapes than conform to anything that is disgraceful.[16]

Governor Caswell brought General Shelby's communication before the council of state, specially summoned for its consideration, and replied May 31st, giving the results of their deliberations, which, he frankly premises, "may not answer your expectations."

It was no part of Caswell's policy to attempt a subjugation of the separatists. He knew that his State was in no condition to support an armed conflict. He was for holding consistently to his policy of conciliation. He, therefore, wrote:

It would be very imprudent to add to the dissatisfaction of the people there by showing a wish to encourage the shedding of blood, as thereby a civil war would eventually be brought on, which ought at all times to be avoided if possible, but more especially at the present as we have great reason to apprehend a general Indian war, in which case there is no doubt that they will meet with support from the subjects of foreign powers; or at least they will be furnished with arms and ammunition. And if the western and southern tribes should unite with your neighbors you will stand in need of all your force; and therefore recommend unanimity amongst you, if by any means it can be effected, as you will be thereby much more able to defend yourselves than you possibly can be when divided, but also save the circumstances of cutting each other's throats. Besides this, it would be impracticable to raise an armed force at this time, if we were ever so much disposed thereto, for the following reasons: the people in general are now engaged in their farming business, and if brought out would be very reluctant to march; there is no money in the treasury to defray the expenses of such as might be called out; nor in fact, have we arms or am-

---

[16] *N. C. St. Rec.* XXII, 679; Ramsey, 362.

munition. Under such circumstances it would be madness to attempt it.

I must therefore recommend to you the using every means in your power to conciliate the minds of the people, as well those who call themselves Franklinites as the friends and supporters of government. The measures you took with Mr. Sevier and his party, of which you first acquainted me, if again they could be adopted, would be best under the situation that things now are. If things could lie dormant as it were till the next Assembly, and each man's mind be employed in considering your common defense against the savage enemy, I should suppose it best. And whenever unanimity prevails among your people and their strength and numbers will justify an application for a separation, if it is general, I have no doubt of its taking place upon reciprocal and friendly terms.[16]

Governor Caswell enclosed with the above communication an "open letter" to the inhabitants of the western counties, in which he made the same arguments, and urged that if disputes and confusion lasted, private interests would suffer.

Is there an individual in your country who does not look forward to such a day [of separation] arriving? If that is the case must not every thinking man believe that this separation will be soonest and most effectually obtained by unanimity? . . . 'Tis my opinion that it may be obtained at an earlier day than some imagine, if unanimity prevailed amongst you. Altho' this is an official letter, you will readily see that it is dictated by a friendly and pacific mind. . . I will conclude by once more entreating you to consider the dreadful calamities and consequences of a civil war. Humanity demanded this of me; your own good sense will point out the propriety of it. At least, let all animosities and disputes subside till the next Assembly; even let things remain as they are, without pursuing compulsory measures until then, and I flatter myself that honorable body will be disposed to do what is just and right and what sound policy may dictate.[17]

Caswell a few weeks before had written to Sevier, as one old friend to another, in terms of assurance: "I cannot account for the conduct of our Assembly at this last session. I know that some of the gentlemen's sentiments did not coincide with my own, but still think if the people on your side the mountains had have been more unanimous, the measures of separation would have been pursued. . . . You may only rely upon it that my sentiments are clearly in favor of a separation whenever the people to be separated think themselves of sufficient strength and abilities to support a government. My idea is, that nature, in the formation of the hills between

---

[16] *N. C. St. Rec.*, XXII, 687; also *Draper Coll. Shelby Mss.*
[17] *N. C. St. Rec.*, XXII, 686.

us and directing the course of the waters so differently, had not in view the inhabitants on either side being longer subject to the same laws and government... I conclude by recommending unanimity among you as the only means by which your government can obtain energy even when the separation is effected by consent of North Carolina."[18]

The wisdom of Caswell's policy was demonstrated by the event. A constantly increasing number of the friends of Franklin became persuaded that separation would be consummated at the next Assembly. Why not acquiesce in the course suggested by such a fair man as Governor Caswell? Had not Governor Sevier himself shown that at heart he was for conciliation when he signed the conference agreement? True to human nature, not a few of the Franks saw personal advantage in the tax remission granted by North Carolina. How could the Franklin Commonwealth survive if her Assembly should carry out in good faith her pledge to release the taxes in the years 1788 and 1789? Besides, the thirteen original States had appointed delegates to a convention which was to assemble in May—the month when Governor Caswell's proclamation was published in Franklin—to remodel and strengthen the federal government. Might not that body in some way be induced to satisfy the aspirations of the western peoples for separate governments?

Fortunately for North Carolina's cause her adherents were able to point to the fact that Governor Caswell was sending a troop of militia, commanded by Major Thomas Evans, to aid the inhabitants of the Cumberland counties, and that Colonel Anthony Bledsoe was at that time waiting in Sullivan county to pilot the militia to Nashville. Here at last was a manifestation of the strong arm of government reaching across the mountains![19]

The drift of sentiment during the summer of 1787 was in favor of the old State. As the partisans of Franklin dropped away the remnant became deeply resentful of the defection and made no effort to hide their umbrage. Recriminations and factional bitterness resulted (save only in the lower counties) which tended to undermine the new Commonwealth.

---

[18] *N. C. St. Rec.*, XXII, 681; *Caswell to Sevier*, April 24th, 1787.
[19] Proof that the North Carolina militia would not march to *subdue* the Franklinites is furnished by Maj. Evans who complained of "so many officers declining to serve" in the battalion for the *defense* of the Cumberland Settlements. May 21st, 1787. *N. C. St. Rec.*, XX, 703.

CHAPTER XX

A High Debate—1787

In May a convention was held at Greeneville to consider the final adoption of the Constitution promulgated at that place on November 19, 1785. It was resolved that that instrument should be the Constitution of the State, "until the people of said State are received into the Federal Union; or a majority of the freemen of the State of Franklin shall otherwise direct." Several amendments were proposed for consideration by the people and their ratification, or rejection at the polls. A search has not brought to view these amendments; they probably were of minor import.

Before the convention closed, Cocke brought before the body a motion in substance as follows: "In view of the fact that Franklin's commissioners who waited on the Assembly of North Carolina last year were not attended to with that respect due to commissioners; and, notwithstanding the illegal manner in which the members from the western counties had been elected in the name of North Carolina, yet they were permitted to take their seats as legislators; and as those members were mortal enemies to our rising Republic, whose citizens the Assembly of North Carolina called their western inhabitants, a separation was thereby prevented. But as we find that some individuals of the said Assembly now warmly express themselves in favor of a separation, upon condition that Franklin would join North Carolina, and send from Franklin members to take seats in their Assembly to effect a separation, such separation would undoubtedly be granted. Therefore, the holding of an election on the same day appointed for the election for the State of North Carolina would enable us to send members to negotiate a separation, and thus we could easily obtain our wish without trouble or hazard."

Governor Caswell had held out to the Franks the hope that the next Assembly of his State might consent to a separation, and Cocke's idea was that that result would be the more likely if tried friends of an independent government in the West should hold seats in that body and advocate the cause from the floor.

A warm debate followed Cocke's brief remarks in support of the motion, and the substance of the speeches has been preserved in a contemporaneous newspaper report of the convention, though the same escaped the research of our historians.[1] Interest is lent to the debate by John Sevier's participation. He was not given to public speaking, and in likelihood this is the only speech by him that has been preserved in print. Fortunately, in their remarks he and others adverted to the history of the region and gave a glimpse of its first settlement.

This, being the only account of a Franklin parliamentary proceeding in anything like detail, is given in full and as reported.

The entire debate evinces the ability of those who took part in it, and goes far toward demonstrating that they were by no means as rude as their surroundings. The account is almost certainly Elholm's and is as follows:

Col. Wear said, he did not approve of the motion in any sense; that, besides, the motion required the greatest deliberation and more time for consideration than what the House would admit at present, and that we ought to be exceedingly careful of our safety and of the growing Commonwealth; and he would therefore vote against it.

The Hon. Gen. Cocke observed that he thought the plan not dangerous, but he considered the motion as the only plan whereby we might obtain our wishes through a peaceful channel; and he confessed that, from every observation he had made as a commissioner who had waited on the North Carolina Assembly, he had every reason to believe that numbers of individuals of their legislative branches were warm for a speedy separation and reconciliation with us; and from those circumstances, he thought it his duty to support the motion in its present nature.

The Honorable George Elholm signified his greatest amazement that a debate of this nature should be carried on in this assembly; that to take seats merely as pretended friends of North Carolina, was inconsistent with the character of a people whose bravery in the field had changed the most gloomy aspect to that the most pleasing. They could not sit like old women in council when their

---

[1] Georgia *State Gazette* (Augusta) issues of July 14th and 28th, 1787, in DeRenne Library, "Wormsloe," Savannah, Ga. The space given to the debate, in the few columns devoted to news by the press of that day, demonstrates the deep interest of Georgians in the progress of events in Franklin.

rights and privileges were in question. He wished of heaven that a few ancient Roman senators might arise to teach this council to claim their rights with a spirit compatible with their martial prowess; and, although North Carolina refused to attend to the proposal of our commissioners last session, she might from a second thought receive them; and, even if she should not with a due respect, that so far from its proving fatal, it could in his opinion but turn out at worst an ill conveniency to the State of Franklin, which in a short period could not fail to vanish. He wished, therefore, the motion might not be carried.

The Honorable General Cocke was astonished that prudence in this council should be held out an odium, and not be preferred to the method the honorable gentleman who spoke last highly recommends to this Assembly. He recommended to consider how the interest of North Carolina stood respectively with the State of Franklin. You will find that the latter adds to the former an addition of charges annually to the amount of upwards of 9,000 pounds. If then you will admit North Carolina to possess wisdom in her council, you must also adjudge her as ripe to confirm a separation as ourselves; and I have been an eye-witness that several gentlemen in that State by their conduct confess themselves sensible of their errors; and I am certain if any member from this quarter will ask a separation, it will be readily granted.

It is true that North Carolina would catch at a straw last session in order not to separate us; but now she has had an opportunity of seeing her mistake; and, therefore, will more readily comply; for which reason I recommend the mode held forth: to carry our own friends in an election, which will simply answer our purpose.

His Excellency, Governor Sevier, who had been waited on by a committee for his opinion, observed that it was well known in general that North Carolina, in compliance with a requisition made by Congress in June, 1784, passed a cession act, which gave us the privileges which we now unhappily are obliged to contend for. He then cited the clauses that give those rights to the people of Franklin; and further observed that, on the fourteenth of July following, Mr. Spaight, from North Carolina, laid the act before the Committee of States under the great seal of North Carolina State; and, therefore, he was fully satisfied that, after being thus received, the virtue of the very act itself, deprived North Carolina of the right they presumed in repealing the said cession act on the 20th of November following. And that Congress is sensible that they have complied with the requisition of the said act is fully ascertained by their frequent demands on North Carolina to comply agreeable to the tenor of the same. This cession act, therefore, he said, cannot be compared to any common statute, made only for the regulation of their own internal police, which only respects her own citizens; but it was no sooner constitutionally passed than it became a sacred charter for three different powers, viz., the Congress, the people of the State of Franklin, and North Carolina. Of course it can never be lawfully repealed without the consent of the said three different powers. The people of the West had not released North Carolina from her sacred pledge of an independent separation; and, what was of more importance in regard to the benefit of the Union, neither had the United States relinquished their claim; and he was highly prompted to believe they never would; but, should such a thing happen, it would then be time enough for the people of Franklin to consult as to what measures to pursue. But as to the independency of Franklin, it existed in full force undeniably. He referred the Convention to take a view of the Constitution of North Carolina, where they would find a clause which mentions that there may be a State or States erected in the West, whenever the legislature gives consent to the same. Now for North Carolina to attempt to insinuate that the said cession act had not been constitutionally passed, and that another is still wanting for that purpose, can only serve to expose themselves in a disadvantageous way to a just and sensible world. He well perceived that tools were set at work among us, but he was sure that North Carolina would stop rather than run the risk of quarreling openly with the United States; that the people of this country have ever proved good, faithful and powerful citizens to the interests of the United States; and they only contended now for the sacred rights and privileges given them already. It was his opinion, however he might be for unanimity, that further application was unnecessary, and that the act of cession and the Constitution of North Carolina were plenary proof of his assertions.

Col. Cage was of the opinion that if we did not hold the sham election proposed under the authority of North Carolina, thereby to get friends to represent us in that Assembly, we should never bring about a reconciliation; and as a friend to peace as well as a faithful friend to the State of Franklin he heartily wished that the motion now in question might be carried; thus, with their own weapons we should prove victorious over our enemy.

Col. Amis endeavored to support the same very powerfully.

The Honorable George Elholm said that he deemed it miraculous that men of understanding should so largely differ in reference to a plain and simple fact, who were all staunch friends to Franklin and patriots to freedom, and so closely connected in the independence of their country. It was plain that if we suffered any of our friends to represent us in the Assembly of North Carolina, by choice of our citizens under any pretence whatever, we had in fact made void the cession act on our part, and of course reverted insensibly to North Carolina government. Good God of heaven, how long shall the spirit of ill-timed prudence prey upon us to diminish a former conduct? Let us consider that the esteem conferred on us is the fruit of justice, generosity and our own independent spirit; and if we fly those virtues will we not deservedly sink into disgrace? His Excellency has plainly demonstrated that our government is legal. Let us, therefore, avoid a conduct for which we would have cursed our fathers. We have spent our youth in pursuit of liberty, and let us now in our experienced days support our freedom and leave it an inheritance to our posterity. We have neither sumptuous buildings nor towns that can serve to damp our spirit if we are threatened with an invasion; while our internal riches, on the other hand, are enchanting enough to convert any hostile force sent among us into a real present to strengthen our growing republic. We have a line of conduct drawn before us by the ablest politicians the world had ever produced. If Franklin will pattern them she will prosper. It has been mentioned that North Carolina was as ripe for separation as Franklin, but he thought that argument was an insult to the house; for separation was already effected, which North Carolina endeavored to annihilate. But the cry of that State was, "join us, and then we shall separate immediately." This is another of a grosser nature. We should have been perfect dupes, indeed, to believe that gentlemen in North Carolina who, it was well known, had ever conducted themselves with every sense of delicacy and honor in private life, should indifferently expose themselves in a public character, without an expectation of making a second separation a better bargain at the expense of the people of Franklin. Again, it has been observed that they used our commissioners with every mark of friendship and civility; but it is well known that the same polite gentlemen had suffered our public officers, chosen by the voice of our good citizens, to be loaded ungenerously with insults in their legislature, with impunity, by men who even violated the laws of their State in taking their seats;[2] and this was a truth too glaring to be denied. Franklin had been constitutionally separated from the government of North Carolina, in every sense, as much as two nations merely in alliance ought to be. Therefore, the State of Franklin could not honorably treat with North Carolina on any other terms than what she could with any other sister State in the Union; and that on such footing he recommended Franklin to send commissioners to endeavor to negotiate peace between Franklin and that State.

The Honorable General [Cocke] in the manner he expressed the word *odium*, seemed to intimate that an ungenerous expression had been made use of. If the cap fitted any, it could be but few; and he was confident that the honorable General, a gentleman of the law, who knew how statutes must be interpreted, must even confess it ungenerous to judge of sayings in any other light than one in which they were commonly understood; and he hoped if an apology were requisite, it would be sufficient to confess that the expression arose from a warmth occasioned by a surprise at the nature of the debate. He was as much disposed for peace as any other gentleman present, and only differed about a mode to procure it. This assembly was entrusted with the welfare and rights of about thirty thousand souls, placed in a garden of Columbia, protected by upwards of 9,000 free, able-bodied citizens, and it was the duty of every member to watch each other's conduct with vigilance and in a republican spirit as guardians at this time for their constituents and a free-born offspring.

The Honorable General Kennedy advised the gentleman to withdraw his motion, for he might easily perceive it would not be carried; for it could not be surmised that a plan of that nature could be conducted to any advantage whatsoever to the people of Franklin. A scrutiny must condemn it. He noticed that a few leading persons, of the small inconsiderable faction of deluded citizens on this side of the Appalachian mountains, had joined North Carolina in an endeavor to effect confusion and anarchy in this State. They were, at our first convention, friends to our new Republic; and, it was well

---

[2] The reference here is to Tipton and the other members from the western counties in the 1786 Assembly.

known, they had changed their conduct merely through a disappointed ambition; by which means they became indefatigable political tools for our enemies in North Carolina. Those leaders, in violation of the laws of that State, got themselves secretly elected under a sham sanction of said laws, last year; and the Assembly of that State allowed them seats, pretendedly believing those men to be our representatives of what they styled their "reverted western citizens," and showed themselves careless to every reason, and deaf to every conviction displayed by the commissioners sent by the General Assembly of Franklin. Notwithstanding these illegal members openly confessed that the opposition of only three hundred Franks, commanded by General Cocke, had obliged them to hold their election secretly, yet North Carolina received those persons politically as members and protected them as if they had been representatives of the general voice of the western citizens. This being premised, to suppose then that the scheme now debated in the House could prevent that party from sending members to the North Carolina Assembly would be truly ridiculous. Besides, they were now assisted by a late act in favor of secret elections. Should we now, as a convention of the State of Franklin, through folly pass a resolve for our citizens to hold a sham election, under the sanction of North Carolina, in order to chose our friends on the day appointed to elect members of the Assembly of that State? It would certainly give the enemies to the confirmation of separation straws enough (to use the gentleman's own phrase) to fire the government of Franklin with. As they have not convinced us as yet that they will not be as ready in the next Assembly to catch at straws as they were in the last, it would be a crime to believe that it would not leave us, on its vestiges, objects for the laughter of the world. I will admit that we by that means might carry friends to the confirmation of our separation act; but the opposite party, secretly at another place, would surely do the same. What then would be the consequence? North Carolina would then receive the members of that party, announce us as reverted rebels, and have a plea to use us accordingly. If North Carolina will not receive commissioners from Franklin, it should convince us that that State will not negotiate a confirmation; persuade us, in such a case, to rely on it that justice will not let the State of Franklin suffer because North Carolina piqued up a difference with Congress and refused to give her a deed for the western land. Our steady and uniform proceedings since the adjournment of the North Carolina Assembly must have convinced that State that the citizens of Franklin are determined to live independent of North Carolina. Therefore, members from this quarter could only ask what our conduct had claimed and confirmed; when commissioners, on the other hand, can demand our privileges, and negotiate peace to the honor of our State. But, laying aside all those objections, the measures proposed could never be excusably executed, but to save a government on the verge of destruction. But as this is not our situation at present, then, as a citizen of a brave people who ever scorned duplicity, he utterly condemned the motion, and agreed fully with the gentlemen who would not enter into negotiations with North Carolina, on any other terms than with other sister States in the Union.

His Excellency, the Governor, here taking the floor again, produced an act passed in the last General Assembly of Franklin, which directed the executive to make use of hostility, if nothing else would do, to prevent elections within the limits of the State of Franklin under the authority of North Carolina. Therefore, the tenor of the motion now before the House would bring the friends of independency under the rigor of that act. It is extraordinary that the conduct of the citizens who had sent members here should uniformly support the independency of Franklin, and that those members should also unanimously express themselves in favor of supporting the same, and yet at the same time blindly pursue a method which could not fail to bring about reunion with North Carolina. Let us suppose for a moment that the scheme now in agitation would answer the end supposed by some among us, which it certainly never would. It would in fact only alter our condition from independency to dependency, and ourselves from freemen to servants, and the course would disqualify us from every privilege above mere favors. But let us suppose that it would bring about a second separation as apparently favorable to our Commonwealth as the cession act. The quota of our debt would then be laid proportionally to the number of citizens we have now, which is on a ratio as is four to one to what they were at the time of our separation. Of course in the midst of our frugality we would be obliged to bear part of the expense requisite to support the extravagance and luxury of North Carolina government, besides our proportion to Congress for discharge of the foreign Continental debt. Thus situated, we are equally interested in the character of the cession act with the honorable Congress; and thereby bound in honor to give it a mutual support. Therefore, were we now to revert, it would remove us from all confidence due to a spirited power, to wallow in disgrace forever. A concise narrative of the settling of Franklin would show that the first colony in the country was settled by Virginians, about fifteen years ago, and that a line afterward run by Virginia and North Carolina left a helpless number of industrious citizens destitute of any more protection than what their own inconsiderable strength afforded them against the outrageous warlike tribes of Indians. That, in this situation of that settlement, the British superintendents, Cameron and Stuart, offered them protection on condition that they would transplant themselves further down toward West Florida, which their abhorrence of British tyranny at that time made them refuse. Soon after, in the year 1776, they applied to a convention held at Halifax, North Carolina, to become citizens of that State, in order to prevent that they might be thought inimical to the Revolution, which would have added to their distress. Their petition underwent a high and long debate before it was favorably received by North Carolina;[3] and in that convention the clause was inserted in the North Carolina Constitution which makes the cession act constitutional and just. The people of Franklin territory had paid large sums of money for the greatest part of their land before the Revolution of North America took place. Besides this, the settlers had held it by the sword, a mode that has confirmed the most powerful charters round the globe. Now going on ten years, the savages laid waste their buildings, carried off their stock and other movable property, killed and scalped several families and obliged the rest to fly to the safety of forts for the space of twelve months. In their helpless condition, the Virginians had proved their warmest supporters. He was, therefore, fully satisfied that if the matter were thoroughly discussed no impartial judicial power would judge North Carolina entitled to govern that territory which nature had formed a castle for a Commonwealth. Our enemies would find to their sorrow that it is garrisoned by brave, independent people should they concern unjustly with the western citizens, and we adhere to our former virtue. But should this day involve an offspring into slavery, it would fall a heavy curse on our own heads.

---

[3] Gov. Sevier was a delegate to the Convention and Provincial Congress of 1776, and he speaks from personal knowledge of the debates.

Colonel Doherty begged the House to beware of a danger not yet noticed. After the lower [seaboard] interest in North Carolina had made an instrument of the requisition of the United States to curtail the frontier, and thereby balance the scale of politics in favor of the seaboard citizens, a company of land speculators arose and formed a plan to throw us into confusion wherewith to prevail on us to revert to North Carolina to give them an opportunity of locating our land and improvements over our heads.[4] We must countermine that danger or a few years will bring a deluge of those speculators on our territory, who will infest our country with slavery that will be an evil equal to the thraldom inflicted formerly on the English by a swarm of Norman barons. He recommended it to every Frank, like men of spirit, to guard against it.

Major Newell perfectly agreed with Colonel Doherty, and added that we were constitutionally placed in an independent condition, and that we had both the spirit and the power within ourselves sufficient to support the independency of our rising Republic; and that as his sentiments on this were already sufficiently expressed, he would only mention that he could not agree to any other mode of negotiation with North Carolina than on terms claimed by any other sister State; and he called for the ayes and nays.

Colonel Barton agreed that Franklin had sufficient strength within herself to support independency, but he urged that that strength ought to be nourished by sound policy. He was not the least apprehensive that the petition sent by the small inimical party to North Carolina for men, ammunition and arms to subdue our infant Republic would meet with success. For, laying aside the Continentals of that State, and a few counties besides which had joined with patriotism and resolution in the last war, North Carolina had not proved to be very alert. He was certain that those men would not now assist to enthral those of their brethren who received and protected the records of North Carolina when Governor Caswell could raise only about twenty-five men among themselves to escort the records over the mountains to Franklin.

He feared the plan in debate would tend to check our government by confusing weak minds, and therefore condemned it utterly and recommended their uniform conduct to be ardently pursued. It had already brought Franklin respectable and powerful friends and the applause of justice.

[4] For justification of this charge, see *ante*, p. 20 and *post*. p. 191.

Captain Chisholm was tired of the state of administration in Franklin as it now stands; and was, therefore, urgent for a reconciliation; but he declared himself incapable of pointing out the readiest mode to obtain a better, and therefore called for a decision of the house.

The Honorable General Cocke, next speaking, said he found that the plan was discovered and had, therefore, lost its virtue; and he now condemned it as useless. But he still believed it might, undisclosed, have conducted peace smoothly into our Commonwealth. His argument in support of the motion had been severely handled; not more so than he knew it would suffer from undergoing debate. But, in regard to duplicity, he scorned it equally with any member on the floor. No less despicable conduct than that practiced by those inconsiderable characters, attended to by General Kennedy, could have made him support such a scheme to counteract an enemy.

The motion was withdrawn and another agreed to: That Commissioners be appointed to wait on the North Carolina Assembly with instructions from the General Assembly of Franklin to negotiate peace with the State of North Carolina consistent with the honor of, and with justice to, those two States as independent of each other.

It will be seen that, speaking broadly, those who favored the plan of Cocke represented the upper and longer-settled counties, while those who opposed were from the lower or frontier counties of Franklin.

Governor Sevier communicated to General Shelby a copy of the resolution that was adopted, along with a friendly letter which also sheds some light on the failure of the Sevier-Shelby compromise of March. Under date of May 30th, Sevier wrote:

I have the pleasure to enclose you a copy of a resolve of our last convention which will discover to you the friendly disposition of the Franklin people towards you, and evince to the world that the wish for peace and unanimity in the Western Country. Your letter by Mr. Bowman, I have before me. I must inform you that Parkinson[6] refused to comply with your orders. Informed Mr. Bowman that had such orders been issued from any of his superior officers of his own county, that he would have obeyed them; but that you have

---

[6] Captain Peter Parkinson; see sketch, *post.* p. 337. Sevier here imputes blame to Parkinson for the failure of the March compromise.

been much censured, and he thought himself not bound to obey you; therefore sold the guns for a trifle. I wish you, once more, to quash such rash proceedings, and to call them to an account yourself for such conduct, otherwise, however disagreeable it may be to me, I shall be under the necessity of doing it.

CHAPTER XXI

Defeat of Compromise and Resulting Violence

In June Sevier was hopeful of an accommodation with his opponents. He wrote to General Kennedy, of the Washington District, on July 6th:

"I met with the Old State party on the 27th of last month; few of our side met, not having notice. I found them much more compliable than I could have expected, except a few. I have agreed to a second conference, which is to be held at Jonesborough the last day of this month. You will please to give notice to all those appointed by the convention that may be in your District to be punctual in attending at the time and place. I shall earnestly look for you there, and as many other of our friends as can possibly attend; and I flatter myself something good for the public may be expected."[1]

The purpose of the projected conference was to arrange a compromise before the election in August for representatives in the assemblies of the two States. Conflicts of a serious character were expected, if no agreement was reached.

When, therefore, the August election came on (the third Friday and Saturday) discord and strife marked the occasion in several of the counties in the northern part of Franklin. In the lower counties of Caswell, Sevier and Blount the opposition to Franklin was a negligible quantity.

Disappointed and confused by the failure of the conference, the Franklinites hurriedly fell back on Cocke's strategy which had been discussed and discarded in May. The plan itself is surprising to one of to-day who contemplates it: Franklin leaders offered themselves for election to the North Carolina Assembly!

In Hawkins county (Spencer county in the Franklin government) Stockley Donelson (Franklinite) was a candidate against Thomas Amis (Carolinian). The polls were opened and the North Carolina sheriff made proclamation that no person would be

---
[1] Ramsey, 391.

allowed to vote unless he had paid taxes to North Carolina. When three votes had been cast, Colonel Wm. Cocke appeared on the scene with a number of men, some of whom were from Greene county as claimed by the opposition. The sheriff, apprehensive that a riot would ensue, adjourned the election to the next day. Fear of violence prevented the polls being opened the following day or at all.

Peter Turney,[2] the Spencer sheriff, was asked by Thomas Henderson, "who was to open the election, the sheriff of the old State or the sheriff of the new?" And was answered by Turney: "By both, agreeable to a resolve of the convention." When informed that only such as had given in their property for taxes could vote, Turney replied: "If that is the case, the strongest party shall take the house"—a decision by physical strength.

The polling place having been abandoned by the Carolinians, Donelson was declared elected; and the sheriff of North Carolina gave him a certificate of election which the North Carolina Assembly refused to recognize, but declared the election void, and ordered a new writ to be issued. Thus far the Franklinites' plans had succeeded.[3]

In Sullivan, the Franks attempted to use like tactics, and Sevier charged that they would have been successful but for the opposition tearing up tickets, denying the franchise to those who had not given in their taxable property to North Carolina, and using foul play.[4]

Landon Carter and—strangest of all—Sevier stood for election from Washington county. "I wrote him [Governor Caswell] I was elected, and also mentioned the other gentlemen, and wished his advice whether it would be expedient for me to attend. He writes pressingly for myself to attend, and promises every assistance to compromise matters, and seems to have no doubt of it being done.

---

[2] The first of the name later made familiar to all Tennesseans by Peter Turney, colonel of the First Tennessee Regiment, C.S.A.; chief justice, and finally governor of Tennessee. For a sketch of Turney, see *post*, p. 327.

[3] In Hawkins (Spenser) county, Peter Turney, the sheriff under the Franklin regime, at first advertised an election under Franklin authority, but on change of the plans allowed the sheriff of Hawkins county under North Carolina authority to conduct the election. *N. C. St. Rec.*, XX, 322.

[4] *N. C. St. Rec.*, XX, 322. Roosevelt in error, treats this as an election held for members of the Franklin Assembly and frustrated by the adherents of North Carolina.

Also that we be prepared with petitions, &c., to show the great majority that is in favor of the separation. I cannot be so well determined whether to attend or not, until I hear from Georgia."[5]

Judge David Campbell was elected to the senate from Greene county, in pursuance of this plan; and it is probable that, at the time of his election, he did not intend to take the seat.

Now began the resort to violence in the form of forays of armed men. Colonel John Tipton, although not colonel of the county, appeared in Hawkins county with a force of about fifty men, "under a pretense of redressing a quarrel" between the two sheriffs, though the principal purpose was to get possession of the county records held by the Franklin officers. This conduct gave rise to a rumor that they had made a prisoner of Governor Sevier with purpose to carry him to North Carolina. Two hundred Franks hurried to the home of Tipton, only to find that the report was baseless. "It was only through the influence of his Excellency that the opposite party did not fall a sacrifice to our Franks. During that time a body of about fifteen hundred veterans embodied themselves to rescue their governor (as they thought) out of the hands of the North Carolinians."[6]

In July, the sheriff of Washington county, Andrew Caldwell, was incarcerating in jail the sheriff who represented North Carolina's authority, Jonathan Pugh, thereby demonstrating that the Franks prevailed there, in actual exercise of power, though much reduced in numbers.

The Maryland *Journal*[7] quotes a late Virginia newspaper as stating that "the State of Franklin has sent, or is to send, two deputies to Kentucky, to meet a convention of all the western settlements for the purpose of consulting on proper measures respecting navigation of the Mississippi."

---

[5] Sevier to Gilbert Christian, Mount Pleasant, Oct. 20, 1787, in *Am. Hist. Mag.*, VI, 381. John Tipton and Landon Carter contested for the seat in the senate of North Carolina, with result that the election was held void and set aside. Tipton was thereby deprived of his seat—a sop thrown to the Franklinites.

[6] Cocke to Elholm, from Mulberry Grove, State of Franklin, August 27, 1787. *Columbian Magazine*, November, 1787; Ramsey, 392.

[7] Issue of Sept. 28, 1787. Shaler in his *History of Kentucky* says that efforts were made to persuade the Kentuckians to join in the Franklin movement. Unless he refers to Arthur Campbell's early scheme for a greater Franklin, this seems to be an error. Shaler may have had in mind the efforts made at this time by the Cumberland settlers to combine with the Kentuckians in government.

The year 1787 witnessed frequent meetings of the Franklin Assembly. A session was held early in August at which General Evan Shelby was elected governor to succeed Sevier on the expiration of the term of the latter, March 1, 1788. The fact was communicated to Shelby in a letter of Franklin's governor, written from Greeneville, August 12, in which acceptance was urged:

At the request of the General Assembly, I do myself the honor to inform you that you are appointed to succeed as Chief Magistrate of this State. You will readily consider it is friends, and not enemies, who would appoint you to this dignified station; and we flatter ourselves that if it will be consistent with your principles and sentiments you would serve a number of your real friends and acquaintances, together with supporting the interests and happiness of our State, and the country you reside in, [rather] than serve a distant set of men, totally unacquainted and unknown. Dear Sir, permit me to solicit your acceptance of this office, as it will give your friends peculiar satisfaction, as well as, I hope, establish unanimity and tranquility in our distracted country. I should have done myself the honor to have waited on you, but am so harrassed with business at this time, that it is out of my power to do so at this period. Our Assembly will meet on the third Monday in next month, at which time your answer is expected. I much wish, for many reasons, to see you, were it possible at this time.[8]

The Franklinites hoped to win over one of the strongest characters in the limits of the State; and through his influence to strengthen the new State at the weakest point—Sullivan county, the home of Shelby. Shelby declined the honor, but the favoritism of the Franks went far toward conciliating him. He shortly afterward resigned as brigadier-general of the Carolina militia, giving his old age as one of the reasons. On October 29th, he sent his resignation to Governor Caswell:

As matters have been in such a fluctuating abyss in the minds of the people on this side of the mountains, together with a desire to lead a retired life, and my old age, induced me to wish that the General Assembly may appoint some other to succeed me in the office of brigadier-general in this district. At the same time I have to observe to your Excellency that there are a number of petitions that are to be preferred to the Assembly for separation.[9] Some of them I have seen, and I am of opinion if we can have a separation upon reciprocal terms, it would not only aleviate the minds of the

---

[8] *Tennessee Historical Society Mss.*
[9] As to these petitions, see page 193.

people, but would terminate in strengthening this part of the community with our parent State.

P.S. If the wisdom of the General Assembly should think Mr. John Sevier a person adequate to succeed me in the office of brigadier-general, I would wish to recommend this gentleman to the honorable, the General Assembly.

Roosevelt clearly misconceived Sevier's letters to Shelby and the latter's resultant attitude. Roosevelt represents Sevier as being suspicious that Shelby was positively hostile: "Sevier warned him that no unfriendly interferrence would be tolerated. Shelby could neither be placated nor intimidated." Sevier certainly did not attempt to intimidate the old general.[10] Roosevelt evidently had not seen the letter of Shelby to Caswell, which plainly shows that the writer was placated to a degree. Certain it is that the sturdy old Welshman would not have recommended for election, as his own successor, a man who had tried to intimidate him.

One likes to think that one of the intermingling influences that prompted Shelby to commend Sevier and to counsel the grant of separation was that of his son, Colonel Isaac Shelby, (now in the Kentucky Country where much the same struggle for separate statehood was going on) interposed in behalf of Sevier, his comrade-colonel on the King's Mountain expedition. After-events showed the Shelbys and Seviers always standing together.

During this year Governor Sevier kept up a correspondence with the gray statesman, now governor of Pennsylvania, in which was solicited support of the cause of the State named in his honor. The letters best speak for themselves:

State of Franklin, Mount Pleasant,
9 April, 1787.

Sir:

Permit me to introduce to your Excellency the subject of our new disputed government. In the Year 1784, in the month of June, the legislature of North Carolina ceded to Congress all their claim to the land west of the Appalachian Mountains, on conditions, I make no doubt you are acquainted with, as the act was shortly after laid before Congress. The inhabitants of this country, well knowing that the Congress of the United States would accept the cession and having no idea that North Carolina would attempt repealing the act, formed themselves into a separate and independent State by the name of *Franklin*.

---

[10] Roosevelt probably got the idea from Sevier's reference to Parkinson's conduct in the letter of May 30th.

In November following, North Carolina repealed the act of cession. In May, 1785, Congress took the several acts under consideration and entered into resolves respecting the same, the purport of which I presume you are acquainted with. The government of Franklin was carried on unmolested by North Carolina until November, 1785, when that legislature passed an act allowing the people in some of our counties to hold elections under certain regulations unknown to any former law; whereby a few, from disaffection and disappointment, might have it in their power to elect persons who were to be considered the legal delegates of the people.

This was done and countenanced; and at their last session, in November, 1786, they have undertaken to reassume their jurisdiction and sovereignty over the State of Franklin, notwithstanding the whole of their adherents do not exceed two or three hundred against a majority of at least seven thousand effective militia. They have, contrary to the interests of the people in the two counties, to-wit, Washington and Sullivan, by their acts removed the former places of holding courts at certain places, to certain places convenient to the disaffected; as we conceive, in order that they might have a pretext to prevaricate upon.

I have thus given your Excellency the outlines of our past and present situation; and beg leave to inform you, that, from your known patriotic and benevolent disposition as also your great experience and wisdom, I am, by and with the advice of our Council of State, induced to make this application, that should you from this simple statement of the occurrences think our cause so laudable as to give us your approbation, you would be pleased to condescend to write on the subject. And any advice, instruction or encouragement, you may think we shall deserve, will be acknowledged in the most grateful manner.

We have been informed, that your Excellency some time since did us the honor to write us on the subject of our State; if so, unfortunately for us, the letters have miscarried, and are not come to hand. Many safe conveyances might be had. A letter may be sent by the bearer, Capt. John Woods,[11] if he should return by way of Franklin; or, if it were directed to the care of the Governor of Georgia, it would come safe; and probably by a number of people who travel this country.

I have the honor to be, Sir, &c.   John Sevier.[12]

                                     Philadelphia, June 30, 1787.

Sir:

I received the letter you did me the honor of writing to me the ninth of April last by the hand of Mr. Woods, who arrived here

---

[11] Woods had been a Continental agent to the Choctaw Indians. He was now going to Philadelphia as guide and interpreter for a delegation of Southern Indians.

[12] Sparks's *Works of Franklin*, X, 290.

about ten days since. You are pleased to ask my advice about the affairs of your government. I am very sensible of the honor your Excellency and your council thereby do me; but being in Europe when your State was formed, I am too little acquainted with the circumstances to be able to offer you any advice that may be of importance, since everything material that regards your welfare will doubtless have occurred to yourselves. There are only two things that humanity induces me to wish you may succeed in: your accommodating your misunderstanding with the government of North Carolina by amicable means, and the avoiding an Indian war by preventing encroachments on their land. Such encroachments are the more unjustifiable, as these people in the fair way of purchase usually give very good bargains; and, in one year's war with them you may suffer a loss of property and be put to an expense vastly exceeding in value what would have contented them perfectly in fairly buying the lands they can spare. There was one of their people who was going to Congress with a complaint from the chief of the Cherokees that the N. Carolinians on the one side, and the people of your State on the other, encroach upon them daily. The Congress not being now sitting he is going back apparently dissatisfied, that our general government is not just now in a situation to render them justice, which may tend to increase ill humor in that nation. I have no doubt of the good disposition of your government to prevent their receiving such injury, but I know the strongest governments are hardly able to restrain the disorderly people who are generally on the frontiers from excesses of various kinds; and possibly yours has not yet acquired sufficient strength for the purpose. It may be well, however, to acquaint those encroaching that the Congress will not justify them in the breach of a solemn treaty, and that if they bring upon themselves an Indian war they will not be supported in it.

I am sorry my letter in answer to a former one from your State, miscarried. I cannot at present lay my hands on the copy of it, but will look for it and send it at the next opportunity. I will also endeavor to inform myself more perfectly of your affairs, by inquiry and searching the records of Congress; and if anything should occur to me that I think will be useful to you, you shall hear from me thereupon.

I conclude by repeating my wish that you may amicably settle your differences with North Carolina. The inconveniences of your people attending so remote a seat of government, and the difficulty to that government in ruling so remote a people, would, I think, be powerful inducements with it to accede to any fair and reasonable proposition it may receive from you towards an accommodation.

Your Excellency's most obt. and most humble servt.

B Franklin.[13]

---

[13] *Franklin Papers*, VIII, folio, 1803, MSS. Division Library of Congress.

In replying to a letter from William Cocke about a year before, Franklin had advised the authorities of the new State to submit the points in dispute to the decision of Congress. Franklin now advises Sevier to apply to North Carolina for a satisfactory compromise. The change in Franklin's views was due, doubtless, to what he knew to be the insistence of the landowning States and to his belief that they would prevail in the constitutional convention on the point of the creating new States in the West.

Sevier's next letter was scarcely more than a budget of news:

Franklin, 12 Septem. 1787.

Sir:

Your favor of the 30th of June, I had the honor to receive by the hand of Mr. Droomgoole.

We are under great obligation to you for the trouble your Excellency has been pleased to take in writing, and for the kind advice contained in your letter. It affords us much pleasure to discover that you are disposed to be friendly to our young Republic. We hope to continue to deserve your notice. And any services you are pleased to extend towards us will not be misapplied.

From late accounts, we learn the Creek Indians are committing hostilities and outrages on the people of Georgia; and not long since a party went into the Chickasaw nation, murdered a Capt. Davenport, Commissary for the State of Georgia, also three other persons, wounded three and made one a prisoner. This tribe also, by their predatory excursions in the Cumberland settlements have done much spoil there, by murdering a number of the inhabitants, taking and carrying off their property, burning their buildings, cutting down their corn and wantonly destroying their cattle, &c. Although our frontier is most conveninent to that nation of Indians, yet we have been so fortunate as not to receive any injuries or insults from them.

I have the honor to be, respectively Sir,
With great esteem and regard,
Your Excellency's most obedient and hum. servt.

John Sevier.

His Excellency Governor Franklin.[14]

State of Franklin,
2nd of November, 1787.

Sir:

Since my last by Mr. Martin, nothing very material to acquaint your Excellency with. The Creek Indians continue their partial depredations on the State of Georgia, and a war between that State and these Indians is unavoidable.

I am happy to hear of such unanimity in the late Convention, and

---

[14] American Phil. Soc., *Franklin Papers*, XXXV, p. 140.

have sanguine hopes that you have adopted a plan of government that will add dignity to the rising greatness and happiness of our American Empire.

Permit me to inform your Excellency that the people of this State pray your patronage and attention to such matters as you may judge consistent with their interest, and the nature of their case may deserve. It might become a matter of much regret, should these people be unnoticed by Congress. They are firmly attached to the Continental measures and have been particularly active and serviceable in the late war; but at the present time there appears to be a general uneasiness among a number of the Western Americans through a jealously that their interest is neglected.

This, I expect, will be handed you by Major Droomgoole, on his way to Congress with letters from the Cherokee Chiefs. Mr. Droomgoole informs me that he is desirous of acting as superintendent over some of the Southern tribes. Should this appointment be not already filled, beg leave to introduce him to you as a gentleman, much noticed among the Cherokee Chiefs, and from his general deportment toward the interest of the United States, I have every reason to believe would discharge the duty required in this office, with satisfaction to the tribes and to the power thay may employ him.

The Cherokees complain that no persons attend them, and consider themselves neglected, and as Mr. Droomgoole has been at trouble and expense in quieting the minds of these people and keeping down all kinds of animosities that have been liable to rise in consequence of their being stimulated by some other power against the Americans, I hope your Excellency will not consider it impertinent in me to solicit your attention in his behalf.

I have the honor to be Sir,
  With great respect and esteem
    Your Excellency's mo. obedt. & hum. servt.

John Sevier.

His Excellency, Governor Franklin.[16]

---

[16] American Phil. Soc., *Franklin Papers*, XXXV, p. 276.

CHAPTER XXII

A Cry for Help from the Cumberland—1787

Colonel Bledsoe, after waiting in Sullivan county for nearly a month for Major Evans' battalion, left in disgust for his home on the Cumberland. June 1st, as he passed through Kentucky he wrote to Governor Caswell:

At this place I received accounts from Cumberland that, since I last did myself the pleasure of addressing you, three persons have been killed at that place within seven miles of Nashville, and there is scarcely a day that the Indians do not steal horses in either Sumner or Davidson counties; and I am informed the people are exceedingly dispirited: had accounts that the several northern tribes, in conjunction with the Creek nation, have determined the destruction of that defenceless country this summer; and their hopes seem blasted as to Major Evans's assistance. Colonel Robertson has lately been to this country to get some assistance to carry on a campaign against the Chickamauga towns and got some assurance from several officers; and the time appointed for the rendezvous was fixed to the 15th inst. but find the men cannot be drawn out at that season of the year. I have thought it my duty to ask your advice in the matter, whether or not we shall have leave of government to carry on such a campaign if we can make ourselves able, with the assistance of our friends, the Virginians [Kentucky district] as they promise us immediately after harvest.

I am fully convinced that it is the perfidious Chickamaugas that annoy our frontiers, tho' some of them wish to have the Creeks charged with the whole of the damage. As it is always my desire to act advisedly, I should thank you to advise me as to carrying on an expedition as it appears to me and to the people in the counties of Davidson and Sumner counties, that nothing can give security to them but to carry the war into the enemy's own country. . . .

Self-preservation and the distress and cries of a bleeding country make it absolutely necessary to preserve it from ruin and destruction.[1]

Major Evans had seen fit to journey by way of Richmond, Virginia, from which place late in May he wrote that he was trying to collect men for his battalion and that he was in need of funds for

---

[1] *N. C. St. Records*, XX, 712.

the purchase of supplies "before the troops can possibly go through the wilderness."[2]

Governor Caswell in his reply confessed his great uneasiness to find the major's letter dated at Richmond, and to learn the causes of the delay; and expressed fear that Bledsoe had lost patience and gone west.[3]

The middle of August found the major yet lingering east of the Blue Ridge, as Caswell charged, "engaged in making an attack on a lady whom he has lately reduced into possession by making her his wife."[4]

On Colonel Bledsoe's reaching home, he and Colonel James Robertson joined in reporting to Governor Caswell the distressed situation of their people. A rumor, believed by them to be true, was that the Spaniards were doing what they could to encourage the several savage tribes to war against the American settlers, by offering a reward for scalps. "A disorderly set of French and Spanish traders are continually on the Tennessee, ... a great means of encouraging the Indians to do much mischief."[5]

The day after this was written, the Indians killed Mark Robertson, the younger brother of Colonel Robertson, near the latter's home. Without waiting for authority from Governor Caswell a spirited campaign was launched against the Chickamauga town of Coldwater.

Through the friendly Chickasaws, news reached Colonel Robertson that the Creeks had planned to raid the Cumberland settlements. The North Carolina battalion had not even been heard from. In his dilemma, Robertson addressed an urgent letter to Governor John Sevier, Mount Pleasant, Franklin, as follows:

Nashville, August 1st. 1787.

Sir:

By account from the Chickasaws, we are informed that at a grand council held by the Creeks, it was determined by that whole nation to do their utmost this fall to *cut off this country;* and we expect the Cherokees have joined them, as they were to have come in some time ago to make peace, which however, they have not done. Every circumstance seems to confirm this.

The 5th of July, a party of Creeks killed Captain Davenport,

---

[2] *N. C. St. Records*, XX, 704.
[3] *Ib.*, 714, June 2nd.
[4] *Ib.*, 758.
[5] Ramsey, 465.

Agent for Georgia, and those men in the Chickasaw nation, wounded three and took one prisoner; which the Chickasaws are not able to resent for want of ammunition. The people are drawing together in large stations and doing everything necessary for their defense. But I fear, without some timely assistance, we shall chiefly fall a sacrifice. Ammunition is very scarce; and a Chickasaw now here tells us they imagine they will reduce our station by *killing all our cattle, etc. and starving us out.*

We expect, from every account, they are now on their way to this country to the number of a thousand. I beg you to use your influence in that country to relieve us, which I think might be done by fixing a station near the mouth of Elk, if possible, or by marching a body of men into the Cherokee nation. Relieve us in any manner you may judge beneficial. We hope our brethren in that country will not suffer us to be massacred by the savages without giving us any assistance; and I candidly assure you that never was there a time in which I imagined ourselves in more danger.

Kentucky being nearest, we have applied there for some assistance, but fear we shall find none in time. Could you now give us any? I am convinced it would have the greatest tendency to unite our counties, as the people will never forget those who are their friends in a time of such imminent danger. . . . I have written to General Shelby on this subject, and hope no division will prevent you from endeavoring to give us relief, which will be ever remembered by the inhabitants of Cumberland.[6]

It must have been with some hesitation that Robertson wrote this to Sevier, his comrade of the old Watauga Association whose gallant efforts in behalf of Franklin had more than once been chilled by Robertson's people. There is more than a hint here of a union with Franklin in the future as there had been once before in 1786.

Another Cumberland leader at the same time appealed to Governor Sevier—Anthony Bledsoe, who had but a few months before joined General Shelby in urging Governor Caswell to "act a decided part" in putting down the Franks:

When I had last the pleasure of seeing your Excellency, I think you were kind enough to propose that, in case the perfidious Chickamaugas should infest this country, to notify your Excellency and you would send a campaign against them without delay. The period has arrived that they, as I have good reason to believe, in combination with the Creeks have done this country great spoil by murdering numbers of our peaceful inhabitants, stealing our horses,

---

[6] For accounts of the Coldwater campaign, see Ramsey, 465; Goodpasture, Indian Wars, *Tennessee Historical Mag.*, IV, 120; *N. C. St. Rec.*, XX, 730.

A CRY FOR HELP FROM THE CUMBERLAND 173

killing our cattle and hogs, and burning our buildings through wantonness, cutting down our corn, etc. . . . Our dependence is much that your Excellency will revenge the blood thus wantonly shed."[7]

Putnam states that Governor Sevier was able to assure Colonels Robertson and Bledsoe: "Let matters occur as they may here (in Franklin) if I am spared, I propose joining the Georgia army with a considerable number of volunteers, to act in concert against the Creeks, though many of our enemies are making use of every diabolical plan in their power in order to destroy our laudable intention."[8] Putnam also says that a number of the men of Franklin enlisted in the battalion of Evans.[9]

And to Governor Mathews, of Georgia, Sevier wrote enclosing the communications of Robertson and Bledsoe, and saying: "It is our duty, and highly requisite in my opinion that such lawless tribes be reduced by dint of the sword. . . Be assured we will encounter [surmount] every difficulty to raise a formidable force to act in conjunction with the army from your State."[10]

The danger on the frontiers passed without the necessity of the troops taking the field. The plans of Sevier included the erection of a fortified station in the vicinity of the Chickamaugas, as Robertson had asked.

The men on the Cumberland were thoroughly disgusted and ireful over the failure of the North Carolina troops to come to their rescue. The battalion raised in February had been scheduled to arrive on the Clinch river in April. In point of fact, Major Evans reached General Shelby's (Bristol) August 18th and halted there until the 29th, and only reached Moccasin Gap on September 10th, headed for Nashville through Cumberland Gap and Kentucky, and arrived at his destination October 16th, 1787.[11] Virginians and

---

[7] Putnam, *History of Middle Tennessee*, 285-6.

[8] Putnam, 286.

[9] *Ib.*, 276. Gilmore, in the *Advance Guard of the Western Civilization*, 110, seizing upon this fact, enlarges upon it, and represents Sevier as calling for volunteers to fill up the battalion in response to the appeal for aid, and that the "tall Watauga boys" sprang up at the call of Sevier, two hundred and fifty strong. Roosevelt's strictures on Gilmore as a romancer are justified.

[10] August 30th. Ramsey, 392.

[11] Major Evans reported Nov. 10th, vindicating his delays east of the mountains. He makes a strong case against the North Carolina authorities: "I have done my duty to the utmost of my power, and can assure your Excellency that few men would

Franks had been enrolled,[11a] yet the battalion was reduced in number, and in a bedraggled, half-clad condition—truly not an imposing representation of the strong arm of a sovereign State when Nashville was reached.

After-history records still less to the credit of North Carolina in respect to her treatment of the men of this battalion. Survivors of Evans' force were compelled to petition the first legislature of the Territory South of the Ohio River (September, 1794) for compensation for the services they had rendered, payment of which had been pledged by North Carolina out of the taxes to be collected west of the mountains. By irony of fate, it fell to the lot of North Carolina's champion in the Franklin State contest, John Tipton, as chairman of the committee, to report upon the petition to the Assembly. That report can scarcely be conceived of as being purposely unfair to the obligor State:

The said batallion was raised on the faith of the State of North Carolina as appears by their act of 1786, and was destined for the protection of their then frontiers. The soldiers did their duty faithfully, and in discharging the same many of them lost their lives, but have received no part of their pecuniary pay.

It would be dishonorable and iniquitous for the government of this Territory not to pay these troops had its public faith been pledged for that purpose, nor could the failure of any particular fund have in that case been with propriety alleged as a pretext to evade the debt.

Your committee are forced to recall to remembrance that this Territory has never been protected in a state of peace and security, without which it was not reasonable to expect from it finances equal

---

have ever attempted to march the men I did from Holston without a more ample supply than I was furnished with, as your Excellency will see by a return of commissary and quarter-master, transmitted to you by Mr. Markland, who left me with no other supply than what is contained in said return, and not one shilling of money, quite contrary to orders, to perform a march of near four hundred miles, and that cheerfully, through a wilderness and in a strange State where no supplies could be had either on public or private credit. This was my situation when I arrived at Kentucky; was therefore obliged to furlough my men in order that they might work for a sufficiency of provisions to carry them to Nashville, which they did, and returned, chiefly, agreeable to my orders. . . . The men are so bare for every necessary of clothing, that unless they are supplied soon they will be entirely unable to perform any kind of duty, and they murmur much that they have not got, or any prospect to get, what was promised them when they entered the service."
N. C. St. Rec., XX, 786. For confirmation in part: Putnam, 278.

[11a] Wm. Martin, son of Col. Joseph Martin, was captain of one of the companies of thirty-three men. George Doherty, yet a major, was paymaster of the battalion.

to the payment of such troops as North Carolina might think proper to enlist: besides that, the inhabitants of this country contributed equally with said battalion to afford security and peace to the interior parts of North Carolina.

The most natural fund for the payment of the soldiers aforesaid would have been derived from the vacant lands which those soldiers helped to protect and secure, which fund has been disposed of for other purposes by the government which raised the battalion; that as for any other fund established for this payment by the State of North Carolina, if said fund has not proved effectual, the default did not arise from any misconduct in this government, or in the citizens thereof, but either through the neglect of the officers of that State, or the deficiency might be fairly ascribable to this, that the lands on which the taxes ought to have been collected were chiefly in the hands of citizens of North Carolina whose absence from the Territory enabled them to evade the taxes imposed on and paid by the people of this Territory.

Neither do we see any equitable circumstances which ought to induce this Assembly to discharge a debt contracted by and justly due from the State of North Carolina.[12]

The words of the Tipton report, "the neglect of the officers" of North Carolina, may refer to a series of frauds which were being uncovered about the year now under review (1787) in the office of John Armstrong, entry-taker for the western lands under the act of 1784. The deficit in the accounts of that officer was reported to the Assembly to be £6732.[13]

The rank injustice to the trans-Alleghany people worked by this act of 1784 and its snap repeal seems to have invited peculation, the result of which came upon the Commonwealth as retribution. The added charge that the North Carolina grantees of such lands had evaded taxation is sustained by the record, which denounces their claim of justification as "groundless pretense."[14]

The Cumberland folk proposed to a new-state convention, held in Kentucky in September, that they be included in the new government. "The Cumberland people have sent two gentlemen to wait on our convention to try if Kentucky will allow them to join with it in government; and, if so, on what terms, they first obtaining leave from North Carolina. What may be done I cannot tell at this time."[15]

---

[12] *Journal of Legislative Council, of Territory South of the Ohio*, (reprint 1852), 10.
[13] *N. C. St. Rec.*, XXI, 133.
[14] *N. C. St. Rec.*, XX, 396-7.
[15] Samuel McDowell to Arthur Campbell, Sept. 23, 1787. *Draper MSS.*, 9, D. D. 46.

In pursuance of this purpose, doubtless, Colonel James Robertson, who was senator in the North Carolina Assembly (November, 1787) aided by Col. William Blount, prepared a statement to that body of the situation and sentiments of his constituents. In it he set forth the people's harassment by the Indians. "They have cheerfully endured the most inconquerable difficulties in settling the Western Country, in full confidence that they should be enabled to send their products to market through the rivers which water the country; but they now have the mortification not only to be excluded from that channel of commerce by a foreign nation, but the Indians are rendered more hostile through the influence of that very nation probably with a view to drive them from the country, as they, the Spaniards, claim the whole soil." Robertson then called upon the humanity and justice of the State to prevent further massacres and depredations, and recommended as the most convenient and the safest means of relief compliance by North Carolina with the resolves of the Continental Congress which had urged the cession to the nation of their western lands by the States which owned them.[16]

---

[16] Ramsey, 502-3; *Tenn. Historical Mag.*, III, 231.

CHAPTER XXIII

Franklin and Georgia—1787

If the old-state partisans on the frontiers looked to Virginia for support in periods of stress, the Franklinites turned southward to Georgia for an ally. As Roosevelt observes, Georgia was a frontier State in spirit, particularly at this period when political sway was passing from her leaders of the seaboard region to those of the North Georgia hill country who had come in from the frontiers of Virginia and the Carolinas. Backwoodsmen felt toward Georgia as they did toward no other member of the old Thirteen.[1]

Governor Sevier had a warm friend in blunt George Mathews, now elected governor of that State, who, like Sevier, had come out of the Valley of Virginia.

At the time of the surrender of the gubernatorial chair by Edward Telfair to Mathews, the Georgia Assembly took favorable action on a mission of Major Elholm, in the following report:

> That the letters from John Sevier, Esq., evince a disposition which ought not to be unreguarded by this State, particularly in the intention of settlers in Nollichuckey, etc., to co-operate with us during the late alarm with the Indians, provided the necessities of the case required it; they, therefore, recommended to the House that his Honor, the Governor, inform the Honorable John Sevier, Esq., of the sense this State entertains of their friendly intentions to aid in the adjustment of all matters in dispute between us and the hostile tribe of Creek Indians that were opposed to this State.
>
> That in regard to Major Elholm, who has been so particularly recommended, they cannot forbear mentioning him as a person entitled to the thanks and attention of the legislature, and recommend that his Honor, the Governor, draw a warrant on the treasury in favor of Major Elholm for the sum of fifty pounds.[2]

Governor Telfair in the same month wrote Governor Sevier of

---

[1] *Winning of the West*, pt. IV, ch. III.
[2] Ramsey, 384; Steven's *Georgia*, 380, *et seq.*

the attention and respect the legislature had paid to the proffer of "aid you were authorized to afford the State."[3]

Other distinguished men of Georgia wrote to express their esteem and good wishes for Sevier and for the new State of Franklin. Col. Walton presented him with a neatly bound volume of the constitutions of the thirteen States, accompanied by a complimentary address. The Society of the Cincinnati of that State elected Sevier an honorary member, at Augusta, February 12th. Ramsey, possessed of the certificate of membership at the time he wrote, gives its recitation of Sevier's record: "that he had a principal merit in the rapid and well conducted volunteer expedition to attack Colonel Ferguson, at King's Mountain, and a great share in the honor of that day, which, as is well known, gave a favorable turn to our gloomy and distressed situation, and that an opportunity never yet appeared but what confirmed him as an ardent friend and a real gentleman."

Major Elholm was able to inspire enthusiasm, if not to win outright support for the State of Franklin, in Georgia. Haywood says that a common toast there was, "Success to the State of Franklin, his Excellency Governor Sevier, and her virtuous citizens."[4]

Sevier had sent by Major Elholm a letter to his old friend of the trying revolutionary days, Col. Elijah Clarke, who replied (February 11th) in expressions of warm regard that must have been, above almost any other thing, pleasant to Sevier:

Augusta, Feb. 11th, 1787.

Dear Sir:—I received your favour by Major Elholm, who informed me of your health. Assure yourself of my ardent friendship, and that you have the approbation of all our citizens, and their well wishes for your prosperity. We are sensible of what benefit the friendship of yourself and the people of your state will be to Georgia, and we hope you will never join North-Carolina more. Open a Land Office as speedily as possible, and it cannot fail but you will prosper as a people; this is the opinion current among us.

I have considered greatly on that part of your letter which alludes to politics in the Western country. It made me serious, and as

---

[3] Ramsey, 385. Haywood says that this communication was addressed to Sevier in the character of Governor of the State of Franklin. (Haywood, 172). The Assembly, however, appears to have safeguarded its phrasing.

[4] Haywood, 172. William Downs assured Gov. Sevier (May 21st) that "the greatest politicians give it as their opinion that Franklin will support itself without a doubt and, from what I can understand, would give every assistance in their powers." Ramsey, 386.

seven states have agreed to give up the navigation, it is my friendly advice that you do watch with every possible attention, for fear that two more states should agree. I only observe to you, that the Southern States will ever be your friends.

It was reported that East and West Florida were ceded by the Spaniards to France, but it is not so. I know that you must have the navigation of the Mississippi. You have spirit and right; it is almost every man's opinion that a rumour will arise in that country. I hope to see that part myself yet. Adieu; Heaven attend you and every friend, with my best respects.

In a second letter, (May 22, 1787), Clarke said:

Should any further appearance of war be apparent, I shall take the earliest opportunity of communicating it to you, with the expectation of acting in confidence and concert with your State in operations taken against the Creeks.

I am very sorry to hear you have not peaceably established yourselves in the State of Franklin, and that the unhappy contention yet prevails between that and the State of North Carolina, and more particularly when they think of reducing you by force. These ideas have not proceeded from any assurance from this State, as it is the received opinion of the sensible part of every rank in Georgia that you will, and ought to be, as independent as the other States in the Union.[5]

On his return to Franklin, the ebullient Elholm proved that he, too, could write inspiring letters to his recent hosts.[6]

---

[5] Ramsey, 386. The spirit of independence shown in this letter was, in a later year (1794) to manifest itself in an attempt of Clarke, the war-hardened, imperious and stern, to establish "a separate and independent government on the lands allotted to the Indians for their hunting-grounds without the limits of Georgia, with a legislative body, a constitution and a committee of safety." Steven's *Georgia*, 33; Alston, *Ga. Bar. Asso. Rep.* (1912), 137-54. John Clarke, his son, was afterward elected governor of Georgia.

[6] Writing, probably from the present Knoxville, under date line: "Tennessee, in the State of Franklin, June 10, 1787," "a gentlemen of the State of Franklin to an officer in Georgia" affords no little sidelight on the spirit of almost the entire West:

"I had the pleasure of your friendly favor of the 26th. ult., in which I was happy to observe that the State of Georgia bids fair for becoming the first of the confederacy, with the respect to its policy, commercial staples, military strength, and number of officers trained in the late war, whose experience and courage fit them for reaping a harvest of glory in any military enterprise, to which their country may call them.

The fall session of the Franklin Assembly provided for the forwarding of aid to Georgia of nine hundred men, thought to be sufficient for the purpose; and Sevier informed Mathews that the force awaited the determination of Georgia officials, but that the Creeks had abated their hostilities on the Cumberland.

Major Elholm was sent (June 24th) on a second mission to Georgia, carrying a letter to Governor Mathews from Governor Sevier in which was incorporated an appeal that Georgia intervene to bring about a reconciliation between Franklin and the parent State. Sevier wrote that a reunion on just terms would prove agreeable. Short of this—"the sword cannot intimidate us."[7]

"By accounts the most authentic from all the Southern Indians, we are assured, beyond all doubt, that an opportunity will shortly be given to those heroes, to acquire fresh laurels in a war which the Creek nation is determined to create.

"The emissaries of the Spanish Governor at Pensacola and New Orleans, have long been indefatigable in their exertions of exciting all the savage tribes south of the Ohio and east of the Mississippi, to raise the hatchet against your state in particular, as the only one whose claims of territory, enterprising spirit, and strength they affect to dread. By them, the Creeks are actually supplied with everything for a long, vigorous, determined series of hostilities, and it is more than probable that before this letter may reach you the Creeks may be in the heart of your settlements. This insidious interposition of Spanish jealousy, as well as the usurpations of the Spaniards on our rights of territory and navigation, will (and we here [and] in Kentucky hope that it shall) rouse the Georgians to retaliate on the Dons at the Natchez and New Orleans. In such event, no doubts can exist but that the hardy warriors of Franklin, Kentucky, and those of all the other settlements on the western waters, will effectually co-operate in such a measure. And were the force of 30,000 men necessary to the project of subjugating the Creeks, storming New Orleans, and opening the navigation of the Mississippi, such force could, I am persuaded, be called forth, and with alacrity would turn out from the states and settlements just mentioned. I shall be more diffuse on this topic in my next, and am in the meantime, my dear sir, Yours, etc." Charleston (S. C.) *Morning Post*, June 29, 1787.

[7] "Franklin, 24th. June, 1787.
"*Sir:*—The Honourable Major Elholm waits upon your Assembly in character, of Commissioner from this State, with plenary powers.

"The party in opposition to our new republic, although few and inconsiderable, yet, by their contention and disorder, they occasion much uneasiness to peaceable minds. We are friendly citizens of the American Union, and the real desire we have for its welfare, opulence, and splendour, makes us unwilling and exceedingly sorry to think, that any violent measures should be made use of, against the adherents of any of our sister states; especially the one that gave us existence, though now wishing to annihilate us. And what occasions in us excruciating pain is, that perhaps we may be driven to the necessity, unparalleled and unexampled, of defending our rights and liberties against those, who not long since, we have fought, bled and toiled together

Sevier realized that the State of Franklin was to fall into a rapid decline unless something could be done to bolster it. He knew the welding influence on all frontiersmen of an Indian campaign, particularly if land were held out as service-bounty. He, therefore, equipped Elholm with a letter addressed to the Georgia Assembly, in which he reviewed the subject of using the territory of Georgia in the Bend of the Tennessee as a place for settlements by the outflow of emigrants from Franklin, and gave assurance that his State would aid in affording them protection from the hostile Indian tribes; that this would be effected in a large measure "by erecting

with, in the common cause of American Independence, or otherwise become the ridicule of a whole world. This I hope, however, God will avert; and that a reunion will take place on honourable, just, and equitable principles, reciprocally so to each party, is our sincere and ardent wish.

"When we remember the bloody engagements in which we have fought together against the common enemy, the friendly, timely and mutual supports afforded between the State of Georgia and the people of this country, it emboldens us to solicit you, sir and through you the different branches of your government, that you will be graciously pleased to afford to the State of Franklin such of your countenance as you may, from your wisdom and uprightness, think, from the nature of our cause, we may deserve,—in promoting the interest of our infant republic, reconciling matters between us and the parent state, in such manner as you, in your magnanimity and justice, may think most expedient, and the nature of our cause may deserve.

"Permit us to inform you that it is not the sword that can intimidate us. The rectitude of our cause, our local situation, together with the spirit and enterprise of our countrymen in such a cause, would inflame us with confidence and hopes of success. But when we reflect and call to mind the great number of internal and external enemies to American Independence, it makes us shudder at the very idea of such an incurable evil, not knowing where the disorder might lead, or what part of the body politic the ulcer might at last infect.

"The nature of our cause we presume your Excellency to be sufficiently acquainted with. Only, we beg leave to refer you to the Cession act of North-Carolina, also the constitution of that government, wherein it mentions that there may be a state or states erected in the West whenever the legislature shall give its consent for the same.

"We cannot forbear mentioning, that we regard the parent state with particular affection, and will always feel an interest in whatever may concern her honour and prosperity, as independent of each other.

"For further information, I beg leave to refer you to Honourable Major Elholm." Ramsey, 390. The Council of the State, at Augusta, resolved that it entertained a high sense of the friendly intentions of the people of Franklin. *Draper MSS.*, IX, 45. The Land Board at Washington, Ga., having accounts from the State of Franklin and the settlements on the Cumberland that a number of settlers from those sections were contemplating removal to the Tennessee District, ordered surveying in that District to be proceeded with immediately. Ramsey, 377.

some garrisons on the frontiers of this State, which we have lately resolved to do."

Major Elholm in reporting the action of the Franklin Assembly requested that the men coming for service from Franklin should be granted bounty lands in the Bend; and he was called upon by the Georgia Council of State to furnish a *project* of the military preparations necessary for the campaign, and also for the settlement of the Bend of Tennessee.[8]

---

[8] Elholm and Sevier continued efforts to establish claims in the Great Bend after statehood, (1798). *Cal. King's Mountain Papers, Draper MSS.*, 219, 221.

CHAPTER XXIV

FRANKLIN AND THE WEST IN THE CONSTITUTIONAL CONVENTION—1787

Having failed to get favorable action on the part of the Continental Congress, the Franklin leaders ventured now to hope that the convention, called to consider how the frame-work of the national government could be strengthened, might do something for them.

A writer from the State of Franklin, in the *Maryland Journal*, of July 27, 1787, observed that the people of that Commonwealth "are in hopes that the Federal Convention will invest Congress with power to have a deed executed to them for the territory ceded by the State of North Carolina on the 2nd of June, 1784, as Congress was in possession of the act of cession of said State at the time it was repealed; and, also that it could not with propriety be repealed as the time Congress had to consider of and accept the territory so ceded was made one of the stipulations of said act. . . . They have opened an office in the State of Franklin for the disposal of the lands given up to them by the Cherokee tribe; the money arising from the sale of said lands is to be reserved in the treasury for the express purpose of paying their quota of the federal debt, as they are friends to the federal government, if they can enjoy it."

This provision for covering the proceeds of the domain into the treasury was a bid for national favor, and was meant to be in contrast to the attitude of North Carolina toward the central government.

The North Carolina delegation to the federal convention, in its personnel, was not friendly to the aspirations of the western people. Caswell had declined the appointment as a delegate, and Blount took but little part in the deliberations. These two men had some appreciation of what the great hinterland was and was to be. And William Richardson Davie had been on the Watauga as a practicing lawyer at an earlier day and was well disposed; but he, too, took but a small part in the debates. Alexander Martin, Richard Dobbs Spaight and Hugh Williamson, as may well be conceived, were adverse—the last named in particular. He was by far the most active member of the delegation in debate and in the molding of policies. He it was, who had intervened to bring about the repeal of the North Carolina cession act of 1784, while Alexander Martin was governor.

So far, therefore, as this delegation was concerned, nothing could be expected.

Jealousy on the part of some of the delegates from the seaboard States toward the rising West was first exhibited in a debate on the basis of representation in Congress.

Gouverneur Morris, of Pennsylvania, looking forward "to that range of new States which would soon be formed in the West" thought that the rule of representation should be so fixed as to secure the Atlantic States a predominance in the national councils. The new States would know less of the public interest than these; would have an interest in many respects different. This would not be unjust as the western settlers would previously know the conditions. The busiest haunts of men, not the remote wilderness was the proper school of political talents.

John Rutledge, of South Carolina, agreed that if numbers should be made the rule of representation, "the Atlantic States will be made subject to the Western."

Gorham, of Massachusetts, made the point that the States would vary in relative extent by separations of parts of the largest States. "A part of Virginia is now on the point of separation. In the province of Maine, a convention is at this time deliberating on a separation from Massachusetts." King, of the same State, insisted that Jefferson's scheme for new States was impolitic, in that it amounted to a compact with the settlers that as soon as their number reached the size of the smallest of the original States admission into the Union might be claimed. "The plan as it respects one of the new States, is already irrevocable, the sale of lands having commenced, and the settlers will immediately become entitled to all the privileges of the compact."

Williamson, of North Carolina, urged that the Western States should stand on a different footing since their property was not rated as high as that of the Atlantic States.

Madison was opposed to determining "human character by the points of the compass." No discrimination against the West was admissible either in point of justice or policy.

Gerry, of Massachusetts, agreed that new States in the West "will oppress commerce and drain our wealth into the Western Country. There was a rage for emigration from the Eastern States into the Western Country, and he did not wish those remaining behind to be at the mercy of the emigrants."

As to the number of senators, Gorham preferred two to three from each State. "The number of States will increase. Kentucky, the province of Maine, and Franklin will soon be added to the present number."[1]

Touching the admission of new States, Butler was opposed to recognition of their equality in the Union being anchored in the Constitution.

Madison insisted that the Western States neither would nor ought to submit to a Union which degraded them from an equal rank with other States.

Mason, of Virginia, said: "If it were possible by just means to prevent emigrations into the Western Country, it might be good policy. But go the people will as they find it to their interest, and the best policy is to treat them with that equality which will make them friends, not enemies."[2]

Williamson was against treating the Western States on terms of equality with even the small States of the East.

When it was proposed to make the admission of new States, erected within the limits of then existing States, dependent upon the consent of the legislature of such State, that old lion, Luther Martin, of Maryland, came into the arena roaring opposition. Nothing would so alarm the limited States (with no western lands) as to make the consent of the large States, claiming western lands, necessary to the establishment of new States within their limits. "Shall Vermont be reduced by force in favor of States claiming it? Franklin and the western country of Virginia (Kentucky) were in a like condition."

The proposition, notwithstanding, was carried by the reason of the voting strength of the States that asserted title to the western regions as against the Nation: New Hampshire voted no; Massachusetts, aye; Pennsylvania, aye; Delaware, no; Maryland, no; Virginia, aye; North Carolina, aye; and Georgia, aye.

Article XVII, as amended, stood for consideration as a whole.

---

[1] *Doc. Hist. Constitution*, III, 410-412.
[2] *Ib.*, 643.

Langdon, of New Hampshire, agreed with Martin: "dangerous opposition to the plan would be excited."

G. Morris: "If the forced division of the States is the object of the new system, and is to be pointed against one or two States, I expect the gentlemen in the chair [George Washington] would pretty quickly leave us."

This intimation, if meant to imply opposition to new States in the West, was distinctly not justified. Washington shared Jefferson's views as to the new-state movement, even when it affected his own Virginia. He was on record,[3] time and again to the contrary, and never more plainly than in these words to Jefferson: "The inhabitants of Kentucky have held several conventions, and have resolved to apply for a separation. Opinions, as far as they come to my knowledge, are diverse. I have uniformly given it as mine to meet them upon their own ground, draw the best line, and make the best terms we can, and part good friends."[4] Nor was Washington frightened by the spectre of separation. To Jefferson he had written: "I am not less in sentiment with you in respect to the impolicy of the States grasping at more territory than they are competent to the government of; and, for the reason you assign, I very much approve the mouth of the Great Kanawha as a convenient and very proper line of separation."[5]

In the progress of the debate Rutledge ventured the assertion that there could be no room to fear that North Carolina would call on the United States to maintain her government over the mountains.

Mr. Williamson protested that North Carolina was well disposed to give up her western lands, but attempts at compulsion was not the policy of the United States. He was for doing nothing in the Constitution in the present case and for leaving the whole matter *in statu quo.*

Luther Martin urged the unreasonableness of forcing the people of Virginia beyond the mountains, the western people of North Carolina and Georgia, and the people of Maine, to continue under the States then governing them. The majority might place the seat of government among themselves for their own convenience and still keep the injured parts of the States in subjection, under

---

[3] *Ante.*, p. 27.
[4] Sparks's *Writings of Washington*, IX, 134.
[5] *Ib.*, 33.

the guaranty of the general government against domestic violence. "When the great States are to be affected, political societies are of sacred nature."

The Articles of Confederation had made the admission of a new State to depend upon the affirmative vote of nine States; but, following the action taken at the close of the debate, such admission, practically speaking, was made to depend upon the consent of that old State which claimed sovereignty over it, since little, if any, of the western lands was unclaimed by some one of the Thirteen States.

The debate has been outlined somewhat at length for the reason that the result sealed the fate of the State of Franklin, in that it placed her recognition and admission securely at the option of North Carolina. It remains only to be observed that in this convention of patriots no voice was raised to urge an equitable right to self-determination on the part of the western people, since they by their bravery and fortitude had conquered the western wilderness and given it value in the esteem of the claimant States; and more, had turned to aid in prizing the foot of the British invader from seaboard soil, which the invader was determined to claim on the basis of *uti possidetis*.

Luther Martin refused to sign the Constitution and went home resolved to prevent the ratification of that instrument by the legislature of Maryland. In making a report to that body, under the title of "Genuine Information" (November 29, 1787) he said: "The States of North Carolina and Virginia . . . reach from the seacoast unto the Mississippi. The hardship, the inconvenience, and the injustice of compelling the inhabitants of those States who dwell on the western side of the mountains . . . to remain connected with the inhabitants of those States, respectively, on the Atlantic side of the mountains and subject to the same State governments, would be such as would, in my opinion, justify even recourse to arms to free themselves from and to shake off so ignominious a yoke.

"It would be too absurd and improbable to deserve a serious answer, should any person suggest that these States mean ever to give their consent to the erection of new States; but should this Constitution be adopted, armed with a sword and halter to compel their obedience and subjection, they will no longer act with indecision; and the State of Maryland may, and probably will, be called upon to assist with her wealth and her blood in subduing the inhabitants of Franklin, Kentucky, and Vermont, and the provinces of Maine and Sagadahoc, and in compelling them to continue in subjection to the States which respectively claim jurisdiction over them."[6]

Martin's statement was overcolored. He mistook, so far as North Carolina was concerned, the marrow of the policy to be there pursued: that of holding under leash the Western Country for further exploitation of the land, to the acquisition of which the Trans-Appalachians were regarded chiefly as way-breakers. There was little or no concern for the continuance of mere political control of the people beyond the mountain ranges.

---

[6] Farrand, *Records of the Federal Convention*, III, 224, *et seq.*

CHAPTER XXV

Close of the Crucial Year—1787

The federal constitutional convention adjourned September 17th. On the same day, the fall session of the Franklin Assembly opened at Greeneville. Charles Robertson was speaker of the senate, and John Menifee speaker of the house of representatives.

It is probable that news of the action touching the admission of new States, taken at Philadelphia on August 30th, reached Franklin while the Assembly was in session. How ominous it was could not have been unappreciated, especially by Cocke and Judge Campbell, men trained in the law. Ramsey[1] says that the legislature of Franklin manifested a strong tendency to dismemberment. From some of the older counties there were no representatives, while some of the delegates from others exhibited indecision. The legislation was confined for the most part to unimportant amendments of the laws of North Carolina which had been adopted as the basis of the system of jurisprudence of the Commonwealth.

Governor Sevier was pledged to Georgia to carry forward plans for a joint campaign against the Creek Indians, but it was now with difficulty that he procured the passage of assenting and enabling acts. Finally a bill was passed for embodying troops and for their descent by the waters of the Tennessee river, in case of a call from Georgia, but as the result of a compromise with the more conservative element. "The *quid pro quo* given to the dissentients was the appointment of two delegates to attend the legislature of North Carolina to make such representations of the affairs of Franklin as might be thought proper." Under this final adjustment, Judge Campbell and Landon Carter were named to so serve.

A bid for Judge Campbell's return to his allegiance to North Carolina had been made by Governor Caswell in February, 1787,[2] but he had not then seen fit to accept the tendered commission.

No doubt, Campbell had advised Sevier of the predicament of

---
[1] Page 401.
[2] *N. C. St. Rec.*, XX, 617.

Franklin consequent on the action of the constitutional convention; but at the time personal animosities were rampant, particularly between Sevier and Tipton. In a personal encounter, the latter, "thanks to his superior physical strength, did not come off second best." This, in part, accounts for Sevier's persistence in the struggle against odds to establish a State in the West.

Another, and a more cogent reason was, that the settlers in the lower counties, who were almost to the man standing faithfully by him, would be abandoned to the workings of Carolina's policy for their removal from their homes, deemed by that State to be on lands reserved for the Cherokees. The same borderers of the South had been his chief support in the later campaigns against the Indians. They had not deserted him, and they were looking to him for succor. Could he afford to abandon them? Sevier, always loyal to his friends, determined that he would not, and he held to his course.

Sevier now saw more than a ray of sunshine coming out of Georgia, after two long months of waiting. A letter reached him from Governor Mathews saying that at last the Assembly of his State "are now fully persuaded that they never can have a secure and lasting peace with the Creek Indians till they are well chastised and severely feel the effects of the war. They have passed a law for raising three thousand men for that purpose, and have empowered the Executive to call for fifteen hundred men from Franklin.... The Bend of Tennessee being allowed for your men, I flatter myself, will give pleasure; and, as the bounty is given for fighting our common enemy, will be, I am persuaded, thought generous and liberal."[3]

Georgia sent to Franklin, a young officer of great force and capacity, Lieutenant-Colonel George Handley,[4] who was to act as commissioner on the part of Georgia in the preparations for hostilities then going forward.

Former Governor Telfair also wrote to Sevier that Georgia had taken measures that would "prove extremely beneficial to Franklin, inasmuch as to evidence to the Union that one of the members of it has full confidence in the valor and rectitude of the people and gov-

---

[3] November 12th. Ramsey, 395.
[4] Handley became governor of Georgia at the early age of 36 (1788). He came from England in 1777; became a captain, and soon reached the rank of lieutenant-colonel in the Revolutionary War.

ernment thereof. It is a crisis by which a young people may rise in estimation, and it will give tone to Franklin."[5]

Ramsey states that proffers were made to Governor Sevier by the Chickasaw Indians of assistance in the war against the Creeks.

Martial ardor marks the following letter (November 11th), from Elholm, to Major-General Moultrie, from Augusta:

The savages are daily committing new marks of cruelty on the inhabitants of this State (shocking to humanity): the other day they tortured a prisoner as long as they could continue to give pain, and then left the unfortunate victim with a stake drove through his bowels. Every possible preparation to bring the Creeks to justice is made; one-half of the militia immediately ordered into the field; recruiting officers industriously engaged in raising four regiments, consisting of 750 men each, and, I am informed, with great success. I have engaged (authorized by my fellow citizens for that purpose) to act in concert, with 1,500 Franks, with the movements of Georgia, to be commanded by a general of their own to the west of the mountains. A commissioner is sent to the Spanish government to request of that government not to assist our common enemy with any arms or ammunition.[6]

Sevier lost no time in sending a circular to the military forces in Franklin, in which he outlined the objects of the campaign, the bounty offered, etc.[7] This call to arms thrilled the frontiersmen,

---

[5] Ramsey, 396.
[6] *Maryland Journal*, of December 11th.
[7]   28th November, 1787.

Major Elholm is just now returned from Georgia with expresses from the governor of that state, requiring an aid of fifteen hundred men from the State of Franklin, to co-operate with them against the Creek Indians, under the following conditions, to wit:

All that will serve one campaign, till a peace is made, shall receive as follows:

A colonel, one thousand two hundred acres; a lieutenant-colonel, one thousand one hundred; a major, one thousand; a captain, nine hundred; first-lieutenant, eight hundred; second-lieutenant, seven hundred and fifty; non-commissioned officers, seven hundred; privates, well armed and accoutred, six hundred and forty.

Any general officer, called into the service, to have the following proportions:—

A major-general, fifteen hundred acres; a brigadier general, fourteen hundred acres.

The Bend of Tennessee is reserved for the troops of Franklin, which is a desirable spot, and will be of great importance to this state. We are to have an additional bounty of fifty acres on every one hundred acres, in lieu of rations, and all other claims against the State of Georgia, which makes our proportion of lands amount to half as much more as what is above allotted. A private man's share, if he finds himself, amounts to nine hundred and sixty acres, and officer's in proportion.

particularly the younger men of daring and enterprise. Volunteers were recruited under the direction of Colonel Handley and Major Elholm, and by December 2nd a letter was forwarded, announcing to Georgia readiness for the campaign.

A chill followed this fever. Not until February, 1788, did a reply come, and it announced that the campaign had been abandoned on

---

This great and liberal encouragement will, certainly, induce numbers to turn out on the expedition, which will not only be doing something handsome for themselves, but they will have the honour of assisting a very generous and friendly sister state to conquer and chastise an insolent and barbarous savage nation of Indians.

I now request that you will, with the utmost despatch, cause a general muster to be held in your county, and endeavour to get as many vulunteers to enter into and engage in the aforesaid service, and under the above conditions, as in your power. You may, also, encourage active persons to turn out and recruit; and both yourself, and those that may recruit, to transmit to me, immediately after the general muster, your numbers of recruited volunteers. If I am spared, I think to take the field once more, and wish we may be able to march about Christmas, if possible, for the sooner we march, the sooner the people can return in time to put in their spring crops.

I congratulate you, and every true friend, on the success of our Commissioner in the State of Georgia, and am happy to inform you that our situation as a state is now secure and on a permanent footing—much occasioned by one of the members of the Union, through her liberal and sisterly affection, having taken us by the hand, and noticing us as a people, of which you will be convinced by the copies, &c., accompanying this. The good people in this country are under high obligations to our trusty and worthy Commissioner, Major Elholm, whose acquaintance and abilities have enabled him to accomplish for us most desirable purposes.

I have not time to transcribe and send, for your's and the people's perusal, a copy, in full, of the Georgia act, respecting Franklin, but hope the outlines, herein inserted, will be satisfactory. I also recommend that the recruiting officers might apply and take a copy for the satisfaction of those who may be inclined to enter into the service.

The State of Georgia has appointed Col. Handley, a respectable character in that state, to attend the State of Franklin in character of Commissioner. I expect him in a few days, and shall be desirous of giving him every information before his return. I recommend the information herein contained, through your patronage, to the people, who, I hope, after seeing the great notice and respect shewn them by the State of Georgia, in her application to us for our assistance, and the high confidence they place in the spirit and bravery of the people here, that they will be animated with the idea, that they are now capable of evincing to the world that, like a young officer who first enters the field, they are competent, from their bravery and merit, to make themselves known and respected amongst the nations of the world; and, though we have not large cities and sea-ports, which generally sink into wealth and, luxury, by which means the offspring dwindled into effeminacy and dissipation, yet I hope, we shall always remain as happy, free and independent as any other people; If not, sure I am, it will be our own fault, and we ought never to be pitied.

account of the fact that Congress had ordered three commissioners, one of them from Georgia, to hold a treaty with the Indians, "and we now only suspend our operations till their determinations are known."

The delay, and the suspension, which proved to be a final one, defeated the hopes of the militia and thwarted the design of their leader.

In certain quarters the rumors of this raising of troops in Franklin took the color of preparations for hostilities against the Spaniards—"to thrash those perfidious Castilians into better conduct toward the subjects of the United States." So reported a correspondent to the Maryland *Journal*.[8]

Pursuing a suggestion in one of Governor Caswell's letters, the Franklin leaders circulated a number of petitions to the North Carolina Assembly for a separation, in which were incorporated portions of the recent memorial to Congress and some of Caswell's own arguments in favor of separation:

We hope that having settled west of the Appalachian mountains ought not to deprive us of the natural advantages designed by the bountiful hand of Providence for the convenience and comfort of

---

[8] Issue of Nov. 6th, 1787. It may be that it was a part of the plan to challenge and attack the Spaniards should they give aid to the Creeks despite the request made of them not to do so: "By late advices from the State of Franklin, we learn of their Assembly being convened by a special call from the Governor and Council. The principal business of this meeting was to take into consideration the hostile behavior of his Catholic Majesty's subjects in the Floridas and Louisiana toward the good people of that State in particular, and the Western States in general. It is said that they have it from an undoubted authority that many of their citizens have been deprived of their lives, liberties and properties, within the jurisdiction of the United States, by persons acting under the authority of his Catholic Majesty's government; and that although many remonstrances have been made by them to his Catholic Majesty's governors, and to Congress, to remove those grievances, their just demands have not been attended to. It is added, that their Assembly, as the fathers of the people, thinking it their indispensable duty to put a stop to all further depredations, have passed a law which provides for a body of 1,500 men, to be immediately enlisted as regular troops, for three years, to be embodied in one legion and to be commanded by a general of experience. They are to be joined by 500 men from the Cumberland settlements. That they will be in readiness to march this month, and mean to thrash (by Divine Blessing) those perfidious Castilians into better conduct towards the subjects of the United States; and that they received a supply of arms and ammunition from Charleston before the law was passed." The chances are, however, that the information was sent to the *Journal* from Virginia by one who misconceived or exaggerated the situation.

all those who have the spirit and sagacity enough to seek after them. When we reflect on our past indefatigable struggles; both with the savages and other enemies during the late war, and the great difficulty we had to obtain and withhold this country from those enemies at the expense of the lives and fortunes of many of our dearest friends and relatives; and the happy conclusion of peace having arrived, North Carolina has derived great advantages from our alertness in taking and securing a country from which she has been able to draw into her treasury immense sums of money, and thereby become able to pay off, if not wholly, yet a great part and sink her national debt. . . . We, therefore, humbly conceive you will liberally think that it will be nothing more than paying a debt in full to us, only to grant, what God, Nature, and our locality entitle us to receive. Trusting that your magnanimity and justice will not consider it a crime in any people to pray their just rights and privileges, we call the world to testify our conduct and exertions in behalf of American Independency; and the same to whether we ask more than free people ought to claim agreeable to republican principles. . . . Congress hath, from time to time, explained their ideas so fully, and with so much dignity and energy that if their arguments and requisitions will not produce conviction, we know of nothing that will have a greater influence, especially when we recollect that the system referred to is the result of the collected wisdom of the United States; and, should it not be considered as perfect, must be esteemed the least objectionable.

The text of this petition is carried into the Appendix[9] with the signatures attached thereto. The petition was presented to the senate of North Carolina in December, 1787.[10]

The names of Andrew Jackson and Archibald Roane appear alongside as signers—evidently of that copy which was circulated in Greene county. The two men, so distinguished in state and nation in after years, appeared for the first time in the region in 1788.[11] The explanation must be that, on so arriving, their and other signatures were procured and sent forward to be attached, thus extending the petition which should stand for use at some later session of the North Carolina Assembly. The name of Joseph McMinn is also affixed. The fact that these ambitious young men, two of whom were to become governors of Tennessee and one president of the United States, joined promptly in the movement

---

[9] Appendix B.
[10] *N. C. St. Rec.*, XXII, 714.
[11] Jackson was admitted to the bar at Jonesborough, May, 1788, and to the bar at Greeneville, in August, 1788.

for separation argues cogently that they found favoring sentiment strong.

The Assembly of North Carolina met in November. Governor Sevier named an additional commissioner to attend and make an effort to procure consent to separation, hope of which Governor Caswell had so frequently held out earlier in the year. Francis A. Ramsey, a member of the Council of the State, and father of the historian, was selected. He was authorized to propose as an inducement to separation *the assumption by the State of Franklin of the Continental debt of North Carolina.*

The upper counties of Franklin were represented by delegates; Sullivan county by Col. Joseph Martin (senate) John Scott and George Maxwell; Washington county by Col. John Tipton (senate) James Stuart and John Blair; Greene county by Daniel Kennedy (senate) and Judge David Campbell; Hawkins county by Nathaniel Henderson (senate) and William Marshall. General Kennedy appears to have hesitated and delayed his appearance in the senate until late in the session. He and Martin from the senate, and Judge Campbell and Maxwell from the house of commons, served on a committee appointed "for quieting the tumults and disorders in the western parts of this state." The act of pardon and oblivion of the offenses of the insurgents was extended to all who wished to avail of it.[12]

Another request came from Congress to this Assembly urging the cession of the western lands.[13] The petition that came from the West for a separation was disregarded.

Tipton was deprived of his seat as senator, because of illegality in the election; and that he felt the sting was evident from the course he pursued in sending in protests against other proceedings that were intended to lure back the separatists.[14]

The senate passed on the first reading, by a vote of 23 to 22, an act to repeal the repealing act of 1784, and the house of commons did likewise. This would have brought about a cession and separation. Among the leaders of the senate opposing this action was General Thomas Person. General Kennedy, of Greene county, of course supported it; but Colonel Joseph Martin, of Sullivan county, voted against it. Colonel James Robertson of Davidson county,

---

[12] *Acts*, 1787, ch. 27.
[13] *N. C. St. Rec.*, XX, 248, 276.
[14] *N. C. St. Rec.*, XX, 202, 279-80.

stood with the friends of Franklin, though Colonel Anthony Bledsoe of Sumner did not.[16]

The measure was defeated by being left to sleep on the table—whether of purpose from the outset will never be known. But it is manifest that the politicians from the Atlantic counties were too much for those of the western counties. It was no part of their purpose to lose hold on the tempting field. The representations made to the Assembly by Burton, Blount and Hawkins, the States delegates to Congress, had no effect. In an address of the three to that body, read by Benjamin Hawkins, it was said: "The States which have ceded western lands complain pointedly and heavily against North Carolina for claiming a part of the lands in possession of Congress without ceding any part of her claim."

A stinging protest against the course pursued at this session was entered by a man who had lived among the Wataugans and was now residing in, and representing one of the eastern counties of North Carolina, William Tatham. Opposing the action looking to perfection of western titles and the favoring of John Armstrong, entrytaker for western lands, by giving him further time for settling his accounts, Tatham filed a written protest in which he denounced the original opening of that land office as an infringement of the constitutional rights of the people; a premeditated plan having been "laid previous to the opening of said office" to the end of monopolizing the lands; and that the State had been much injured by the speculation consequent thereon.

He referred to grants based on entries of lands in the far-away country of the friendly Chickasaws (now known as West Tennessee) in these words:

"The indulgence granted Colonel Armstrong will be productive of further jealousies and discontents between the white people and the Chickasaw Indians, if not wars, aided or assisted by our Catholic neighbors on the Mississippi; because every future warrant from that office or entries made on the same, will be a further indulgence to our speculators to encroach on the Chickasaw Indians who have so gloriously boasted their friendship for the white people; and, instead of deserving the ingratitude we have shown in trespassing on their lands and taking their lands away without their consent without cause or provocation, have ever shown us an

---

[16] *N. C. St. Rec.*, XX, 241.

CLOSE OF THE CRUCIAL YEAR

example worthy of imitation, and a specimen of magnanimity far above our reach."

Tatham closed by inveighing against the course determined upon as a subordination of the public interest "for the speculation of a junta of individuals."[16]

He, better than any other member, was able to speak from the vantage-ground of knowledge of both the peoples of the West and the East.

By this Assembly, Judge Campbell was elected a judge of the superior court at Jonesborough for the District of Washington, which office he accepted. His action was bitterly resented by his former associates. Haywood quaintly says that Colonel James White, the father of Knoxville and an unyielding Franklinite, "whose yea was yea, and nay was nay, throughout his whole life, deemed the acceptance of this office by Campbell an unpardonable dereliction of duty. Meeting Campbell on the road, as he returned from Tarborough, he upbraided the latter with a desertion of his friends in very undisguised terms of reprobation."

Campbell's action paralyzed the judicial department of the infant Commonwealth of which he had been the head. The courts were to the people the most visible manifestation of government. The defection was as shard in the souls of Sevier and those closest to him. Judge Campbell's course was not disgraceful, but it was both ungraceful and ungracious.

The year 1787 closed, leaving Governor Sevier distraught if not dismayed. Every card dealt by Fate had been against him and his State.

---

[16] *N. C. St. Rec.*, XX, 249. For biographical sketch of Tatham, see Williams, *William Tatham, Wataugan.*

CHAPTER XXVI

THE SEVIER-TIPTON SKIRMISH—1788

Colonel John Tipton, after his rebuff by the Assembly of Carolina, returned home, intent upon pressing his fight to a successful issue. He was left in authority as colonel of his county and clerk of its court, held at Davis's. It was determined that the most effective way of delivering a telling blow at the State of Franklin was to stop the functioning of her courts. Therefore, at the February term of the Carolina court of Washington county, an order was entered "that Jonathan Pugh, Esq., sheriff take into custody the court docket of said county, supposed to be in the possession of John Sevier, Esq." Raids to get possession of court records were now resumed. A correspondent of the Winchester (Virginia) *Advertiser* wrote that "the disturbances for some time past have been very alarming. The Tiptonites and the Franklinites have been constantly in arms against each other. The former have two or three times taken possession of Jonesborough; the Franklinites were lately in possession of the same place. Their succors came in so slowly that they thought it prudent to evacuate the town, and in the evening about 240 Tiptonites appeared so suddenly that the few who were in it were captured." Andrew Caldwell, Francis Baker and Ambrose Yancy were taken and obliged to appear at court where they engaged thereafter to be inactive in the dispute.[1]

Sevier was in Greene county where he had gone to hearten the new-State followers. A few days before (January 24th) he had written to General Daniel Kennedy with the same end in view:

"I have lately received some favorable news from Doctor Franklin, and other gentlemen; also, am happy to inform you that I find our friends very warm and steady—much more so than heretofore. My son can inform you of some late particulars. Anything material your way, will thank you for a sketch of it by my son."

The Franklinites driven from Jonesborough fell back to Greeneville where their leaders were.[2] Word was sent to the strongholds

---
[1] See also same quoted, *Maryland Journal*, Apr. 11, 1788.
[2] *Ib.*

in the lower counties of a rendezvous at Greeneville;[3] and soon the clans under Captain Nathaniel Evans were gathering on the waters of the French Broad to join Sevier.[4]

Sevier had another and personal grievance to be redressed. In the early part of 1788 an execution from a court sitting under the authority of North Carolina had come into the hands of Sheriff Pugh, who levied it on a number of Governor Sevier's slaves, and removed them from his Mount Pleasant farm on Nolachucky river to the home of Colonel Tipton for safe-keeping. Deeming this action illegal, Sevier determined to put an end to the raids on the courts, to suppress open opposition to the authority of the courts of Franklin and to recover his slaves, all in one blow.

Having gathered about one hundred and fifty men, from Greene, Sevier and Caswell counties at Greeneville, he marched to the home of Tipton on Sinking Creek, about one and one-half miles from the present Johnson City. Other men from Washington county joined the force as it passed. In Tipton's house was a guard of about forty-five men.[5]

---

[3] One of the calls for aid was sent by Sevier from the home of Major Christopher Taylor, west of Jonesborough (Feb. 11th) probably as Sevier was *en route* to Greene county. It was addressed to Captain John Zahaun (Seehorn) Caswell county (Seehorn's Ferry, near the present town of Dandridge): "I am informed that the Tipton party has got very insolent, and have been guilty of several cruelties and barbarous actions. I have ordered fifteen men out of each company to turn out; and am well satisfied that the men of Sevier county will turn out bravely. I beg you will use your influence to get as many men out of your neighborhood to turn out as may be in your power. I shall expect your company up. I am satisfied that a small exertion will settle the matter to our satisfaction. Pray speak to Mr. Allen and let us raise as many men as in our power. For further particulars, I beg leave to refer to the bearer [James Sevier]. Ramsey, 413.

[4] "Coming to one of my appointments on French Broad, in the afternoon of one of the coldest days I ever witnessed in that country, I found a large company of armed men there, going to attack Colonel Tipton in his own house where he had fortified himself." Rev. Thomas Ware, *Sketches of Life and Travels*.

[5] This account of the Sevier-Tipton battle is based on the accounts given by Haywood, who was followed in the main by Ramsey; by Colonel Tipton in his report to General Joseph Martin, *N. C. State Records*, XXII, 691; by Maxwell to Colonel Arthur Campbell, Mar. 10, 1788, *Draper MSS.*, Vol. IX, 47; by General Wm. Russell in *Maryland Journal*, Apr. 8, 1788; Statements of Major John Sevier, *Draper MSS.*, 32 S, pp. 140, 180, 210-213; Rev. Thomas Ware, *Life and Travels;* communication from Washington county, June 10th, *State Gazette*, South Carolina, Sept. 1, 1788; Statement of son of Col. John Tipton, *Draper*, XX, vol. 5, p. 40; *Maryland Journal*, Apr. 11, 1788. The last account says Tipton had "not more than 60 or 70 men" but Tipton's son says 45. Haywood gives 15 as the number. Tipton

Sevier's force arrived in the afternoon of February 27th and first took a position about a quarter of a mile away from Tipton's house. Sevier then sent in a flag with a communication requesting a surrender within thirty minutes.[6]

Tipton gave only a verbal reply: that he asked no favors, and if Sevier would surrender himself and his leaders they all should have the benefit of North Carolina's laws. At this time a company from the eastern part of Washington county (now Carter county) under Captain Peter Parkinson, responding to a call for aid from Tipton, appeared upon the scene. The Sevier troopers opened fire on this company and killed three horses. Parkinson's contingent was driven back, temporarily at least. Two women coming out of Tipton's house were fired upon by mistake, and one was wounded in the shoulder.

Sevier seems now to have proposed a siege of the Tipton house.

---

had been busy ordering in reinforcements. He had kept in touch with the plans of the Franks. On Monday, February 25th, he wrote to Colonel Robert Love, in command of the militia of Greasy Cove, Washington county (now Unicoi county) as follows: "The rebels are again rising; Sevier is now making his last effort; he has given orders to his officers below to draft fifteen men out of each company, and to take property from those that will not serve and give to those that will. This day they are to meet at Greene; tomorrow at Jonesborough, and Wednesday, if not before, make a push here. I therefore request you to give orders to officers in the Cove to collect their men with the greatest expedition and march to my house tomorrow, fixed in ample manner; as I propose to defend this quarter, without making any excursions, unless I can get further information. N. B. Let no time be lost." Ramsey, 414.

[6] "State of Franklin, February 27th, 1788. In a Council of the Officers to secure the rights of the Citizens in this State, and from Motives to Establish Peace and Good Order:

"It is our request to Colonel John Tipton that he and the party now in the house surrender themselves to the discretion of the people of Franklin within thirty minutes from the arrival of the flag of truce.

"John Sevier, C. Gen'l.

"Honored by Colonel Conway."

The officers in command under Sevier were Col. Henry Conway, Col. Charles Robertson and Major George Elholm.

The house of Tipton is standing today. The log house has, however, been covered with weatherboarding. It is said that the bullet marks may be seen in the logs beneath. In after years, the farm of Tipton was owned and the house occupied for many years by Landon C. Haynes, Confederate State Senator from Tennessee. The house stands on the right of the highway and of the line of the Carolina, Clinchfield and Ohio Railway, running from Johnson City to Erwin, and in sight of the former place.

He ordered all passes to that house guarded. A party of which his son James was a member, occupied a rocky eminence west of the house the night of the 27th. Colonel Love secretly escaped from the house and under cover of darkness made his way toward Greasy Cove to raise more men. He met his brother, Thomas Love, with ten or twelve men coming to join the Tiptonites. The night being exceeding cold, the guard under young Sevier had left their post and gone to the camp-fire to warm. In this way the men under the Loves reached the home of Tipton unobserved.

The next morning Sevier sent in another flag with a communication of milder nature. Tipton replied demanding submission and said: "if they would acquiesce I would disband my troops and countermand the march of the troops from Sullivan." This was directed to "Colonel" John Sevier. Sevier's officers, offended at this, pretended to believe that the message was for Valentine Sevier, a brother of the governor, and it was by them replied that Colonel Sevier was not in camp and that they undertook to answer themselves to say: that as they were not uneasy about the forces now on the grounds; and, as to the troops on the march from Sullivan, they could countermand the march themselves, without putting Colonel Tipton to any trouble. It is probable that the officers in the Sevier camp thought that Tipton referred to Parkinson's company which, they knew, had been turned back.

A light field piece was placed on a hill overlooking the Tipton place. Major Elholm, second in command, in order to make short work and obviate the danger incident to delay proposed the erection of a light movable overcover, and a prompt advance of the troops under its protection; but Sevier did not assent. A part of the command was engaged in foraging for supplies for the troops and their horses. Certificates of the State of Franklin were given for the supplies impressed for that purpose.[7]

Toward evening William Cox came into the Sevier camp and gave information that the militia of Sullivan was embodying to

---

[7] One of these certificates reads:

"State of Franklin, February 28th, 1788.

"Received four bushels of meal at two shillings per bushel for the use of said State. Given under my hand this said date.
"Received from Jonathan Pugh.

"Drury Robertson, Captain."

Pugh, who as sheriff had levied on Sevier's slaves, was thus made to aid the effort to retake them. He was to forfeit his life, in the battle of the next day.

reinforce Tipton, and would that night cross the Watauga river at Dungan's mill ford,[8] about six miles distant. "Cox was thought to act a doubtful if not double part, and many gave no heed to his information." However, two of the young blades, Captain Joseph Hardin, son of Colonel Joseph Hardin, and John Sevier, Jr., with a party of forty men started, out of abundance of caution, for the ford to dispute the passage of the Sullivan troops should they attempt it. When within half a mile of the ford, the men under Hardin and Sevier, suffering from the bitter cold, refused to go further, seeing no signs of a foe and believing the intelligence to be a hoax.

Cox, however, had acted in good faith, and the men under Colonels Maxwell and Pemberton were allowed to collect in a body at Dungan's on the night of the 28th in response to urgent appeals from Colonel Tipton. From this rendezvous they marched at an early hour the next morning, undiscovered and unmolested. Before sunrise they were at Tipton's. A very heavy fall of snow aided in screening them from the view of Sevier's pickets and troops. A party of Franks composed of Captain John Sevier, Jr., and his brother James, and thirty others, all mounted, at daybreak "went out on a scout, and as they passed along the lane fronting the house of Tipton, they were fired upon, the balls rattling on the fence, they at full gallop. None was injured."

The troops under Maxwell, says Haywood, fired a volley and raised a shout which seemed to reach heaven, announcing that deliverance was at hand for the besieged. From the house the shout was reëchoed as the force under Colonel Tipton sallied, joining the Sullivan troops in an attack on the dismayed Franks in Sevier's camp.

The battle now commenced. After the first volley from the Carolinians, the Sevier forces, abandoning the small piece of ordnance, camp equipment, saddles, etc., retreated to an eminence not far from their camp which being gained a number of shots were returned on the attacking force. Webb, of the Sullivan county force was killed and Jonathan Pugh, high sheriff of Washington county, was wounded and died eight days after the action. About six other Tiptonites were wounded. The attack being pressed with firmness, the Franks were soon dislodged, and, not able to discern in the blinding storm the size of the attacking force, beat a retreat

---

[8] On the place of James P. St. John, near Watauga station of the Southern railway, and just below the railway bridge that spans the Watauga river.

toward Jonesborough. In this action John Smith, on the side of Sevier, had his thigh broken and died from the effects a few weeks afterward. Henry Polley was wounded in the hip.

The casualties would have been greater but for the heavy snowfall. Ramsey, however, on the authority of men who were in the engagement, says that many men, of both parties, fired into the air purposely, to avoid the shedding of blood; and this seems probable when we recall how expert all were in the use of firearms.

The scouting party out under Captain Sevier, on hearing the volleys near the camp, hastened back and on riding up saw the flag of the Franklinites still flying above the camp. They did not suspect that so sudden and complete a change had taken place. But a volley from the Tiptonites arrested them and "some few, amazed and wondering, were pulled from their horses and called upon to surrender, among these John Sevier, Jr., James Sevier, and their cousin, John Sevier," and sixteen others. Gasper Fant of this party was wounded in the arm, and "Samuel Beard, who had on a red overcoat received several balls through it but escaped unhurt."

That night, on the intercession of Colonel Love, the young Seviers were permitted, on pledge of honor to return, to go with the wounded John Smith to the home of the latter. They returned on the next day and gave bond for their appearance at court and were set at liberty. Colonel Love signed as their surety.

Haywood is authority for the statement that Tipton was determined to hang the two sons of Governor Sevier:

"Apprized of the rash step he intended to take, the young men sent for Mr. Thomas Love, and others of Tipton's part, with whom they had a good understanding, and solicited their intercession with Tipton. Those persons went directly to him and represented in strong terms the rashness, illegality and impolicy of the intended execution. They urged their arguments so effectually that, with tears flowing down his cheeks at the mention of his own sons, supposing them to be in possession of Sevier about to be executed by him for offenses imputed to their father, he pronounced himself too womanly for any manly office, and desisted from his purpose."[9]

---

[9] In his letter to Draper, a son of Colonel Tipton, Jonathan Tipton, undertakes to correct errors in Haywood's account of the Sevier-Tipton battle, but he registers no denial of this statement. He construes Haywood to mean that two sons of Tipton were, in fact, taken prisoners by Sevier, and denies that such was true. *Draper MSS.*, XX, vol. 5, p. 40.

However, the little battle was not without its humorous phases. Major John Sevier left on record the story that when the rout of the Franks began Major Elholm bawled out: "Halt, form, Colonel Robertson!" Robertson, who talked through his nose and had not time for extended remarks, replied gruffly: "Damnation, I'll halt for no man!"

George W. Sevier, a son of the governor, related this incident to Draper: Sevier's negro servant, Tobe, was among the prisoners taken and conducted to Tipton's front yard to be there guarded. Strolling about the lawn, Tobe was asked by one of the guards to whom he belonged. "To the Sullivan troops, sir," was the quick-witted reply. Surveillance being relaxed, Tobe sauntered off, soon saw his opportunity, mounted a good horse and dashed off, leaping the yard fence. A gunshot failed to hit him or to stop him.

Ramsey describes the demeanor of Sevier during the siege, as represented by those who were of his party, to have been very different from that which was usual. He was silent and morose. In his abstraction even Elholm's vivacity failed to arouse him. He communicated little with his officers and suggested no plans, either of attack or defense. The fact that in the besieged house and opposing force were many of his former friends, who could no longer follow his fortunes, grieved him to the point of making him no longer the purposeful and resourceful campaigner.

Colonel Joseph Hamilton, Sr., is quoted to the effect that Sevier made repeated efforts to compromise, sending Captain John Cowan time and again, under flag, for that purpose; but without avail.[10]

Tipton's forces followed in pursuit of the retreating Franks, but before going far they were met by Robert Young, Jr., with a verbal message from Sevier, asking for time to consider terms. Colonels Maxwell and Tipton replied, giving until the 11th inst., for the purpose.

Sevier's reply has been preserved. It was addressed to Tipton: "I received the flag sent by yourself and Colonel Maxwell. The answer thereto is sent by Messrs. Young and Evans. You can discover the purport and sentiment of the officers. As to my own part, I am at liberty to do for myself. I wish you would be so good as to write me particularly from under your own hand, setting forth the

---

[10] Ramsey, 412.

terms in plain manner, and let me know what I have to depend on, and I shall answer you by the 11th inst., agreeable to your flag."[11]

Colonel Tipton stated to his brigadier-general that he proposed a submission to the laws of North Carolina. Sevier and his followers went south to Greeneville, where, on March 3rd, a council of officers was held and its conclusion was forwarded to Colonels Tipton and Maxwell by Young and Evans:

"We have received your flag of truce, dated 29th February, 1788, but as we do not fully comprehend its contents you have not put it in our power to give any answer thereto. But it is the sentiment of our council, equally now as heretofore, to be amenable to the laws of the Union for our conduct; and flatter ourselves that you will be answerable to the same laws for your proceedings. And, actuated by the principles of humanity and justice and discretion of the people, and honor of both parties, this council wishes that a convention of the people may be called at the earliest opportunity. In the meantime, this council remains peaceably disposed until the arrival of another flag of truce from you. As a proof of our peaceable disposition, we have already given up some property taken, and are willing to give up the rest; and hope that your party will also return the property that fell into your hands.

"John Sevier, P."[12]

Sevier, conceiving that his term of office as governor expired March 1st, no longer undertook to act in that capacity. He signed as president of the council.

Neither party could assure the other; at base was a deep distrust of the other's intentions. And, in fact, not without some reason. Tipton and Maxwell had on the 10th sent a call on Colonel Arthur Campbell for volunteers from Virginia, to "quell the insurrection"; satisfied as they were that "Sevier is trying to raise another party."[13]

This was not true of Sevier, but General Cocke, in Spencer (Hawkins) county, was (17th) issuing "orders to Thomas Henderson to raise the militia of their party to march against Colonel Tipton."[14]

Tipton in particular, was for punitory action. On March 11th,

---

[11] *N. C. State Records*, XXII, 695.

[12] *N. C. State Records*, XXII, 715.

[13] *Draper MSS.*, XX, 47. Another call, it seems was sent on the 12th, in which it was stated that Parkinson's home had been fired on.

[14] Hutchings to Martin, *N. C. State Records*, XXI, 716.

he issued to Colonel Robert Love an order: "You will cause the men of Greasy Cove to be notified to appear at my house on Saturday evening next, well equipped with arms and ammunition, and six days provisions. Those that have arms, etc., and do not comply, take and give to those that will serve."

On the 16th he with his force was at the home of Abednego Inman, from which he wrote to General Kennedy of Greene county that his business was not to disturb or molest the inhabitants, but rather to protect them. "As I am persuaded that you have the interest of the country at large at heart, if it should coincide with your approbation you should bring the commissions to Greene Court House tomorrow, for the purpose of establishing a court, so that the inhabitants may be exempt of the penalty prescribed by law."

Both Sevier and Kennedy had been away on the frontiers since the 10th; and Colonel Tipton's march was fruitless.

Joseph Martin, the successor of Evan Shelby in command of the brigade west of the mountains, had been absent. On his return, he asked for a report from Tipton as one of his colonels and seemed a bit querulous in respect of Tipton's actions; particularly about his treatment of Gilbert Christian, a follower of Sevier. Martin, from frequent consultations with the executives of North Carolina, knew that diplomacy and not war was the policy of the State. He conceived himself fitted by long experience to play the part of diplomat and now essayed the role. From this time forward Tipton was to play a minor part.

Knowing that Sevier and Kennedy were closely knit in friendship, General Martin wrote the latter on March 21st:

> I am greatly distressed and alarmed at the late proceedings of our countrymen and friends, and must beg your friendly interposition, in order to bring about a reconciliation, which, you well know, was my object in accepting the brigadier's commission. I am, perhaps, as little afraid of stepping forth in the field of action as any other man; but I would be sorry to imbrue my hands in the blood of my countrymen and friends, and will take every method in my power to prevent anything of that nature. In our present situation, nothing will do but a submission to the laws of North-Carolina, which I most earnestly recommend to the people. You well know this is the only way to bring about a separation, and also a reconciliation for our worthy friend, whose situation at this time is very disagreeable. I most sensibly feel for him, and will go very great lengths to

serve him. Pray see him often, and give him all the comfort you can.

I am told that a certain officer says, that if I issue an order for a reconciliation, that it shall not be obeyed; but I shall let that gentleman know that I am not to be trifled with. Pray write me all what the people will do, and whether you will accept your commission, which I hope you will. Have the militia immediately officered and prepared for action, as I expect a general Indian war shortly. Please give my best respects to the people in general. Tell them my object is reconciliation, not war.

Martin wrote to Governor Samuel Johnston, successor of Caswell (March 24th) that "confusion in the West was truly alarming."

I sent Saturday last to Sevier and his party requiring them to lay down arms, but can get no answer, only from Colo. Joseph Hardin which I forward. Though I know that on Friday last they [the Franklinites] met in convention to concert some plan. The bearer of my express informs me that he understood that Sevier had gone towards French Broad river since the 10th instant; that Colonel Kennedy and several others had gone the same way to carry on an expedition against the Cherokee Indians, which I am well assured wish to be at peace except the Chickamauga party, which could be easily drove out of that country if your Excellency should recommend it. I am somewhat doubtful that Sevier and his party are embodying, under the color of an Indian expedition to amuse us, and that their object is to make another attack on the citizens of this State, to prevent which I have ordered the different colonels to have their men in good order until I could hear from your Excellency. . . .

Private papers are in circulation in many parts for the people to sign in opposition to the laws of this State, setting forth that the taxes are heavier than they can bear; that the poll-tax is four dollars, etc. . . .

Should the Franklinites still persist to oppose the laws of this State, would it not be well to order General McDowell to give some assistance, as a few men from there [North Carolina] will convince them that North Carolina is determined to protect their citizens. The leaders of the rebel party assure the people that North Carolina will not interfere, and that we are to settle the dispute among ourselves.[15]

Sevier himself had not gone on an Indian campaign. He wrote, on March 27th, from Greeneville to Martin, in reference to the latter's letter of solicitation to Kennedy:

Yours of the 21st instant is now before me. I consider myself

---

[15] *N. C. State Records*, XXI, 459.

under obligations to any friend for his interposition in time of distress, but in the meantime beg leave to assure you that, in my opinion, I have acted no part in behalf of Franklin but what I have been justly authorized to do by the laws of North Carolina, which State is the author of all these disturbances. I have served North Carolina in public character for many years. In the height of her calamities I was faithful; and you are well acquainted that I made every exertion where few others dared to mention the name of Independence. Yourself are a witness that I was dragged into the Franklin measures by a large number of the people of this country. I have been faithful, and my own breast acquits myself that I have acted no part but what has been consistent with honor and justice, tempered with clemency and mercy. How far our pretended patriots have supported me as their pretended chief magistrate, I leave the world at large to judge.

I never meant to spill blood on any occasion to the latest period of my time in office, though, unfortunately for some, it has been the case, but contrary to my orders; and their fate I do sincerely lament. I am now a private citizen sometime since. I have supported the authority of Franklin during my continuance in office; and, if the people have not spirit enough to support it further, I shall not concern myself more than to secure my person and friends from the hands of ruffians and assassinators. It is my wish that a peace and good order may take place in this country.

If it is your wish that hostilities cease, you must request your officers to act accordingly. Otherwise, should armed men range through the country it will exasperate the people, and I know not what may be the consequence. If myself and friends can be protected and unmolested until your North Carolina Assembly, we shall let all matters lie, and the people at large must act as they see fit. What I mean by my friends is, those that have been active in behalf of Franklin. I am determined to share fate equally with those that have stood by me, and live and die together.

If you think proper, I will meet you at any time. Colonel Hardin will inform you where we can have an interview, and you may rest assured that you will suffer no insults whatever. And I shall be glad how soon you can make it convenient to attend in order to compromise the irksome dispute.[16]

Sevier felt confident in appealing to Martin's own recollection for confirmation of the fact that he had been dragged into the Franklin movement. Martin's reply to this manly letter is not preserved, but its contents may be gathered from Sevier's next communication to him of date April 3rd:

I have just been honored with your letter with respect to an

---

[16] *Calendar Virginia State Papers*, IV, 416.

accommodation of our unhappy disturbances. I am ready to suspend all kind of hostilities and prosecutions on our part, and bury in total oblivion all past conduct. If you and the officers under your command will accede to like measures until the rising of the next North Carolina Assembly, and be guided by the deliberations of that body, peace and order may immediately take place."[17]

Both Martin and Colonel Arthur Campbell wrote to Governor Randolph of Virginia, assuring him that the commotions in Franklin had subsided.

But the tumult and violence, once started, were not so easily and promptly quelled.

Bishop Asbury, writing in his journal of preaching at Nelson's, in Colonel Tipton's immediate neighborhood, made this entry under date of May 6, 1788: "The people are in disorder about the old and the new State.... At Nelson's I had a less audience than was expected, the people having been called away on an expedition against the new-State men."[18]

On April 10th, Sevier wrote to the Governor of Georgia that "our country is, at this time, almost in a state of anarchy, occasioned, as we suggest, by the North Carolinians stimulating a party to act in a hostile manner against us;" and once more he expressed the purpose to aid with a considerable number of volunteers in any campaign against the Creeks.[19]

The stipulation of the pact of accommodation against straggling bands and molestation was not kept; but not because of blame immediately attributable to either Martin or Sevier. The animosities engendered in the little civil war now found vent in feuds in the upper counties; and in some instances no doubt bad men availed of the opportunity offered to wreak private vengeance. It was difficult for the law to set bounds to the forces that had been loosed. The compact failed; and seemingly neither Sevier nor Martin reproached the other as blameworthy because of it.

---

[17] *Calendar Virginia State Papers*, IV, 421.
[18] *Asbury's Journal*, II, 32.
[19] Ramsey, 414.

CHAPTER XXVII

Occurrences on the Border—1788

Sevier not unwisely determined that his presence in his home county would not tend to tranquillize the turmoil. He, therefore, made headquarters at Greeneville. Soon there was need of his services as leader in a campaign against the Indians, who were tempted to activity by the fratricidal strife among the white people. Evidence that the danger from the savages was real and imminent comes from leaders of both factions. March 17th Colonel Hutchings reported to General Martin that the situation in his quarter bore "a very disagreeable aspect. The inhabitants within six miles of my house have forted on account of the Indians. ... I daily am pressed upon to carry a campaign against Chickamauga."[1]

Martin (April 17th) reported to the governor of Virginia the alarmed state of the frontiers throughout the whole of Franklin on account of the incursions of Indians. "Mr. White,[2] in particular, who has been a great advocate for the State of Franklin, sends to James Robertson for aid;" and in a later communication to the governor he said, "I fear it will be out of my power to keep the people back much longer."[3]

On April 24th Martin went to the settlement on the lower Holston to make an effort to allay the excitement, only to find on arrival that a man and a boy had been recently killed and a number of men were in arms for an avenging foray. He finally persuaded this party to choose four of their number to accompany him to the Cherokee towns to ascertain whether the nearby Cherokees were guilty of the murders. Martin believed that the Chickamaugas were responsible. On investigation the whites were satisfied that this was the fact, and Martin prevailed on the Cherokees to remain in their towns and plant corn, he agreeing to stay among them at the request of the Cherokees and their white neighbors.

---

[1] *N. C. St. Rec.*, XXII, 715.

[2] James White, the founder of Knoxville.

[3] *Calendar Virginia State Papers*, IV, 424, 428, 432.

Unfortunately, about the 15th of May, a white family was killed within nine miles of Chota, and two parties gathered to chastise the Cherokees. Martin met one of these and turned it back. The other proceeded to attack and burn one of the towns; and the Indians, believing that Martin was deceiving them, were incensed. They put Martin under guard for several days. He finally persuaded them that their suspicions were baseless, and "they let him go, but told him had any of their men been killed, his life must have gone for theirs."[4] The murders were the work of the Chickamaugas and Creeks, Martin persuaded himself but not the border people.

General Martin being unwilling to act as brigadier against the Indians without authority from the far-away government of North Carolina,[5] Sevier's work was cut out for him both by circumstance and the will of the people.[6]

Martin left Chota on May 24th, and on reaching the French Broad river learned that Sevier was at the head of a force raised to go against the Cherokees. Martin turned back to the Indian towns to move off his negroes, horses, etc. Then turning again northward, he met and endeavored to dissuade Sevier, but to no purpose. At the head of one hundred mounted riflemen Sevier pressed forward to find Chota abandoned. He then struck a town on the Hiwassee river. Surprising the Indians, he killed a number and burned the town, which, Colonel Hutchings reported, "so raised him in the esteem of the people of the frontier that the people began to flock to his standard."[7]

Returning to Hunter's Station, the next day they made a push up the Little Tennessee river to Tallassee town, from which the Indians fled to the nearby mountains pursued by the white troops. Many of them were killed.

Next came a deed of grievous cruelty, news of which was received with horror by the saner inhabitants of Franklin and the entire western people, and stained the records of the campaign. It

---

[4] *State Gazette* of South Carolina, Sept. 1, 1788. See also *State Dep. MSS.*, 150, Vol. II, Martin to Secretary Knox, July 15, 1788. Martin had just been appointed assistant to the superintendent of the Southern Indians.

[5] *Calendar Virginia State Papers*, IV, 424, *et seq.*

[6] Martin wrote to the governor of Virginia in April that he "expected nothing but a troublesome, bloody war with the savages this summer." *N. C. St. Records*, XXII, 693.

[7] *N. C. State Records*, XXI, 718; Roosevelt, *Winning of the West*, IV, ch. IV.

can only be fully understood when its background is seen, as given by Haywood.[8]

In the raids, made by the Indians in May and now being punished, there had been an act of atrocious treachery and murder committed by them. The Kirk family lived on the southwest side of Little river, twelve miles south of the present site of Knoxville. While Kirk was away from home an Indian, Slim Tom, or Chilhowee, well known to the family, came to the house and asked for food, which was given him. He withdrew, having noted the defenceless situation of those in the house. Slim Tom soon returned from the woods with a party of Indians, fell upon the family and massacred the whole number present, eleven. John Kirk, upon returning home, saw the dead bodies lying on the ground. He gave the alarm, and word was sent to the militia under the command of Sevier, who collected a force at Hunter's Station, on Nine Mile Creek, which runs into the Holston on the south side. The troopers, with this outrage rankling in their hearts, were now out to administer punishment. John Kirk, a son of him whose family had been massacred, was of their number.

After leaving Tallassee the militia proceeded toward Chilhowee town down the Little Tennessee river. Sevier was absent, which unfortunately left Major Hubbard in command. Abraham, a friendly chief residing at Chilhowee, had declared publicly that if his people went to war he would not quit his home to engage in it. The Tassel (Corn Tassel) who for years had endeavored to keep the peace with the whites, also remained at home. Hubbard sent for Abraham to come over the river to him. White flags had been displayed by the Indians and the troops. Abraham answered the summons and was requested to bring over The Tassel and his son in order that both might be held. When they came, all were put in a house into which young Kirk found his way, Hubbard going in with him. Kirk there drove his tomahawk into the heads of the five or six Indians, including the two chiefs.

Sevier, on his return, saw what would be the result of the rash and savage act, and remonstrated with Kirk who answered that it was an eye for an eye, and that any man, even Sevier himself would have acted in like manner under the same provocation.

The enemies of Sevier charged him with complicity in volition-

---

[8] Haywood, 181; Ramsey, 419; Roosevelt, IV, ch. IV; *N. C. State Records*, XXII, 695; Goodpasture, *Indian Wars and Warriors*, Tennessee Historical Magazine, IV.

ally absenting himself; but this he denied. He was acquitted by those who were on the ground, and by Kirk himself.[9]

This bloody scene, terminating the immediate campaign, shocked the conservative element throughout the western counties; and great indignation was excited throughout the entire country. The Continental Congress passed resolutions condemning the act; and Andrew Pickens in behalf of the justices of Abbeville county, South Carolina, wrote in protest and denunciation "to the people living on Nolechucke, French Broad and Holstein."[10]

Early in June Brigadier-General Martin projected a campaign against the Chickamauga Indians. A council of officers holding Carolina commissions was held at Hawkins's Court House (Rogersville) to make plans. Martin astutely drew Colonel Outlaw into coöperation by asking that he act as commissary officer. By the aid of Colonel Outlaw, Colonel Daniel Kennedy was induced to accept command of the quota of troops allotted to Greene county.[11] A second council was held at Sullivan Court House on the second Monday of June, when the expedition was abandoned. Ardor had cooled.

---

[9] Kirk to John Watts, now become chief warrior of the Cherokee Nation, dated October 17, 1788:

"Sir: I have heard of your letter lately sent to Chucky John [Sevier]. You are mistaken in blaming him for the death of your uncle. Listen now to my story. For days and months the Cherokee Indians, big and little, women and children, have been fed and treated kindly by my mother. When all was at peace with the Tennessee towns, Slim Tom with a party of Sattigo and other Cherokee Indians, murdered my mother, brothers and sisters in cold blood, when children just before were playful about them as friends; at the instant some of them received the bloody tomahawk they were smiling in their faces. This began the war; and since I have taken ample satisfaction can now make peace except with Slim Tom. Our beloved men, the Congress, tells us to be at peace; I will listen to their advice if no more blood is shed by the Cherokees, and the headmen of your nation take care to prevent such beginnings of bloodshed in all time to come. But if they do not, your people may feel something more to keep up remembrance of

"John Kirk, Jun.
"Captain of the Bloody Rangers."

Georgia State Gazette, April 25, 1789.

[10] Roosevelt, citing letter of Justices, July 9, 1788, *State Department MSS*. Roosevelt contends that Sevier should be held responsible for the murders, but Haywood acquits him of blame: "Sevier never acted with cruelty before or since; he was never accused of inhumanity; he could not have given his consent on this occasion." Haywood's *History*, 183.

[11] Kennedy to Martin, June 6, 1788. Library of Congress, *State Dept. MSS.*, II, p. 439.

General Martin left his jurisdiction later in June, and wrote that he was doubtful as to the date of return. Maxwell, one of his own colonels, wrote him to come back. "Your presence was never more wanted than on this occasion. A number of people say you are an Indian's friend, and they'll warrant we won't see you till the campaign is over, while your friends assert the contrary. Your conduct at this crisis will consummate your character in this country."[12]

At this time Sevier was planning to go against the Chickamaugas in their strongholds. A fort, called Houston's Station, was now erected, sixteen miles south of Knoxville and six miles from the present site of the town of Maryville; and Major Thomas Stewart was placed in command. From there (July 8) Sevier and Hubbard addressed an appeal which explains the delay in executing their plan:

To the Inhabitants in general: Yesterday we crossed the Tennessee[13] with a small party of men and destroyed a town called Toquo. On our return we discovered large trails of Indians making their way toward this place. We are of the opinion their number could not be less than five hundred. We beg to recommend that every station be on their guard; that also, every good man that can be spared will voluntarily turn out and repair to this place with the utmost expedition, in order to tarry for a few days in the neighborhood and repel the enemy, if possible. We intend waiting at this place some days with the few men now with us, as we cannot reconcile it to our own feelings to leave a people who appear to be in such great distress.

John Sevier,
James Hubbard.

N.B. It will be necessary for those who will be so grateful as to come to the assistance of this place, to furnish themselves with a few days provisions, as the inhabitants of this part are greatly distressed by the Indians.

J. S.
J. H."[14]

Maxwell attributed the delay of Sevier to "the severity of the Indians and the disaffection of the rubites." But it was the rubes who held the Indians back, turning out time and again under that knight of the saddle, Captain Nathaniel Evans, and his followers to meet repeated onslaughts of the Indians.

---

[12] Maxwell to Martin (July 9), *N. C. State Records*, XXII, 718.
[13] Now known as the Little Tennessee river.
[14] Ramsey, 419.

On Friday, August 8th, a party of thirty-one, under Captain Fain, a part of the guard at Houston Station, joined by a party of settlers, crossed the Little Tennessee at a point about nine miles distant. Tempted by the fruit in an orchard in the vicinity of the abandoned Indian town, Cittico, they stopped to gather apples. The Indians surrounded them, drove them into the river, killed sixteen and wounded four. The Indians had taken possession of the ford, and as the whites endeavored to swim across the stream many were slaughtered in the water.[15]

General Martin on his return to the West found that the Indians were growing bolder and more ferocious in their attacks on the frontier settlements. He was compelled to subordinate the character of Indian agent to that of brigadier, and reluctantly to lead a military expedition against the Cherokees without having obtained the consent of the governor of North Carolina. A second and successful effort was made to organize for an expedition. The council of officers was held at Jonesborough, August 19th, where the result was thus recorded:

That it is the opinion of the council that an expedition is absolutely necessary, and that every exertion ought to be used to carry it into effect.

That it is the unanimous opinion of this council that Brigadier-General Martin ought to command the said expedition.

That the campaign consist of 1,000 men; viz: 700 mounted infantry and 300 foot to go by water.

That Colonel Outlaw be directed to purchase or impress, on the rivers Chucky and French Broad, as many boats and canoes as will transport 150 men with provisions to Chickamauga. That Mr. Doak,[16] commissary for Hawkins, purchase or impress, as many boats and canoes on Holston as will carry a like number.

That the several commissaries will be directed to purchase immediately and have carried to the general rendezvous a sufficient quantity of provisions.[17]

One-half the number of men called for enlisted for the cam-

---

[15] *Maryland Journal*, Sept. 16, 1788. This account gives the names of the killed and wounded: Killed—John Fain, captain; Caleb Jones, Joseph Alexander, Van Piercefield, William Long, Jonathan Dean, John Brannon, William English, John Medlock, Robert Houston, George Matthews, Isaac Anderson, Charles Payne, Luther Johnson, Hermon Gregg, and George Buly. Wounded—John Kirk, Thomas Brown and —— Bullock.

[16] Samuel Doak, but not the minister and educator.

[17] *State Dept. MSS.*, p. 357.

paign.[18] Colonel Robert Love commanded the soldiers from Washington county, Colonel Kennedy those from Greene county, and Colonel George Doherty those from the French Broad section. General Martin led the men of Sullivan county. Colonel Thomas Hutchings, of Hawkins, who had thirsted for the gore of Franklinites, was not on the expedition, it seems.

The rendezvous was at White's Fort (Knoxville) on the Holston, and it is probable that the entire command went as mounted infantrymen.

A rapid march was made down the valley of the Tennessee. Two Indian towns were laid waste as the troops passed. They arrived at Lookout Mountain late in the afternoon, too late to make a crossing of the river. They camped for the night on the site of an old Indian field. A detachment of fifty men under Colonel Doherty was sent forward to take possession of a narrow defile or pass and to hold it until the next morning. But the Indians had anticipated this move, and from a point of vantage on the mountain fired upon the party and drove them back. During the night the Indians reinforced and prepared for a stubborn defense. The troops spent the entire night holding the bridles of their horses. Early next morning spies were sent out to reconnoitre. They also were fired upon, and William Cunningham, of Doherty's command wounded. A large division was now ordered forward to force a passage. The men had to march single file, zigzagging among the rocks between the bluff and the river. It was the custom of the captains to march at the head of their companies in attacking. The Indians, concealed behind rocks and trees, poured down on them a sudden and destructive fire. Among the many killed were three captains, John Hardin, son of Colonel Joseph Hardin, Fuller and Gibson. Captains Joseph Bullard and George Vincent were wounded. Great confusion followed. The place was such that it was impracticable to rally the men until they were withdrawn to the foot of the mountain. Some fled back to the encampment, declaring that it would prove another Blue Lick affair if they went beyond the pass. General Martin endeavored to rally his force, but most of them refused to follow him farther and broke up into independent

---

[18] The *Martin MSS.* state that the number was 1,000, evidently having in mind the number called; Haywood and Ramsey say 450; Weeks's *Martin* "some 800," and Goodpasture, "about 500."

squads. Left with about sixty men, the commander was obliged to call a retreat.[19]

The situation was a difficult one for General Martin, even if he had made no mistake in directing the attack at such a place. Because of his close personal connection with the Cherokees[20] and because, as long-time agent of the government among them, he had frequently taken the part of the redmen against the whites, he had not the full confidence of his troopers.[21]

He did not have the skill and experience of their tried and trusted "Nolachucky Jack." The failure of the campaign emboldened the Indians to raid the settlements.

The first retaliatory foray was made against Sherrill's Station by two hundred Indians. Sevier, with forty horsemen, out ranging, came upon the trail of the savages. Following the trail they arrived at the station just as the Indians were engaged in setting fire to buildings under cover of darkness. At a given signal Sevier's men charged; the redmen gave way and the rescuers were welcomed with joy by the besieged. The *North Carolina State Gazette* stated that the exploit was "performed to the governor of Franklin's usual good fortune; not a man of his party was hurt."

---

[19] The account of this campaign is based upon that of William Martin, son of General Martin (written for Draper) in *Southern History Association Proceedings*, IV, 464; Ramsey, 517, and Weeks's *General Joseph Martin*, 463.

[20] Martin, while living among the Cherokees, had married a daughter (Betsy) of the celebrated Nancy Ward, and grand-niece of Atakullakulla. She was living as late as 1800, on a fine estate at Wakhovee on the south side of Hiwassee river, fifty miles from Tellico Blockhouse, and was still called Mrs. Martin. Williams, *Early Travels*, 490.

[21] The muster rolls of this campaign, yet in existence, show the following officers under Gen. Martin, down to and including the captains: Colonels: George Doherty, Thos. Gillespie, Daniel Kennedy and John Scott. Majors: Thomas King and John Newman. Captains: Francis Berry, Alexander Brown, Joseph Casey, James Cooper, John Crafford, John Fegan, John Hardin, John Hunter, Samuel McGayha, James Moore, Moses Moore, John Mahon, John Miller, James Richardson, Thos. Vincent and Moses Webb. Capt. Gilbert Christian was the General's aide-de-camp. The roll would have been printed as an Appendix but for its length and the fact that the campaign was not one of the Revolution.

CHAPTER XXVIII

THE LESSER FRANKLIN

A large tract of country lying between the French Broad and the Holston[1] rivers on the north and west, the Little Tennessee river on the south, and the Alleghany mountains on the east, has had a singular and remarkable history. It has sometimes been referred to as the Territory South of the French Broad.

By the North Carolina Act 1783, Ch. 2, Sec. 5, the hunting ground reserved for the Cherokees extended up the middle of the Tennessee and the Holston rivers, thence up the middle of the French Broad to the mouth of Big Pigeon.

By the treaty of Hopewell, as we have seen, the national authority laid off a reservation for that nation of Indians, with its northern boundary located still higher up in the Franklin territory.[2]

Although the North Carolina act prescribed a penalty to be paid by any one who should survey or make entries on the lands below the French Broad, that State, in many instances, granted lands within the reservation and took the purchase money from its grantees.

The State of Franklin early in its history negotiated the treaty of Dumplin Creek in order to open the upper part of that tract of country to settlers. But the rush of emigration in that direction was too strong to be held back by any stipulation of act or treaty, and within less than a year the settlements had passed the last treaty line and each succeeding year they crept farther south.

Those of the settlers who had grants from North Carolina had a right to resent the numerous threats and proclamations of removal made by North Carolina. Other settlers not so situated endeavored to stand under cover of those grantees. A fresh proclamation had issued from the governor of North Carolina for the removal of those in the Territory about the last of the year 1787.

The inhabitants were thus compelled to rely for protection upon

---

[1] Now called the Tennessee at this place.
[2] *Ante*, p. 99.

the State of Franklin and upon the virtue of her treaty of Dumplin Creek.

In the summer of 1788 there was among them their leader, John Sevier, whose fortunes they followed because they admired him almost to the point of idolatry. Added to this was their belief that Sevier and Franklin would save to them their little holdings. Leader and people were well met; both were hard pressed by the same power. Whatever course the upper counties might take, the inhabitants south of the French Broad would not render fealty to North Carolina who disowned them, though she was estopped to do so.[3] This people, therefore, gave a continued allegiance to the State of Franklin.

Haywood, in closing his description of the Sevier-Tipton engagement in February, 1788, says: "With this battle, the government of Franklin came to an end." Every other historian has followed Haywood and so declared: Ramsey, Phelan, Roosevelt, Alden, Henderson and others.

Arthur Campbell planned a "greater Franklin"; now there survived, for a time, to function as a sovereign power, even if fitfully and feebly, a "lesser Franklin"—of the people inhabiting south of the French Broad.

Late in July Governor Johnston referred to John Sevier as one "who styles himself Captain-General of the State of Franklin."

In September, as we shall see, Sevier was writing to Gardoqui the Spanish minister, soliciting a loan for the people of Franklin, for the repayment of which he obligated himself and the "State of Franklin" as an existent power.[4]

October 15th the General Assembly was in session and passed the following act:

In the General Assembly, State of Franklin, October 15th, 1788.
Whereas, the collection of taxes in specie, for the want of a cir-

---

[3] Governor Johnston of North Carolina, a learned lawyer, in an official communication of date Sept 22, 1788, after pointing out that fifteen hundred families had settled in the strip of country, said: "The people inhabiting the lands on the fork of the French Broad and Holston rivers claim under grants from this State, regularly issued from the secretary's office and executed by the governors. The people are, therefore, as much under the protection of the State as any other of her citizens. For this reason, as well as others I have heard, the treaty of Hopewell will probably ever be reprobated by every good citizen of this State." *N. C. Rec.*, XXI, 501.

[4] *Post*, p. 240.

culating medium, has become very oppressive to the good people of this Commonwealth; and

Whereas, it is the duty of the legislature to hear at all times the prayers of their constituents and apply as speedy a remedy as lays in their power,

Be it enacted by the General Assembly of the State of Franklin, and it is hereby enacted by the authority of the same, That, from the first day of January, A.D. 1788, the salaries of the civil officers of this Commonwealth be as follows, to wit:

His excellency, the governor, *per annum,* one thousand deer skins; his honor, the chief justice, five hundred do. do.; secretary to his excellency, the governor, five hundred racoon do. do.; the treasurer of the State, four hundred and fifty otter do. do.; each county clerk, three hundred beaver do.; clerk of the house of commons, two hundred beaver do.; members of the assembly, three do.; justices for signing a warrant, one muskrat do.; to the constable for serving a warrant, one mink do.

Enacted into a law this 15th day of October, 1788; under the great seal of the State.

Witness his Excellency, &c.

. . . .
Governor, captain-general, commander-in-chief and admiral in and over the same State.[5]

---

[5] This act was published as a news item by newspapers of that period which gave attention to affairs in Franklin: Augusta *Chronicle and Gazette,* May 2, 1789. See also *American His. Association Rep.*, 1898, p. 322. Judge Simeon E. Baldwin, referring to this statute, there says that "it is probable that no statute in this precise form was ever passed, or, indeed, any statute of so late a date," but he too follows Haywood.

The statute probably was printed in one of the Boston journals, because Daniel Webster made it a topic of debate in the United States Senate, when in March, 1838, the establishment of a sub-treasury was under discussion. He said:

"Most members of the Senate will remember that, before the establishment of this government, and before or about the time that the territory which now constitutes the State of Tennessee was ceded to Congress, the inhabitants of the eastern part of that territory established a government for themselves, and called it the State of Franklin. They adopted a very good constitution, calling for the usual branches of legislative, executive and judicial power. They laid and collected taxes, and performed other usual acts of legislation. They had, for the present, it is true, no maritime possessions, yet they followed the common forms in constituting high officers; and their governor was not only captain-general and commander-in-chief; but admiral also, so that the navy might have a commander when there should be a navy.

"Well, sir, the currency in the State of Franklin became very much deranged. Specie was scarce, and equally scarce were the notes of specie-payment banks. But the legislature did not propose any divorce of government and people; they did not seek to establish two currencies, one for men in office and one for the rest of the

THE LESSER FRANKLIN 221

In reply to remarks of Webster touching this act of Assembly, in the United States Senate, Hugh Lawson White, of Tennessee, gave an account of Franklin which is the more interesting because of the fact that the speaker was a son of Colonel James White, a Franklin leader who founded the city of Knoxville in the territory now under discussion. Senator White, who had been reared among these bordermen, said:

The Senator from Massachusetts [Mr. Webster] at the close of his reply to the Senator from South Carolina, [Mr. Calhoun] 'for his special benefit' in very good temper, and in a most happy manner, referred to the early history of that portion of my State, now called East Tennessee, once known as the State of Franklin. He read us a part of one of her acts of assembly which fixed the salaries of some of her officers, and directed the species of currency in which they were to be paid.

I always feel gratified when I know or hear that my State has done anything that benefits any portion of my fellowmen. 'Blessed be the peacemakers' is the language of Holy Writ. On this occasion the two honorable and distinguished Senators had assumed an attitude so belligerent that I really feared it might end in something worse than words. But no sooner were the labors of my State fifty years ago brought to the notice of this grave body, than we all forgot that any of us had been out of temper, and so soon as we could

community. They were content with neighbors' fare. It became necessary to pass, what we should call, now-a-days, the civil list appropriation bill. They passed such a bill; and when we shall have made a void in the bill now before us by striking out specie payments for government, I recommend to its friends to fill the gap by inserting, if not the same provisions as were in the laws of the State of Franklin, at least something in the same spirit.

"The preamble of that law, sir, begins by reciting, that the collection of taxes in specie had become very oppressive to the good people of the commonwealth for the want of a circulating medium. A parallel case to ours, sir, exactly. It recited further, that it is the duty of the legislature to hear, at all times, the prayers of their constituents, and apply as speedy a remedy as lies in their power. These sentiments are very just, and I sincerely wish that there was a thorough disposition here to adopt the like.

"Acting under the influence of those sound opinions, sir, the legislature of Franklin passed a law for the support of the civil list, which, as it is short, I beg permission to read. It is as follows:

(Mr. Webster here read the body of the act as set out in the text.)

"This, sir, is the law, the spirit of which I commend to gentlemen. I will not speak of the appropriateness of these several allowances for the civil list. But the example is good, and I am of the opinion that, until Congress shall perform its duty by seeing that the country enjoys a good currency, the same medium which the people are obliged to use, whether it be skins or rags, is good enough for its own members."

recover composure enough to adjourn, we separated like a band of brothers—no two leaving the chamber in better temper with each other than the two honorable Senators.

But sir, the Senator knew nothing under the practice of the state law; therefore we have not the full benefit which we ought to derive from his reminiscences. He could have related the whole incident so much better than I can that I regret he did not mention the subject to me before he addressed the Senate; if he had, I would have given him the additional facts, that the whole might have been detailed to the Senate in his good-tempered and felicitous manner.

It will be remembered that the governor, chief-justice, and some other officers, were to be paid in deer skins; other inferior officers were to be paid in raccoon skins. Now at that day we were all good whigs, although we had some of the notions of the democrats of the present day.

We thought those taxes might safely remain in the hands of the collectors until wanted for disbursement. The taxes were, therefore fairly collected in the skins and peltry pointed out in the law. But the collectors knew, report says, that although raccoon skins were plenty, opossum skins were more so, and that they could be procured for little or nothing. They therefore, procured the requisite number of opossum skins, cut the tails off the raccoon skins, sewed them to the opossum skins, paid them into the general or principal treasury, and sold the raccoon skins to the hatters.

The treasurer had been an unlucky appointment, although a worthy man; he was a foreigner, knew nothing of skins or peltry, and was, therefore, easily deceived by the sub-treasurers. When this imposition was discovered, the whole system went down, and we never had a greater fancy for leaving the taxes in the hands of the sub-treasurers or collectors from that day to this.

But sir, those old proceedings more clearly develop the true character of my State than almost anything of the present day.

The territory or tract of country called Franklin, was composed of four counties of North Carolina, and separated from the body of the State by the great ledge of mountains, called at different places by different names, and from what is now called West Tennessee by the Cumberland mountains and a wilderness of two hundred miles.

The Revolutionary War had terminated with Great Britain in 1783, but it continued with the powerful tribes of Indians who had been in alliance with her. The depredations of these Indians were so serious that aid to arrest their ravages was desired from North Carolina; that state was not in a situation to furnish that protection, and instead thereof, from good motives, no doubt, but without due consideration, passed an act ceding us to the United States. When the news was received, the leading men, who were King's Mountain men—Sevier, the companion of the gallant Campbell and Shelby at their head—took fire; the discontent ended in a declaration of independence, and the formation of the state called, to perpetuate whig principles, 'Franklin.'

North Carolina discovered her error and before Congress could act on the subject, repealed her act of cession. But it was too late. We had been disposed of without our consent. Though but a handful, with a powerful savage enemy infesting our whole frontier, and without a dollar to begin with, we set up for ourselves. We would not brook the indignity; we had begun the fight for liberty and liberty or death we would have. We continued the controversy until 1789, when an accommodation with our parent state took place; and with our own consent, and upon terms thought just, we, with other portions of territory, were ceded, in 1789, to the United States.

In 1796, we became the State of Tennessee, and how we have since continued, I willingly leave to the judgment of our sister States.

I confess that, instead of feeling humbled, I feel proud that my ancestor was one of that unyielding band; that I now find myself associated here with a Sevier and a Tipton; and although I sometimes think that two generations back those of their name would not have worked so tamely in party gear, yet every once in a while *the blood shows itself*, and you can see that if their home concerns are not attended to here, according to what is just, they break party bandages and walk abroad in that freedom for which their fathers periled everything.

It is thus seen that "the controversy continued until 1789." The treasurer referred to was Elholm.[6] Henry Conway, of American ancestry, had been the treasurer under the Greeneville Assemblies.

Again, it has already been noted that the Greeneville government made payment to the civil officers of the State in specie or current notes.

Sevier's last battle under the flag of Franklin was fought in January, 1789; and he reported it in writing to the "Privy Council of the State of Franklin," in the following:

Copy of a letter from Gov. Sevier to the privy council of the new state of Franklin, dated at Buffalo Creek, January 12, 1789.

It is with the utmost pleasure I inform your honors, that the arms of Franklin gained a complete victory over the combined forces of the Creeks and Cherokees, on the 10th inst. Since my last, I received information that the enemy were collecting in a considerable body near Flint Creek, within 25 miles of my headquarters, with an intention to attack me. To improve this favorable opportunity, I immediately marched my corps towards the spot and arrived, after

---

[6] See sketch of Major Elholm, *post*, p. 309.

enduring much hardship by [reason of] the immense quantities of snow and the piercing cold. On the morning of the 10th inst., we were within a mile of the enemy. We soon discovered the situation of their encampment by the smoke of their fires, which we found extended along the foot of the Appalachian Mountain. I called a council of war of all the officers, in which it was agreed to attack the enemy without loss of time; and in order to surround them, I ordered Gen. M'Carter,[7] with the bloody rangers and the tomahawk-men, to take possession of the mountain, the only pass I knew that the Indians could retreat by; while I with the rest of the corps formed a line, nearly extending from the right to the left of their wings.

The arrival of Gen. M'Carter on the mountain, and the signal for the attack, was to be announced by the discharge of a grass-hopper, which was accordingly given and the attack began.

Our artillery soon roused the Indians from their huts; and, finding themselve pretty near surrounded on all sides, they only tried to save themselves by flight, from which they were prevented by our riflemen posted behind the trees. Their case being desperate, they made some resistance, and killed the people who were serving our artillery. Our ammunition being much damaged by the snow on the march, and the enemy's in good order, I found it necessary to abandon that mode of attack, and trust the event to the sword and the tomahawk; accordingly gave orders to that purpose. Col. Loid, with 100 horsemen, charged the Indians with sword in hand, and the rest of the corps followed with their tomahawks. The battle soon became general, by Gen. M'Carter's coming down the mountain to our assistance; death presented itself on all sides in shocking scenes, and in less than half an hour the enemy ceased making resistance, and left us in possession of the bloody field.

The loss of the enemy sustained in this battle is very considerable; we have buried 145 of their dead, and by the blood we have traced for miles all over the woods it is supposed the greatest part of them retreated with wounds. Our loss is very inconsiderable; it consists of five dead, and sixteen wounded; amongst the latter is the brave Gen. M'Carter, who, while taking off the scalp of an Indian, was tomahawked by another whom he afterward killed with his own hand. I am in hopes this brave and good man will survive.

I have marched the army back to my former cantonment, at Buffalo Creek, where I must remain until I receive some supplies for the troops, which I hope will be sent soon. We suffer most for the want of whiskey.[8]

---

[7] The name M'Carter still survives in Sevier county, Tennessee. James McCarter, an early Scotch settler in that county, is here referred to. E. T. Hist. Soc. Pub., III, 64.

[8] *City Gazetter and Daily Advertiser*, of Charleston, Apr. 21, 1789; and *Augusta Chronicle*, May 2, 1789.

It seems that the inhabitants of the territory, along with those of the upper counties, were led to believe that separation by act of North Carolina was near at hand, when the Greene county delegates to the Carolina Assembly returned home and made report of the proceedings and sentiment of that body. Sevier was willing to give over the unequal contest if this people could be satisfied in respect of their occupant and preëmption claims, and not be dispossessed of holdings that had been cleared by their axes and defended by their rifles in numberless contests with their savage neighbors. Could a diagram be drawn, accurately designating every spot signalized by an Indian massacre or depredation, or by courageous attack, defense, pursuit or victory by the whites, the whole of that section of country would be studded over by delineations of such incidents.[9]

It is probable that Sevier counseled the dropping of the name, State of Franklin, in petitions to North Carolina in order that the border people might shape for adoption by and reconciliation with the mother State. He himself contemplated taking the oath of allegiance to that State at an early date.

On January 12, 1789, representatives of the inhabitants met to consult on some "voluntary plan" of safety and defense. They placed on record the information they had received of the proceedings of the North Carolina Assembly; and, particularly the facts that a treaty was to be held, in May following, with the Cherokees "to fix out a certain boundary betwixt us and the Indians," and that the commissioners had been instructed "to purchase the lands south of the French Broad, if possible, and that the people in that quarter were directed to continue in possession of said lands until the treaty."

The members of this convention conceived General Martin to be a "person unworthy our confidence as an officer, from the partial representation he has given us—witness his conduct at the treaty of Hopewell; his not residing in the district, and the declaration of the Assembly that he had not acted agreeable to the orders of the government." They agreed that John Sevier "should keep the command of the inhabitants on the frontier, or any that may come to their assistance." They declared in favor of a "Council of Safety" for the regulation of their affairs, *as the laws of French Broad*

---

[9] Ramsey, 370.

requires; and that the Assembly of North Carolina be petitioned to cede the territory west of the mountains to Congress.

John Sevier, Alexander Outlaw, Archibald Roane, David Campbell and Joseph Hamilton were requested to draw up a representation of their situation and of their earnest desire to be in the Federal Union. William Nelson (Alexander Outlaw, alternate) was named to wait on Congress; and Joseph Hardin was appointed to wait on the Cumberland Settlement with such instructions as the council of safety might give.[10]

It is the opinion of the writer that at the same or at a later meeting of this group of pioneers, they adopted "Articles of Association," which had been drafted to be the complement of the "Proceedings" above described. The latter document, intended for use in support of the petition to North Carolina,[11] was purposely silent in respect to the operations of the Franklin government among them; while the Articles provide, in express terms, for the continuance in power of "the officers appointed under the authority of Franklin."

The one document was a plan of safety; the other a compact for the government of their internal affairs.

The Articles may be taken to embody some of the leading features of the Watauga Articles of Association. However, the laws of North Carolina, and not those of Virginia, were adopted by way of reference. As given by Haywood[12] the fundamental agreement reads:

ARTICLES OF ASSOCIATION

We, the subscribers, inhabiting south of Holston, French Broad and Big Pigeon Rivers, by means of the division and anarchy that has of late prevailed within the chartered limits of North-Carolina, west of the Apalachian Mountains, being at present destitute of regular government and laws, and being fully sensible that the

---

[10] The proceedings are given in full, Appendix C.

Gen. Joseph Martin thus reported to Governor Johnston, Feb. 5th: "A party of men have lately met on French Broad and called themselves a convocation of the people and have passed several resolves, one of which is to raise a number of men by subscription, and to be commanded by Col. Sevier, saying that North Carolina refused to aid the people over the mountains, and, in consequence the Assembly's not making any allowance to the people who went against Chickamauga. I was in doubt for some time that a general revolt would take place." *N. C. St. Rec.*, XXI, 523.

[11] Therefore found in the archives of that State. *N. C. St. Rec.*, XXII, 722.

[12] Page 193, Ramsey, 435.

blessings of nature can only be obtained and rights secured by regular society, and North-Carolina not having extended her government to this quarter, it is rendered absolutely necessary, for the preservation of peace and good order, and the security of life, liberty and property to individuals, to enter into the following social compact, as a temporary expedient against greater evils:

Article I. That the Constitution and Laws of North-Carolina shall be adopted, and that every person within the bounds above mentioned, shall be subject to the penalties inflicted by those laws for the violation thereof.

Article II. That the officers appointed under the authority of Franklin, either civil or military, and who have taken the oaths of office, shall continue to exercise the duties of such office, as far as directed and empowered by these Articles, and no further, and shall be accountable to the people or their deputies for their conduct in office.

Article III. That militia companies, as now bounded, shall be considered as districts of the above territory, and each district or militia company chall choose two members to represent them in a General Committee, who shall have power to choose their own president and clerk, to meet on their own adjournments, and the president shall have power to convene the Committee at any time when the exigencies of affairs require their meeting, and shall have power to keep order and to cause rules of decorum to be observed, in as full a manner as the president of any other convention whatever. And in all cases of mal-administration, or neglect of duty in any officer, the party grieved shall appeal to the Committee, or a majority of them, who shall be competent to form a board of business. And upon such application, the Committee shall cause the parties to come before them, and after examining carefully into the nature of the offence, shall have power to deprive of office, or publicly reprimand the offender, as the demerit of the crime may deserve, or otherwise to acquit the party accused, if found not guilty.

Article IV. Where vacancies happen in the military department, the same shall be filled up by election, as heretofore used, and the officers thus elected shall be the reputed officers of such regiment or company, as the case may be, and shall be accountable to the Committee for their conduct as other officers.

Article V. The civil officers shall have power to take cognizance of breaches of the peace or criminal offences, and where any person is convicted of an offence not capital, the officer before whom such offender is convicted, shall immediately inflict the punishment directed by law for such offence. But where the crime is capital, the officer shall send such criminal, together with the evidences for or against him or them, to the highest justice of the peace for North-Carolina, there to be dealt with according to law; but no civil officer shall decide upon cases of debt, slander, or the right of property.

Article VI. Militia officers shall have power to collect their regiments or respective companies, emergencies making it necessary, and in case of invasion by the common enemy, shall call out their companies regularly by divisions, and each militia man shall give obedience to the commands of his officer, as is required by law, or otherwise be subject to the penalties affixed by law for such neglect or refusal, at the judgment of a court martial.

Article VII. And, whereas, it is not improbable that many horse thieves and fugitives from justice may come from different parts, expecting an asylum amongst us, as we are destitute of a regular government and laws by which they may be punished, each and every of us do oblige ourselves to aid and assist the officers of the different state or states, or of the United States, or any description of men sent by them, to apprehend such horse thief or fugitive from justice. And if any of the above characters should now be lurking amongst us, or shall hereafter be discovered to have taken refuge in this quarter, we do severally bind ourselves, by the sacred ties of honour, to give information to that state or government from which they have fled, so that they may be apprehended and brought to justice.

Article VIII. United application shall be made to the next session of the Assembly of North-Carolina to receive us into their protection, and to bestow upon us the blessings of government.

Article IX. The captains of the respective militia companies shall each of them procure a copy of these Articles, and after calling the company together for the purpose, shall read them, or cause them to be read, distinctly to said company; and each militia man or householder, after hearing them read, if he approve of them shall ascribe his name to the articles, as a proof of his willingness to subject himself to them; and said Articles shall be the temporary form of government until we are received into the protection of North-Carolina, and no longer.

Ramsey surmises that the seat of government under the Articles was at Newell's Station. The tradition in Sevier county is that for six months Sevier made his headquarters on the Robertson farm, one-half mile east of Seymour Railway Station, in the ninth civil district of that county.

Sevier continued to befriend the people who had settled this beautiful and attractive country. He presented a memorial in their behalf to the Carolina Assembly of 1789, in which he urged that body to recognize the validity of the treaty of Dumplin Creek, which, he declared, had been fairly and openly negotiated.[13] It seems that Sevier influenced that body to reserve the right to

---

[13] *N. S. St. Rec.*, XXII, 727.

Carolina, in the last cession act,[14] to open an office for the entry of preëmptions by the people of this section, but the Assembly adjourned without making specific provisions for the office; and it never did so thereafter. This entailed on the people long years of anxious waiting before their titles were validated.

In 1794, when a member of the Legislative Council of the Territory South of the River Ohio, Sevier aided in procuring the legislature of the Territory to represent to Congress that the inhabitants South of the French Broad ought to be secured in their rights of preëmption.[15]

As the first governor of Tennessee, and in one of his first messages, he urged the Assembly of 1796 to remind the senators just elected to Congress of the "embarrassed situation" of this people.[16]

He again showed tenderness for those who had stood by him in the hour of stress and strain, when in addressing a special session of the Tennessee legislature, in 1806, he said in his message: "Among the very great objects you will have before you for legislative consideration will be the situation and circumstance of the people settled on the south side of the French Broad and Holston, and west of Big Pigeon rivers. They are respectable and worthy inhabitants, who have suffered by Indian depredations too deplorable to relate. They are justly deserving of the patronage and indulgence of a liberal and patriotic legislature; and I entertain every hope that the paternal care of the Assembly will be tenderly exercised towards such a deserving and worthy class of citizens."[17]

---

[14] *N. C. Act 1789*, ch. 3, sec. I, sub. sec., 10; Scott's *Revisal*. I, 408.

[15] *Journal*, 12; petition of inhabitants, pp. 23, 24.

[16] *Senate Journal, 1796*, 24.

[17] Governor's message, submitted July 29, 1806. *Senate Journal*, 5. The history of this district is interestingly set forth in a rare pamphlet "An Address to the Citizens of Tennessee by a Citizen, South of French Broad and Holston. Knoxville, 1823." The writer states that the district began to be populated in 1783. In three or four years the country fringing the south bank of the French Broad was settled by a class of citizens "who were most of them refugees from the poverty and ruin in which they were involved by the calamities of a destructive war which they had just before successfully concluded with one of the greatest powers of the world. Danger had taught them enterprise; and urged by the calls of necessity, they were willing to encounter the most formidable perils ... for the sake of obtaining a little spot of earth upon which they and their families might subsist. This country formed a frontier of near one hundred miles in length and an average breadth of from fifteen to twenty miles." For further light on this section: Sanford, *Blount College*, 28; and cases in the United States Supreme Court, Preston v. Browder, 1

It was not a matter of surprise that the citizens of one of the counties in that district, when the county was regularly formed, insisted upon retaining for it the old Franklin name of "Sevier." Common gratitude prompted the action; theirs was a deeper sense of obligation.

At the February (1789) term of the Greene County Court, John Sevier, Joseph Hardin, Henry Conway and Hugh Wear, "came into court and took the oath of allegiance, agreeable to the Act of the Assembly in such cases made and provided."

Then, truly, the State of Franklin had come to an end. Governor Caswell's policy of conciliation had at last vindicated itself, and it continued to be the policy of the mother State until the second cession act was passed.

Wheaton Rep. (14 U. S.), 115; Danforth v. Thomas, *Ib.* 155; Danforth v. Wear, 9 Wheaton (22 U. S), 673; also Profit v. Williams, 1 Yerger (Tenn.), 92.

CHAPTER XXIX

The Arrest of Sevier—1788

The success that Sevier and his followers had in every contest with the Indians was not sufficient to keep him inspirited. As one after another of his supporters in the older settlements of Franklin fell away and acknowledged allegiance to North Carolina, he became despondent, and for a time lost grip of himself while among the rough fighters of the lower country. He drank freely.

Added pressure was now brought to bear upon Sevier. In July, 1788, Governor Johnston issued an order to the authorities of Washington District that, on facts being made to appear, a warrant issue for his arrest on the charge of treason to the State of North Carolina, the military force to aid if necessary. Such order coming to Judge Campbell, he withheld action, he being so close to Sevier and his former conduct as to render adverse action unseemly if not openly hostile. The matter laid over until the arrival from across the mountains of Judge Samuel Spencer, who issued the required writ.

Early in October Sevier resolved to visit Jonesborough. On the 9th a council of the Carolina militia officers was held in that village to consult as to the feasibility of a second campaign against the Chickamaugas, General Martin, Colonel Tipton, Colonel Love and others attending. Sevier late in the afternoon of the same day appeared in the little town, and in an ugly mood. The council had adjourned and Tipton had left for his home ten miles away. Sevier engaged in a wordy altercation with Major David Craig and David Deaderick, a merchant. After nightfall he rode to the house of the widow of one of his old captains, Jacob Brown, to spend the night. News of his presence was borne to Tipton who left his home to collect a force of ten men to effect Sevier's arrest. This group went first to the house of Colonel Charles Robertson, who was then living five miles south of Jonesborough. There, however, on thorough search of the house, they failed to find the governor. The pursuers went next to Mrs. Brown's, reaching there about sunrise. Recognizing Tipton and seeing that his party was armed, Mrs. Brown seated herself in the front doorway to obstruct Tipton who endeavored to force a passage. The bustle roused Sevier from slumber; looking out and seeing Colonel Love who had attached himself to Tipton's party, he opened a door and surrendered to Love. Tipton, upon seeing Sevier, was greatly enraged and swore that he would hang the prisoner. He ordered Sevier to get his horse to go to Jonesborough. On reaching that place, by Tipton's command iron handcuffs were put on Sevier, who now asked Love to intercede to prevent his being carried across the mountains, far away from family and friends. Love urged upon Tipton that this would be bad policy as Sevier's friends would undoubtedly attempt a rescue and bring on a serious conflict. Under Tipton's orders a deputy sheriff with two other guards, started with Sevier for Morganton, North Carolina, to be carried farther east if it should be thought necessary. Colonel Love traveled with the party as far as his estate in the Greasy Cove and treated the prisoner with consideration and kindness.

As the guard and prisoner passed through Burke county, the McDowell neighborhood was reached. Colonel Charles McDowell, who with his companions had been given shelter under Sevier's roof when harried and driven to cover in 1780 by the British forces, and Joseph McDowell, a comrade-in-arms of Sevier in more than one battle of the Revolution, went with the prisoner to Morganton and became sureties on a bail bond until Sevier procured a Carolina kinsman who could sign as surety for his appearance. Court was in session and Sevier attended as his bond required.

By this time a group of Sevier's relatives and friends had crossed the mountains intent upon a rescue. Joseph Sevier, the governor's brother, John Sevier, Junior, Nathaniel Evans, George North, James Cozby, Jesse Green and William Matlock composed the party. After crossing the mountains they separated and went into Morganton singly. They went to a tavern where they found Sevier in company with Major Joseph McDowell. They frankly disclosed that they had come for him and that he must go. After tarrying for an hour or two, Sevier ordered his horse and all openly rode out of town headed for the mountains.

The sheriff of the county, William Morrison, himself a participant in the battle of King's Mountain, did not order a pursuit.[1]

---

[1] Based, for the most part, on the account of John Sevier, Jr., to Draper, in

After reaching home, Sevier was constrained to write a letter (October 30th) to the Carolina Assembly, soon to convene, protesting against the "rigid persecution carried on to gratify the ambition and malice of an obscure and worthless individual"; and saying that, in opposition to the Constitution and laws of that State, he had been subjected to wanton cruelty and savage insults and borne out of the district for trial at a distance from his neighbors who could best judge of his innocence or his guilt.[2]

Towards the end of the year, so full of strife between Sevier and his opponents and of bloody battles with the redmen, the murk lifted at last to bring into view a pleasing scene of frontier life. On his return from Morganton large numbers of Sevier's friends and acquaintances, whole families, without preconcert paid him a visit of cheer and welcome at his Mount Pleasant home where at all times unstinted hospitality was dispensed by his wife, "Bonny Kate." The horses of all who came from distant points were turned into the cornfield, and all gave themselves over to gaieties. "An old fiddler from Virginia, of the name of Black, happened along at the time, and Colonel Sevier got the old musician to tune up his violin, and for nearly a week it was a jubilee. Colonel Sevier led off in the old country dances, such as 'The White Cockade' and 'The Flower of Edinburgh.' Sevier liked to make others happy and mingled with young and old—the life of all. The bright-eyed fair ones lent helping hands in providing substantials and luxuries for the table."

While Sevier was yet held at Morganton, the Indians made an attack on Gillespie's Fort, below the mouth of Little river on Holston, about eight miles from the present Knoxville. An onslaught was made at sunrise of October 17th, by above two hundred Cherokees and Creeks, under the command of John Watts (Kunoskeskie). The small garrison was overpowered after a short resistance, ammunition being expended; and twenty-eight persons, mostly women and children were killed.[3] The Indians left behind a letter addressed to Sevier and Martin and "the inhabitants of the New State" in which the reasons for their attack were given.[4]

Draper's MSS. The alternative account given by Ramsey (p. 428), based on the William Smith MS., while picturesque, is not authentic.

[2] *N. C. State Records*, XXII, 697.

[3] Letter of October 25th, in Georgia *State Gazette*, of Dec. 27, 1788.

[4] Ramsey, 519. Forty-two killed and taken prisoners. D. Kennedy's account, Oct. 22, 1788.

Stark terror ran through the frontier south of the French Broad. An appeal for succor went to Colonel Daniel Kennedy, of Greene, who in turn wrote urgently to Colonel John Tipton, of Washington County: "The Indians are a thousand strong and reinforced by a large body of Creeks; they intend driving all the white people out of this country.... I hope you will exert yourself on this occasion, so very important and distressing. The stations are, chiefly, evacuated south of the French Broad and the road crowded with women and children making their escape, many of them on foot, who have lost all but their lives. The women carry their tender babies in their arms.... The inhabitants are in great want of provisions."[5]

Sevier returned to the southern border settlements, and in December conceived a design to acquire from the friendly Chickasaw Indians the lease of a body of land on the lower reaches of the Tennessee river, and to colonize it.[6] He counted largely on the coöperation of the inhabitants south of the French Broad river for settlers. The scheme was abandoned when he was able to descry not far off a turn in the tide of adversity.

---

[5] From Evan's Ferry, Oct. 22nd. N. C. Hist. Com. MSS. Kennedy took the lead in sending a memorial to the N. C. General Assembly asking military aid from the State.

[6] *North Carolina State Records*, XXII, 719, *et seq.*

CHAPTER XXX

The Spanish Intrigue—1788

Reports of the increase in the vindictive feeling of the inhabitants of the western waters toward the Spaniards gave concern both to the American government and to the authorities of Spain. It was feared that assertion of their supposed rights might take the form of a military invasion of Spanish Louisiana and a seizure of the port of New Orleans, even in defiance of the Federal government. There already existed in several quarters local movements for separation from the Federal government, itself. In Vermont, under the leadership of the Revolutionary hero, Ethan Allen, and his brothers the movement was toward a connection with Great Britain; and in the Valley of the Mississippi it was toward alliance with the government that controlled the navigation of the Mississippi.

The Spanish authorities were aware of their government's weakness and feared the result of a combination of the mounted riflemen living on the Kentucky, Cumberland and Tennessee rivers, and an invasion by them. But they were also aware of elements of strength on the part of themselves in their ability to let loose or restrain the Creeks and other Indian tribes, near neighbors of the western peoples; and to hold out as a temptation the free navigation of the lordly Mississippi.

It had now become the policy of Spain, by the use of these factors of strength, to win over the frontier communities, if not to a political incorporation then to independence and an alliance of some sort with Spain.

The Intendant Navarro, writing to Spain in 1788, urged the necessity of inducing the Westerners to separate from the people of the seaboard by the grant of commercial privileges and of coöperation to hold in check the Indians who were under Spanish influence. Gardoqui, the Spanish minister in this country, gave a ready assent to the policy as did also Miro, governor of Louisiana.

When the shrewd Gardoqui learned of the bitter breach between the old-and new-state men in Franklin he judged that the time was ripe to avail of the disaffection. In that quarter, as on the Cumberland, he used as emissary Dr. James White, a resident of the Cumberland Settlement, who was a member of the Continental Congress—the only representative Trans-Alleghany Carolina ever had in that body; therefore, the first in any national council. White was at the time also superintendent of the Southern Indians for the general government.

Active intrigue was begun in April, 1788, occasion being afforded by the appeal of Governor Johnston, of North Carolina, through White for Spanish coöperation in restraining the Indians. On the 18th, Gardoqui wrote letters to Governor Johnston, James Robertson and John Sevier. In the letter to Sevier he adroitly said: "His Majesty is very favorably inclined to give the inhabitants of that region all the protection they ask for; and, on my part, I shall take very great pleasure in contributing on this occasion and on other occasions."[1]

On the 21st, White addressed a communication to Governor Johnston in which he announced his purpose to leave the sittings of Congress for a period; "in the present state of the treasury no services to the United States can be rewarded." He assured Johnston that the Spanish officials were beginning to be convinced that people of the Western Country were to be restrained rather by benevolence than violence; and that the attitude of the Eastern States toward the West as to the formation of new States in that region was based on jealousy of additional weight and influence to the southward. "If their partial views are indulged, affection, fear nor interest will not long hold the trans-mountain people dependent on the Atlantic States."[2]

This accords with what Gardoqui wrote home to Floridablanca, on the 18th: that the future policy of Spain's representatives would be to treat the Westerners with the greatest generosity; that he did not believe Spain could force the frontiersmen out of Franklin, which was yet actually claimed to be a Spanish territory, but that he had secret advices that by proper treatment they might be brought under Spanish influence.[3]

At this very time, a special agent of the Secretary of War was in Franklin to investigate how much truth there was in the repre-

---

[1] Henderson, The Spanish Conspiracy in Tennessee, *Tenn. Historical Mag.*, III, 233, quoting Gardoqui MSS., in Durrett Collection.
[2] *N. C. St. Rec.*, XXI, 465, White to the Govenor of North Carolina.
[3] Roosevelt, *Winning of the West*, IV, 229.

sentations of Captain John Sullivan and others, which had been given wide publicity by the press: that preparations for an armed conquest of Louisiana were going forward in Franklin.[4]

Lieutenant John Armstrong, of the First Regiment, U. S. Army, arrived in Franklin April 8th, 1788, and visited the counties of Sullivan, Washington and Greene, interviewing the most intelligent men. He reported his conviction that "there is not, and has not been, any design formed or forming of the nature mentioned in the letter signed John Sullivan, nor has he ever been in that settlement. I could not learn that any British agents had been in the settlements of Holston." Armstrong, commenting on the division of sentiment and the Sevier-Tipton battle of February 29th, states that from the nature "of this dispute, had any such design been on foot, I should have been informed by one party or another." He expressed the opinion that "the interposition of the United States will be necessary to put a stop to the effusion of blood in this quarter."[5]

Sevier, as has been seen, was in the spring and summer of 1788 on the frontier of Franklin struggling valiantly to defend the settlers south of the French Broad against the Indians; and there Dr. White found him, a proscribed man, but still holding to the vestiges of the State of Franklin in hope that by some fortuity at this critical and changeful period in governmental structures, the State might yet be securely established. In near-desperation and seeing the national situation as it was painted by White, Sevier wrote to Gardoqui about June 1st, and again on July 18th. Of these communications no trace seems to have been found. Doubtless by them Sevier sought, without compromising committal, to procure much needed supplies of ammunition from the Spaniards and to secure their influence in curbing the Indians, particularly the Creeks and the Chickamaugas.

After he learned of the failure of the North Carolina convention (August 1st) to ratify the Federal Constitution, there was presented to Sevier, outlawed by that State, no alternative to yielding allegiance to it as a State out of the Union but continued resistance. He thought that the refusal to enter the new Federal Union was probably final. The majority in convention against ratification was so large as apparently to be thus far decisive.

---

[4] This is the rumor referred to, *ante*, p. 138.
[5] *State Dept. MSS.*, Vol. III, 551, April 28, 1788.

One chance of securing for Franklin federal recognition was perceivable. With North Carolina out of the Union the Congress might conclude to admit the State of Franklin on the basis of the irrepealability of the first cession act. On the other hand should North Carolina later on reconsider and become a State of the Union then one of the provisions of the new Federal Constitution would acknowledge that State's ultimate sovereignty over the western lands, and give her the power to veto the admission of a new State in the West.

By reason of his successful campaigning against the Indians Sevier had now "regained his influence to a great degree" and "put himself at the head of the Federalists, and menaces the State of North Carolina for putting themselves out of the Union by rejecting the new Constitution."[6]

On September 12th, Sevier in the changed circumstances, adopted a radical course, more with intent to defy the old State than to swing Franklin to a new allegiance. He wrote two letters to the Spanish minister. In one, he solicited the good offices of that official to prevent an alliance of the Creeks, Choctaws and Chickasaws with the Cherokees who "continued the war with all liberty." He suggested that the inhabitants of Franklin might form a new settlement in the Great Bend of Tennessee; and intervention to obviate opposition was sought.

Two historians who have made a close study of this period and phase, James and Whitaker, are in agreement that aid in carrying out the long-cherished project of settlement of the Great Bend was the chief motive that prompted both White and Sevier. Indeed, White's disclosures to Gayoso were full enough to convince the latter that the Franklinites' desire was for that region, and Gayoso was convinced that it was not compatible with the real interests of Spain. In May, 1789, Gayoso wrote to Valdes a letter which sheds valuable light on the men and their motives:

"White is thoroughly republican at heart. The movement that is taking place in the State of Franklin has as its object the establishment of independence rather than a *rapprochment* with Spain. The Franklinites know that it is to their interest to form a connection with this province [Louisiana] and they wish to do so, but they are extremely ambitious and their principal object is to extend their territory so that it may draw near the Mississippi

---
[6] Gilmore, *Advance Guard of the Western Civilization*, 333.

and Mobile Rivers, in the hope that this advantage will attract many immigrants from other places, and enable them to build up an opulent State."[6a]

The second letter should be read in the light of the fact that the original of it does not exist. A copy of it, translated into Spanish, is preserved in the Gardoqui manuscripts; and this translation was made by Spanish officials who were interested in placing upon the original the construction that would be the more likely to bring favorable action from the home government in behalf of the plan which Gardoqui had formulated and sponsored. The translation of this letter back into English is that of Henderson:

Franklin, September 12, 1788.

Sir:

Since my last, of the 18th of July, upon consulting with the principal men of this country, I have been particularly happy to find that they are as well disposed and willing as I am in respect to your proposals and guarantees. You may be sure that the favorable hopes and ideas that the people of this country maintain with respect to the future probability of an alliance and concession of commerce with you in the future are very ardent and that we are unanimously determined to that effect. The people of this country have come to realize truly upon what part of the world and upon what nation depend their future happiness and security, and they readily infer that the interest and prosperity of it depend entirely upon the protection and liberality of your government. We must expect it of our situation and circumstances that they will lead us on in the most effective manner to look for the long security and prosperity of your government in America, and, being the first to resort in this way to your protection and liberality from this side of the Appalachian Mountains, we feel encouraged to maintain the greatest hope that we shall be granted all reasonable helps by him who is so amply able to do it and give the protection and help that is asked in this our petition. You know our delicate situation and the difficulties in which we are in respect to our mother State, which makes use of all stratagems to impede the development and prosperity of this country. In spite of the fact that we possess some of the most fertile lands on this continent and easy means of exportation, yet we cannot dispose of a single article of its products (which would be almost innumerable) unless we have authority to make use of our rivers toward the ports below. Seeing us in these embarrassments, it is easy for you to realize the great scarcity of specie

---

[6a] Whitaker, *The Muscle Shoals Speculation*, Miss. Valley Hist. Review, XIII, 365, 384, citing the National Archives at Madrid. In 1789 White was dissuading Cumberland people from removing to the Spanish possessions. *N. C. St. Rec.*, XXII, 792.

in this country, of which there is very little among us. Nothing else is lacking in order to assure our mutual interests but a small sum of this article (the quantity of which I leave to your prudent judgment) and such other, military, assistance as your understanding deems it necessary and convenient to supply us with. All that is needed to attain what we want will not be more than a few thousand pounds. We are further encouraged to make this application because of your knowledge that we can pay promptly for whatever you may be able to supply, by sending the products of this country to the ports below. I hope that the payment of this (*i.e* of the loans) will be made with all convenience and that the pledges and receipts of our friend James Sevier (who is our secretary) will obligate both myself and the State of Franklin until they are entirely repaid and satisfied. I do not doubt that the help which is asked will be considered a trifle that is taken out of the treasury, especially when it is compared with the important object to which it is directed, and when we can repay so soon the sum that is advanced and when it will leave us under the greatest obligation of gratitude and perpetual friendship. We are determined, in so far as it is possible for us, that you shall so regard us; and when you see the advantages that will regularly arise from this connection, you will consider that our interests, which run in the same channel, will last and be inseparable. It behooves us to make the most prompt and necessary preparations for defence. If any break should happen, we must be prepared in time—the reason for which will necessarily be very obvious to you. Therefore, it is not necessary for me to say anything else about the subject and I beg of you to inform me from time to time, whenever opportunity offers and circumstances require it. I leave to you the choice of any other, more easy mode of communication than the present one, and for other matters I refer you to my son James, who is a competent person to give a perfect account of whatever concerns the Western Country. Before finishing, it may be necessary to inform you that there will be no more favorable occasion than the present one to put the plan into action. North Carolina has rejected the Constitution, and at the least a considerable time will pass before it becomes a member of the Union, if this ever happens. I beg you to supply James with whatever you think will be useful to us. If perchance you could get a passport, it would be of great profit to this country, because it is probable that some of us will find it convenient to go down to the Spanish ports; and if we are allowed to ship products of this country it will be a matter of great importance for us. I have the honor to be, Sir, with great esteem and consideration, your most respectful servant,

(Signed)   JOHN SEVIER

To Senor Don Diego de Gardoqui, Minister of Spain.[7]

---

[7] Henderson, *The Spanish Conspiracy*, 234; *Conquest of the Old Southwest*, 334.

This document has been referred to or quoted by Gayarre and Winsor as evidence that Sevier proposed to throw the State of Franklin into the arms of Spain. Even as rendered by the Spaniards, it is not properly susceptible of such a construction. Its writer was intent on procuring prompt aid; to that end he went as far in statement and implication as his ultimate purpose would admit. He proposed an alliance of friendly sovereignties, not an incorporation. He solicited a loan, not a grant. The preparations were for defense, not attack, and against North Carolina. The small amount of aid asked clearly so shows. Roosevelt, fairer to Sevier in this than in some other matters, thus summarizes: "He jumped at Gardoqui's cautious offers; though careful not to promise to subject himself to Spain, and doubtless with no idea of playing the part of Spanish vassal longer than the needs of the moment required."[8]

Sevier did not intend to play the part of vassal at all, in any true sense of the word. Gayoso did not so conceive.

Gilmore, on the authority of the historian Ramsey, in a statement of the facts as Sevier himself had detailed them, says that at the time Sevier wrote the above letter he also communicated by Captain Nathaniel Evans to General Shelby what was being done by himself.[9] The meaning of this act is clear when Evans' and Shelby's attitude toward North Carolina is remembered and considered.

Recalling that North Carolina had voted herself out of the Union, what could the western people expect of her in the matter of forcing open, single-handed, the great waterway to New Orleans? James Robertson, who went further than Sevier in treating with the Spaniards, said that he had earnestly endeavored to convince the members of the Carolina Assembly of 1788 who were opposed to ceding the western lands that the Westerners who had the greatest aversion to taking the protection of Spain would be compelled to leave their country or become Spaniards. These mem-

---

[8] *Winning of the West*, IV, 230. Roosevelt represents that Sevier because baffled by the occurrences of October and November, suddenly became a Federalist; and, strangely in the same connection, quotes apt authority to the effect that Sevier had been an advocate of the Federal Constitution in August. "This particular move was fairly comic in its abrupt unexpectedness," he says. It is submitted that the comic role is Roosevelt's own, in this instance. For evidence of prompt advocacy of the work of the constitutional convention of 1787, by Sevier and his followers, see p. 64, *ante*.

[9] *Advance Guard*, 333.

bers of the Assembly he says "were indifferent as to what became of us"; and all that was done was the passage of a resolution declaring that the citizens of the State had an indisputable right to the navigation of the Mississippi.

As a spur to cession General Daniel Smith, writing from the Cumberland, gave directly to Governor Johnston the assurance that "many of the settlers have been worn out with war; nothing being done by government for our protection; the Federal Constitution not being agreed to; no cession made to Congress—all these evils operated so forcibly on their minds that had the Spaniards offered us effectual protection, I am persuaded many here would have been for coming under their government in hopes of getting their calamities alleviated."[10] General Smith himself was of the number.

One of these patriots may not be indicted without indicting all. The Cumberlanders did not act without notice to North Carolina and their plans had in contemplation efforts to gain the consent of that State before any other further decisive step should be taken. As for Sevier: North Carolina was out of the Union, and Franklin was out of North Carolina. "If this be treason, make the most of it." In a communication (October 30th) he said, pointedly enough for apprehension of his meaning by the Carolinians addressed:

Can it be that North Carolina is so void of understanding as to think she is so permanently fixed as not to be shaken? Has she not discovered that there are formidable and inveterate enemies around her watching to take advantage of our divisions, which I am sorry to say are too numerous? Have you not discovered that those people have it in their power to do as much, at least, if not a great deal more, for the Western Americans than you can yourselves? Have you not seen the most affectionate child become sour and inveterate against the parent when the parental, tender ties of humanity have been refused?[11]

As for another, the champion of North Carolina in Franklin, and his connection with Spain: Joseph Martin, then brigadier-general of Carolina on November 8, 1788, wrote to McGillivray, who was in the employ of the Spanish authorities:

I must beg that you write me by the first opportunity in answer to what I am now going to say to you. I am daily applied to by a body of very respectable people to make application to you for

---

[10] *N. C. St. Rec.*, XXII, 790.
[11] *N. C. St. Rec.*, XXI, 559, and XXII, 697, 787.

liberty to settle on Tombigby. If you give me proper indulgence, I make no doubt of 500 families removing there under my directtion. . . . I hope to do honor to any part of the world I settle in, and am determined to leave the United States for reasons that I can assign to you when we meet, but durst not trust it to paper."

General Martin was acquitted of wrongdoing by the Carolina Assembly which could not fail to see that if there were dereliction that body could not itself escape a measure of condemnation.

A new would-be factor in Spanish intrigues in the West was the mendacious Irishman, Dr. James O'Fallon, of Charleston and later of Kentucky. He was the agent for the South Carolina Yazoo Company. In a letter to Gardoqui, of date May 26, 1788, he outlined an ambitious project for a colony of Catholics, to be mostly Irish, on a grant of land from Spain sufficient to give 857 acres each to 5,000 heads of families to be settled within a period of seven years. The location of the proposed concession was across the debatable northern margin of East Florida. O'Fallon urged upon Gardoqui the need of political relations with the Anglo-Americans living on the western waters, and he mentioned propositions he claimed to have received from Kentucky and Franklin.[12]

In Kentucky intrigue was taking on the deeper color of conspiracy, under the machinations of Wilkinson. Restless Arthur Campbell was taking it on himself to advise Innes that there should be "a general coalescence of the Western Countries," and Innes in reply bemoaned the eclipse of the State of Franklin. "I have been expecting such an event. In cases of that kind if discord takes place, the whole system becomes distorted and it generally ends in lasting factions." Innes expressed the view that no relief could be expected from the new national constitutional system. "There may be a change of men but their ideas will be the same, and when you reflect that the promoting of the interest of the Western Country will tend to almost a depopulation of the Eastern, we cannot even hope that our interests will be considered."[13]

There was not lacking some justification for the last statement

---

[12] *Gardoqui Papers*, I, 198, Durrett Coll., Univ. of Chicago; Parish, *Intrigues of Dr. James O'Fallon*, Miss. Valley Hist. Review, XVII, 230; Whitaker, *Spanish-American Frontier*, 129; Serano y Sanz, *Espana y Los Indios Cherokis y Chactas*, 47, 52. O'Fallon twice visited the Franklin region in the interest of his designs, which as time ran took on kaleidoscopic changes.

[13] Innes to Campbell, September 19, 1788, *Draper MSS.*, 9 DD 51.

when such views obtained in the East as Governor Clinton had openly professed to Gardoqui—that the peopling of the West from the East was a national calamity. When such sentiments were purposely passed on to penetrate the frontiers, irritation and indignation could but result.[14]

---

[14] Hamilton's opinion was that if Spain were allowed to persist in her policy of barring the Mississippi to navigation, the result would be "a war with Spain, or a separation of the Western Country. This country must have an outlet for its commodities. This is essential to its prosperity and if not procured to it by the United States, must be had at the expense of the connection with them." (1790).

CHAPTER XXXI

North Carolina Convention and Assembly—1788

The proposed Federal Constitution was submitted to North Carolina for adoption, and on December 5, 1787, the two houses of the Assembly met in joint conference to take into consideration the mode of action thereon. A state convention was called for July, 1788, to be composed of delegates from each county.

Undoubtedly the discussion of the Constitution and the election of delegates had some effect in bringing back to allegiance to the old State many men of the West who otherwise would have been without voice and influence in the solution of the great problems involved in the proposed national fundamental law.

All the western counties of Carolina sent delegates; Greene county: Ashael Rawlings, James Wilson, and James Roddy; Hawkins county: Stockley Donelson, Thomas King, and William Marshall; Sullivan county: Joseph Martin, John Scott, John Dunkin, David Looney, and John Sharpe; Washington county: Robert Allison, James Stuart, John Tipton, John Blair, and Joseph Tipton.

Sevier and his partisans indulged a faint hope that this convention might in some way cede the western territory, or otherwise provide for a separation; but the body adjourned without doing anything in furtherance of their desire; and, indeed, without taking any step favorable to the ratification of the Federal Constitution. Tipton and his friends voted against favorable action.

Sevier and his friends had been advocates of the Constitution, and now sought to make capital of the convention's failure to ratify.

Roosevelt incorrectly states that Sevier suddenly became a Federalist; and, "doubtless, not because of Federalism, but to show his hostility to North Carolina."[1]

As early as December, 1787, the Sevier element had spoken out in favor of the new system of government in the petition presented to the Assembly of Carolina, praying for separation,[2] and the same

---

[1] *Winning of the West*, IV, ch. IV.
[2] Appendix.

sentiment was reflected in the vote taken in the Assembly upon the call for a second convention to consider ratification.[3]

In the Carolina Assembly of 1788 (November) a majority of the delegates from the trans-Alleghany country were friends of Franklin and in favor of separation. In the senate from Greene county was James Roddy; from Hawkins county, Thomas Amis; from Washington county, John Tipton. James Robertson represented the counties on the Cumberland river. In the house of commons, Greene county was represented by Joseph Hawkins and Alexander Outlaw; Washington county by James Stuart and John Blair; Sullivan county by George Maxwell and John Scott; Hawkins county by Thomas King and Wm. Cocke. The last named, it seems, delayed attending until near the end of the session (ten days). Davidson county sent Elijah Robertson and Thomas Hardiman, and Sumner county sent William Walton and James Clendenning.

In the senate, on the second day of the session, a committee was appointed to take under consideration the situation of "the inhabitants on the Western Waters," Amis and Tipton of the number. Fortunately, Richard Caswell and Wm. Blount were also members.

Willie Jones, another friend of the western people, promptly presented a bill in the senate providing for once more pardoning and consigning to oblivion the offenses of certain persons in the counties of Greene, Hawkins, Sullivan, and Washington. On a motion to amend so as to except John Sevier and to exclude him from the benefits of the act, Tipton alone of all the members from the West, gave the amendment support. During the debate on this measure[4] Amis warmly opposed the amendment which would except Sevier, and in doing so gave offense to the irascible Tipton. A personal encounter on the floor of the senate was with difficulty prevented. Further discussion was postponed until the following day. Roddy, senator from Greene, during the evening, made an effort to mollify the enraged disputants. He reproached Amis for having used language calculated to exasperate Tipton and urged him thereafter to pursue a course that would "soothe his feelings." It was agreed

---

[3] *N. C. St. Rec.*, XXII, 48, and *post*, p. 250.

[4] Ramsey erred in following the statement of Isaac Lane which related the debate to the 1789 Assembly. Tipton, Roddy, and Amis were members of the 1788 Assembly, while only Amis, of the three, was in that of 1789. So the incident could not have occurred at the time stated in Ramsey's *Annals*, 432.

that on the next day Roddy should conduct the debate from the standpoint of Sevier's western friends, as less likely to give further offense to Tipton. When next morning, the discussion was resumed, Roddy took the floor but he had not proceeded far when Tipton became enraged, sprang from his seat and seized Roddy by the throat. Amis now called out to Roddy, "Soothe him, Colonel, soothe him!" The combatants were separated, but a challenge for a duel was issued. Mutual friends interfered and composed the controversy.

The vote in the senate following the debate was 24 to 19 against Tipton's contention.

In the house of commons an effort was made to defeat outright the pardon bill, but it was passed by a vote of 52 to 33, the friends of Tipton voting in the negative, and the friends of separation, joined by the delegates from Davidson and Sumner counties, voting aye.[5]

Willie Jones also introduced in the senate a bill to cede to Congress the Western Country.[6] Tipton seconded an amendment by which the words "west of the Alleghany Mountains" should be deleted and "west of the Cumberland Mountains" should be inserted.[7] Tipton would have thus severed and held for all time the Franklin counties and all of what is now East Tennessee under the jurisdiction of North Carolina. His motive was apparent. The amendment met a decisive defeat, 15 to 30. All the western senators voted in the negative save Tipton.

The isolation of Tipton was further emphasized when the senate acted on the bill providing for a second convention to consider the ratification by North Carolina of the Federal Constitution. He alone of the western senators voted against it;[8] and his bill "to prevent vexatious lawsuits" in the four Franklin counties was rejected on the first reading.[9]

A majority of the eastern members shared the view of the majority of those who represented the West, that Tipton was not blameless in respect of the disorders across the Alleghanies. He and

---

[5] *N. C. St. Rec.*, XXI, 77.

[6] *Ib.*, XX, 513.

[7] *Ib.*, 535.

[8] *Ib.*, 514. The Tiptonites in the house of commons also opposed a further consideration of the Federal Constitution, while the friends of Sevier favored it. *N. C. St. Rec.*, XXI, 130.

[9] *Ib.*, 577.

his followers were rebuked when the Assembly came to elect officers for the western territory, and in a way that caused them to wince. William Cocke was elected State's attorney; Thomas King, colonel; Landon Carter, first major, and Francis Alexander Ramsey, second major of cavalry, for Washington District—all Sevierites.

The Assembly passed an act providing for the establishment of a military station at a proper place on the north side of Tennessee river for the protection of the frontiers, to be garrisoned by a company of thirty-six officers and men. The expenses, however, were to be payable from taxes in Washington District, and "out of no other fund whatsoever." Regulation from eastern Carolina was imposed; but financial support withheld.

The cession bill was laid over till the next session; and the act of oblivion as finally passed censured Sevier's course by declaring him barred of the enjoyment of any office of profit or trust in the State.[10]

On the whole, the western people were pleased; they were led to believe that separation, now urged by the Cumberland people as well as by those of Franklin, was not far off.

---

[10] *N. C. Act 1788*, chapter 4. Sevier stood pardoned and no longer an outlaw, under this act; though his biographer says he continued to be an outlaw. Turner, *Life of Sevier*, 183.

CHAPTER XXXII

THE SECOND CESSION AND AFTERWARDS

Despite the legislative bar of the "enjoyment of any office of profit or trust" by Sevier in North Carolina, the people of the Greene senatorial district elected him to represent them in the Carolina state senate of 1789. His friends, Thomas Amis and Landon Carter, were returned from the Hawkins and Washington districts, respectively; and only General Joseph Martin, of Sullivan, was chosen from the opposing faction to sit as Sevier's third western colleague in the senate.

Sevier appeared with his credentials when the Assembly met in November, and was "qualified," sworn in and seated weeks before an act could be passed to remove the disqualification. The election of Sevier and two of his followers by the western electors made it clear to the senate that the conciliation of the people across the mountains could best be effected if the disabling clause of the act of 1788 should be disregarded.[1]

Sevier was also elected as a delegate to the Convention called to reconsider the ratification of the Federal Constitution, and was allowed to take his seat, in spite of the inhibition.

The Assembly and the Convention met at the same time and place. Both bodies had some delegates in common. The Assembly was confronted with another call from Congress for a cession of western territory.[2] Only North Carolina and Georgia had failed to make cessions and a pointed appeal was made to the magnanimity and sense of justice of the laggard State. Though North Carolina was out of the Union, to contribute toward the liquidation of the continental debts continued as an unchanged obligation.

Another spur to the making of a cession was the presentation for payment of large claims incurred in the conduct of General Martin's campaign against the Chickamauga Indians, under the State's military authorities. The members from the seaboard counties

---
[1] *N. C. St. Rec.*, XXI, 584-5.
[2] *Ib.*, 503.

winced when they saw the magnitude of these claims. Haywood, who was at the time yet a resident and active in the affairs of North Carolina, afterward wrote of this situation: "The Atlantic members labored to find ways and means, and still more, to avoid making contributions from the counties east of the Alleghanies" to liquidate these claims.

The two bodies, Assembly and Convention, coöperated in trying to solve the serious problems involved in the former refusals, to ratify the Federal Constitution and to cede the western domain. The swing of sentiment was now distinctly away from localism to the federal system. That further severance from the sister States was deemed unwise is shown by a pronounced reversal—the Constitution was ratified by a vote of 195 to 77, whereas in the previous year ratification had failed by a vote of 184 to 83.

Plans were matured for a second cession to the United States of America, though a considerable element in the Assembly favored a proposition advanced in the house of commons: to cede directly to the citizens who resided west of the mountains the territorial or political rights over the western domain, which was to be erected into a separate State, North Carolina to reserve the right to open a land office and dispose of the unappropriated lands for the purpose of satisfying specie certificates issued by the State and redeeming her paper money then in circulation.[3]

This would have been to affront the national government. It might lead, it was thought, to a serious breach, and to the possible loss of all control of the lands across the Alleghanies. There was deep solicitude that this point be safeguarded; an extensive control of the disposal of these lands must be retained. Land control had been throughout the crux of the cession problem.

An act to cede the Western Country to the United States was passed. John Sevier had the satisfaction of recording his vote in favor of cession even though on onerous terms;[4] and, in the Convention, in favor of ratifying the National Constitution.

The cession act, and the deed executed in pursuance thereof, incorporated as safeguarding conditions, the following:

---

[3] The bill so providing, passed two readings in the two houses. *N. C. St. Rec.*, XXI, 257, 271, *et seq.*

[4] The measure passed in the senate by a vote of 30 to 13, and in the house of commons by a vote of 68 to 30, John Rhea, representative from Sullivan county, being the only western delegate to vote in the negative. General Martin, in the senate, did not vote.

THE SECOND CESSION AND AFTERWARDS 251

1. That the military reservation[5] should inure to the benefit of the officers and soldiers of the continental line of North Carolina, their heirs and assigns; and if that reservation should not be found to contain a sufficient quantity of land fit for cultivation to satisfy the several provisions of law for their benefit, the deficiency might be made good by resorting to other parts of the territory ceded, not already appropriated.[6]

2. That entries and grants of lands made agreeable to law prior to the cession should have full force subsequently; and power was reserved to the governor of North Carolina to perfect titles under entries that had not ripened into grants.

3. That entries in John Armstrong's office (under Act 1783) located on land already entered by another should be allowed to be shifted to land on which no entry had been specially located.

The passage of but few years sufficed to raise a grave issue between the mother State and Tennessee as to the operative force of these reservations, leading to an acrimonious debate, and to legislative acts of retaliation that were in a way reminiscent of the Franklin State struggle.[7]

---

[5] About 3,000,000 acres bounded as stated in a previous chapter.

[6] *Act of North Carolina*, 1784, Ch. 19, Sec. 17, had made a similar provision to cover such deficiency.

[7] At the date of cession the laws of North Carolina required all surveys for grants to be finished and grants procured by the end of 1792. Tennessee claimed that North Carolina had no power to enlarge the limitation, none having been reserved in the cession act. North Carolina was insistent and persistent in the assertion of the power.

Thomas Jefferson, Secretary of State, after a thorough investigation, reported to the President, in 1791, a detailed estimate of the acreage in the West that had been entered or passed to grant under North Carolina's authority. He found the total to be 8,177,598 acres, which naturally was of the best lands. In resistance of the efforts of North Carolina, the legislature of Tennessee penalized in the sum of $5,000 any person subsequently surveying any land in the State "for the purpose of obtaining a title for such lands from North Carolina." Again (in 1811) North Carolina renewed the claim and effort, this time to bring from the Tennessee legislature a prohibitory act, imposing a penalty of $5,000 on any surveyor who should survey North Carolina entries, and on any register of deeds who should record any grants based thereon, and also a fine of $1,000 and disbarment upon any lawyer who should begin a suit upon such a claim. See *Acts of Tennessee*, 1801, ch. 2; *Acts*, 1812, Ch. 86; Sanford's *Blount College*, 83 *et seq*.; American State Papers, *Public Lands*, I, 18; Whitney, *Land Laws of Tennessee, passim; Memorial of North Carolina to Congress*, of 1824; *Memorials of Tennessee*, of 1817 and 1825; Hoyt, *Murphey Papers*, II, 320, 328. The United States was magnanimous toward Ten-

Cession thus provided for, the Assembly proceeded to a disposition of the claims of the soldiers who held certificates for service issued by the officers in the Chickamauga campaign. Their payment was imposed on the people of the Washington district (the Tennessee Valley)—made receivable for taxes in that district and no other. In substance, those who fought were directed to pay themselves.[8]

As if to forestall opposition from the western people to the terms of the cession act respecting lands in the western domain, pains were taken by the Assembly to conciliate them by means of the treatment accorded the most popular man in the West, Sevier. This leader was now formally found "not as highly responsible as many others" who had engaged in the Franklin movement, which at first (it was resolved) "he did oppose in such a manner as actually to prevent elections from being held in the new government [Franklin] in two of the counties; and when at last he joined them it was in obedience to the entreaties of several of the most influential persons in that part of the country."[9]

Joseph Martin, who had stood for years in the breach in favor of the restoration of North Carolina's sovereignty in the Franklin territory, was now in disfavor with the western inhabitants. Not withstanding his valuable service to the Carolina Commonwealth, he, while a member of the senate, was removed from the office of brigadier-general of western forces without any accusation being lodged against him as such. The senate by a vote of 28 to 7 con-

---

nessee and endeavored to make amends for any injustice done, even though the national government should take little of benefit as the result of the cession. Referring to the final cession, it has been said: "In accepting the cession offered by North Carolina, Congress made a bad bargain. In the deed of cession North Carolina stated certain conditions by which Congress had to satisfy a number of claims before it should make any disposition of the ceded lands. It proved afterward that Congress could hardly make any disposition whatever of the acquired lands for the claims were in excess of lands whose Indian title had been extinguished by that State. Being thus covered by reservations, the cession made by North Carolina was only nominal, and no public lands were created out of the ceded territory"—meaning none for disposal by the Federal Government. Sato, *History of the Land Question in the United States; Johns Hopkins Hist. Ser.*, V, 38.

[8] This, though the campaign was quite as much for the protection of Mero district (the Cumberland Valley) as of the district onerated, in which lived the Franklinites.

[9] *N. C. St. Rec.*, XXI, 285.

curred in the passage of this remarkable resolution that effected his removal:

"Resolved, That it is the sense of this General Assembly, that John Sevier is the brigadier-general of the district of Washington, and ought to be obeyed as such *according to the date of his commission issued in the month of November, 1784;* and that the governor issue his proclamation requiring all the good people of that district to pay due regard thereto and govern themselves accordingly."

What must have been the feelings of the aged and true-hearted Evan Shelby when he learned that his loyalty and services and his commission as brigadier-general of the same district had been thus discredited? And what the emotions of Martin, his successor, as he rode his horse through the solitude of the wilderness to his home in the West? Whatever may have been the desert of either, it was not this at the hands of Carolinians.

The Assembly formed a new congressional district out of the transmontane counties; and in the succeeding February John Sevier was elected to serve as its delegate—the first member of the Congress under the Constitution to represent a part of the Mississippi Valley.

Congress accepted the cession and soon established in the region a territorial form of government under the formidable and misfit title "Territory of the United States of America, South of the River Ohio"—frequently for convenience designated as the "Southwest Territory." William Blount was chosen by President Washington to serve as the first governor, in preference to General Martin whose claims and application failed, though supported by Patrick Henry. Sevier, who was the choice of the western people for the governorship of the Territory,[10] was appointed as brigadier-general of territorial forces by the President, and he and his friends were in the ascendency in the new government. Tipton and other opponents of the Franklin leader received honorable though secondary recognition, from either constituencies or the appointing power.

---

[10] In convention at Greeneville May 5, 1790: "No other man on the continent, the President of the United States not excepted, can give as general satisfaction to the people... Party heat and civil commotions are not yet assuaged, so that a long acquaintance must be essential to govern a people martial in their nature and heretofore in a kind of anarchy." Hardin, chairman, to Samuel Johnston, Hayes Coll. of MSS.

Finally the people realized their desire for separate statehood, when, on June 1, 1796, Congress admitted the State of Tennessee into the Union—the first member erected out of a territory of the United States.

John Sevier was elected by the people as the first governor almost as of course and without opposition, and served six terms of two years each—an honor never bestowed on any other Tennessean.

The legislature and the judiciary of Tennessee had to solve a number of problems that were the results of the Franklin regime: the status of marriages consummated under Franklin licenses;[11] of judgments rendered by the courts;[12] of administration of estates,[13] etc. The situation dealt with was one without parallel in American jurisprudence, since Franklin was and is the only example of a *de facto* American State that functioned in every aspect of statal power.

---

[11] All marriages validated by Tennessee Act, 1803, Ch. 25.

[12] The *North Carolina Act of 1786*, Ch. 23, had provided that where any judgments in the courts of Franklin respecting property were incompatible with justice, the person aggrieved should have his remedy at common law. The court of last resort in Tennessee construed this to mean that the proceedings of the courts of Franklin were of obligatory force when substantial justice had been attained. The western inhabitants had been under the protection of the State of Franklin during its existence, and a presumption of law arose that such proceedings were compatible with justice, subjecting the claimant to the burden of proving the contrary. *Ingraham's Heirs v. Cocke*, 1 Overton (1 Tenn. Rep.), 22.

[13] Validated by Act 1801, Ch. 24. An instrument of conveyance admitted to record under Franklin authority was treated as if recorded in Tennessee. *Tennessee Act*, 1815, Ch. 1.

CHAPTER XXXIII

Modes of Life

As settlements progressed further and further down the valleys of the Nolachucky and Holston rivers, in the upper and older section of Franklin, freed from the terror of Indian invasions by the buffer vanguard a distinct advance was made in the scale of living. Many of the houses were enlarged, the single-room log cabin with its "lean-to shed" giving place to double log houses, each unit having a loft, or garret. These units were connected by a roofed passage-way open at both ends, which served as a porch and storage place for the family tool-chest, the water-bucket and a day's supply of wood. Sawmills were not in use in the earlier days, but the whipsaw contributed to the making of more comfortable houses. The whipsaw was operated by hand. The timber was first squared with adze or broad-axe, then raised to a scaffold six or seven feet high. Two strong men operated the saw, one standing on the scaffold, the other below it. To turn off one hundred feet of boards for flooring and trim was a good day's work for two men. Some of those better circumstanced erected stone houses of the native blue limestone; these almost invariably were two-story structures. No use was made of bricks.

Bloomeries and forges for the production of iron were established on a small scale about 1786–7, and iron nails, hinges and other structural parts came into more general use. Improvement, too, was made in agricultural implements and household utensils.

In the manufacture of bread-stuffs, the sweep and pestle were superseded by small water-mills which served neighborhoods. The franchise to operate these mills for toll was grantable by the county courts in their legislative capacity.

Far removed from markets, effort was directed toward the production of the essentials of life. Sugar was made from the sap of the maple trees which grew in abundance. The season for tapping was about the middle of February when the frost of the night followed by sunshine produced a free flow of sap. The sugar-making season continued for four or six weeks, after which the sap was too poor to make sugar but was capable of being made into molasses, vinegar, and a species of table beer.

Salt was obtained from the nearby salt-works on the Holston in Virginia, owned by the minor daughter of General William Campbell, but operated at this time on an enlarged scale by Colonel Arthur Campbell, her guardian.

There were few skilled artisans in Franklin. The blacksmith and the gunsmith plied their trades and were looked upon as men of consequence. Colonel George Doherty was an expert gunsmith and marksman. Woodenware, such as tubs, buckets and barrels, was made by general artisans, as were also, to some extent, chairs. The last were usually of oak or hickory, bottomed with splints of white-oak or slippery-elm. Baskets and hampers were woven of white-oak or hickory splints.

Handcraft in the homes was forced upon the families by necessity. The clothing was almost wholly home-made. Linsey-woolsey was the cloth usually worn by both sexes. Linen made from home-grown flax furnished the chain and wool supplied the filling or woof. A rough jeans was the cloth out of which the stouter garments of the men were made. Home tanning and cobbling customarily supplied the shoes, or shoe-packs fashioned somewhat after the moccasin of the Indians.

Land was cleared for cultivation by burning; generally the trees were belted or girdled and after dying they were felled, cut into logs, rolled into piles and burned. At times when burning was resorted to, the fire would get beyond control and a large area would be burned over, thereafter to be called a barren. Michaux, the younger, describes such a barren, produced in Franklin days in clearing land just north of Holston river. Wild strawberry vines matted the earth, and in season the "berries covered the ground as with a red cloth."[1]

Fine apples were produced; and the Franklin people were indebted to the friendly Chickasaws for species of superior peaches and plums.

From the same Indian nation was obtained a fine breed of horses highly valued by the Franklin people. These horses are said[2] to

---

[1] Hence the name of Strawberry Plains for this locality.

[2] Hugh Williamson in his *Observations* (1811), p. 80. The breed was in repute in East Tennessee in the latter decade of the eighteenth century. A Rogersville breeder advertised a celebrated sire named Piomingo; "a fine Spanish horse raised

have been derived from a breed of Spanish horses left among the Chickasaws by De Soto, and to have been unmixed with any other strain. They furnished speed and stamina as mounts for Sevier's troopers.

A custom incident to warfare between the bordermen and the Cherokee Indians was, that the horses captured by the bordermen from the Indians were put to auction sale, but not until after those who had lost horses to the Indians had been compensated by an allotment in kind.

The frontiersmen, as hunters and soldiers, relied for a supply of bullets largely on a vein of lead ore found on the lands of John Sevier in the mountains about two and one-half miles from his residence in Washington county.[3]

Powder was as necessary as lead and, as merchandise, was at times not procurable. Necessity forced a home production. Charcoal, of course, was readily obtainable. Saltpetre was made from nitrous soil taken from local caves and submitted to a process of leaching and boiling. The manufacture was at rude water-mills. A mill consisted of a pole suspended at the middle by means of a white-oak pin which rested in the two forks of timber. Another pin was placed perpendicular in the front end, forming a pestle. The back end of the pole carried a box into which the water poured, by its weight raising the front end; as the water rushed out the pestle fell upon the charcoal, saltpetre and sulphur in a log trough used as a mortar. The sulphur was brought hundreds of miles, on packhorses usually.

The soldiers under Sevier went to war as mounted infantrymen. Men to hold and guard the horses were counted off. The onslaught was one of surprise and accompanied by a piercing yell that carried terror to the enemy—doubtless the same as the famous rebel yell of the Civil War. Indeed, the methods and strategy of Sevier may well have passed, as by descent cast, to that other great commander of Tennesseans, Nathan Bedford Forrest.

The highways were few and poor. The upkeep devolved upon "warned in" hands who labored an allotted number of days under

---

in the Chicksaw nation." *Knoxville Gazette*, of March 24, 1792. See also Smith's *Tour*, I, page 139.

[3] In this immediate section iron ore was later found and reduced to pig iron in furnaces for several generations; and in recent years immense deposits of zinc have been discovered and mined.

an easy-going supervisor of the neighborhood section. The road ended in a blazed trail which terminated in a bridle path, beyond which was the wellnigh trackless forest. There were scarcely any bridges over the streams and few ferries.

Several streams were navigated by flat-boats, usually of forty or sixty tons burden, since they were more wieldy and safer. The boats were constructed of oak, and were proportioned twelve by forty feet for a forty-ton craft. Only larger ones had any covering. Most of them were purposely of cheap construction because they were destined for sale as plank at the down-stream destination. Boats of sixty tons employed six hands, particularly if a cargo of goods was to be brought back—poled up-stream.

Few of the villages of Franklin were located on navigable streams so as to have their goods brought in entirely by boat; but from a very early day the Boat Yard (Kingsport) at the junction of the two forks of Holston river was a center for water transportation, and commerce. Lieutenant Armstrong, of the United States Army, in giving a report of his official visit to Franklin (April, 1788) calls "Sullivan Court House the metropolis of the new State."[4] The other villages were, in the order of their size, Jonesborough, Greeneville, and Hawkins Court House (Rogersville). Goods sold in these places were purchased in Richmond, Baltimore and Philadelphia.

Each village had one or more taverns, the rates fixed by public authority for entertainment being: Diet, one shilling; lodging, four pence; liquor, half pint, six pence; pasture and stable, six pence; corn per gallon, eight pence; oats per gallon, six pence.

One traveling between villages or on the frontier could always find entertainment in the homes of the people. Hospitality was the unwritten law. Bishop Hoss says: "To have turned a hungry man from one's door, would have been to pay a premium for general contempt, and 'light, stranger, hitch your horse and come in,' was the salutation most in use when anybody that was unknown by face rode up to the door."

---

[4] This indicates that the first regular seat of justice in Sullivan county was at Kingsport prior to the laying out of Blountville in 1792.

CHAPTER XXXIV

Travelers in Franklin

Few travelers visited Franklin. The barrier interposed by nature between it and North Carolina in two lofty mountain chains deflected the strong current of travel from Carolina to Kentucky and the Cumberland country, through Flour Gap, Abingdon, Martin's Station and Cumberland Gap, and away from the territory of the Franks. The main wilderness road through these places was reached by a lateral road from Franklin which passed near the Long Island of Holston, forming the junction at the North Fork of Holston a few miles southeast of Moccasin Gap in Virginia. Most of the travelers to the West in the years 1784-1789 passed over the main road; and therefore few journals or diaries of travel relate to the comparatively secluded country of Franklin; and as the Cherokees occupied the country to the south, few travelers to Georgia passed through the territory of Franklin.

It so happens that the only visitors who made anything like ample records of their visits to Franklin were ministers of the gospel—men of intelligence, whose comments are illuminative of life on the frontier.

The Moravian Brethren, who had settled their Wachovia grant around Salem, North Carolina, in 1753, from the outset had it in purpose to spread the gospel among the Cherokee Indians. In 1783, they sent one of the brethren, Martin Schneider, on a visit to the Overhill Cherokees to propose the establishment of a mission in their country. Brother Schneider set out from Wachovia December 19th with letters of introduction from Colonel Martin Armstrong to Colonel John Sevier and Colonel Joseph Martin, intending to meet a delegation of the Indians at Long Island. Passing through Flour Gap, by Christmas eve he reached the neighborhood of Colonel Evan Shelby, where he learned that three weeks before nine of the Chickamauga Indians had been at the home of Colonel Sevier, complaining that the white people were settling on their lands. "But Colonel Sevier would not hear them and made as if he did not understand them, on account of which the Indians grew very angry and said that next spring they would find the scalps of the white people... In the neighborhood were frolics, shooting and fighting. My companion went to one of the frolics at Colonel Shelby's where General Rutherford, of Salisbury, lies with his people, with whom he intends to go to Muscle Shoals in Cumberland where land is measured out for the soldiers.[1]

Dec. 26th. I pursued my journey alone and arrived in the evening safely in the house of Colonel Joseph Martin, two miles to the right hand of Long Island and one hundred and eighty miles from Salem. Here I found not the least appearance of the treaty which was the occasion of my journey. Colonel Martin himself had set out for the Cherokee towns on the 22nd; but his people believed that he was still with Mr. Harland,[2] an Indian trader, forty miles from his home. I set out early on the 27th... This morning, I passed the north fork of the Holston river and came in the evening to Captain Amis'[3] where I met a young Indian trader whose name was Grantham. He was a very welcome man, for upon my desire he told me the names of the Indian towns and Colonel Martin's Indian name[4] that, in case Colonel Martin should be gone and I be obliged to travel alone, I could tell the Indians whom I might meet whither I was going. He also went with me on the 28th over the Holston river, which is here a quarter of a mile broad, as far as Mr. Harland's. Here I found that Mr. Harland had set out with Colonel Martin on Christmas day. I was at a loss what to do... It was impossible for me to return without executing my mission... Towards evening I came to Colonel Smith's which is the last house on the road and where the wagon road ceases. He showed me the footpath to his father's[5] where I stayed all night.

The 29th. In the morning my horse was nowhere to be seen. I looked for it two miles around but could not find it. A neighbor's

---

[1] Br. Schneider evidently was confused by the talk he heard of the country in the Big Bend of Tennessee, and thought the Muscle Shoals were in the Cumberland river. Rutherford was on his way to Nashville.

[2] Ellis Harland or Harlin.

[3] Later, Rogersville.

[4] Gluglu, as given by Schneider in another part of his journal. Probably gulkalu (tall) as it sounded in the ears of the traveler.

[5] James Smith, Senior and Junior, were from North Carolina. The one was on the Wautauga in the early part of 1775. He served as the first clerk of the land office under Charles Robertson, Trustee; was a member of the Committee of Safety of 1776; and coöperated in defense of Fort Caswell, on the Watauga in the same year. The other remained longer in North Carolina where he commanded a company under the Carolina Committee of Safety, and in the same year became a member of the Committee. *N. C. Col. Rec.*, X, 309, 311. He arose in rank to a majority which he resigned January 2, 1779. *Ib.*, XIV, 6. Both father and son were advocates of separation.

wife told me that the same had happened to another man a week ago, and at last it was found that a negro had rode it a side way and then tied it to a tree. I was therefore obliged to offer a reward for my horse, and in an hour's time it was brought to me. I came till in the evening fifteen miles, but my path became so undiscernible that I saw no other way but to return the next day to Colonel Smith's. It continued to snow very fast. I therefore made a fire before a leaning or bended tree, which was burnt hollow, and set myself during the night in that hollow tree where I was kept dry, but was dyed pretty black. The next morning the snow was of good service to me, for I had forgot to take my night's lodging near a water, and I could melt snow for my coffee.

The 30th. I arrived again with Colonel Smith, and was obliged to resolve to take a man and horse as guide with me to Island Ford on French Broad forty-five miles hence, for which they asked three dollars.

The 31st. I set out anew with my guide and came in the evening, to Mr. Jesse Gentry's[5a] twenty-six miles farther. Between Messrs. Smith and Gentry there are about three or four new settlers.

The New Year of 1784 found the traveler at the French Broad river. He comments upon the clearness of the western streams, with their stone or gravel beds.

The country from Flour (Flower) Gap hitherto is very hilly, on which account most of the plantations lie between two ridges, and are very narrow and long. But the wood, even on the highest mountains is very thick and good, and the land in the valleys is very fertile. Often I wished that we had one of their many limestone hills in our neighborhood. The people there make scarcely any use of it. Towards evening I went into a house to warm myself a little because it was very cold. The man whose name was Happert [Hubbard][6] asked me about my business with the Indians, which I told him. He did not seem to be satisfied. He, however, bid me a forced civil farewell; but I was scarce gone a hundred steps when he called me back in anger and said he must know my business better, for as I was going to Colonel Martin I could have no good intention. I did all I could to pacify him, and assured him that I knew nothing at all of their land affairs, whereby I brought it at last so far that he dispatched me with some curses. This man and many others are such enemies to Colonel Martin that he has reason to be very much on his guard on his journeys, and that merely because he takes the part of the Indians and has effected it with the government that the country of the Cherokees has been con-

---

[5a] Of the Jefferson county family of Gentry, among the earliest settlers in that region.

[6] James Hubbard, elsewhere mentioned.

firmed to them by an act of Assembly, and will not suffer that the white people settle on their hunting grounds. But these people would rather like to extirpate them altogether and take their land themselves. They scarce look upon them as human creatures, which I could often perceive in their conversations.

In the evening I went to the ford of French Broad river to an island about three-fourths of a mile broad. The river is but narrow; I tried to ride through it, but in vain, because my guide was not acquainted with it. He showed me the path to Captain Guest's[7] three miles down the river, and then returned home. In the midst of the wood when I had lost my path I met the first Indian who in a very friendly manner showed me by signs the right road. He thereupon shaked my saddlebags, out of which I gave him some bread and meat, and it seemed it was what he wanted. With Captain Guest I stayed all night. His old father,[8] who is still living, was in the first times a beloved neighbor of Bethabara[9] and knew still the names of all the brethren who then lived there; he rejoiced also heartily to see once more a brother.

The 2nd. Captain Guest brought me over the French Broad river; the ford goes over an island belonging to Colonel Sevier containing nine hundred acres and is as smooth as a meadow. Captain Guest told me that eight miles farther up the river was another island of eight hundred acres, and in the midst of it a whole acre dug out, eighteen feet deep. This round hole is full of water and the earth dug out so that in the edge still a ditch remained. On the top of it [the earthworks] was formerly a house of earth of which still something is to be seen. Over the whole island there is a ditch and a breastwork but the Indians themselves don't seem to know by whom or for what purpose all this work has been done. The common report is that once an Indian king had his dwelling there. In the evening I found a fine camp eleven miles on the other side of Little river, where I could hide myself in a little hut from a heavy rain.

The 3rd. At ten o'clock in the forenoon I came to the first Indian house on this side the Tennessee [Little Tennessee] river, one hundred and twenty miles from Long Island. One of them showed me the ford; I gave him a tobacco pipe and he explained to me by signs in which house on the other side, which is called Sitiko, Colonel Martin was to be found. Having got on the other side, I saw him creeping out of an Indian hot-house;[10] and he came to wel-

---

[7] Joshua Gist (sometimes Gest). See sketch, *post*, p. 314.

[8] Benjamin Gist. See sketch, *post*, p. 314.

[9] One of the Moravian churches in Wachovia Settlement. For the Gists in that neighborhood see Fries, *Moravian Records*, I, *passim*. They were relatives of Christopher and Nathaniel Gist.

[10] "Every family has, besides the dwelling house, a still smaller hot-house. This has but a very small opening to creep into it, and this is their abode in cold weather,

come me in a very friendly manner, and, having read Colonel Armstrong's letter, he said that he would be at my service in my concern as much as he possibly could. He inquired in a very friendly manner about the brethren in Salem, where he gladly had visited long ago and intends soon to do it... He took me with him to his lodgings in the house of a trader, Mr. Springston[11] who was married to an Indian woman, but whose father-in-law was not at home during my stay there.

Brother Schneider remained among the Cherokees until the 11th day of January, and gives an interesting account of their customs and mode of life. Not being able to bring the Indians to a final decision in favor of a mission, he set out alone on the return journey, notwithstanding a snow covered the ground and obscured the path. Reaching Sevier's Island he selected a camping place on the lower end. He records in his journal:

12th.... Having forgot on the other side my tow and dry chips, and here being all wet, it was almost midnight before I could cook my supper. The wild geese and swans flew about me in great numbers. I could scarce get any sleep and spent the night in much perplexity, for the water grew higher and more rapid and roared beside me most frightfully. There is almost nobody living in the neighborhood of whom I could expect any help, and I saw before my eyes that I would not get over safely, but yet I believed our Savior could help me.

13th. I breakfasted before break of day and put as few clothes on as possible... Three-quarters of the way [crossing over the stream] it went very well, but now two large cakes of ice between which I must pass got hold of my horse and with a violent current down the stream till into a hole twelve or fifteen feet deep, in which but lately a man was drowned. My horse which otherwise could swim very well could scarce keep up on account of the pointed rocks, on which account I was several times in water until under my arms. On the shore there was no place for landing, because there was nothing but rocks which are as straight as a wall and some are hollowed out twenty feet deep by the violent current. At last I saw a little opening between the rocks where, to my good fortune, was also so much ground that my horse could stand in the water above his belly. I jumped down into the water, took my things off and tied my horse to a piece of wood fastened by the ice, and climbed up through the narrow pass, but which was too straight for my horse... All was to me like a dream, and now I had to run three miles through the snow over hills, without roads or paths in wet

etc." (Schneider's *Journal*.) See on the hot-houses, Williams, *Memoirs of Lt. Timberlake*, 61.

[11] A trader and trusted messenger of Colonel Martin.

clothes to Captain Guest's... Captain Guest and his family were frightened, seeing me coming without coat and quite covered with ice, and cared for me in a most loving manner and gave me dry clothes. I was so fatigued that I could scarce speak a word. Captain Guest and another man went to fetch my horse out of the water ... by tying the bridle to a long pole and in this manner swim it to the ford, one pulling before and the other pushing behind.

The stout-hearted Brother, traveling up Dumplin Creek then down Long Creek, a distance of twenty miles, came again into the "plantations." He notes the courtesy shown by the settlers in accompanying him over obscure parts of the trail, until he again reached the home of Colonel Smith; thence he passed on to Long Island where he stayed on the night of January 17th.

In going and coming, Schneider did not pass through the more closely settled portions of the country. He notes regretfully the failure to see Sevier "because he lived twenty-five miles out of my way, on Chuckey river."[12]

In July, 1785, Governor Sevier was visited at his home on the Nolachucky by Piomingo, the greatest chief produced by the bravest and most chivalrous of all the Southern tribes, the Chickasaws. He was accompanied by several other Chickasaw chiefs and went as high up as Long Island of Holston while in Franklin. Everywhere he was given a cordial reception. Piomingo made a distinctly favorable impression. A letter from Franklin in the *Pennsylvania Packet*,[13] reporting his visit, says: "He seemed to be a man endowed with more than ordinary prowess of mind and humanity, for an Indian. In his speeches, he delivered himself fluently and with great force of argument, disclosing a clear knowledge of the strength and interest of the Southern tribes, and of the causes and effect of the late Revolution. These people are more comely in their persons and kindlier in their dispositions than any of the nations I have been acquainted with. If their present temper is well improved by the commissioner of Congress very valuable effects may be produced."

In another account it is said that Piomingo spoke freely of the

---

[12] MSS. of "Br. Martin Schneider's Report of His Journey to Long Island on Holston River, and from thence farther to the Upper Cherokee Townes on Tennessee River, from Middle of December, 1783, till January 24th, 1784." The entire Journal appears in the author's *Early Travels in Tennessee*, published in 1928.

[13] Issue of September 30, 1785.

growing power of the Americans and of the danger of his people having their country wrested from them. "He is urgent in soliciting a trade down the Tennessee, and says he will protect it from the plundering parties of the Cherokees. A small essay may be made. If it succeeds well it will be an inducement for the merchants on James river to embark largely, as it is certain the Tennessee is the nearest and best communication between the eastern navigation and the Mississippi."[14]

The object of this visit was to seek the opening of a trade with Franklin and to form a sort of alliance against the Creek Indians. The following year the king and chiefs of the Chickasaws sent a talk to Governor Sevier in which the visit of Piomingo was referred to. "As Piomingo and you promised to let each other know any news that would be worth sending, and as the Creeks have since got mad, we beg to know what time you intend to destroy them; or, if you intend to let them always kill your white people and yet make up with them."[15]

A young Methodist preacher from New Jersey, Thomas Ware, rode the Nolachucky circuit for one year, in 1787-8. He was educated and observant, and in later years recorded his experiences which are interesting in that they give the impressions made upon one of a sensitive nature, unaccustomed to the rude life and the ruder conditions of the frontier. He says:

In the fall of this year (1787) our presiding elder received letters from persons low down the Holston and French Broad, deploring their destitution of the gospel, and entreating him, if possible, to send them a preacher. These letters he read at a quarterly-meeting conference; and it was agreed that I should go and see if I could form a circuit in those parts. Accordingly I went. There are many things which rendered itinerating in that section of the country, at the time I went, peculiarly painful to a person like myself. I was still young in the ministry, and deeply sensible of my want of qualifications to act well the part of a pioneer; but, having pledged myself to go and having evidence that my feeble efforts had been crowned with some success, nothing could deter me from redeeming my pledge.

The winters are shorter and the climate less frigid in East Tennessee than in New Jersey; but sometimes the cold for a few days is intense. At these times, especially when I had to ford rivers and creeks at the risk of life, as I often had to do, and to lodge in open

---

[14] *Pennsylvania Packet*, October 27, 1785.
[15] *Ib.*, December 30, 1785.

cabins, with light bed-clothing and frequently with several children in the same bed, I was much exposed to taking cold, and traveling there on these accounts was rendered exceedingly crossing to my nature. But, in addition to these, much of the time my path was infested with savage men, the deadly foe of white men who had but too justly incurred their resentment; and more subtle and terrible enemies among human beings could not be imagined than were the native red men, incensed at the wrongs inflicted upon them by the whites. Several families and individuals had been murdered by them in places directly on the routes I had to travel; and once, at least, I narrowly escaped being murdered or taken prisoner. My course led through a fine bottom covered chiefly with crab-apple trees. I passed along very slowly, making my observations on the richness of the soil, the timber and grass which at that late season was yet green, and had thoughts of halting to muse a little in the grove; but, recollecting at the moment that I had heard a rumor about hostile Indians in that vicinity, I concluded not to stop, but rather mend my pace. I had now approached a lofty grove when suddenly my horse stopped, snorted and wheeled about. As he wheeled, I caught a glimpse of an Indian but at too great a distance to reach me with his rifle. I gave my horse the reins and hastened to the nearest settlement to give the alarm. I had been told that some horses were singularly afraid of an Indian. Be that as it may, I have reasons to suppose that the sudden fright which mine took at seeing one was the means, under God, of saving me from death or captivity.

At another time while I was preaching at the house of a man who had invited us by letter to visit their settlement, we were alarmed with the cry of "Indians!" The terror this cry excited at that time, none can imagine except those who witnessed it. Instantly every man flew to his rifle and sallied forth to ascertain the ground for the alarm. On coming out we saw two lads running with all speed and screaming, "the Indians have killed mother!" We followed them about a quarter of a mile and witnessed the affecting scene of a woman weltering in her blood. It was what the people called a good sugar day, and Mrs. Carter, a brother's wife of the man at whose house we had met, chose to stay at home for the purpose of making sugar rather than go to the meeting, though it was in sight, and several of her friends had tried to persuade her to go with them.

The maple grove, or sugar bush was, near their dwelling, skirted on the side next to the river by what is called a canebrake. Here Mrs. Carter sat by the side of a large buckeye tree which had fallen down, spinning and watching her sugar while her sons were gathering wood. They happened at the time to be at a distance and in the direction of their uncle's house. The Indians were concealed in the canebrake and, coming up slyly behind the fallen tree, drove the tomahawk into her head before she knew they were near. The Indian who did the bloody deed was seen by the boys just as he struck their mother, but they were at a sufficient distance to make their escape.

Ware gives an account of the Sevier-Tipton skirmish, but from hearsay. He was filling an appointment on the French Broad at the time and there came in contact with what he describes as "a large company of men going to attack Colonel Tipton." Ware endeavored to dissuade them from their purpose, and in such a way that they concluded he was a friend of Tipton. Some of them proposed (probably for sport) to take him before the governor, who was about ten miles distant, for trial as a spy. He proceeds with the narrative:

While they disputed I withdrew to an adjoining room, hastened to the stable by a back way, saddled my horse and was out of their reach before they knew I was off. Thus I escaped the vengeance of infuriated men, but became exposed to imminent danger from another quarter. It was now near night; and I had twelve or fifteen miles to ride in order to reach the first settlement. The river I had to ford was fifty rods wide and filled with floating ice which in some places was congealed into large cakes, rendering the passage extremely difficult and dangerous. But my noble beast carried me safely over.

I had a very imperfect knowledge of the way, and as the marks of the trees were my principal guide, it was a matter of much doubt whether I could find it in the night. As I feared, it so happened. I took a path which soon came to an end. By this time I had become so chilled that I could scarcely keep myself awake upon my horse. I was apprized of my danger, dismounted immediately and ran to and fro until I became warm. After taking several cow-paths which led into the forest from the river, all of which shortly came to an end, I concluded to throw the bridle on my horse's neck and let him have his course, and a little before midnight he brought me to the house where I wished to go. The night was so exceedingly cold, and the house of my friend so open, that he and his family had found it more comfortable to remain up and keep a good fire than to retire to rest. In this condition I found them; and never was a good country fire and a kind reception by friends more welcome to my feelings.[16]

To conserve and advance the work of Ware and his fellow-laborers, Bishop Asbury, the first apostle of American Methodism, made a journey across the mountain ranges and organized the first annual conference in the West. From that time until the close of his life he continued, in feebleness of body, to make those journeys

---

[16] Ware, *Sketches of Life and Travels.*

which in the history of Christian heroism are unmatched except by those of the apostle Paul and Livingston.

Starting westward from North Carolina, April 28, 1788, the good Bishop records in his journal:[17]

After getting our horses shod, we made a move for the Holston, and entered upon the mountains, the first of which I called Steel, the second Stone, and the third Iron mountain: they are rough, and difficult to climb. We were spoken to on our way by most awful thunder and lightning, accompanied by heavy rain. We crept for shelter into a little dirty house where the filth might have been taken up from the floor with a spade; we felt the want of fire, but could get little wood to make it, and what we gathered was wet. At the head of Watauga we fed, and reached Ward's that night. Coming to the river next day we hired a young man to swim over for the canoe, in which we crossed, while our horses swam to the other shore. The waters being up we were compelled to travel an old road over the mountains. Night came on—I was ready to faint with a violent headache, the mountain was so steep on both sides. I prayed to the Lord for help; presently a profuse sweat broke out upon me and my fever entirely subsided. About nine o'clock we came to Greer's. After taking a little rest here, we set out next morning for Brother Cox's on Holston river. I had trouble enough; our route lay through the woods, and my pack horse would neither follow, lead nor drive, so fond was he of stopping to feed on the green herbage. I tried the lead and he pulled back. I tied his head up to prevent his grazing, and he ran back. The weather was excessively warm. I was much fatigued and my temper not a little tried. I fed at I. Smith's and prayed with the family. Arriving at the river, I was at a loss what to do, but providentially a man came along who conducted me across. This was an awful journey to me, and this a tiresome day, and now, after riding seventy-five miles, I have thirty-five more to General Russell's. I rest one day to revive man and beast.

Friday, May 2. Rode to Washington,[18] where I met brother Tunnel on the way to Mr. C's. We have to put up in houses where we have no opportunity for retirement.

Virginia:—Saturday 3. We came to General Russell's—a most kind family, in deed and in truth.

Sunday, 4. Preached on Phil. II, 5-9. I found it good to get alone in prayer.

Tuesday, 6. I had many to hear me at Easly's on Holston. I was much wearied riding a strange horse, having left mine to rest. It is some grief that I cannot be so much in prayer on the road as I would be. We had a good time, and a large congregation at K's.

---

[17] Asbury's *Journal*, II, 31, 32.
[18] Washington Court House, now Abingdon, Virginia.

Tennessee.[19]—The people are in disorder about the Old and New State: two or three men, it is said, have been killed.[20] At Nelson's[21] I had a less audience than was expected; the people having been called away on an expedition against the New State men: my subject was Hebr., VI, 11, 12. Rode to Owen's, and met our brethren from Kentucky, where I preached on Psalm CXIV, 17, 18, 19, with some fervor. Came to Hubbard's and Keywood's where we held conference three days, and I preached each day. The weather was cold; the room without fire, and otherwise uncomfortable; we nevertheless made out to keep our seats until we had finished the essential parts of our business.

---

[19] The word "Tennessee" was evidently inserted by Bishop Asbury in a revision of his journal at a later date when that name had been adopted for the Commonwealth.

[20] Reference is to the skirmish at Tipton's house in February.

[21] William Nelson's home was on a ridge, northwest of and just outside the limit of the present Johnson City, and on the farm now owned by Richard Carr. The Nelson house was a favorite stopping place of the Bishop—described by him, in 1806, as "an ancient home and stand for Methodists and Methodist preaching." *Journal*, III, 206. A marker of granite is on the farm, commemorating the fact.

CHAPTER XXXV

RELIGION IN FRANKLIN

The Revolutionary War, like all long-continued wars, was followed by a period of moral unrestraint; tension broken, a rebound followed. Dr. Alexander, of Princeton, of the Presbyterian church, and the Methodist Bishop Asbury are in accord in the view that in the period succeeding the War of the Revolution, vital piety was at a low ebb. The people were insensible to the genuine spirit of religion, and "full of the spirit of the world."[1]

A like condition obtained among the people of Franklin who had derived from the older sections, and who had removed to the border in search of fortune. They plunged whole-heartedly into a conflict with the forces of nature. The reckless hardihood bred by the war now found vent in grim struggling with elemental forces for the right to exist. Their spiritual natures, if clamant at all, might wait until tyrannous necessity relaxed its hold. Men were compelled to think more of the means of living than of the meaning of life.

And with this border people another war was unending. The redmen to the south were ever-threatening and often out-breaking foes. War-strain did not cease. This condition was a challenge to the churches. It was not unheeded.

The Presbyterian church had been first in the field; and it now saw that there was need of an augmented ministerial force if the ground was to be held. From Liberty Academy in the Valley of Virginia Revs. Samuel Houston and Samuel Carrick came to aid Samuel Doak in spreading the gospel among the people; and Rev. Hezekiah Balch came across the mountains from the stronghold of Presbyterianism, Mecklenburg county, North Carolina, on the same mission.

It is interesting to note that contemporary with the declaration of separate statehood in this region, there was a demand for a new ecclesiastical jurisdiction in the Presbyterian church. Prior to 1785, the Presbytery of Hanover was regarded by the Synod of

---

[1] Dr. Archibald Alexander in *Biblical Repository*, April, 1848; Asbury's *Journal*.

New York and Philadelphia as including the settled parts of Tennessee and Kentucky. In that year, Doak laid before the Synod an application, signed by Balch, Cummings and himself, that Abingdon Presbytery be created; to be bounded on the north by New River, and on the east by the Appalachian mountains, the southern and western limits left unfixed. The request was granted, and the first meeting of the new Presbytery was appointed to be held in the bounds of Franklin, at Salem church, Doak to preside as moderator. The time fixed was the first Tuesday in August, 1785. It is not improbable that the idea of the new ecclesiastical jurisdiction was suggested to Doak by the establishment of Franklin in which he was taking part at this time. The planting of new churches kept pace with the outward flow of population; and when the State of Franklin came to an end, there were more than twenty churches of this denomination established within the limits of that State.

Two other denominations came to dispute, and not without success, this undoubted earlier supremacy of the church of the Scotch-Irish settlers. That deep student of American institutions and government, James Bryce, has well characterized the South as a region of "high religious voltage"; commenting upon which, Frederick J. Turner says the characterization is especially applicable to the Upland South, which has always been responsive to emotion and intensely democratic.[2]

In the efforts to cover so wide a field with a corps of well-educated ministers of the Presbyterian faith, these few perforce were well nigh as much itinerants as the circuit riders of another church came to be. But as towns were established and demanded the continuous services of pastors, the country districts and far-flung settlements were left more and more to the ministrations of the Methodist circuit-riders and the Baptist preachers who, with a zeal worthy of admiration, preached a soul-stirring gospel that was gladly heard by the common people of the hill country.

The Baptists had come into the region before the Methodists; and, as early as 1779, established a church at Buffalo Ridge in Washington county, with Tidence Lane as pastor. They were only one year later than the Presbyterians in forming a separate and independent association in the new State. Holston Association was organized October 30th, 1786, at the Cherokee Meeting House, in Washington county, Tidence Lane serving as moderator and Wil-

---

[2] *The Frontier in American History*, 167.

liam Murphy as clerk. The following churches were in the Association: Kendrick's Creek (Double Springs); Bent Creek (Whitesburg); Beaver Creek; Greasy Cove (Unicoi county); Cherokee Creek; North Fork of Holston (near Kingsport); Lower French Broad River (Dandridge).

In the original minute book, yet preserved, is the "Plan of Association" of this first Baptist association in Franklin, and one of the earliest, if not the first, west of the Alleghany mountains:

1st. We hold it necessary to associate together in council in order to give counsel to the respective churches that compose this Association, in order to maintain our Christian fellowship.

2nd. Not as a legislative body to impose laws or exercise any supremacy, each church being an independent body.

3rd. We are not an association of ministers, but of churches, each church being represented by her own delegates, freely chosen.

4th. Whereas, a church is constituted externally by the parties entering into mutual agreement in writing to maintain the worship of God, according to the Gospel order, and referring to the articles of their faith; so churches by their delegates constitute themselves an Association by the confession of their faith maintained to each other.

The independence and individualism manifested in these articles accorded with the spirit of the frontiersmen; and has remained to the present time a distinctive feature of the polity of the denomination. A more rapid growth would have resulted but for the anti-missionary and non-progressive spirit of the early Baptists. In 1788, according to Morse's Geography, there were but ten Baptist churches in Franklin, and those of small membership, as against twenty-three large Presbyterian congregations.

Most of the Baptists were of the Separate order; a few were Regulars, and the tenets of all were essentially Calvanistic.[3]

The ministers at this period were: Tidence Lane from North Carolina; William Murphy, Isaac Barton, Jonathan Mulky, James Keel, John Frost and Alexander Chambers, from Virginia. Most of them continued to be permanent residents of the country.

A Methodist circuit was formed in the country the year preceding the formation of the new State. In 1783 the Holston circuit embraced a portion of Southwest Virginia along with the Holston-

---

[3] Benedict, *Baptist Denominations*, 790-4. The Holston and Watauga Baptists came from the Sandy Creek church or Association in North Carolina founded by Stearns and his company of Separates or New Lights from New England.

Nolachucky country. Rev. Jeremiah Lambert was appointed to take charge of it, and was the first Methodist preacher in what is now Tennessee. At the end of the first year of his labors he reported a membership of seventy-six. Rev. Henry Wills succeeded him in 1784. In 1785, the year in which American Methodism was placed on an independent foundation, Wills was presiding elder, and Richard Swift and Michael Gilbert were the senior and junior circuit riders. In 1787, the circuit was divided into two, Holston and Nolachucky circuits. Bishop Asbury sent south to serve on the Nolachucky circuit, a well-educated young man from New Jersey, Rev. Thomas Ware, aged twenty-eight years. Ware left an interesting relation of his experience among the frontiersmen, which appears in another chapter. He was the first preacher to visit and to minister to the people south of the French Broad (in the fall of 1787). The gospel of free grace and free will met with a ready acceptance, and Methodism grew rapidly. It reached an element of the population to which Calvinism did not appeal, and vitalized the experience and rendered less sombre the lives of many.[4]

Colaborers with Ware, under Rev. John Tunnel as presiding elder, were Jeremiah Mastin, Nathaniel Moore and Micajah Tracey, circuit riders, and several zealous "local preachers," some of whom had preceded the itinerant preachers and broken the bread of life to the settlers in the cabins and woods.

Bishop Francis Asbury did not come to the region until the spring of 1788, but he had, on journeys through Virginia and Carolina, conceived that a second great epoch in American history would be the conquest of the wilderness beyond the Alleghanies and sensed the importance of tincturing that conquest with religious idealism; and he had urged young ministers in the older States to accept appointments on the frontier.

The Lutherans and the Quakers were yet to send ministers into the country; and the Episcopalians seemingly did not seek an opportunity to reach out from their stronghold on the seaboard and serve the needs of the backwoodsmen.

The Moravians, in 1784, sent Rev. Martin Schneider on a visit to the Overhill Cherokees to ascertain the feasibility of establishing a mission among the Indians. He found few of the brethren in Franklin, and it was no part of the plan of his church to begin religious work in the borders of that State.

[4] Price, *Holston Methodism*; McFerrin, *History of Methodism in Tennessee*.

There can be no disguising of the fact that a considerable fraction of the population felt little or no concern about religion. In the nature of things, some wild and turbulent characters were drawn to the border and some of higher type found vent in the adventurous activities of border life, and in breasting the blows of circumstance, looking chiefly to the acquisition of lands as reward for their aggressive courage.

CHAPTER XXXVI

THE PEOPLE OF FRANKLIN

The population of Franklin was composed almost wholly of emigrants from Virginia and North Carolina. Each of those States contributed approximately equal parts. The Virginian element slightly preponderated in the earlier years of settlement when the Holston-Watauga region was believed to be within the bounds of that Commonwealth, and later migrations did not bring the Carolinians to a predominance. Two things conduced to this result:. The trough-like Appalachian Valley gave direction to migration from the north toward the southwest. The current flowed as did the streams that had their sources in Virginia. It was easier to follow the great longitudinal valley to the southwest than to cross the mountain ranges and come out on the west, or for Carolinians to make the long detour through Flour Gap and the lower counties of Virginia.

Moreover, the location on the waters of the Cumberland river of the reservation of bounty lands for North Carolina's revolutionary soldiers caused a large stream of settlers to flow past the borders of Franklin.

The population of the State in 1788 was, at lowest reckoning, 25,000 souls. Brissot de Warville, the French traveler, thus fixes it in round numbers. He did not visit Franklin but reached the Shenandoah Valley and evidently based his estimate on information gained while there. The people of that Valley were in close touch with those of Franklin.

The estimate of Major Elholm (in the Greeneville Convention of 1787) was 30,000 inhabitants, and 9,000 free citizens, and this finds strong corroboration in the figures given by Imlay who wrote about four years later.[1]

The population of 1790 was, however, only 28,650 as ascertained by a loosely taken census. During the two intervening years there had been a steady drift of settlers into the region, but quite as

---

[1] *Winterbotham's View*, III, 171. See also Ramsey, 544.

distinct and persistent an outflow of Franklin's inhabitants westward, particularly after the opening of the wilderness road to the Cumberland Settlements.

The twenty-five thousand inhabitants were distributed among the counties of Franklin approximately as follows: Sullivan, 4,300; Washington, 4,500; Wayne, 1,700; Greene, 4,200; Caswell, 2,700; Spencer, 3,700; Sevier, 2,400; and Blount, 1,500.[2]

Several racial stocks were represented, but the principal strains were the English and the Scotch-Irish. Over-emphasis has been given to the weight of the Scotch-Irish element, both as to numbers and to influence. It did not preponderate in either regard.[3] A fairer statement is, that those who were of Scotch-Irish extraction exercised an influence out of proportion to their numbers. This was due in part to their sturdiness and restless energy, and quite as much, to the superior educational advantages many of them had enjoyed. Intermingled with these were families of Irish, of German, of Huguenot and of Welsh stock. The Germans were few in comparison with their numbers in the same region a generation later, and they furnished few leaders. The Welsh in the Shelbys, Conways, Evanses and Williamses, and most of all the Huguenots, in the Seviers, Vincents and Amis, were the most prolific of leaders, their total numbers considered.

The coincidence of these varied racial stocks naturally resulted in a cross-fertilization—a blending that tended to strength and sym-

---

[2] The distribution as of 1790 among the counties of the Territory South of the Ohio River which had been in the bounds of the Franklin State is thus given by Stephen B. Weeks who doubtless had access to the census returns: Sullivan, 4,447; Washington, 5,872; Greene, 7,741; Hawkins, 6,970; Sevier, 3,619. Why Sevier county should appear in such tabulation is not apparent; the reëstablishment of the county was not effected until 1794. Week's Tennessee's Population, *Tennessee Historical Magazine*, II, 243. A proper reckoning of the population in the period of 1780–1790 must have in consideration the fact that the increase in the inhabitants of Tennessee in the decade of 1790–1800 was 195.9 per centum—greater by far than the growth registered by the nation as a whole.

[3] Rossiter, an expert of the Census Bureau, estimates that there were in the bounds of what is now Tennessee, in 1790, 26,519 inhabitants of English extraction as against 3,574 of Scotch-Irish extraction. *A Century of Population Growth*, 121. He applies the proportions found in North Carolina in the same year, but this was an incorrect basis. The more populous tidewater sections of Virginia and North Carolina sent comparatively few representatives, and the Scotch-Irish of the piedmont and valley regions of those States did contribute largely to the peopling of Tennessee.

metry and to make a fit foundation for a democratic commonwealth.

They had come into the great valley as the result of individual initiative and enterprise; theirs was not even a community migration. They had come, too, of choice. They were not sent out as colonists—projectiles across intervening space—by skilful promoters or speculators intent upon winning a principality for themselves under the guise of colonizing the West.

They had not come full-handed; cheap land was the attraction, and homes for selves and the oncoming generation was the goal of the typical settler. The economic structure was essentially agricultural. There was almost no servant or tenant class; land was too cheap or easily preëmpted for even those of lowly birth to be content to serve. Cheap land promoted individualism and economic equality, which along with an innate spirit of independence generated an intense democracy. Early marriage was the rule; frequently the groom was not of age, and the bride was burdened by not more than the weight of sixteen years. Large families resulted, and thus was supplied the manpower for tilling the fields. The owners of the larger farms in the fertile valleys were also holders of slaves. Negro slavery had been in existence in the region from the days of the Watauga Association, and by 1788 the number owned in the State of Franklin was around fifteen hundred.[4]

The women of the period were accustomed to the performance of many forms of labor. Young girls, of the average family, gave some assistance in the fields, such as the dropping of seed corn, and the gathering of flax which they later hatchelled, spun and wove. No small part of woman's domestic service was that rendered at the loom and dye-pot, and with the needle. They slaved to make

---

[4] Rossiter, in his *A Century of Population Growth, 1790–1900*, 132, 133, states that the number of slaves in the Southwest Territory in 1790 was 3,417, and that by 1800 they had increased to 13,584. While the soil and the crops in the Cumberland Country made slave labor more profitable there than in the higher altitudes of the eastern parts, it is believed that 1,500 slaves in Franklin in 1788 is not an under-estimate. A negro, belonging to William Evans, was executed by hanging under the authority of the State of Franklin. The owner petitioned the first General Assembly of the Southwest Territory for redress by way of compensation. *Journal of House of Representatives*, 10. The claim was disallowed. *Ib.*, 15. In 1786 the average price of land in North Carolina was two dollars per acre, while it might be purchased on the Tennessee river west of the mountains for a shilling and six pence per acre. Watson, *Men and Times of the Revolution*, 292.

clothing for the slaves as well as for members of their immediate families. The care of the vegetable gardens and of the dairying and the poultry also fell to their lot, as did also the making of sugar from maple sap. A high order of managerial skill, therefore, marked the womanhood of Franklin. This, transmitted to their offspring, in some measure accounts for the executive ability demonstrated by so many of the sons of this border people.

Hemmed in by the Alleghanies on the east and by the Cumberland mountains on the west—between the hot lowlands of Carolina and the further Mississippi Valley—the region had a bracing climate. The mean altitude was about fourteen hundred feet above sea level; the mean temperature about sixty degrees. The diseases most common were rheumatism, agues and fevers. Smallpox was the dreaded scourge. Tuberculosis was almost unknown. So healthy were the inhabitants that from the first settlement of the country to 1788, not a single trained physician had settled in the district. One of its inhabitants is quoted by Winterbotham as writing: "Our physicians are a fine climate; healthy, robust mothers and fathers; a plain and plentiful diet, and enough exercise. There is not a regularly bred physician residing in the whole district."

Schools were few, especially so among the inhabitants out on the fringe of settlement. In the older neighborhoods, the instruction given was elementary, except that afforded by the academies of Doak and other parsons. In the upper section of the State as early as 1784, the young people enjoyed the privilege of instruction in a dancing-school conducted in Sullivan county by Captain Barrett,[5] a young English officer who had served under the King's standard in the War of the Revolution.

The percentage of illiteracy was large. Ramsey and Roosevelt underestimate it. The people, speaking in the large, had few opportunities for an education, either in their old home communities or in the new. They were in close conflict with the forces of Nature, and the old Dame was not in one of her gentler moods. Elemental rawness and crudity appeared in the background and in the foreground. The tranquillity of pastoral scenes—of peaceful herds and flocks

---

[5] Ellett, *Pioneer Women of the West*, 162. Probably Captain Samuel T. Barret, of the 37th Regiment, born June 22, 1761. Another school teacher whose name and service are preserved was Humphrey Hogan who taught at King's Mill, Reedy Creek, Sullivan County. Wm. L. Lovely, of the Virginia forces in the Revolution is said to have been another.

and well-filled granaries and barns—was not for them an inherited environment. Even the boundless forest was an enemy to be attacked with axe while the redman was held back with rifle. A self-reliant and purposeful, if not a cultured, race of men was developed.

It would be a matter of surprise if under such conditions and among so many stout-hearted men, there should not be a few raw-hearted ones. Every sector of the frontier, whether at the Northwest or at the Southwest, produced a clearly marked type, the Indian hater, such as James Hubbard and John Kirk. Usually he was a man who had suffered agony of soul in the blotting out of loved ones at the hands of the savages. That agony hardened into a spirit of revenge that bordered on monomania. He struck in retaliation at times so blindly and fiercely as to bring mischief upon his own race.

Another factor that made for the virility of this people of the backcountry was the comparative youthfulness of the settlers. Very few old folk and few past middle age removed to that region. A new country was peopled by hardy, buoyant and enterprising youth. No one placidly looked forward to the enjoyment of a patrimony, except it be one to the creation of which his own hands contributed. A beautiful valley and the almost boundless West lay before them, beckoning all to adventure themselves. The thing most worthy of remark is the far reach and wide range of the vision and plans of the people of Franklin, and the projective power that gave them and their descendants a very considerable mastery of men and measures throughout the generations that have followed.

It may be doubted whether any other population of twenty-five thousand souls at any time in American history has produced more men of force and influence.[6] The records made by the leaders of Franklin themselves, is elsewhere noted. One president of the United States, Andrew Jackson, and two governors, McMinn and Roane, appear on the petition for separation. What of their descendants? Taking into account only those who bore or bear the surname of their paternal ancestor of Franklin days, among the descendants are found:

Cabinet members: D. M. Key, postmaster-general; Wm. G.

---

[6] Disproving the assertion of Gouveneur Morris, that "the busy haunts of men, not the remote wilderness, is the proper school of political talents."

McAdoo, secretary of the treasury; Isaac Shelby, secretary of war (declined); John H. Reagan, postmaster-general, C.S.A.

Diplomats: A. H. Sevier, minister to Mexico, and James Williams, minister to Turkey.

Senators: Hugh L. White, Spencer Jarnagin, Hopkins L. Turney, David T. Patterson, David M. Key, E. W. Carmack, Robert L. Taylor and J. B. Frazier, of Tennessee; David Barton and John B. Henderson, of Missouri; John Tipton, of Indiana; Ambrose H. Sevier and James Henderson Berry, of Arkansas; John H. Reagan, of Texas; Wm. Kelly, of Alabama; John Martin, of Kansas; Jeter C. Pritchard, of North Carolina, and Landon C. Haynes, C.S.A.

Governors: Wm. B. Campbell, Robert L. Caruthers, Robert L. Taylor, Peter Turney, James B. Frazier, John I. Cox and Alfred A. Taylor, of Tennessee; Elias N. Conway, James Sevier Conway and James H. Berry, of Arkansas; Austin A. King, of Missouri; Wm. L. Sharkey, of Mississippi; Isaac Shelby, of Kentucky; Joshua L. Martin, of Alabama; Mathew Talbot and Nathaniel E. Harris, of Georgia.

Supreme Judges: Hugh L. White (also candidate for the presidency), Wm. B. Reese, Jacob Peck, Robert L. Caruthers, A. O. W. Totten, Samuel Milligan, James W. Deaderick, Thomas A. R. Nelson, Peter Turney, Robert McFarland, D. L. Snodgrass, William K. McAlister and N. L. Bachman, of Tennessee; Edward Cross, Wm. Conway and Elbert H. English, of Arkansas; Harry Cage and Wm. L. Sharkey, of Mississippi, and Anthony Bledsoe Shelby, of the Republic of Texas.

Federal Judges: D. M. Key, James H. Peck, D. D. Shelby, Edward Cross, Jeter C. Pritchard, Samuel Milligan (Court of Claims), R. M. Barton (U. S. Labor Board).

Members of Congress: Adam R. Alexander, Josiah M. Anderson, John Blair, Reese B. Brabson, Samuel Bunch, Brookins Campbell, Thos. J. Campbell, Wm. B. Campbell, E. W. Carmack, R. L. Caruthers, Wm. B. Carter, John Cocke, W. M. Cocke, David Crockett, John W. Crockett, John H. Crozier, Wm. Fitzgerald, A. E. Garrett, L. C. Houck, John C. Houck, Abram McClellan, William McFarland, O. B. Lovett, Thomas A. R. Nelson, John Rhea, Samuel A. Smith, Charles E. Snodgrass, Henry C. Snodgrass, James Standifer, Wm. Stone, Nathaniel G. Taylor, Robert L. Taylor, A. A. Taylor, J. M. Thornburg, John Trimble, Isaac Thomas and Hopkins L. Turney, of Tennessee; David Hubbard,

John McKee, Joshua L. Martin, John M. Martin and Wm. R. W. Cobb, of Alabama; A. H. Sevier, Edward Cross and Henry W. Conway, of Arkansas; Campbell P. Berry, of California; Andrew Humphreys, of Indiana; Wm. D. Vincent, of Kansas; Vincent Boering, of Kentucky; G. W. Anderson, Samuel Caruthers and Austin A. King, of Missouri; Harry Cage, of Mississippi; John H. Reagan, of Texas; and Arthur S. Colyar, C.S.A., of Tennessee.

Army and Navy: David Farragut, admiral; Samuel P. Carter, rear-admiral (also brigadier-general); Valentine Sevier Nelson, commodore; John Cocke, major-general of militia; Nathaniel Taylor, brigadier-general; Julius C. Robertson, brigadier-general; Robert Patterson, J. O. Shelby, C. S. A., and Jacob Tipton, brigadier-generals; Alex. P. Stewart, major-general, C.S.A.

Religious Leaders: David Nelson, Presbyterian, author of *Cause and Cure of Infidelity;* John Rankin, Presbyterian, anti-slavery leader; John W. Doak, Presbyterian; E. E. Hoss, bishop of the Methodist Episcopal church, South; Elbert F. Sevier, Methodist.

Business: C. M. McGhee, Hugh T. Inman, S. M. Inman, Robert Lowry, capitalists; W. C. Patterson, president Pennsylvania Railroad; Wm. R. Shelby, railroad president; Samuel B. Cunningham, railroad president; Samuel Tate, railroad president.

General Sam Houston, of Tennessee and Texas, and General Edmund P. Gaines, came with their parents into the region shortly after the collapse of the Franklin government. They grew to manhood alongside the sons of the Franklin leaders, among whom, from an early day, had been the relatives of Houston.

The forcefulness of the Franks and their sons manifested itself most of all in the earlier days when political conditions in the Southwest were in the formative stage and new States were being created. They furnished the first governors for Tennessee, Kentucky and Arkansas, and first senators in Congress from Tennessee, Arkansas, Missouri and Indiana.

CHAPTER XXXVII

Survival of the Conception and Spirit

The concept of Franklin as a State did not die, but survived to appear at later stages of the history of East Tennessee. The joinder of what was Franklin territory in government with the Cumberland Country and West Tennessee never accorded with the dictates of nature.

Gilbert Imlay, who watched the development of affairs on the frontier in behalf of Great Britain, about 1790 predicted that the Cumberland Country would form the next State to follow Kentucky into the Union, the difficulty of communication between it and North Carolina being so great as to compel its separation. "The mountains [Cumberland] will most likely be its eastern limits; its southern limits will be, either the partition line continued between North Carolina and Georgia, or it will be run southerly until it strikes the ridge of hills which divides the Tennessee [river] country from the country of the Choctaws; thence a due west course to the Mississippi, or following some one of those branches which rise in those hills and pursuing its course to that river."[1]

Imlay's was an approach to Arthur Campbell's conception of Franklin's proper domain. Thus:

The country upon the headwaters of the Tennessee stands next in the list of advancement [into the Union]. This country includes the settlements of Clinch, and the settlements of Powell's valley which are part in Virginia and part in North Carolina; besides the settlements of Nolachucky and French Broad. This last settlement

---

[1] Imlay, in *Winterbotham's View*, III, 170. Imlay's forecast of the future of the Indian tribes proved truer to the event. He foresaw that the settlers in North Georgia would in a very few years bid defiance to the Cherokees in that quarter. "The settlement of [French] Broad, aided by Holston, have nothing to fear from them [the Cherokees] and the Cumberland is too puisant to apprehend any danger. . . . The settlements at the Natchez and above will soon extend do the southern boundaries of Cumberland; so they will be completely enveloped in a few years. Our people will continue to encroach upon them on three sides and compel them to live more domesticated lives and assimilate them to our mode of living or to cross to the western side of the Mississippi." *Winterbotham's View*, III, 175.

will be extended to the borders of the Cherokee country which will bind this State to the southward. Its western boundary will be the Cumberland mountains... Its northern limits will be the ridges of hills that divide the waters of Tennessee and the Great Kanawha, and its eastern boundary will be the high hills that divide the eastern and western waters... This State will be in extent upwards of two hundred miles north and south, and the average width from east to west nearly an hundred and fifty.

This country has mountains on every side but the southwest, and is interspersed with high hills in most parts of it. The valleys are extremely fertile and everywhere finely watered. The climate in the upper part of the country is not so temperate as that of Kentucky, though it lies in the same latitude, which is owing to the neighboring mountains. Many parts of this district are well settled, and cultivation was brought to such considerable perfection that the inhabitants had it in contemplation to become independent seven years since, under the distinction of the State of Franklin. Its population is not only considerable, but its respectability in every consideration will very soon entitle it to the rank of a distinct State; though it may require some time to effect a unity of sentiments and a consolidation of its various and detached settlements into that order which the organs of government require.

A distinguished Frenchman, Francois A. Michaux, in his Travels of 1802, recorded his impressions of East Tennessee.[2] After referring to the frustrated attempt to establish the State of Franklin, he says:

It is still very probable, and has already been in question, that East and West Tennessea [West Tennessee as descriptive that time of all the country west of the Cumberland Mountains] will ultimately form two distinct States, which will each enlarge itself by a new addition of part of the territory belonging to the Cherokee Indians. The natives, it is true, will not hear the least mention of a cession being made, objecting that their tract of country is barely sufficient to furnish, by hunting, a subsistence for their families. However, sooner or later, they will be compelled to yield. The division of Tennessea[3] cannot be long before it takes place, whether under the consideration of convenience or the enterprising dispositions of the Americans. It is commanded, on the one hand, by the boundaries that Nature herself has prescribed between the two countries, in separating them by the Cumberland mountains; and on the other, by their commerce, which is wholly different, since Cumberland carries on its trade by the Ohio and Mississippi, while

---

[2] Michaux, *Travels*, 248. Thwaite, *Early Western Travels*, III, 281.

[3] So written by Michaux, the younger. His father, in his earlier *Travels*, spells the name "Tennasse" and "Tenassee." Thwaite, *Early Western Travels*, III, 74.

Holston does most by land with the seaports belonging to the Atlantic States, and has very little to do with New Orleans by the river Tennessea, and scarcely any with Cumberland and Kentucky.

In 1796, in the Constitutional Convention met to organize the State of Tennessee, Alexander Outlaw moved, and Joseph Anderson seconded, the insertion in the document of a clause providing "that, if we be not admitted by Congress as a member State of the General Government, we should continue to exist as an independent State."

The next proponent of a new State was Andrew Johnson, who at that time, as a member of the Tennessee senate, was barely started on a career that led to the presidency of the nation.

As early as 1809, the State of Tennessee in her polity was compelled to reckon with the geographical peculiarities that had from the outset presaged three grand divisions; and the Constitution of 1834 gave formal recognition to such divisions. Divisional feeling appeared first when the Cumberland Settlements failed to join in the Franklin movement, and again when a large majority of their inhabitants voted against statehood in 1795. The Chickasaw purchase of 1818 gave rise to a third grand division, West Tennessee, between the rivers Tennessee and Mississippi.

As Middle Tennessee and West Tennessee developed, and population increased, primacy in State affairs passed from East Tennessee. In 1840 the control was, for all practical purposes, with the middle division. It was felt by the other two divisions that this power was unfairly wielded.

The year 1841 was marked by high tension in politics in Tennessee. In October of that year, the first suggestion of a division of the State, in order to the creation of new ones, came from West Tennessee.[4]

An editorial in the *Nashville Whig* (December 6, 1841) commenting upon the proposal expressed the opinion that it was impracticable, since "East Tennessee intends to set up for herself and become a free, sovereign and independent member of the Confederacy." It was not suspected by the writer that there might come about an alliance for dismemberment between the East and the West.

---

[4] The *Huntingdon Advertiser* proposed the formation of a new State by adding to the western division, the northern portion of Mississippi and that part of Kentucky which lies west of the Tennessee river. Thus was purposed the consolidation into a State of the domain of the Chickasaws.

That stormy petrel, Andrew Johnson, now offered in the senate a joint resolution which called for the appointment of a joint committee to take under consideration the propriety of ceding East Tennessee to the general government for the purpose of forming an independent State to be called the State of Frankland.[5] The *Whig* at once perceived and declared that the separation of East Tennessee was "in serious contemplation."

Johnson's plan was a reversion to Arthur Campbell's State of Franklin. One of the ablest West Tennesseans, John A. Gardner, of Weakley county, offered a similar resolution on the 15th, which looked to the creation of the new "State of Jacksoniana" out of the territory of the Chickasaws.[6]

On January 18th Johnson called for a consideration of his resolutions, and in a speech which consumed an hour urged their passage. He wished the deliberate vote of the senate on the subject; the project did not originate with him, he said, but with the people of East Tennessee. He adverted to the period when that part of the State had been under the sovereignty of the State of Franklin, and to the republican simplicity to which his people would return.[7]

The resolutions were adopted by the senate, there being seventeen "ayes" and six "nays." All of the six negatives were cast by senators from Middle Tennessee. A combination between the other grand divisions was evident. The *Nashville Whig*, granting that Johnson had placed the claims of East Tennessee "in a strong light" and that the people of that division were anxious for a separation, continued to combat the proposal as impolitic.

---

[5] "*Resolved* by the General Assembly of the State of Tennessee, that there be a joint select committee appointed to consist of two members on the part of the Senate, and three on the part of the House of Representatives to be chosen from the eastern portion of the State (commonly called East Tennessee) to memorialize the general government for the purpose of being formed into a sovereign and independent State to be called the State of Frankland; and said Committee shall report by bill or otherwise.

"*Resolved*, That his excellency, Governor James C. Jones, be and he is hereby required to open and hold a correspondence with the Governors of the States of Georgia, North Carolina and Virginia for the purpose of ascertaining their opinions in relation to ceding a portion of the territory of their respective States, to the general government, to be included in the State of Frankland when formed, and for the further purpose of requesting them to lay the subject before their respective legislatures at their next ensuing session." *Tennessee Senate Journal*, 1841-2; *Nashville Whig*, of December 10, 1841.

[6] *Tennessee Senate Journal* of 1841-2, 288, 345.

[7] *Nashville Whig*, January 18th, 1842.

Samuel Milligan[8] of Greene, called up the senate resolution in the house of representatives on January 22nd, and advocated concurrence. Brookins Campbell,[9] of Washington county, urged, favorable consideration, "not upon the ground that East Tennessee was disposed to complain of her connection with Middle and West Tennessee, but because of the dissimilarity of her interests and of the difficulty of legislating for a people separated from the balance of the State by a great natural barrier, and whose local wants could not be correctly appreciated by their brethren west of the Cumberland mountains."

The resolution was finally approved by the house of representatives, after amendments, one of which was the striking out of the direction that the governor open a correspondence with Virginia, North Carolina and Georgia. The resolution as amended did not reach the senate in time for action before the adjournment of the Assembly. The increasing importance of Tennessee as a pivotal State in national campaigns, and the close and bitter contests between the Whigs and the Democrats for control of the State, shunted aside the separation issue for two decades.[10]

Another period of stress and turmoil once more brought the separation of East Tennessee to serious discussion. Strangely enough, the movement for the separation or secession of Tennessee from the Union precipitated it. After the passage of the ordinance of independence by the legislature of Tennessee, a convention was held

---

[8] Afterward an associate justice of the Tennessee Supreme Court and a judge of the Court of Claims at Washington.

[9] Member of Congress, 1852-3. The advocates of emancipation had their stronghold in Upper East Tennessee and they favored separation. At the Anti-Slavery Convention which met in London in 1843, Joseph Leavitt, of Boston, made the interesting statement that "the people of East Tennessee, a race of hardy mountaineers, find their interests so little regarded by the dominant slaveholders of other parts of the State that they are taking measures to become a separate State. They are holding anti-slavery meetings and meetings of political associations with great freedom, discussing the question, rousing the people and showing how slavery curses them, in order to bring them to the period of action." *Proceedings of the Anti-Slavery Convention*, London, 1843. A contemporary (Nov. 27, 1841) argument in favor of a separate State is found in *Letters of an East Tennessee Abolitionist*, E. T. Hist. Soc. Pub., III, 144-5.

[10] The resolution for the establishment of the "State of Jacksoniana" was defeated in the Senate by a vote of nine to fourteen. But recurrently and to the present time, agitation has been renewed for a new State covering the same territory with the city of Jackson or Memphis as its capital.

(May 30, 1861) in Knoxville, composed of members who were loyal to the national authority. A vigorous "declaration of grievances" was promulgated and published in pamphlet form. Commissioners were appointed to appear before the State legislature, then in session, to ask "its consent that the counties composing East Tennessee . . . may form and erect a separate State." "Desiring, in good faith, that the General Assembly will grant our reasonable request, and claiming the right to determine our own destiny"—was a declaration, and steps were taken for the holding of another convention in case the legislature refused independence.[11]

In the debate in the Assembly at Nashville, following the presentation of the memorial, the name of Franklin was proposed for the projected State.

After the Civil War was ended, the newspapers of that division announced that "East Tennessee will ere long take the preliminary steps for a separate State organization"—encouraged, doubtless, by the successful rape of Virginia in the organization, recognition and admission of West Virginia as a State.[12]

Even in recent years there have been suggestions of the revival of the Franklin Commonwealth—faint echoes of the early period that has always appealed to Tennesseans. The mountain and hill country of greater Franklin is today often referred to as the "State of Appallachia." A community of feeling and interest—a real homogeneity—is demonstrated by the fact that several of the most influential churches disregard state lines and maintain conference and synod boundaries in keeping with geographical, social and economic demands.

The Frank's spirit of independence, the passionate and not sterile restiveness under undue restraint or dictation, has time after time burst into flame in the history of Tennessee as a Commonwealth.

Andrew Jackson was made to feel its power when he sought to compel Tennesseans to support Van Buren, as his own successor, against Hugh Lawson White, the able and beloved Tennessean, son of a devoted Franklinite. White carried the State by a majority of 10,039 over Van Buren and Harrison, and the party of Jackson was unable to carry the State in a national contest until 1856.

The same characteristic was manifested by the State in her with-

---

[11] *Journal of Convention*, pamphlet, in Lawson McGhee Library, Knoxville.
[12] Draper Collection; newspaper clippings.

drawal from the Union in 1861, and, in turn, by the eastern division in resisting secession and itself seeking separation.

In 1910 and 1914, the dominant political party was brought to defeats in the assertion by the people of the State of their faith in a free and independent judiciary.

The genius of the people has always been of an intensely democratic type. They have been responsive to leadership, but susceptible to waves of punitory resentment when that leadership has shown a tendency to harden into dictation.

THE FRANKLINITES

JOHN SEVIER

The grandfather of JOHN SEVIER, or Xavier, was a native of France, a Huguenot, and is said to have been related to Saint Francis Xavier, and to have lived in the village of Xavier in the French Pyrenees. On the Revocation of the Edict of Nantes the grandfather and a brother fled to London where the former became a prosperous merchant. His son, Valentine, emigrated to America, and about the year 1740 settled in the Valley of Virginia where he acquired several tracts of land. Valentine Sevier was enrolled as a member of Peter Scholl's military company in 1742. He married Joanna Goode.

John Sevier, their son, was born September 23, 1745, in Augusta county (that part now in Rockingham county) in the Long Meadows district. After a short schooling in Fredericksburg and Staunton young John served as a clerk in his father's store. About this time he went out on short excursions against the Indians.

In 1761, at the age of sixteen, he married Sarah Hawkins. After farming for a short while, he, about 1765, bought a tract of land and laid out and established the village of New Market. Here he kept a store and an inn, and donated three acres of land as a church site to the Baptists. In 1770, he removed to Millerstown (supposedly Woodstock).

On invitation of Evan Shelby, who as merchant at Sapling Grove passed occasionally on his way to the markets up the Valley of Virginia, John Sevier visited the Holston country in 1771 and 1772 and decided to locate there. His brother, Valentine, Jr., was there as early as February 2, 1773, as is shown by a charge entry on the books of Shelby of that date "Valentine Savayer to Evan Shelby, Dr." The Seviers, the father and sons, first located at Keywood's, about six miles from Shelby's, but soon removed to a farm on the east bank of Watauga river, between the present cities of Elizabethton and Johnson City.

Before his removal from Virginia he had been commissioned a captain of militia by Governor Dunmore. Sevier was one of the thirteen who composed the "committee of safety" west of the Alleghanies in Salisbury District of North Carolina about the beginning of the Revolution. The year 1776 was a full one for the young Virginian. He commanded as captain a company of mounted militia on the Christian expedition of that year. He also aided as an officer under Colonel John Carter in the defense of Fort Caswell (Watauga Fort) against the Cherokees, July 1, 1776; and in the preparation of the memorial to the legislature of North Carolina asking to be brought under the government of that State (July 5, 1776). He was, in the same year, one of the first representatives of Washington District in the Provincial Congress of North Carolina. By that body, he was elected lieutenant-colonel of Washington District. He also served in the State's first constitutional convention in the same year.

Sevier lived for a few years on Little Limestone creek, about five miles below Jonesborough, where he farmed and ran a water-mill. Thence he removed to a large plantation on the Nolachucky, "Mount Pleasant," Washington County, (1778). In 1779, he served under Colonel Evan Shelby on a campaign against the Chickamauga Indians; and the next spring commanded an expedition against the Cherokees. The signal service of Colonel Sevier at King's Mountain in October, 1780, and his subsequent career are too well known to be even outlined in this sketch. He was engaged in thirty-five skirmishes or battles with the Indian tribes, and never suffered a defeat. Roosevelt ranks him as first of all the Indian fighters of the West.

Sevier was the idol of the people of his day. In person he was tall, handsome and graceful. A charm of manner made him irresistible with soldiers or with civilians. No man ever succeeded in efforts of rivalry, and few tried. He was most fortunate in his matrimonial connections. After the death of his first wife, he married Catherine Sherrill, "Bonny Kate," the heroine of Fort Caswell-on-Watauga who was ever thereafter to her husband a true and capable helpmate and counselor.

Strange as it may seem to non-residents of Tennessee, Sevier has continued through succeeding generations to hold the first place in the hearts of the people of the Commonwealth. He and Andrew Jackson came into collision before 1800; and a few years later Jackson defeated him, by one vote, for the major-generalship of militia, only to have the result rebuked by Sevier's election for the fourth, fifth, and sixth times as governor, despite all the influence that Jackson could command.

No other American has served his people in the capacity of chief executive of a State as long as Sevier. Adding his tenure as governor of the State of Franklin to the terms as governor of Tennessee, above noted, he was in such service for approximately sixteen years. Too, Sevier was the choice of the Westerners for governor of the Southwest Territory, expressed in convention at Greeneville, May 5, 1790.

The legislature of Tennessee has chosen the two men, Sevier and Jackson, as the State's representatives in the group of statues in the Hall of Fame in the Capitol at Washington. Having regard to the bitter enmity that marked their careers, the sculptor may achieve a master-stroke by causing the two marble effigies to look in opposite directions.

General Sevier died near Fort Decatur, Alabama, where, while a member of Congress, he had gone as a commissioner appointed by President Madison to fix the Creek Indian boundary according to treaty. His death was on September 24, 1815—one day past his birthday—and the burial was at Fort Decatur. In June, 1889, the remains were removed and re-interred in the grounds of the courthouse at Knoxville. A graceful marble shaft was erected above the grave, in 1892, upon which appears this inscription:

"Pioneer, soldier, statesman, and one of the founders of the Republic; governor of the State of Franklin; six times governor of Tennessee; four times elected to Congress; the typical pioneer who conquered the wilderness and fashioned the State; a projector and hero of King's Mountain; thirty-five battles, thirty-five victories; his Indian war-cry, 'Here they are! Come on, boys, come on!'"

ARTHUR CAMPBELL

ARTHUR CAMPBELL, the son of David Campbell, was born in 1742 in Augusta county, Virginia. When a boy of about fifteen years, he volunteered as a militiaman to aid in protecting the frontiers from the Indians. Stationed at a fort near where the road from Staunton to Warm Springs crosses Cowpasture river he with his companions wandered in search of wild fruit. While in a plum thicket the party was fired upon by Indians lying in ambush and young Campbell was slightly wounded and captured. He was taken to the region of the great lakes and held a prisoner for three years. During that period Arthur Campbell traversed much of the country which now constitutes the States of Michigan, Ohio, Indiana and Illinois.

He was subjected to great hardships until he fortunately came under the protection of an aged chief who took him to the French fort at Detroit. The Jesuit fathers had at the time a mission at that fort. The bright English boy attracted attention and so pleased the fathers that they gave him instruction. Young Campbell's captivity, therefore, gave him an intimate knowledge of the western country, and he received a better education than the average boy of his day on the western frontier of Virginia. A glimpse of the boy among the Indians is given by James Smith, of Pennsylvania, who was in captivity at the same time:

"Wyandott Indian warriors had divided into different parties, and all struck at different places in Augusta county. They brought in with them a considerable number of scalps, prisoners, horses and other plunder. One of the parties brought in with them one Arthur Campbell, that is, Colonel Campbell who lives on Holston river, near the Royal Oak. As the Wyandotts at Sunyendeand and those at Detroit were connected, Mr. Campbell was taken to Detroit, but he remained some time in this town (Sunyendeand). His company was very agreeable and I was sorry when he left me. During his stay at Sunyendeand, he borrowed my bible and made some very pertinent remarks on what he had read. One passage was where it is said, 'It is good for a man that he bear the yoke in his youth.' He said that we ought to be resigned to the will of Providence, as we were now bearing the yoke in our youth. Mr. Campbell appeared then to be about sixteen or seventeen years of age."

Campbell escaped from the Indians and made his way through a wilderness of two hundred miles to a detachment of the British army that was then on a march into the country of the western Indians. He was at once engaged as a guide, for which service he was later rewarded with a grant of one thousand acres of land near the present city of Louisville, Ky.

On his return to his parents, who had mourned him as dead, he applied himself to study with a capacity enlarged by his experiences, and made marked progress.

About six years before the Revolution, he removed to the Holston country, settling on a fine tract of land known as Royal Oaks, his father and family soon following. In 1776, he was chosen to represent the county of Fincastle in the General Assembly, in which his attention was drawn to the region of Kentucky and Tennessee by the petition of Richard Henderson and associates in behalf of the Transylvania Company. On July 4, 1776, Campbell was named as one of the commissioners on behalf of Virginia to take evidence touching the validity of the claims of the promoters of Transylvania, and he aided in the taking of many depositions. It was at this session that the Assembly dissolved the relations of Virginia to the British crown and instructed the delegation in Congress to bring a similar measure before that body.

Campbell had prior to this served as a member of the committee that drafted the Address of the Freeholders of Fincastle, in January, 1775. He was a member of the first house of delegates under the Constitution, and threw his influence in favor of the liberal ideas in respect to religious freedom championed by Thomas Jefferson.

On the organization of Washington county, Virginia, in January, 1777, Campbell was appointed county lieutenant and commander in chief of the militia. He served for many years as the presiding judge of the court of that county. He was also the commanding colonel of the 70th Regiment of militia.

He joined Sevier (1780) in an expedition against the Cherokees following the former's victory at Boyd's Creek, and carried war into the Indian towns as far south as Coosa river, Georgia.

Colonel Campbell aided in formulating plans and raising troops for the King's Mountain expedition. General Nathanael Greene appointed (February 26, 1781) Campbell, along with Evan Shelby, John Sevier and others, commissioners on the part of the United States to negotiate treaties with the Cherokee and Chickasaw Indians.

For thirty-five years Arthur Campbell resided on the Royal Oaks estate, eight miles east of the home of his first cousin, General William Campbell, Aspindale. He devoted himself to the cultivation of his farms, and, after the death of General Campbell, to the management of the extensive saltworks at Saltville, he serving as the guardian of General Campbell's daughter and heir. Residing on the main highway between the Southwest and the East, Colonel Campbell entertained on a liberal scale. From his visitors he gathered information respecting their home communities. He was also an extensive reader. Thus he became the best informed of all men concerning affairs in the Kentucky and Tennessee regions. He also conducted a wide correspondence. Indeed there would be no extravagance in the statement that he made his home the clearing-house for information regarding Indian and civil affairs throughout a wide area of country. His correspondence with officials and leading politicians has served to preserve much of historical interest that would otherwise have been lost. He was fluent in conversation and capable of entertaining the most intelligent.

In temperament Colonel Campbell was unfortunate. He was irascible, jealous, litigious and over-bearing, and was often at breach with other leaders. He was not popular with them or with the people. His kinsman, David Campbell, governor of Virginia, writing in appreciation of his good qualities, was forced to say: "He had more bitter enemies than any man I ever knew in my life."

He twice offered for preferment without success; once to be appointed southern superintendent of Indian affairs, and, late in life, to be elected to Congress. Strongly imbued with the spirit of independence, Campbell could not resist dipping into movements that looked to separate statehood, both in the Tennessee and the Kentucky regions. He was, in a true sense, a self-constituted adviser of the frontier people, and for the most part a capable one. A few years before his death he removed to Kentucky, settling on Yellow creek (the present city of Middlesborough) where he had a very considerable landed estate. He died of cancer at the age of seventy-three.

Arthur Campbell married a sister of General William Campbell. Two of his sons lost their lives in the war of 1812. Captain James Campbell died at Mobile, Alabama, and Colonel John B. Campbell fell at the battle of Chippewa where he commanded the right wing under General Scott.

Campbell county, Tennessee, lying just across the Kentucky-Tennessee line from his last home, was named in his honor.

WILLIAM COCKE

WILLIAM COCKE was a remarkable man with a career quite as remarkable. He was born in 1748 in Amelia county, Virginia, the youngest son of Abraham Cocke, who was a descendant of Richard Cocke, the earliest of the name to settle in Virginia, about 1630.

The Cocke family emigrated from Devonshire, England, and from about the time of his arrival in Virginia Richard Cocke was lieutenant-colonel commandant of Henrico county, and member of the house of burgesses for the years 1632-1644. Stephen Cocke, the grandfather, inherited Malvern Hill, famed in the Civil War.

William Cocke married Sarah Maclin and, about 1773, removed to the West, first settling on Renfro's creek, in Washington county, Virginia, and later lower down, in North Carolina in the present county of Sullivan as a subsequent projection of the state line demonstrated.

William Cocke in the spring of 1774 was captain of a company of irregular militia raised for the defense of the Holston settlers. A formal commission was issued to him (August 1774) by Colonel William Preston, he succeeding Captain Anthony Bledsoe resigned. The next month Captain Cocke made a journey into North Carolina for the purpose of soliciting military aid for the frontiersmen who were then hard pressed by the several hostile Indian tribes. His company was active in defending the border, as was also one under Daniel Boone.

In the spring of 1775 Cocke was employed by Colonel Richard Henderson to accompany the latter in his march through the wilderness into the Kentucky country there to found the Transylvania government.

Cocke's first legislative experience was in the house of delegates of the Colony of Transylvania, May, 1775. Cocke in later years brought a suit in equity against Henderson and his associates to have decreed a specific performance of a contract for a large boundary of land, promised as compensation for his services.

On his return to the Holston-Watauga settlement Cocke led his company in the battle of Eaton's Fort (1776). A charge that he was guilty of cowardice in the action was denied by Cocke; and it turned up to embarrass him several times in his after-career. He was, by order (December 9, 1776) of the Privy Council of Virginia suspended until a court of inquiry should pass on his conduct. Cocke found almost immediate vindication at the hands of his neighbors who elected him, along with Anthony Bledsoe, a delegate to the Virginia legislature of 1777, against Arthur Campbell and William Edmiston. The defeated candidates filed a contest in the house of delegates, in which they contended that Cocke and Bledsoe were ineligible. The report of the committee was to the effect that Long Island of Holston was situated in Virginia and in favor of the contestees. Thus two North Carolinians (later Tennesseans) furnished Washington county, Virginia, her first representatives in the General Assembly of Virginia. Two years later, 1779, it suited Cocke's purpose to shift, and he contended that taxes could not be legally collected in the strip where he resided on the north side of Holston river in Carter's Valley. Cocke resisted the sheriff who was undertaking to collect taxes in behalf of Virginia, "as it was in Carolina and never was in Virginia." Cocke had already acknowledged allegiance to North Carolina and entered the public service of that State. He had, in August 1777, been elected clerk and then made an unsuccessful race against John Sevier for the clerkship of the Washington County Court in 1778. In the same year he had been elected to represent his district in the Assembly at Newbern. After taking his seat he was deprived of it on the ground that he occupied the office of clerk.

As a captain, Cocke was on the campaign to relieve the South Carolinians in the earlier part of 1780. At Thicketty Fort he was deemed the fittest officer to send forward to demand of Colonel Patrick Moore the surrender of the fort. Cocke was not on the King's Mountain expedition.

On February 26, 1782, Cocke was admitted to the bar at Jonesborough, and in the same month to the bar of Sullivan county. In April of the same year he was a member of the General Assembly. Cocke's connection with the State of Franklin is shown in preceding chapters. As a member of the Council of State and of the several conventions he was second only to Sevier in influence.

He was in June, 1784, elected judge of the court of oyer and terminer of Davidson county, but, owing to his connection with the Franklin movement, did not qualify.

Cocke held a seat in the Carolina Assembly of 1788, by which body he was elected State's attorney for Washington District.

Under the territorial form of government, Cocke was a member of the first legislature, 1794; he was by that body made attorney of Washington District and a trustee of Blount College, for the establishment of which he introduced the bill.

In the constitutional convention of 1796, he was a delegate from Hawkins county. By the first legislature he was elected to represent Tennessee in the United States senate, and served until July, 1797. He was elected a second time, serving 1799–1805.

In 1797 a new county was created and named Cocke in his honor.

In 1807 Cocke announced his candidacy for the governorship of Tennessee, but soon saw that he could make no headway against John Sevier, in whose favor he withdrew.

In 1809 he was appointed judge of the first circuit—a position he was not adapted to temperamentally. He was essentially an orator and advocate. He was impeached in 1812, and on trial found guilty of misconduct in office, though his offending appears to have been a refusal as judge to grant a writ of *certiorari*, on an unsworn petition.

Cocke found a measure of vindication in an election by the people of his county to the legislature of 1813.'

Smarting from what he conceived to be, and what today appears to have been, an unjust impeachment, Cocke despite advanced age volunteered to serve as a private in Colonel John Williams' Regiment of Volunteers and went to Florida on a campaign against the Seminole Indians, and the next year served as a private in the Creek War. A deep gratification must have come to him with the following note of commendation from his commanding general, Andrew Jackson:

"January 28th, 1814.

"Sir: The patriotism that you brought into the field at your advanced age which prompted you on with me to face the enemy in the late excursion to the Tallapoosie river; the example of order, your strict admonition throughout the lines; and, lastly the bravery you displayed in the battle of Enotochopco by recrossing the creek, entering the pursuit and exposing your person and thereby saving the life of Lieutenant Moss, and killing the Indian, entitle you to the thanks of your general and the approbation of your country."

He was in 1814, perhaps through the instrumentality of General Jackson, appointed by President Madison agent to the Chickasaw Indians. He made his home at Columbus, Mississippi. Cocke served a term in the Mississippi legislature.

William Cocke died August 22, 1828, and is buried under a monument erected by the State of Mississippi, on which appears this inscription:

"Here lie the remains of William Cocke, who died in Columbus, Miss., on the 22nd of August, 1828. The deceased passed an eventful and active life. Was Captain in command during the war of 1776. Was distinguished for his brave daring and intrepidity. Was one of the pioneers who first crossed the Alleghany mountains with Daniel Boone into the wilderness of Kentucky. Took an active part in the formation of the Franklin Government, afterward the State of Tennessee. Was the delegate from that free limit to the Congress of the United States. Was a member of the convention which framed the first Constitution of Tennessee, and was one of the first Senators from that State to the Congress of the United States, for a period of twelve years, and afterwards one of the Circuit Judges. He served in the Legislatures of Virginia, North Carolina, Tennessee, and Mississippi, and at the age of 65, was a volunteer in the war of 1812, and again distinguished himself for personal bravery and courage. He departed this life in the 81st year of his age, universally lamented."

When there is added Cocke's further legislative service in Transylvania, the Territory South of the Ohio, and Franklin, it may safely be stated that his record is unique among American legislators.

The best estimate of Cocke's powers is that of Caldwell in his *Bench and Bar of Tennessee:* "He is remembered as the great orator of his time, and, by consent of his contemporaries, he had no equal as a popular speaker. A remarkable readiness and brilliancy of speech has been characteristic of his family in all succeeding generations."

His son, John Cocke, was major-general in command of the East Tennessee troops in the Creek War and distinguished himself as a gallant soldier. He served in Congress from the second district of Tennessee four successive terms, from 1819.

William Michael Cocke, a grandson, was a member of Congress two terms, 1845–1849; and his son, Sterling, was chancellor of Mississippi.

JUDGE DAVID CAMPBELL

DAVID CAMPBELL, the chief judicial officer of the State of Franklin, was born in Virginia in 1750. He was a younger brother of Colonel Arthur Campbell. In 1776 he joined the Continental army and rose to the rank of major.

Campbell was elected clerk of the Washington county court (Virginia) in January, 1777, and, studying law the while, served until August, 1780, when he resigned to begin the practice of law under a license issued to him by Governor Thomas Jefferson. While yet a young man he removed across the State line into the Tennessee country, settling in Greene county prior to 1783. He was elected by the Carolina Assembly of 1784 assistant judge of Washington District, but declined to qualify as he had joined in the State of Franklin movement; and he was made chief judge of the new State, and also a member of the Council of State. He attended the Carolina Assembly of 1787, as a representative from Greene county, and being elected by that body assistant judge again, he accepted the place, thereby giving umbrage to his former Franklin associates.

He was appointed by the President one of the judges of the Territory South of the Ohio River. In 1792 he was one of the commissioners on the part of the national government to run and mark the line between the whites and the Cherokee Indians.

Judge Campbell was nominated for senator in Congress in the first legislature of Tennessee, but was defeated by William Cocke. He was continued as a judge of the Superior Court—not Supreme Court, as has been stated by others. In 1803 an attempt was made to impeach him for misconduct in office, but it proved unsuccessful. Campbell, however, was (1809) defeated for reëlection by James Trimble. He was nominated to a federal judgeship in the Mississippi Territory, March 3, 1811, but falling into bad health he did not live to serve.

Judge Campbell resided in the later years of his life on a fine estate opposite the junction of the Little Tennessee and the Tennessee rivers (the site of the present Lenoir City). He died in 1812.

Judge Campbell was of the noted Campbell family of Southwest Virginia. Practically his entire adult life was devoted to judicial service. But for lack of decision of character he would have been a greater favorite of the people and a more outstanding figure in the history of his State.

A son of Judge Campbell, Thomas J. Campbell, was elected a member of Congress from Tennessee (1841–1843), and later was clerk of the National House of Representatives in the Thirtieth and Thirty-first Congresses, serving until his death, April 13, 1850.

LANDON CARTER

LANDON CARTER, the son of Colonel John Carter, chairman of the Watauga Association, was born in Virginia, and removed with his father, first to Carter's Valley and then to Watauga. He was educated at Liberty Hall, Mecklenburg county, North Carolina (now Davidson College). He was more adequately equipped than any of his contemporaries for a diversified public career to which he was later called.

He was one of the petitioners to have the Watauga Settlement annexed to North Carolina. In 1780 he served as a captain under Sevier on the Boyd's Creek campaign, and was in the same year with Major Charles Robertson's command in South Carolina. In the same year he succeeded his father in the office of entry-taker for Washington county—an office of great responsibility, the immense extent of that county considered. On the death of his father in 1781, he was appointed administrator of the estate which was the largest then in existence in North Carolina west of the Alleghany mountains. This tended to develop the business capacity of young Carter. In 1782 he was appointed by the North Carolina legislature auditor for Washington District; and the following year he was named one of the incorporators of Martin's Academy (later Washington College). For years he served that institution as an active trustee.

Carter was in command of a company under John Sevier in the South Carolina campaign of 1781, and he and his company remained there with Sevier after the expiration of their term of service, and after a majority of the western troops had returned home. He fought under Marion until January, 1782. On the march back home his company was ambushed by the Indians at the eastern part of Yellow Mountain.

In 1784 he represented Washington county in the house of commons of the Carolina General Assembly.

Landon Carter was a thorough-going supporter of the State of Franklin. He was secretary of the first convention at Jonesborough; speaker of the first senate; member of the first council of state, and later secretary of state, and entry-taker.

He was in the Carolina senate of 1789, and supported the cession bill and Sevier's reinstatement as brigadier-general of Washington District over Joseph Martin.

One of the first steps (1790) of Wm. Blount as governor of the Territory South of the Ohio was the appointment of Carter as lieutenant-colonel commandant of the Washington District militia. He was also commissioned a justice of the peace of Washington county. Carter was later elected treasurer of Washington and

Hamilton Districts of the Territory, and continued to serve until the Territory became the State of Tennessee.

He served as colonel on the campaign of 1792; and was made a member of the first board of trustees of Greeneville College.

Colonel Carter represented Washington county in the first constitutional convention of the State of Tennessee. His son, William B. Carter, was president of the second (1834) constitutional convention; and his grandson, William B. Carter, Jr., was a member of the convention of 1870. The name of Carter is therefore connected with the molding of the fundamental law of the Commonwealth, from the Articles of the Watauga Association and the Constitution of the State of Franklin to the latest constitutional convention.

The first legislature of Tennessee (1796) created Carter county, and named it in honor of Landon Carter. The name of his wife, Elizabeth, is borne by its county site, Elizabethton. Both he and his father were partners of John Sevier in land speculations.

Landon Carter died June 5, 1800.

JAMES WHITE

JAMES WHITE, the son of Moses White, was born in Rowan (that part which is Iredell) county, North Carolina, about the year 1747. He joined the Continental army and gained the rank of captain of militia (1779-81). For his military service he was entitled to locate a land warrant under N. C. Act of 1783; and in August of that year he made a tour of exploration for desirable lands in company with Robert Love and Francis A. Ramsey, the latter a surveyor. On the way westward to the frontier they crossed the French Broad at Rutherford's War Ford, and followed that stream to the mouth of Dumplin creek, where they recrossed the French Broad and traveled as far south as the mouth of Holston (Lenoir City). It was then that White and Ramsey first saw the lands upon which they afterward laid grants and upon some of which the present city of Knoxville stands.

Captain White returned to his home in Carolina, and made preparations to move his family to the West. In 1784 he made his way to Fort Chiswell in Virginia, where he made a crop and left his family for one year. In the following year he was a member of the Franklin Convention. His first residence was at a point four miles above the junction of French Broad and Holston rivers; but he remained there only one year. White and an old Carolina neighbor, James Conner, had begun to clear for a settlement on the present site of Knoxville, to which they removed in 1786. White's cabin stood on the west side of First creek, near its junction with the Holston; and, it is said, constituted one of the corners of White's Fort. This fort became a rendezvous for immigrants and rangers, since it was easy of access by water and by trails down the rivers. White's Fort settlement was destined to become the first capital of the State of Tennessee. It occupied a strategic position between the settlements on the upper reaches of the Holston and those on the Cumberland. The first hint of its future destiny was in the North Carolina Act, 1789, chapter I, which fixed "the house of James White, in Hawkins county" as the place where election returns from the districts of Washington and Mero should be canvassed to ascertain who was entitled to be commissioned representative in the Federal Congress from the trans-Alleghany region. James White was a representative in the Carolina Assembly in 1789, and doubtless aided in molding this legislation.

Shortly after the organization of the Territory South of the Ohio Governor Blount fixed upon White's Fort as the site of government, giving it the name of Knoxville, in honor of General Knox, then secretary of war. On November 3, 1780, Blount commissioned James White first major and a justice of the peace of Hawkins county; and later when Knox county was created White was given the highest miliary rank—lieutenant-colonel commandant of the county. His was the first name among those commissioned justices of the peace, and he was the presiding justice of Knox county.

White was a member of the constitutional convention of 1796, and of the first legislature held under the Constitution. He was senator in the second General Assembly of Tennessee, and speaker of the next, which position he resigned in order that Wm. Blount, recently expelled from the senate of the United States, might be elected to the vacancy. White sympathized with Blount and opened the way for the attempted vindication of the latter by the people of the State. White also served as speaker of the senate of Tennessee in 1801 and 1803.

He, in later life, was elected brigadier-general of the militia of Hamilton District and as such led his troops in the Creek War of 1813. In 1798, he was agent of the State of Tennessee to attend on the negotiation of a treaty with the Cherokee Indians.

In the State of Franklin he was one of the earliest speakers of the senate, and remained throughout a firm friend of Sevier and the new Commonwealth.

General White, while a man of great firmness, was philanthropic. He owned two grist mills, and in times of scarcity would give of their product to those of his neighbors who were in need. He donated the land on which the first Presbyterian church in Knoxville was built; and a city block to Blount College, upon which a two-story wooden building was erected to serve that institution, of which he was a trustee.

Living to see the city of his founding well started on its career, and his son, Hugh Lawson White, rising to eminence, General White died in Knoxville, August 14, 1821. Of him Ramsey, the historian, says: "to extreme old age, he retained the esteem and affection of his fellow-citizens, and never had a stain on his unsullied good name."

GILBERT CHRISTIAN

GILBERT CHRISTIAN was a descendant of Gilbert Christian who emigrated from the Ulster district of Ireland in 1726, settling near Lancaster, Pennsylvania, and removing thence to the Valley of Virginia in 1732.

Gilbert Christian, the son of Robert Christian, was born in Augusta county, Virginia, about 1734. As early as 1774 he was as a lieutenant in command of King's Mill Station in Sullivan county.

He had participated in the border wars of 1755–63. He settled on the Holston near the above station, and the place, now known as Kingsport, was called Christiansville. He commanded a company in the Cherokee campaign of 1776, under Colonel William Christian, his uncle; also in the campaigns against the Chickamauga Indians in 1779 and 1788, and was at King's Mountain. He served as a major on Colonel Arthur Campbell's expedition against the Cherokees in 1780–1; and was colonel of Sullivan county in 1782–3 A warm friend of Sevier, he joined in the new-state movement. He was the speaker of the Franklin senate of 1786. Sevier turned to him for aid and comfort in the trying days of the Commonwealth's dissolution, and never in vain.

Governor Blount chose him in 1790 for the highest honor in his county of Sullivan—lieutenant-colonel commandant of territorial militia, and also for justice of the peace.

In 1793, despite his age, Colonel Christian took the active command of his regiment on the Hightower (Etowah) campaign. He contracted a fever and died at Knoxville on the return journey. Fittingly he was with Sevier until the last battle the latter ever fought had ended in success.

Gilbert Christian married in June, 1763, Margaret, daughter of George Anderson, of Middle river, Augusta county, Virginia. One of his sisters married William Anderson.

Christian and William Anderson in 1761 were among the troops of Colonel William Byrd at the fort at Long Island. About this time, these two young men, along with John Sawyers, explored the valley of the Holston south of Long Island as low down as Big creek, in Hawkins county where they met a party of Indians and turned back.

Of the many stout-hearted men who have passed in review before the mind of the writer, the most consistently admirable is Gilbert Christian. His memory deserves to be perpetuated by a suitable monument, erected by the county of Sullivan and the thriving city of Kingsport. His is a record worthy of commemoration.

JOSEPH HARDIN

Joseph Hardin was born near Richmond, Virginia, April 18, 1734. When the Revolutionary War broke out he was residing in Tryon county, North Carolina. In August, 1775, he participated in the organization of a Committee of Safety in that county, and signed the document known as the Tryon Association, in which it was declared that the signers faithfully united themselves to resist force by force and defend their natural freedom and constitutional rights, and take up arms and risk lives and fortunes in maintaining the freedom of their country.

He represented Tryon county in the Provincial Congress of North Carolina, held in 1775 and 1776. In September, 1775, he was appointed by that Congress major of the regiment of Salisbury District. When in the following year troops were raised and sent to aid the hard-pressed South Carolinians, Hardin was a captain in the Second (Locke's) Battalion of General Allen Jones' Brigade. He was captain of a company of Light Horse in service under General Griffith Rutherford on the Cherokee expedition. He represented Tryon county in the Assemblies of North Carolina in 1778 and 1779. When his section was overrun by the British and Tories, he fled across the mountains and settled at first on the waters of Lick creek in Washington (now Greene) county. He was soon afterward sent as Washington county's delegate to the Assembly of 1782. On the organization of Greene county he was commissioned one of the first justices of the peace, and his son, Joseph, Jr., was appointed entry-taker.

In the Franklin Assembly he was honored by election to the speakership. He was an active and faithful new-state adherent. He represented Greene county, as a friend of separation, in the Carolina Assembly in 1788, and was one of the last to take the oath of allegiance to North Carolina in the Greene county court. When the second cession act was passed, and before acceptance by Congress, Hardin showed his consistency. Being a magistrate, at the next succeeding term of court an entry of record shows that "Colonel Joseph Hardin withdraws himself from the bench, being convinced in his own mind that the jurisdiction of North Carolina has ceased in this territory ceded to the Congress of the United States."

Hardin was chairman of a convention of the inhabitants of the ceded territory held at Greeneville, May 5, 1790, which chose John Sevier as their preference as governor of the Territory recently erected by Congress. "No other man on the Continent can give as general satisfaction in that office," the convention resolved.

Governor William Blount in organizing the government of the Territory South of the Ohio, appointed Hardin a justice of Greene county; and in 1791, under the direction of Governor Blount, he partially ran one of the Indian boundary lines, fixed by the treaty of Hopewell. It was run southeasterly from Camp creek, a distance of about fifty miles to Rutherford's War Trace.

Hardin represented his county in the lower house of the first Territorial Assembly, held at Knoxville in 1794. He was among the most influential members of the body. He was speaker of the house of representatives of the second Territorial Assembly.

In 1795, he purchased two thousand acres of land in Knox county, in what is known as Hardin's Valley, and he shortly removed and spent the remainder of his days there.

He located his military claim to two thousand acres on the lower Tennessee river, along with grants of one thousand acres to each of his sons. In the year 1816, his son James conducted a party of twenty-six—four families—by boat down the Tennessee river and settled these lands, which lie in what is called, in honor of Colonel Joseph Hardin, Hardin county, Tennessee.

Joseph Hardin was a staunch Presbyterian, and one of the first elders in the Mount Bethel church at Greeneville. He was one of the original trustees of Greeneville (now Tusculum) College; and always a leader in his community. His son, Robert Hardin, D.D., attained eminence as a minister of the Presbyterian church. His son, John, was killed while on the Lookout Mountain campaign of 1788. Another son was captured and held a prisoner by the Chickamauga Indians in campaign of 1782.

CHARLES ROBERTSON

CHARLES ROBERTSON, of Washington county, was one of the leaders of the Watauga Association. He acted as trustee for the early settlers, taking the title to the lands purchased of the Cherokee Indians in March, 1775; and the records of Washington county show that he faithfully executed the trust by conveying tens of thousands of acres of land to the various settlers. By an ordinance of the constitutional convention of North Carolina of 1776 he was named as one of the justices of "Washington District." Robertson was one of the four delegates from Washington District admitted to membership in the Provincial Congress of 1776. By that body he was appointed first major of the district militia. On the establishment of Washington county he was continued in that office; and by an act of Assembly the court was to be held at his house then on Sinking creek, near the present Johnson City, until a court house should be built. In 1777 he marched a body of troops to Long Island of Holston to act as a guard while a treaty was being there negotiated with the Cherokee Indians.

He was in the Carolina senate of 1778 and 1779. The Assembly of 1778, in an effort to keep the Cherokee Indians quiet, appointed Robertson to go to the Overhill Cherokees with a friendly talk from the governor. By the Assembly of 1780 he was appointed lieutenant-colonel in command of two hundred men of Washington county to coöperate with Colonel Evan Shelby's forces on an expedition against the Cherokee Indians. Washington county sent him to the house of commons in 1784, where he voted in favor of the first cession act.

Charles Robertson, having had previous experience in legislative bodies was honored with the speakership of the senate of the State of Franklin. To him was awarded also the colonelcy of Washington county. He continued to serve as a magistrate under the new State government. His daughter had married Robert, the brother of John Sevier, and Colonel Robertson stood by the fortunes of the governor of Franklin until the last; he participated in the Sevier-Tipton engagement of 1788.

On the organization of the county of Washington, as a part of the Territory south of the Ohio River, Colonel Robertson was commissioned a justice of the peace.

Robertson had an honorable military record in the Revolution. He was sent in command of a part of John Sevier's regiment in July, 1780, to the relief of the Carolinians. His troops aided in the capture of Thicketty Fort where ninety-three loyalists surrendered; and in the battle of Musgrove's Mill.

In his later years Colonel Robertson lived south of Jonesborough, on Cherokee Creek. He died about 1800.

DANIEL KENNEDY

DANIEL KENNEDY was born in Virginia about the year 1750. Family tradition is to the effect that he served in Lord Dunmore's War (1774) as a private in the company of Captain Evan Shelby. In 1776 he aided in the defense of the Watauga Fort when it was attacked by the Cherokee Indians. Sometime after July, 1777, he settled at Milburnton, then Washington but now Greene county, and the next year he served as a grand-juror in the Washington county court. In 1770 he removed to a large tract of land he had entered, near the mouth of Camp Creek, south of Greeneville. This homestead remained in the family over one hundred years, passing to others in 1898.

Kennedy marched with John Sevier to the battle of King's Mountain (1780) as a lieutenant, to be promoted to a captaincy for gallantry in action. On his return he was honored with a seat on the bench of Washington county court, in 1781.

He represented Washington county in the North Carolina General Assembly of 1783, and was influential in the passage of an act to establish Greene county. On the organization of that county he was elected clerk of its court, an office he held for the remainder of his life under the several changes in the forms of government.

In the State of Franklin he served as a member of the council of state and as brigadier-general. With John Sevier and Alexander Outlaw he served as commissioner of that State in negotiating the Dumplin Creek treaty with the Cherokee Indians.

Elected by the friends of Franklin, he at a late day of the session took a seat in the Carolina senate of 1787. Both the Tipton and the Sevier forces were solicitous for the support of General Kennedy, because of his great popularity in Greene county. His heart was with Sevier as his speech in the Franklin convention of 1787 evidences. That speech also demonstrates the ability of Kennedy, and that he could have risen high in the affairs of State and Nation had he not preferred to retain in comfort the clerkship of his county.

When the Franklin government was virtually doomed by the action of the Federal constitution convention, General Kennedy acted under a colonel's commission from North Carolina on General Martin's campaign against the Cherokees, on the failure of which Kennedy joined Sevier under whom he had often campaigned.

General Kennedy was a friend of education. As early as 1783, he was named as an incorporator of Martin's Academy (Washington College) and he was also a trustee of Greeneville College.

General Kennedy died in consequence of a bruise on the hand from a forge hammer, and was buried at Mount Zion church, six miles from Greeneville. Above his grave there was recently erected a monument—a large native rock embedded in which is a bronze tablet bearing this inscription:

To the Memory
of
Col. Daniel Kennedy
1750–1802
Soldier, Patriot, Statesman,
Revolutionary Soldier,
Pioneer of Tennessee
First Clerk of Court
Greene County
Served Under Four Forms of Government
1783–1802.
Supported State of Franklin
Made Peace With Indians
Trustee
Greeneville and Washington Colleges
Erected by Descendants
1920.

AUGUSTUS CHRISTIAN GEORGE ELHOLM

GEORGE ELHOLM was a native of Duchy of Holstein, which at the date of his birth was under the dominion of Denmark. He came to America early in the Revolutionary War and received a captain's commission in Count Pulaski's corps. In September, 1779, General Lincoln and Count d'Estaing made an attempt to retake the city of Savannah by siege. Learning of the purpose of the allied forces, the British general hurriedly ordered in all outposts. A portion of Colonel Cruger's command under Captain French attempted to comply with the order by passing in armed vessels through the inland channels. Intercepted in their course up the Ogechee river, the British troops were compelled to land and entrench. Colonel John White, of the Fourth Georgia Battalion, in consultation with his officers concerted a plan for their capture. On the night of October 1, Colonel White and Captain Elholm, with five others of the American troops, reconnoitered and kindled many fires to give the impression of a large encampment. Another bit of strategy was resorted to—the giving of commands in a loud tone as if directing the disposition of a considerable body of soldiers, the hurry and bustle of staff officers being imitated. Colonel White, unattended, dashed up to the British troops and demanded a conference with the commander. Just at this time Captain Elholm rode up and urgently inquired of his colonel where he should place his artillery. Captain French, convinced that a large force had surrounded his camp, surrendered his detachment of one hundred and eleven, and five vessels with their crews, arms and munitions.

Elholm was later attached to the command of Colonel Horry under General Francis Marion, and behaved with great gallantry in the operations against the British in South Carolina, 1780–81. For a time he was a captain in the legion of Colonel "Lighthorse Harry" Lee. It is probable that Sevier and Elholm first met while campaigning under General Marion; and the friendship then formed may have led Elholm to go to Franklin when he learned of Sevier's effort to found a new State. It seems that, for a time, Elholm was adjutant-general of Georgia, and his going to Franklin, more than likely, was with the consent, if not by the procurement, of Georgia's then governor, Telfair, the purpose being to effect some sort of military alliance with the new government.

Besides acting as Franklin's commissioner to Georgia, Major Elholm served quite effectively as adjutant and drill-master of the

Franklin militia. His buoyant nature and his ebullience cheered Sevier and his followers when the trend of events was against their cause. He stood for heroic measure in times of crises, and had his advice been heeded Franklin might have had a different fate. As it was, he was an influential factor. This is shown by the hatred of him manifested by the opponents of Franklin in letters written at the time. An unknown writer, in August, 1788, refers to Elholm's great influence in Franklin affairs, and declares "he is cordially despised," by those in opposition.

The gallant Major by his imperturbable good humor and his talent as a musician won to himself the young people and was given a welcome in the homes of the border. He had a warm place in the regard of Sevier, and in later years when Sevier was governor of Tennessee, Major Elholm came from his home in Georgia to visit his old friend and leader.

He remained in service with Sevier until the last of Lesser Franklin, and on returning to Georgia served as adjutant-general under Governor George Mathews. A disagreement between Mathews and Elholm led to the court martialling and cashiering of the latter.

Major Elholm then entered on the practice of law at Augusta. He left a journal "valuable for the amount of information it contained, and curious on account of the grandiloquent style in which he was in the habit of expressing himself." A search for this journal was made by the author in hope that it might be found, to shed additional light on the affairs of Franklin. It was according to White in his *Historical Collections of Georgia* in the State Library at Milledgeville when White wrote. It was perhaps taken away or destroyed by troops during the occupancy of Milledgeville by the Federal army in December, 1864. A large number of the most valuable records in that library were then lost.

The *Augusta Herald*, of Wednesday, November 27, 1799, gave two lines to the passing of this man of heroic mold, who had in days of stress and need given valuable service to the State and Nation:

"Died, on Saturday night last, Augustus Christian George Elholm, Esq., attorney at law."

HENRY CONWAY

HENRY CONWAY was born in Virginia, and removed to the lower part of the Nolachucky settlement before 1783, in August of which year he was appointed one of the tax-assessors of Greene county, and at the November term of court was on the grand jury.

He served as treasurer of the State of Franklin (1787); as one of the commissioners who signed the treaty of Coytoy (1786) and as speaker of the senate of 1786.

Two of the sons of Governor Sevier married his daughters. James Sevier's wife was Nancy Conway; Major John Sevier's first wife was Elizabeth Conway. A third daughter married John Sevier, son of Colonel Valentine Sevier, II, and became the mother of Senator Ambrose Hundley Sevier, of Arkansas. The wife of Henry Conway was Sarah Hundley of Virginia.

Through his son, Thomas, Henry Conway was progenitor of other grandsons who rose to eminence in the State of Arkansas. Henry W. Conway served with distinction under General Jackson in the War of 1812, and was member of Congress from Arkansas, from 1823 to 1827, when he was killed in a duel with Robert Crittenden. James Sevier Conway was founder of the city of Little Rock, Arkansas, and first governor of that State, 1836-1840. Elias Nelson Conway was the fifth governor of Arkansas.

George Conway, a brother of Henry Conway, was of the commission that laid out the town of Greeneville. He served as colonel on the Cherokee expedition of 1793, and was first major-general of the State of Tennessee. Joseph Conway, another brother, served the State of Franklin.

Without doubt, the Conway family produced more men of ability than any other Greene county family.

Henry Conway remained throughout all vicissitudes firmly attached to the State of Franklin. Not until the February term, 1789, of the Greene county court did he take the oath of allegiance to the State of North Carolina.

There is more than a hint of record that Henry Conway was a man of full habits. He lived well, and extended a gracious hospitality. Bishop Asbury was his guest on one of his visits to Tennessee, and Governor Sevier made the Conway home a stopping-place in his frequent journeying between Washington county and Knoxville.

FRANCIS A. RAMSEY

FRANCIS ALEXANDER RAMSEY, son of Reynolds and Naomi (Alexander) Ramsey, was born near Gettysburg, Pennsylvania, May 31, 1764. An uncle, John Alexander, had located on Big Limestone Creek near the present village of Limestone, in Washington county, North Carolina, where other Pennsylvanians had formed the nucleus of a Presbyterian congregation. At the invitation of his uncle, Francis A. Ramsey left his home in Pennsylvania in his nineteenth year, and journeyed five hundred miles to make his home in the Tennessee country, arriving at his destination in 1783. Young Ramsey was fairly well educated and had mastered surveying. He brought compass and chain with him, and was soon employed in surveying entries for the settlers. In November, 1783, he "qualified as surveyor" in the Washington county court.

The skill of Ramsey as a penman and scholar was availed of by the conventions held for the adoption of a constitution for the State of Franklin; he served as secretary. The same qualifications doubtless led to his being made one of the councillors for the new State, and clerk of the superior court of its Washington District. In 1787, he was appointed a commissioner of Franklin to wait on the Carolina Assembly.

In December, 1788, he was elected by the Carolina Assembly second major of the Washington District. In passing from the West to the seat of the government of North Carolina on official duties, he met and later married (April 7, 1789) Peggy, the oldest daughter of John McKnitt Alexander, of Mecklenburg county, North Carolina. The young couple first made their home on Little Limestone creek, in Washington county, at or near Jonesborough.

On the organization of the territory in 1790, Ramsey continued in the clerkship of the court and he was raised to the rank of first major of cavalry of Washington District, next after him, as second major, coming George Farragut, the father of the famous admiral of the navy of the United States. On the organization of Hamilton District Governor Blount appointed Ramsey clerk of its superior court, and in 1792 he removed to Knox county.

As early as August, 1783, Ramsey had accompanied James White and Robert Young on a tour of exploration into what is now Knox county, and Ramsey built a home for his family on lands he then and later on entered for grant. Here were born his sons, James McGready Ramsey, the historian, and William B. A. Ramsey, who became secretary of state of Tennessee.

Ramsey was one of the first trustees of Blount College, now the University of Tennessee.

In 1819 Governor McMinn appointed him a commissioner to examine the offices of the surveyors and registrars of lands in the East Tennessee districts, in order to the prevention of frauds in the granting of lands in West Tennessee purchased from the Chickasaw Indians in that year. In the following year he was made president of the State Bank of Knoxville, but served only for a short time. He died November 13, 1820.

WILLIAM CAGE

WILLIAM CAGE was born in Virginia in 1745. He removed to Chatham county, North Carolina, and served for a time as major in the Revolutionary army. His chief service was against the Tories under the noted Colonel David Fanning. He seems to have been a prisoner of the Tories for a short time. He removed after the war to Sullivan county, North Carolina. That county sent him as one of its delegates to the house of commons of the North Carolina legislature of 1783, his associate being Colonel Abraham Bledsoe. He was returned the succeeding session, along with David Looney. He voted against the first cession act; but became one of the moving spirits in organizing the new State of Franklin. He was elected speaker of the lower house of the first assembly, and was the first treasurer of the State.

In 1785, he removed to Sumner county, probably influenced to do so by the Bledsoes. When the territorial government was organized, he was appointed by Governor Blount sheriff of Sumner county, and by successive appointments he served until 1796, when he was succeeded by James Cage. Another son, Harry Cage, removed to Mississippi where he became supreme judge and congressman. Two of his grandsons were noted men: Harry T. Hays, Major-General, C.S.A., and his brother John Coffee Hays, major of the celebrated Texas Rangers and surveyor-general of California. William Cage died at his home in Cage's Bend (of Cumberland river), March, 1811.

STOCKLEY DONELSON

STOCKLEY DONELSON, born in Virginia, was the son of Colonel John Donelson, the surveyor who in 1771 ran the "Donelson line" between that part of Virginia under civil government and the domain of the Cherokee Indians.

The son followed his father in the profession of surveyor, and like his father was one of the largest and most persistent land speculators in the Western Country. Many of his operations were in partnership with others. In 1783 he engaged with Governor Caswell and James Glasgow to explore the country on the French Broad for proper locations of land warrants, Donelson to receive a one-fourth interest for his services. He was at that time surveyor of Sullivan county; and in 1784, probably because of the influence of Caswell and Glasgow, he was elected by the legislature surveyor for the western lands in the eastern district—a new office of importance since the passage of the act of 1783, opening the West to the entry and grant of lands.

He joined in the Franklin movement and was made surveyor-general of the State. He also was speaker of the house of commons for one term. He represented Hawkins county in the Carolina Convention in 1788, and opposed the ratification of the Federal Constitution.

Governor Blount appointed him to the post of lieutenant-colonel commandant of the forces of Hawkins county at the formation of the territorial government; and he was a member of the first council of state in 1794.

Donelson, it seems, did not figure in the formation of the State of Tennessee. Politics was evidently subordinated to business and the acquisition of a landed estate, estimated to amount to one-half million acres.

JOSHUA GIST

Joshua Gist, who was elected an assistant (lay) judge on the organization of the State of Franklin, and who was a member of one of the conventions, was from North Carolina, where he had been a captain in the Revolutionary War, Brown's Battalion of Ashe's Brigade, and served in the General Assembly.

In 1784 he lived on French Broad and represented Greene county in the Carolina Assembly. He voted in favor of the first cession bill. On the creation of the Franklin county of Sevier he was made a justice of the peace. He was present at the making of the treaty of Dumplin creek.

He was chairman of the convention of January 12, 1789. Under the territorial government he was appointed a justice of the peace for Jefferson county when it was established in 1782; and of Sevier county on its formation in 1794.

He was a son of Benjamin Gist, one of the first justices of Washington county, and also a Franklinite. Joshua Gist appears to have been colonel of Greene county in December, 1784, and as such was ordered to arrest the noted Major Hubbard.

JOHN ANDERSON

John Anderson, named as the second assistant-judge under Judge David Campbell, was of Sullivan county, which he represented in one of the conventions called to consider the Constitution of Franklin. A son of Colonel Gilbert Christian, in writing to Draper, mentioned him as having been one of the leading and consistent supporters of the new State in his county. He was "second colonel" of the militia in Sullivan.

Anderson was made a justice of the peace in Sullivan county by Governor Blount (1790) and he was also one of the magistrates elected by the first legislature of the State of Tennessee. He does not appear to have had aspirations toward a political career.

Presumably he was of the Anderson family of Augusta county, son of Andrew, related by marriage to Colonel Gilbert Christian, and referred to in a letter from Major Arthur Campbell to Colonel William Preston, August 10, 1774: "Capt. Wm. Campbell desires me to recommend one John Anderson to you for ensign to Capt. Looney. I believe you are acquainted with the young gent and I think he may be a proper person." Anderson was so far a proper person as to earn the rank of captain of a company in the War of the Revolution. In 1782 he led the forces of Sullivan county, under Colonel John Sevier, against the Chickamauga Indians. He died October 17, 1817.

JOHN MENEFEE

John Menefee, who was speaker of the house of representatives of Franklin Assembly of 1787, first settled in Sullivan county, which he represented in the first convention at Jonesborough in 1784. In 1790, he was residing in Hawkins (now Knox) county, where he was commissioned a captain of militia by Governor Blount; and on the creation of Knox county, in June, 1792, he was made a justice of the peace and continued in his captaincy. Menefee was Knox county's delegate in the house of representatives of the first, and several later General Assemblies of Tennessee; and was appointed one of the first justices of the peace under the Constitution of 1796. Menefee's Station is named for him. The name is sometimes written "Manifee."

Thomas Amis, son of John and Mary (Dillard) Amis, was of Huguenot family(Amie)which left France on the revocation of the Edict of Nantes for the Barbadoes, in the West Indies, going thence to Virginia. A branch of the family settled in North Carolina. Thomas Amis was in the Provincial Congress of Carolina in 1776, from Bladen county; and in the Third Regiment of the Continental Army. He served quite a time in the commissionary department.

After the war he, having married Mary Gale (or Gayle), removed west of the Alleghanies and settled in Hawkins county where he erected a stone house in which he resided and operated a tavern. He also erected a grist mill and a distillery. It appears that in 1786 Amis was trading in the farther West and that his boats and goods were seized and confiscated by the Spanish commandant at the Natchez, complaint of which was made to Congress.

The good Bishop Asbury, journeying through Tennessee, noted in his journal that at Amis' tavern "we were well entertained for our money" and that Amis was rebuked when he boasted of gaining three hundred pounds per annum "by the brewing of his poison. We talked very plainly; and I told him that it was of necessity, and not of choice, we were there—that I feared the face of no man." Amis also entertained the elder Michaux, Andrew Jackson and John Sevier.

Amis was in the Carolina senate of 1788 and 1789, where his votes were in favor of separation.

Mary, a daughter of Amis, married Joseph Rogers, the founder of Rogersville.

David Campbell, Captain, was a supporter of separation and a member of the Assembly of Franklin. He was born in Augusta county, Virginia, August, 1753, and on becoming of age removed to Washington county of the same State. He participated in the battle of Point Pleasant in Lord Dunmore's War; in the battle of Long Island Flats, in 1776; and in the battle of King's Mountain, with eight others of the name, brothers and cousins. About the year 1782 Campbell having married his cousin, the sister of Colonel Arthur and Judge David Campbell, removed to Washington county, North Carolina; later to Strawberry Plain, and then to Campbell's Station. He served for a time in the Tennessee General Assembly, and as presidential elector. He was the ancestor of Governor William B. Campbell of Tennessee, and of Rev. Dr. David Campbell Kelley, who was known as "the fighting parson," on the staff of General Nathan Bedford Forrest.

Captain Campbell's last home was in Wilson county, where he died, August 18, 1832.

Ramsey says of him: "He left the savor of a good name wherever he was known."

Samuel Doak, the father of education in Tennessee, was born in August, 1749. His parents were Samuel and Jane (Mitchell) Doak, who emigrated from northern Ireland and first settled in Chester county, Pennsylvania, whence they removed to Augusta county, Virginia, where their son, Samuel was born. Young Doak at the age of sixteen was studying the classics under Reverend Archibald Alexander. In 1773 he entered Princeton College from which he was graduated in 1775, during the presidency of Dr. Witherspoon. He was for two years a tutor at an academy in Virginia which later became Hampden Sidney College, and at the same time studied theology under Reverend John Blair Smith, and later under Reverend William Graham in his native county. About this time he married Esther H., the daughter of Reverend John Montgomery; and was licensed to preach by the Presbytery of Hanover. He soon turned southward for a location. After preaching for a time in Sullivan county, then thought to be a part of Washington county, Virginia, he was for about two years at the forks of the Holston and Watauga rivers. He later removed to a settlement on the Little Limestone (below Jonesborough) at the request of the inhabitants. According to the tradition in riding through the forest in that neighborhood he unexpectedly came upon a group of settlers who were felling trees. Learning that he was a minister, they requested him to preach, and this he did, using his horse as a pulpit. He there (1780) organized Salem church, and a school which was later called Martin's Academy and which became Washington College.

In 1818 Dr. Doak resigned the presidency of Washington College to join his son in establishing a classical school in Greene county, Tusculum Academy—now Tusculum College. A volume of "Lectures on the Philosophy of Human Nature" of which he was the author was published by his son, Reverend John W. Doak.

Dr. Samuel Doak was of powerful frame, medium stature, with a short thick neck. His hair was sandy, his complexion ruddy, and his eyes blue. His demeanor was dignified; his countenance grave. His was a stentorian voice, and he was withal a striking individuality.

George Doherty, perhaps the son of George Doherty who was major in the North Carolina troops in the War of the Revolution, settled in the Western Country at an early day. In 1779 he was engaged in the wars against the Cherokee Indians. He served under Sevier as a captain on the King's Mountain expedition. On the establishment of Greene county he was appointed one of the justices of the peace. Early in the life of the State of Franklin he was appointed lieutenant-colonel and later colonel of Caswell county militia. He was on the Hiwassee and Martin campaigns in 1788, and the year following was a member of the North Carolina convention which ratified the Federal Constitution.

When Governor Blount was organizing the government of the Territory in Jefferson county Doherty was made a justice of the peace and lieutenant-colonel commandant.

Colonel Doherty was a representative from Jefferson county in the first Territorial Assembly; and was of that county's delegation in the first constitutional convention of Tennessee. He was in the first senate of that State, and in subsequent years served in sessions of its legislature.

In 1783 he, along with Colonel McFarland, headed a volunteer expedition of two hundred mounted men of the border against the middle towns of the Cherokees in North Carolina, destroying six towns. In the fall of the same year he was on Sevier's Hightower campaign.

Colonel Doherty served on another expedition that has been ignored, seemingly, by the historians of the State. After the acquisition of the Louisiana Territory, in 1803, for a time it appeared to be necessary to compel, by force of arms, the surrender by the Spanish authorities of New Orleans, and the dependent district. The war department (October, 1803) made a requisition on Governor Sevier for a force of mounted infantry to march to Natchez with all possible dispatch. Doherty who was colonel of the militia of the Washington and Hamilton districts embodied a command, described by Governor Sevier as "eight companies of as brave militia as ever went into the field," which reached Natchez in December, 1803, in good health and fine order, though great hardships had been experienced in marching through the wilderness where there was suffering for want of provisions for the troops and their horses. While they were on the march the President learned that New Orleans had been surrendered to the agents of the national government. Colonel Doherty returned with his command, after reaching Natchez, assured of the President's "great pleasure and satisfaction at the prompt manner in which the mounted infantry had turned out."

In the Creek War, Doherty as brigadier-general led an East Tennessee command and his conduct at the battle of the Horseshoe was marked by great gallantry.

Colonel and General Doherty resided on the north bank of the French Broad river. He is described as tall, well-formed and of dark features and as a man of remarkable common sense. Plain and unaffected, he was a natural leader of the border people both in war and in civil life.

Nathaniel Evans was a native of Virginia. It seems he first settled near Jonesborough, later near Bean's Station, and subsequently removed to the country south of the French Broad. He had little inclination to participate in civil affairs. He was a soldier and was justly pronounced by his contemporaries "a good soldier," noted for bravery and daring exploits. He was loyal to Sevier to the last and one of his favorites. A brother, Joseph, settled in Sevier county. In the war of 1792 the two brothers had their horses stolen by the Indians. They disguised themselves by dressing like Indians, stole into the Indian camp, recovered their horses and reached home, one of them having received a slight wound. On the campaign that followed the attack on Houston Station, Evans was in command of a company, and as a reward for his gallantry, it was proposed that he be raised to a colonelcy. He declined the promotion, saying that he could do better service as a captain.

In 1793 Governor Blount made him a captain of the Knox county cavalry, and as such he led a large detachment of mounted troops to aid in the protection of the Cumberland Settlements; and, on his return, was on the Hightower and Etowah campaigns. He was advanced to the rank of first major of the cavalry of Hamilton District, in 1795.

Evans is described as being six feet high and weighing about two hundred pounds.

Samuel Handley, born in Virginia, was as a youth a member of Captain Evan Shelby's company at the battle of Point Pleasant in 1774. He was a lieutenant in the Revolutionary War, and took part in the engagement at King's Mountain. According to a son of John Sevier, he was one of the captains most active under John Sevier in the earlier expeditions against the Indians. He was, among many expeditions, on the Boyd's Creek campaign. The Cherokees came to dread and admire him and to look upon him as a brave and fearless fighter.

Handley was of Sevier's party in the Sevier-Tipton engagement of February, 1788. He represented Washington county in the constitutional convention of 1796. Captain Handley later resided in the vicinity of the Tellico blockhouse, near the present town of Loudon.

Toward the close of the year 1792, while leading a party of men to reinforce the hard-pressed settlers on the Cumberland, his command was attacked by Indians, near the Crab Orchard, on the Cumberland plateau. Becoming separated from his men he was set upon by a brave who had lifted his hatchet to strike, when Handley seized the weapon, crying out "Canaly" (for higinalii) "friend." The Cherokee responded the same word and lowered his arm. Captain Handley was taken a captive to Willstown, in Alabama, where he suffered many indignities and hardships until the next spring. The Cherokees, desirous for peace, made use of his service in causing him to write for them a letter to Governor Blount, and sent him home escorted by eight warriors without any demand for hostage or ransom.

Captain Handley was several times sent by his people as a delegate to the Tennessee General Assembly; and in March, 1798, Governor Sevier honored him by commissioning him to visit the headmen of the Cherokee nation in an effort to prevail on them to sell a portion of their domain that bordered on the white settlements.

He died in Franklin county, aged eighty-two, an honored member of the Society of Cincinnati.

Samuel Houston was born on Hay's creek, in Rockbridge county, Virginia, January 1, 1758, the son of John and Sarah (Todd) Houston. He attended schools in his immediate neighborhood; and November 22, 1776, entered Liberty Academy (now Washington and Lee University) then presided over by the celebrated Wm. Graham. He graduated, with the degree of A.B., in 1780. He at once began the study of theology under Graham, but decided to enter the revolutionary struggle, volunteered as a private in 1781, and as such participated in the battle of Guilford's Court House, in North Carolina. He kept a journal of his experiences as a soldier. In this he recorded the fact that, marching on foot, he discharged his rifle fourteen times, or once for each ten minutes the battle lasted. Houston was in the command of General Stevens. Returning home, the young soldier was received as a candidate for the ministry by the Hanover Presbytery in November, 1781, and licensed to preach the next year. In 1783 he accepted a call to the Providence congregation in Washington county, North Carolina, now Tennessee, and was ordained in August of the same year. Providence church is near the Greene county line. In 1785, Houston was one of the ministers who formed the Presbytery of Abingdon, which he several times represented at the meetings of the Synod. He was a member of the first committee to which was referred the proposal for the formation of a General Assembly for the Presbyterian Church.

In 1789 Houston returned to Virginia to serve the churches at Falling Bridge and Highbridge in his native county. He served these churches many years, and at the same time conducted a classical school. He was elected a trustee of his *alma mater*, then Washington College, October 7, 1791, in place of his father, and served until 1826. He was secretary of the Board of Trustees from 1791 till 1807. He became totally blind before his death, which occurred January 20, 1839.

In personal appearance Houston was tall, erect and square-shouldered, dignified in deportment, but peculiar in his dress. He is described as an earnest preacher and a model pastor. He was a frequent contributor to *Niles' Weekly* and other publications of the day.

It is believed that he began to make contributions to the press while he was living in Franklin State, and that a number of the newspaper articles referred to in the text of his volume were from his pen.

A monument at his grave has this inscription:

Sacred
To the memory
of the
Rev. Samuel Houston,
who in early life was a soldier of the
Revolution
And for fifty-five years a faithful
minister of the
Lord Jesus Christ.
He died on the 20th day of January, 1839
Aged 81 years.

The father of Houston removed from Virginia to make his home in Blount county. Among the delegates in the constitutional convention of 1796, and in the first Tennessee Assembly from that county was James Houston, a first cousin of Reverend Samuel Houston, and the father of Sam Houston, the great Tennessean and Texan.

Moses and David Looney were from Virginia, where Moses had been a captain of militia as early as 1774. They perhaps resided at that time in the western part of what is now Sullivan county, Tennessee. A pass through the Clinch mountains was known as Looney's Gap at an early date. May 3, 1774, the court of Fincastle county ordered Anthony Bledsoe to make the list of tithables in Captain Looney's company. The organization of the first court of Sullivan county was at the house of Moses Looney in the month of February, 1780. David Looney was one of the first justices and major of the militia of the new county. He was advanced to the lieutenant-colonelcy, which office he resigned in 1781. He was a member of the lower house of the Carolina Assembly of 1784. Moses Looney was captured and carried into captivity by the Indians in 1781. Both of the Looneys were in the Franklin movement and sat in the Assembly; and David Looney was one of the first justices of the peace under the new State government.

David Looney was a delegate from Sullivan county to the convention of 1788 which was called to consider the ratification of the National Constitution. He was in 1790 commissioned by Governor Blount a justice of the peace of his county, under the territorial form of government. In the first legislature of the State of Tennessee he represented Sullivan county. In 1796 a Looney was the leading inn-keeper of Knoxville.

Descendants of the Looneys settled in Shelby and Maury counties where they were prominent in the affairs of the State of Tennessee.

Moses Looney was killed while engaged in the arrest of Thomas Faulin, who for a time, held the posse at bay. A parley was proposed on which Faulin came out of his house rifle in hand. While he and Looney were conversing, "a certain red-mouthed Irishman, named Ingram, slipped around and shot Faulin from behind." Before Faulin fell, he raised his gun and shot, the bullet hitting and killing Looney. The two fell dead together.

William Murphey, born March 12, 1759, was reared near Bedford, Va. He volunteered for Revolutionary service August, 1776, and did his first duty as a guard for the lead mines near Fort Chiswell, and later was on Col. Christian's campaign, and did guard duty at the Cherokee treaty of 1777 at Long Island. In the next year he was drafted for five months' service in Capt. Robert Sevier's company of Washington County, N. C., and was in the South Carolina campaign. In March, 1779, Captain Sevier resigned and Murphey was promoted to an ensigncy. He was in a battle on Savannah river and in skirmishes in Georgia. He volunteered to serve three months if necessary as a sergeant in Colonel John Sevier's expedition against the Cherokees in 1780; and again in 1781-82 was on two other Indian expeditions. Murphey was a Baptist minister, a favorite of the Seviers, and a supporter of Franklin State. He served in her Assembly. He died in St. Francis County, Mo., November 2, 1833.

Samuel Newell was born on the Atlantic ocean, November 4, 1754, and his father, first settling in Frederick county, Virginia, soon afterward was one of the early settlers on Beaver Creek of Holston river.

He engaged in service against the Tories in April, 1776, and in the summer of that year was in the battle of Island Flats of Holston. In the same year he was appointed a sergeant in Captain Colvill's company; was promoted to a lieutenancy the following year in which capacity he was for a year or two actively engaged in the protection of the frontier against the Indians. In 1780 he took part in an expedition against the Tories on New river, and was under Colonel Campbell in the battle of King's Mountain, where he received a severe wound early in the action, from the effects of which he never fully recovered. Procuring a horse, after receiving the wound, he managed to continue the combat until the close of the action. He was, notwithstanding, in December following in service on the campaign of Colonel Arthur Campbell against the Cherokees. In 1781 he was advanced to a captaincy, and again was active in protecting the frontier against the depredations of the Indians.

He was one of the early settlers in the French Broad country, and took active part in launching the State of Franklin, as a member of the constitutional convention, and in the legislature. He was one of the first assemblymen from the Franklin county of Sevier.

Under the territorial government Newell was appointed a magistrate of Knox county, and when the county of Sevier was re-created he was appointed to serve there in the same capacity. He was the first chairman of the Sevier county court; and also received Governor Blount's commission as lieutenant-colonel of militia. He was a delegate in the lower house of the first Tennessee General Assembly. In 1797, he removed to Kentucky and later to Indiana where he died September 21, 1841. He is described by Draper as a man of fine presence, six feet one inch in height, and of superior ability.

Alexander Outlaw was born in Duplin county, North Carolina, in 1738. He served for a time (1777) as a captain of militia in the revolutionary conflict. He married Penelope Smith, of his native county and emigrated to the West, first to Washington county, Virginia, where he was on November 24, 1782, commissioned a justice of the peace. He was enrolled in the militia of that county. Attracted by the fine and cheap lands on the lower frontier, he removed to the Nolachucky Settlements in 1783, and located lands in Greene, (now Jefferson) county.

Outlaw was a delegate to the first Franklin convention at Jonesborough, in August, 1784, and served on the committee which had under consideration the situation produced by the cession act of that year. It is difficult to understand his attitude; he alone from the western counties appeared to claim a seat in the Carolina Assembly of 1784 after that body had been in session for some time. He was granted a seat on a certificate of the sheriff of Greene county attesting his election, although the cession act had not then been repealed. Outlaw, strangely enough, voted in favor of the repeal of that act, he having previously, four days after being sworn in, introduced a bill to empower the inhabitants of the Western Country, by and with the consent of the State of North Carolina, to form themselves into a separate State to be known by the name of West Carolina. In 1785, he was in the service of the State of Franklin on a commission to treat with the Cherokee Indians, but the next year he served as paymaster of troops under North Carolina. He also was in the Franklin Assembly of the same year, again acted as a treaty commissioner of the new State, and was a justice of the peace and colonel of the militia in the new county carved out by the Franklin Assembly and named in honor of Governor Caswell.

Outlaw served in General Martin's campaign and in the North Carolina legislature in 1788, and was a delegate in the convention of 1789 which ratified the Federal Constitution. In January, 1789, he was active in the convention held on the border and was by it named as alternate delegate to wait on the Federal Congress to petition for relief.

By Governor Blount he was (1790) commissioned a justice of the peace for Greene county; in 1792 he was admitted to the bar of Knox county; in 1796 he served in the Tennessee constitutional convention, and moved that in the event the State of Tennessee should not be admitted to the Union, the State should continue in existence as an independent State.

Outlaw was a representative from Jefferson county in the first legislature held under the constitution; and in 1799 and 1801 was in the senate and was honored both terms by elections to the speakership.

He developed considerable ability as a lawyer, and was a shrewd and foresighted man of affairs. From his home in the bend of the Nolachucky, he reached out and became the owner of large tracts of the most fertile lands on the Nolachucky, French Broad and Tennessee rivers. Judge David Campbell, Judge Joseph Anderson and Joseph Hamilton married daughters of Colonel Outlaw and his descendants have been influential in the life of the Commonwealth of Tennessee.

Outlaw is depicted as a man of large frame, six feet high, blue eyes, sandy hair and red moustache. He died in 1826, and was buried at Cahauba, Alabama, where he was at the time of his death looking after land purchases in that region.

James Reese, from Mecklenburg county, North Carolina, settled in the western country about 1784. He was a member of the Franklin Assembly; and served as secretary of the Greeneville convention (May 5, 1790) which recommended Sevier for appointment to the governorship of the Territory South of the River Ohio. He resided in Jefferson county, and devoted himself to the practice of law. He does not appear to have aspired to military or political honors. He was the father of Judge William B. Reese, a justice of the Tennessee Supreme Court and president of East Tennessee University, now University of Tennessee.

Charles Robertson (sometimes spelled "Robinson") resided in Greene county. He is not to be confused with Colonel Charles

Robertson, of Sinking Creek, who was a leader of the Watauga Association. The name of each is at times, spelled "Robinson" and it is difficult to distinguish the two when mentioned in records and even in histories.

Robertson appeared in Greene county prior to 1783. His name "Robertson" is on the tax-list of that year in that county. He lived on Meadow creek of Nolachucky river. He, as well as the other Charles Robertson, was in the first Jonesborough convention of Franklin, but this appears to have been his only legislative service.

In 1796-7 the State of South Carolina projected a scheme for the cutting of a highway from Tennessee to Charleston, and proposed to build the road southward provided the State of Tennessee would open and construct the same from Warm Springs on French Broad through the mountains to Sherrill's Cove. Charles Robertson was superintendent of construction of Tennessee's portion of this highway. Governor Sevier in his message (October, 1797) announced that the road was open to traffic by wagons, and spoke in complimentary terms of Robertson.

James Roddy first settled on Roan's creek, of the upper Watauga valley prior to 1778; later he removed to Greene county, and on the organization of Jefferson, he fell in that county. He was on the Boyd's Creek campaign; in the first Franklin convention; a delegate to the North Carolina Convention of 1788; a magistrate and register of Jefferson county under the territorial government; a member of the constitutional convention of 1796 and a senator in the Second General Assembly of Tennessee. From early manhood he was esteemed of sound judgment and trustworthy in all relations of life. Sevier while governor of Tennessee, often made his home a stopping place.

Valentine Sevier, II, was born in the Valley of Virginia in 1747, the son of Valentine Sevier and the brother of Governor John Sevier. His record as a soldier is noteworthy. He was a sergeant in Captain Evan Shelby's company at the battle of Point Pleasant and as spy and combatant was "distinguished for vigilance, activity and bravery." In the act creating Washington county, the Carolina Assembly named him as one of the justices of the peace; and he was elected the first sheriff of the county. As a captain, he was in command of a company in the Revolutionary battles at Thicketty Fort, Cedar Springs, Musgrove's Mill and King's Mountain. He also was active in John Sevier's Indian campaigns. He took part in the attempt to settle the Great Bend of the Tennessee, and was chosen to be major of the militia of that region (January, 1784). When the State of Franklin was established, he served in the legislature and as second colonel of the militia of Washington county. In 1787 the Carolina Assembly named him as lieutenant-colonel of cavalry commandant for Washington District, but he declined to be weaned away from the support of Franklin. The Assembly of the next year declined to reappoint him, "it not appearing that he has availed himself of the act of pardon of the last session." Valentine Sevier emigrated to the Cumberland in 1788, and erected a station near the mouth of Red river, in the county of Montgomery. He endured many and severe hardships on that frontier in the following years. He died February 23, 1800.

Andrew Taylor, of Rockbridge county, Virginia, was the son of Isaac Taylor, of Mill Creek settlement a fine valley in Rockbridge county. He came from county Armagh, North or Protestant Ireland. Unlike many immigrants of that day, they had means, which were invested in lands and slaves. From another branch of this family descended Bishop William Taylor, of the Methodist Episcopal Church, and, according to the family tradition, President Zachary Taylor.

Andrew Taylor married in Virginia, first Elizabeth Wilson, and second her sister, Ann Wilson, and with his young family removed to the Watauga country in 1778, settling in Happy Valley. He was the progenitor of a long line of distinguished men: Brigadier-General Nathaniel Taylor; Nathaniel G. Taylor, Congressman and Commissioner of Indian Affairs; Alfred A. Taylor, Congressman and Governor; Robert L. Taylor, Congressman, Governor and United States Senator.

Andrew Taylor was a member of the Franklin Assembly, and a justice of the peace of his county under the government of the Lost State. Isaac, one of his sons by his first wife, fought in the Revolution under Colonel John Sevier, to whom all of the Taylors were ardently attached. Andrew, Jr., fought in the Indian wars under Sevier.

Peter Turney was an immigrant of French and German extraction, probably from Alsace. He settled in Virginia, and was a private in the company of Captain Evan Shelby at the battle of Point Pleasant, in Lord Dunmore's War. Removing into the Holston country, he became sheriff of Spencer county of Franklin State and, it seems, a captain. In 1796 he had removed west of the Cumberland mountains and lived on the wilderness road, in the present county of Smith of which he was a justice of the peace on its organization in 1799. It appears from Sevier's diary that he did not hesitate to ask official favors of Sevier when the latter was governor of Tennessee, and that they were granted without delay.

Peter Turney was the father of Hopkins Lacy Turney, congressman and United States senator from Tennessee, and grandfather of Peter Turney, chief justice of the Supreme Court and governor of Tennessee.

George Vincent was of North Carolina lineage and probably the son of Thomas Vincent. He was a justice of the peace and a member of the General Assembly of Franklin, and Thomas a captain of a company in Colonel Robert Love's command on General Martin's campaign against the Chickamaugas in 1788; he was badly wounded but brought back on a horse-litter to recover. In the same year he was chosen by the legislature of North Carolina to serve on commissions to run the boundary between Washington and Sullivan counties and to build a court house for the latter county. Both Thomas and George Vincent were petitioners in favor of a separation from North Carolina (1787–88). They lived in the lower end of Sullivan county.

Samuel Wear (sometimes written Weir) was born 1753 in Augusta county, Virginia, the son of Robert and Rebecca Wear. In 1778 he married Mary Thompson in Augusta county, and in 1780 they removed to the French Broad country, where they took up land on the west prong of Little Pigeon river, at the mouth of Walden's creek, five miles south from the present town of Sevierville. He led a company as captain under Sevier at the battle of King's Mountain. The Franklin movement enlisted his support; he participated in the Jonesborough convention; was a member of the Assembly of that State, and was a commissioner to treat with the Indians. He was lieutenant-colonel commandant of Sevier county under the territorial government, and was a representative in the first territorial legislature. On the formation of the State of Tennessee he was a member of the constitutional convention.

In 1793 he led a party on the Tallassee campaign against the Cherokees.

He amassed a considerable body of very choice land; a good portion of which was involved in the case of *Danforth v. Wear*, 1 Wheaton Rep., 155, in the Supreme Court of the United States. His name is borne by Wear's Cove, in Sevier county.

Samuel Wear was a man of much force of character, "brave in battle and wise in council." The Tennessee Society of the Sons of the Revolution has formulated plans for the erection of a monument at his grave on the estate where he died April 3, 1817.

THE ANTIS

EVAN SHELBY

EVAN SHELBY was born in Wales in 1720, the son of Evan and Catherine (Davies) Shelby, by whom he was brought across the Atlantic Ocean about 1732. The family settled in Maryland. He assisted in laying out and constructing the old Pennsylvania road across the Alleghany mountains, and was actively employed as a soldier on the frontier, going out as a scout under General Braddock and commanding a company and showing much gallantry under General Forbes (1758). He was with Washington at Great Meadows and Fort Necessity. At the close of the French and Indian War, he engaged in Indian trade. In 1771 he removed to the Holston where he settled on an estate called by him Sapling Grove (the site of the present city of Bristol) where he later brought his family and engaged in merchandising, farming and cattle-raising. About 1772 Shelby's Fort was erected at Sapling Grove. Shelby and his son Isaac participated in the battle of Point Pleasant, 1774, in which both distinguished themselves, the father being in command of all forces after the disability or death of the three colonels. He was second in command to Colonel William Christian in the Cherokee expedition of 1776, and was himself in command of a successful raid on the Chickamauga towns in 1779.

On June 20, 1775, Captain Shelby joined in the bold Fincastle Address in which it was declared that if "our enemies attempt to dragoon us out of inestimable privileges, we are deliberately and resolutely determined never to surrender them to any power on earth but at the expense of our lives." In 1776 Shelby raised one hundred men to go to the relief of Fort Caswell on the Watauga, where he arrived after the Indians had gone.

On the organization of Washington county, Virginia, Shelby's home was thought to be within its limits, and he was commissioned by Governor Patrick Henry colonel of the county and a justice of the peace, (1777). In 1779 the legislature of Virginia appointed him to explore the country on both sides of the Cumberland mountains for the best location for a road to the Kentucky country, and to open and clear it for the convenience of the great horde of immigrants into that region; but Shelby declined to serve, it having been ascertained that he resided barely across the state line in North Carolina. He was succeeded in the colonelcy by William Campbell. It seems that about this time the governor of Virginia commissioned Shelby a brigadier-general, and the statement has often been made that he was the first officer of that rank residing on the western waters.

Shelby was not long in receiving recognition in North Carolina. He was sent to the senate of 1781, in which he came in close contact with Richard Caswell and Alexander Martin, the last named the speaker of that body.

When steps were taken to establish the new State of Franklin this previous connection with the leaders of Carolina, as well as the conservatism of age, tended to deter him from participation. The Carolina Assembly of 1786 elected him brigadier-general of the Washington District, but he served less than a year. He withdrew from public life and gave attention to the management of his large estate and the enjoyment of well-earned repose. He died December 4, 1794, and his remains lie in East Hill cemetery in Bristol. He left many descendants, of whom the most noted was his son, Isaac, the first governor of Kentucky.

Evan Shelby was well educated for a man of his day. He was of low and heavy build; his countenance was stern—a fair index of his mental traits. He was an outstanding figure at every stage of his long and truly honorable career.

JOSEPH MARTIN

Fortunately for JOSEPH MARTIN his biography has been written in a fairly comprehensive manner and by a friendly hand—Stephen B. Week's *General Joseph Martin and the War of the Revolution in the West*. This biography is of such easy access that a mere outline of Martin's career in this volume seems to be all that is required for an understanding of his participation in the affairs of Franklin.

Joseph Martin, of English ancestry, was born in Albermarle county, Virginia, in 1740, the son of Joseph and Susannah (Childs) Martin. In the years of his boyhood he was wild and ungovernable. He was a truant from school in order to be in the company of other kindred spirits so much that his education was defective. Apprenticed to a carpenter he ran away from his master, in company with

Thomas Sumter, afterward a general in the Revolution and (1756) joined the army at Fort Pitt. His father dying in 1760, Martin came into a respectable inheritance and married (1762) Sarah Lucas. The young couple removed to Orange county, Virginia, but the restless spirit of Martin kept him from the plough, and he spent much of his time hunting in the wilderness to the westward.

In 1763 he made an effort to found a settlement in Powell's valley at what has ever since been known as Martin's Station, on the Kentucky road, twenty miles northeast of Cumberland Gap. The plan was abandoned in a few months because of the hostility of the Indians. In 1773 Martin removed to Henry county, Virginia, and was a participant as a lieutenant in Lord Dunmore's War, though he was not in the battle at Point Pleasant, October 10, 1774. After that war Martin made a second attempt to establish a colony in Powell's valley, this time in 1775, as agent of Henderson's Transylvania Company. It also failed. October 9, 1775, the Virginia Committee of Safety made Martin a captain of militia, and he served as such under Colonel William Christian in the campaign against the Cherokees in 1776. At the close of the campaign Captain Martin was stationed during the winter and spring of 1777 at Rye Cove, on Clinch river. In April he was transferred to garrison a fort near the junction of Big Limestone creek with the Nolachucky river, on the frontier of Washington county, North Carolina. He was in command of troops at the making of the treaty at Long Island in 1777.

In November of that year he was commissioned by Governor Patrick Henry agent to the Cherokees in behalf of Virginia. As such he made his residence and headquarters at Long Island, which continued to be one of his homes for many years. Engaged in efforts to keep the Cherokees at peace, Martin was not on the expeditions in 1780, to South Carolina and King's Mountain; but he was in service as major, and next in rank to Sevier, on Campbell's campaign against that tribe in 1780-81. On March 1781 he was made a lieutenant-colonel of the militia of Washington county, Virginia. The month before he had been named by General Nathanael Greene as one of the commission of eight to treat with the Southern Indians.

Martin, along with Isaac Shelby, represented Sullivan county in the North Carolina legislature; and was state senator in 1783.

In January, 1783, he was one of three commissioners appointed by the governor of Virginia to treat with the Southern tribes, John

Donelson being another, and in November a treaty was effected with the Chickasaws at Nashville. It was while acting under this commission that Martin became interested in the development of the country of the Great Bend of Tennessee. In May 1783, North Carolina also engaged the services of Martin as her agent among the Cherokees and the Chickamaugas.

In 1785 Martin was, as commissioner of the national government, engaged in the negotiation of the treaty of Hopewell, which gave such dissatisfaction to the western people and rendered Martin unpopular. It is likely that one of Martin's motives in this affair was the furtherance of the Great Bend enterprise by forcing the tide of migration to that section, diverting it from the intervening country on the waters of the French Broad and Tennessee rivers.

In 1787 Martin was a representative of Sullivan county in the Carolina Assembly, which body elected him brigadier-general of Washington District. He was commissioned December 15, 1787, and promptly set about negotiating for a cessation of the struggles to establish the State of Franklin. In 1788 he as brigadier-general conducted an unsuccessful expedition against the Chickamaugas.

General Martin represented Sullivan county in the convention of 1788, and in the senate and convention of 1789. He aspired to the governorship of the Territory South of the Ohio River and had the support of Patrick Henry, but also strong opposition on the part of the inhabitants. He removed to Georgia about this time, but remained there for a comparatively short time. Returning to his home county in Virginia, he was commissioned brigadier-general of the Twelfth Brigade of Militia by Governor Henry Lee. He was honored with a seat in the legislature of his State as long as he thought he was fit to serve. He was a commissioner for the survey of the Kentucky-Virginia State line in 1795, and for the location of the Tennessee-Virginia boundary line in 1802. He seems not to have figured in public life thereafter, and died December 18, 1808.

General Martin was a man of rugged, vigorous intellect. He possessed considerable diplomatic skill in handling Indian and frontier problems, though more than once his conduct was colored by self-interest. He made many enemies among the border leaders, but retained his hold on the people of the counties of his residence, as the record of his preferment at their hands shows. He almost continuously had the confidence of the Cherokee Indians, by whom he was given the name Gluglu.

He was six feet tall, and weighed above two hundred pounds. He was reserved and courteous in his bearing and of great energy and force of character. On the whole he was well suited to the sphere which he chose for his life work.

JOHN TIPTON

John Tipton was born in Baltimore county, Maryland, in 1732. In early manhood he removed to Shenandoah county, Virginia. About 1750 he married Mary Butler. In Virginia he made an honorable record as soldier and civilian. He was in General Andrew Lewis' command in Lord Dunsmore's War, 1774; and when the revolutionary struggle came on he served as a recruiting officer for the Continental Army, and as lieutenant and as a member of the committee of safety of Shenandoah county. He was in the Virginia convention of 1776, and in the house of burgesses. Several of his sons, perhaps five, served in the army during the Revolution.

Ramsey is mistaken in the statement that John Tipton was on the King's Mountain expedition; he did not remove to the Watauga country until February, 1782. His brother Jonathan was on the Watauga as early as 1775, and it was he who was in the battle of King's Mountain.

John Tipton settled on a farm on Sinking creek, Washington county, about two miles south of the present Johnson City. He was first brought into prominence in the Tennessee country by the new state movement. He was in the early councils of the State of Franklin, but soon went into opposition, a step attributed by a number of the most fair-minded of his contemporaries to jealousy. As a Carolina factionist he had a seat in the Carolina Senates of 1786 and 1788. He also represented his county in the convention of 1788 and voted against the ratification by North Carolina of the Constitution of the United States.

In organizing the government of the Southwest Territory, Governor Blount did not honor him with any sort of commission, but he was elected to the house of representatives in 1794 and 1795. Tipton was a delegate to the first constitutional convention of Tennessee in 1796; and to the first legislature held under it. He served in the senate of the third General Assembly, and was several times thereafter honored by his county by elections to the legislature. His record, however, has often been confused with those of his

THE ANTIS

brother Jonathan and his son, John Tipton, a resident of Sullivan county which he represented in the General Assembly.

Tipton's title of colonel came from his appointment as Carolina colonel of Washington county militia in 1787. It does not appear that he took part in any of the Indian campaigns in the Tennessee valley.

He was strong-willed and of a jealous and unrelenting disposition, but a man of very considerable native ability. That he was esteemed by his neighbors, his record demonstrates. In person, he was six feet high, spare in early life, but tended to corpulence as age came on. He died in August, 1813, and is buried on the lawn of his estate near Johnson City. That estate, in after years, was the home of Landon Carter Haynes, Confederate state senator from Tennessee. One of his descendants became state superintendent of public instruction in Tennessee. A nephew, John Tipton, was in the Senate of the United States from Indiana. Tipton county, Tennessee, was named in honor of a younger brother of Colonel John Tipton, Captain Jacob Tipton, who raised a company in Washington county, Southwest Territory, and led them to the aid of General St. Clair against the Indians of the Northwest. Captain Tipton lost his life in the battle of November 4, 1791.

All of the numerous branches of the Tipton family have borne honorable parts in the history of Tennessee.

Thomas Hutchings was from North Carolina. He settled in Sullivan county, which he represented in the North Carolina house of commons in 1786. He was later appointed colonel for Hawkins county in the bounds of which he fell, on its being cut off from Sullivan county. He had served as clerk of the court of Spencer county, Franklin, before North Carolina established courts in the same territory (Hawkins county). Hutchings served as clerk of the court and colonel of the latter and was a thorn in the flesh of Cocke. His name appears (1789) as that of a commissioner to lay out the town of Rogersville. He is believed to be identical with the Colonel Thomas Hutchings who married a daughter of Colonel John Donelson, and sister of Mrs. Andrew Jackson. Hutchings later moved to the Cumberland Settlement, and was a justice of the peace of Davidson county in 1796.

His son was a member of the mercantile firm of Jackson, Coffee & Hutchings (his partners being Andrew Jackson and John Coffee) at Clover Bottom on Stone's river, in 1804.

Robert Love, son of Samuel and Dorcas (Bell) Love, was born in Augusta county, Virginia, August 23, 1760. He was on Colonel William Christian's campaign against the Cherokees, 1776; stationed at Fort Patrick Henry, Long Island of Holston, 1775; campaigned under General William Campbell, 1779–80; and under the same leader against Lord Cornwallis, 1781. During this military service his home was in what is now Wythe county, Virginia. Love removed to Washington county, North Carolina, in the fall of 1782, settling in Greasy Cove, now Unicoi county.

He was a magistrate and member of one of the early Assemblies of Franklin, but adhered to the Tipton faction when schism arose, and was major of Carolina militia under Tipton, the colonel for Washington county. He represented Washington county in the North Carolina Assembly of 1789 and in the convention of the same year that ratified the Federal Constitution.

Love, as colonel, commanded the Washington county regiment on General Martin's campaign against the Chickamauga Indians, 1788. Under the territorial government he was justice of the peace and lieutenant-colonel of Washington county, under Landon Carter, commandant. The last place he resigned in 1792, on his removal to the State of North Carolina.

He represented Buncombe county in the senate of North Carolina for several terms had the true distinction of having been elector for the republican (democratic) president from Jefferson to Van Buren, inclusive; and in one of Jackson's contests, Love received every vote cast in his own county. In 1821 he was one of the commissioners of North Carolina who ran the boundary line between North Carolina and Tennessee from Pigeon river south to the Georgia line.

He founded the town of Waynesville, where he died July 17, 1845, "loved by his friends and feared by his enemies," and possessed of a large estate.

Thomas Love, younger brother of Robert Love, by six years, was too young to serve in the Revolution. After residence in the Franklin region he removed about 1790 to Buncombe county, N. C.—that part now Haywood County. These counties he represented in the General Assembly almost continuously from 1797 to 1820. He also served as brigadier-general of militia. Gen. Love removed to Henry county, West Tennessee, and was the first speaker of the State Senate ever elected from that grand division of the State.

George Maxwell was born in Virginia in 1751, removed to the Holston Settlement at an early date, and commanded a company at King's Mountain.

When Sullivan county was organized, he was made one of the justices of the peace; in 1784, he engaged in the effort to establish the State of Franklin, receiving appointment as major of militia and serving in the Assembly. Joining in the Tipton revolt, he represented the county of Sullivan in the North Carolina legislatures of 1787 and 1788, and was appointed colonel of militia in which capacity he led a Sullivan force to the Sevier-Tipton engagement of February, 1788. Under the territorial government he was continued a justice. Living in Hawkins county at the time, he represented it in the Tennessee senate of 1799. He died November 23, 1822.

Peter Parkinson was a native of the Shenandoah valley of Virginia. He served under General Daniel Morgan in the Revolutionary War, and on one occasion was wounded. At the close of the war he removed to the Watauga country. He was in one of the Franklin Assemblies, and in February, 1788, as captain, led a company to the relief of Tipton when the latter was besieged by the followers of Sevier.

He died March, 1792, in what is now Carter county, where at an early date there was a Parkinson fort.

James Stuart was for many years prominent in the civil affairs of Washington county. He was a justice of the peace under North Carolina, Franklin, North Carolina again, the Territory South of the Ohio, and Tennessee. He was on the commission to locate the county site of his county (1777) and to lay out the town of Jonesborough (1779). Stuart was a surveyor and served in running a new line between Washington and Sullivan counties (1788). He had served as one of two commissioners for the purchase and transportation of supplies into the Watauga Settlement during the Indian troubles of 1776, but he does not appear to have figured as a military man. Stuart at first joined in the Franklin movement, but returned along with John Tipton to allegiance to the mother State in 1786. In the Carolina Assembly of that year he represented Washington county, and was returned to those of 1787 and 1788. He was sent as delegate to the Carolina Convention of 1788. Stuart was also one of Washington county's delegates in the Tennessee constitutional convention of 1796; had a seat in the first and second legislatures of Tennessee and was chosen speaker of the lower house at both sessions. He was one of the commission that represented Tennessee in the negotiation of the Cherokee treaty in 1798.

He was a level-headed, conservative man, and of ability considerably above the average.

APPENDIX A

THE CONSTITUTION OF THE STATE OF FRANKLIN

Your committee appointed to collect and adjust the reasons which impel us to declare ourselves independent of North Carolina, report as follows, to-wit:

WHEREAS, we, the freemen inhabitants of part of the country included in the limits of an Act of North Carolina ceding certain vacant territory to Congress, having declared ourselves independent of North Carolina, a decent respect to the opinions of mankind make it proper that we should manifest to the world the reasons which induced us to a declaration, which are as follows:

FIRST. That the Constitution of North Carolina declares that it shall be justifiable to erect new States whenever the consent of the Legislature shall countenance it, and this consent is implied, we conceive, in the cession act which has thrown us into such a situation that the influence of the law in common cases was almost a nullity, and in criminal jurisdiction had ceased entirely; which reduced us to the verge of anarchy.

SECOND. The Assembly of North Carolina have detained a certain quantity of goods, which was procured to satisfy the Indians for the lands we possess, which detainure we fully conceive has so exasperated them that they have actually committed hostilities upon us, and we are alone compelled to defend ourselves from these savages.

3RDLY. The resolutions of Congress held out from time to time, encouraging the erection of new States, have appeared to us ample encouragement.

4THLY. Our local situation is such that we not only apprehend we should be separated from North Carolina, but almost every sensible, disinterested traveler has declared it is incompatible with our interest to belong in union with the eastern part of the State; for we are not only far removed from the eastern parts of North Carolina, but separated from them by high and almost impassable mountains, which naturally divide us from them, which have proved to us that our interest is also in many respects distinct from the inhabitants on the other side, and much injured by union with them.

5TH AND LASTLY. We unanimously agree that our lives, liberties and property can be more secure and our happiness much better propagated by our separation; and consequently that it is our duty and inalienable right to form ourselves into a new and independent State.

A DECLARATION OF RIGHTS MADE BY THE REPRESENTATIVES OF THE FREEMEN OF THE STATE OF FRANKLIN

Section 1. That all political power is vested in and derived from the people.

Sec. 2. That the people of this State ought to have the sole and exclusive right of regulating the internal government and police thereof.

Sec. 3. That no man, or set of men, are entitled to exclusive or separate emoluments or privileges from the community, but in consideration of public services.

Sec. 4. That the legislative, executive and supreme judicial powers of government ought to be forever separate and distinct from each other.

Sec. 5. That all powers of suspending laws or the execution of laws, by any authority, without the consent of the representatives of the people is injurious to their rights, and ought not to be exercised.

Sec. 6. That elections of members to serve as representatives in General Assembly ought to be free.

Sec. 7. That in all criminal prosecutions every man has a right to be informed of the accusation against him, and to confront the accusers and witnesses with other testimony, and shall not be compelled to give evidence against himself.

Sec. 8. That no freeman shall be put to answer any criminal charge but by indictment, presentment or impeachment.

Sec. 9. That no freeman shall be convicted of any crime but by the unanimous verdict of a jury of good and lawful men in open court, as heretofore used.

Sec. 10. That excessive bail should not be required, nor excessive fines imposed, nor cruel and unusual punishments be inflicted.

Sec. 11. That the general warrants, whereby an officer or messenger may be commanded to search suspected places, without evidence of the fact committed, or to seize any person or persons not named whose offense is not particularly described and supported by the evidence, are dangerous to liberty and ought not to be granted.

Sec. 12. That no freeman ought to be taken, imprisoned or disseized of his freehold, liberties or privileges, or outlawed or exiled or in any manner destroyed or deprived of his life, liberty or property but by the laws of the land.

Sec. 13. That every freeman restrained of his liberty is entitled to a remedy to inquire into the lawfulness thereof and to remove it, if unlawful; and that such remedy ought not to be denied.

Sec. 14. That in all controversies at law respecting property, the ancient mode of trial by jury is one of the best securities of the rights of the people, and ought to remain sacred and inviolable.

SEC. 15. That the freedom of the press is one of the greatest bulwarks of liberty, and therefore ought never to be restrained.

SEC. 16. That the people of this State ought not to be taxed, or made subject to the payment of any impost or duty without the consent of themselves or their representatives in General Assembly freely given.

SEC. 17. That the people have a right to bear arms for the defense of the State; and as standing armies in times of peace are dangerous to liberty, they ought not to be kept up, and that the military should be kept under strict subordination to and be governed by civil power.

SEC. 18. That the people have a right to assemble together to consult for their common good to instruct their representatives, and to apply to the legislature for redress of grievances.

SEC. 19. That all men have a natural and inalienable right to worship God Almighty according to the dictates of their own conscience.

SEC. 20. That for redress of grievances and for amending and strengthening the laws, elections ought to be often held.

SEC. 21. That a frequent recurrence to fundamental principles is absolutely necessary to preserve the blessings of liberty.

SEC. 22. That no hereditary emoluments, privileges, or honors ought to be granted or conferred in this State.

SEC. 24. That retrospective laws punishing acts committed before the existence of such laws, and by them only declared criminal, are oppressive, unjust and incompatible with liberty; wherefore no *ex post facto* law ought to be made.

SEC. 25. That the people have a right by their representatives to enact laws to encourage virtue and suppress vice and immorality.[1]

THE CONSTITUTION AND FORM OF GOVERNMENT

AGREED TO AND RESOLVED UPON BY THE REPRESENTATIVES OF THE FREEMEN OF THE STATE OF FRANKLIN, ELECTED AND CHOSEN FOR THAT PARTICULAR PURPOSE, IN CONVENTION ASSEMBLED, AT JONESBOROUGH, THE 17TH DECEMBER, ANNO. DOM. 1784.[2]

SECTION 1. That the legislative authority shall be vested in two distinct branches, both dependent on the people, to-wit: a Senate and a House of Commons.

SEC. 2. That the Senate shall be composed of three representa-

---

[1] Section 25 of the North Carolina Bill of Rights relates to the boundaries of the State. It was omitted and another inserted in its place.

[2] In the North Carolina Constitution of 1776, this caption is followed by a preamble which recited the change of allegiance due to the prosecution of a war against the people of the Colonies by King George the Third; and the necessity for the establishment of a government to prevent anarchy and confusion. The Declaration of Independence of the people of Franklin, serving much the same purpose, precedes the Bill of Rights.

tives annually chosen by ballot from each County[3] until there be ten Counties in the State, after that period, one from each County.

SEC. 3. That the House of Commons shall be composed of representatives chosen by ballot, four[4] for each County, until there be ten Counties within the State, and after that period, two for each County.

SEC. 4. That the Senate and House of Commons assembled for the purpose of legislation shall be denominated the General Assembly.

SEC. 5. That each member of the Senate shall have usually resided in the County in which he is chosen for one year immediately preceding his election, and for the same time shall have possessed and continued to possess in the County which he represents not less than one hundred acres[5] of land in fee.

SEC. 6. That each member of the House of Commons shall have usually resided in the County in which he is chosen for one year immediately preceding his election.[6]

SEC. 7. That all freemen of the age of twenty-one years who have been inhabitants of any one County within the State twelve months immediately preceding the day of any election, and possessed of a freehold within the same County of fifty acres of land for six months next before and at the day of election shall be entitled to vote for a member of the Senate.

SEC. 8. That all freemen of the age of twenty-one years who have been inhabitants of any County in this State twelve months immediately preceding the day of any election, and shall have paid public taxes, shall be entitled to vote for members of the House of Commons for the County in which he resides.

SEC. 9. That all persons possessed of a freehold in any town in this State having a right of representation, and also all freemen who have been inhabitants of any such town twelve months next before and at the day of election, and shall have paid public taxes, shall be entitled to vote for a member to represent such town in the House of Commons; provided always, that this section shall not entitle any inhabitant of such town to vote for members of the House of Commons for the County in which he may reside, nor any freeholder in such County who resided without or beyond the limits of town to vote for a member of said town.

SEC. 10. That the Senate and House of Commons, when met,

---

[3] The words of this section that follow, added to section 2 of the North Carolina Constitution.

[4] North Carolina Constitution "two" and without the words beginning with "until."

[5] North Carolina Constitution stipulated five hundred acres.

[6] The property qualification of one hundred acres was not brought forward. The purpose was to make the lower house representative of all the people.

shall each have power to choose a speaker and other officers, and shall be judges of the qualifications and election of their members, sit upon their own adjournment from day to day, and prepare bills to be passed into laws. The two houses shall direct writs of election for supplying intermediate vacancies and shall also jointly by ballot adjourn themselves to any future day.

Sec. 11. That all bills shall be read three times in each house before they pass into laws, and be signed by the speakers of both houses.[7] On motion and second, the yeas and nays shall be taken on the passing of any act, and printed with the same.

Sec. 12. That every person who shall be chosen a member of the Senate or House of Commons, or appointed to any office or place of trust, before taking his seat or entering upon the execution of his office, shall take an oath to the State, and all officers also shall take an oath of office.

Sec. 13. That the General Assembly by joint ballot of both houses shall appoint Judges of the Supreme Courts of Law and Equity and Attorney General, who shall be commissioned by the Governor and hold their offices during good behavior.[8]

Sec. 14. That the Senate and House of Commons shall have power to appoint the general[9] and field officers of the militia and all officers of the regular army of the State.

Sec. 15. That the Senate and House of Commons jointly at their first meeting after each annual election shall by ballot, elect a Governor for one year, who shall not be eligible to that office longer than three years in six successive years; that no person under thirty years of age and who has not been a resident in this State above one year and shall not have in the State a freehold in land and tenements above the value of two hundred and fifty pounds, shall be eligible as Governor.[10]

Sec. 16. That the Senate and House of Commons jointly at their first meeting after each annual election shall by ballot elect five persons to be a Council of State for one year, who shall advise the Governor in the execution of his office, and that three members shall be a quorum. Their advice and proceedings shall be entered in a journal to be kept for that purpose only, and signed by the members present, to any part of which any member present may enter his dissent; and such journals shall be laid before the General Assembly, when called for by them.[11]

---

[7] The words that follow are not in the Carolina Constitution.

[8] Judges of admiralty courts were provided for in the North Carolina Constitution.

[9] Plural in the North Carolina Constitution.

[10] Five years residence and the ownership of one thousand pounds of real estate in the N. C. Constitution.

[11] The North Carolina Council of State composed of seven members, four to constitute a quorum.

Sec. 17. There shall be a seal of this State, which shall be kept by the Governor and used by him as occasion may require, and shall be called the great seal of the State of Franklin, and be affixed to all grants and commissions.

Sec. 18. The Governor for the time being shall be Captain General and Commander in Chief of the Militia and in the recess of the General Assembly shall have power by and with the advice of the Council of State, to embody the Militia for public safety.

Sec. 19. That the Governor for the time being shall have power to draw for and apply such sums of money as shall be voted by the General Assembly for the contingencies of government, and be accountable to them for the same; and he also may, by and with the advice of the Council of State, lay embargoes or prohibit the exportation of any commodities for any term not exceeding thirty days at any one time in the recess of the General Assembly; and shall have the power of granting pardons and reprieves, except where the prosecutions shall be carried on in the General Assembly or the law shall otherwise direct. In such case, he may in the recess grant a reprieve until the next sitting of the General Assembly; and may exercise all other executive powers of government, limited and restrained as by the State; and on his death, inability or absence from the State, the Speaker of the Senate, for the time being, and in case of his death, inability or absence from the State, the Speaker of the House of Commons, shall exercise the powers of government, after such death or during such absence or inability of the Governor or Speaker of the Senate or until a new nomination is made by the General Assembly.

Sec. 20. That in every case where any officer, the right of whose appointment is made by this Constitution vested in the General Assembly, shall during their recess die, or his office by other means become vacant, the Governor shall have power, with the advice of the Council of State, to fill up such vacancy by granting a temporary commission, which shall expire at the end of the next session of the General Assembly.

Sec. 21. That the Governor, Judges of Supreme Courts of Law and Equity and Attorney General, shall have adequate salaries during their continuance in office.

Sec. 22. That the General Assembly shall by joint ballot of both houses annually appoint a Treasurer or Treasurers for this State.

Sec. 23. That the Governor or other officers offending against the State by violating any part of this Constitution, maladministration or corruption, may be prosecuted on the impeachment of the General Assembly, or presentment of the grand jury of any court of supreme jurisdiction of this State.

Sec. 24. That the General Assembly shall by joint ballot of both houses, triennially appoint a Secretary for this State.

Sec. 25. That no persons, who heretofore have been or hereafter may be receivers of public monies, shall have a seat in either house of General Assembly, or be eligible to any office in this State, until such persons shall have fully accounted for and paid into the treasury all sums for which they may be accountable and liable[12] if legally called upon.

SEC. 26. That no Treasurer shall have a seat in either Senate, House of Commons or Council of State during his continuance in that office, or before he shall have finally settled his accounts with the public for all monies which may be in his hands at the expiration of his office belonging to the State and have paid the same into the hands of the succeeding Treasurer.

SEC. 27. That no officer in the regular army or navy in the service and pay of the United States, of this or any other State, nor any contractor or agent for supplying such army or navy with clothing or provisions, shall have a seat either in the Senate, the House of Commons, or the Council of State, or be eligible thereto; any member of the Senate, House of Commons or Council of State being appointed to and accepting of such office shall thereby vacate his seat.

SEC. 28. That no member of the Council of State shall have a seat either in the Senate of the House of Commons;[13] provided, nevertheless, that the Governor and Council shall attend the General Assembly during the sitting of the same, and that it shall be a part of their official duty to revise all bills before they can be passed and recommend such amendments as they may think proper.

SEC. 29. That no Judge of the Supreme Court of Law or Equity shall have a seat in Senate, House of Commons or Council of State.

SEC. 30. That no Secretary of this State, Attorney General or clerk of any court of record shall have a seat in the Senate, House of Commons or Council of State.

SEC. 31. That no clergyman or preacher of the gospel of any denomination shall be capable of being a member of either the Senate or House of Commons while he continues in the service of the pastoral function.

SEC. 32. That no person shall deny the being of a God or the truth of the Protestant religion or the divine authority either of the Old or New Testament, or who shall hold religious principles incompatible with the freedom and safety of the State, shall be capable of holding any office or place of trust or profit in the civil government within this State.

SEC. 33. That the Justices of the Peace within their respective Counties in this State shall in the future be recommended to the Governor for the time being by the representatives in General Assembly, and the Governor shall commission them accordingly, and the Justices commissioned shall hold their office during good be-

---

[12] The clause that follows was an added condition.
[13] The following proviso inserted.

havior, and shall be not be removed from office by the General Assembly unless for misbehavior, absence or inability.

Sec. 34. That there shall be no establishment of any religious church or denomination in this State in preference to any other, neither shall any person on any pretense whatever be compelled to attend any place of worship contrary to his own faith or judgment nor be obliged to pay for the purchase of any glebe or the building of any house of worship or for the maintenance of any minister or ministry contrary to what he believes right, or has voluntarily and personally engaged to perform; but all persons shall be at liberty to exercise their own mode of worship; provided that nothing therein contained shall be construed to except preachers of treasonable or seditious doctrines from legal trial or punishment.

Sec. 35. That no person in the State shall hold more than one lucrative office at any one time; provided that no appointment in the militia of the office of a Justice of the Peace shall be considered as a lucrative office.

Sec. 36. That all commissions and grants shall run in the name of the State of Franklin and bear test and be signed by the Governor; all writs shall run in the same manner and bear test and be signed by the clerks of the respective courts. Indictments shall conclude against the peace and dignity of the State.

Sec. 37. That the delegate for this State to the Constitutional Congress, while necessary, shall be chosen annually by the General Assembly, by ballot, but may be superseded in the meantime in the same manner; and no person shall be elected to serve in that capacity for more than three years successively.

Sec. 38. That there shall be a sheriff, coroner or coroners and constables in each County within the State.

Sec. 39. That the person of a debtor, where there is not a strong presumption of fraud, shall not be continued in prison after delivering up *bona fide* all his estate, real and personal, for the use of his creditors, in such manner as shall be hereafter regulated by law. All prisoners shall be bailable by sufficient sureties, unless for any capital offenses, when the proof is evident or presumption great.

Sec. 40. That any foreigner who comes to settle in this State, having first taken an oath of allegiance to the same, may purchase or by other means acquire, hold and transfer land or other real estate; and after one year's residence shall be deemed a free citizen.

Sec. 41. That a school or schools shall be established by the legislature for the convenient instruction of youth, with such salaries to the masters, paid by the public, as may enable them to instruct at low prices; and all useful learning shall be duly encouraged and promoted in one or more universities.[14]

---

[14] Some writers express the opinion that the provision for a university was inserted at the instance of Samuel Doak, who was a member of the Convention and the head of the only classical school in Franklin; but the provision was borrowed from the North Carolina Constitution of 1776.

Sec. 42. That no purchase of lands shall be made of Indian natives, but on behalf of the public, by authority of the General Assembly.

Sec. 43. That the future Legislatures of this state shall regulate entails in such manner as to prevent perpetuities.

Sec. 44. That the Declaration of Rights is hereby declared to be a part of the Constitution of this State, and ought never to be violated on any pretense whatsoever.

Sec. 45. That any member of either house of the General Assembly shall have liberty to dissent from and protest against any act or resolves which he may think injurious to public, or any individual, and have the reasons of his dissent entered on the journals.

Sec. 46. That neither house of the General Assembly shall proceed upon the public business unless a majority of all the members of such house are actually present; and that upon motion made and seconded, the yeas and nays upon any question shall be taken and entered on the journals and that the journals of the proceedings of both houses of the General Assembly shall be printed and made public immediately after adjournment.

This Constitution is not intended to preclude the present Convention from making a temporary provision for the well ordering of this State until the General Assembly shall establish government agreeable to the mode herein described.

Resolved, That this Convention recommend this Constitution for the serious consideration of the people during six ensuing months, after which time and before the expiration of the year, they shall choose a Convention for the express purpose of adopting it in the name of the people, if agreed to by them, or altering it as instructed by them.[15]

A true Copy, test:

THOMAS TALBOT, Clk.

---

[15] This paragraph does not, of course, appear in the North Carolina instrument.

APPENDIX B

PETITION OF THE INHABITANTS OF THE WESTERN COUNTRY

The Honourable, the General Assembly of North Carolina now sitting:

The Inhabitants of the Western Country humbly sheweth:

That it is with sincere concern we lament the unhappy disputes that have long subsisted between us and our Brethren on the Eastern side of the Mountains, respecting the erecting a new Government. We beg leave to represent to your Honourable body, that from Acts passed in June, 1784, ceding to Congress your Western territory, with reservations and conditions therein contained; also from a clause in your wise and mild Constitution, setting forth that there might be a State, or States, erected in the West whenever your Legislature should give consent for same; and from our local situation, there are numberless advantages, bountifully given to us by nature, to propagate and promote a Government with us. Being influenced by your Acts and Constitution, and at the same time considering that it is our undeniable right to obtain for ourselves and posterity a proportionable and adequate share of the blessings, rights, privileges, and immunities alloted with the rest of mankind, have thought that the erecting a new Government would greatly contribute to our welfare and convenience, and that the same could not militate against your interest and future welfare as a Government. Hoping that mutual and reciprocal advantages would attend each party, and that cordiality and unanimity would permanently subsist between us ever after, we earnestly request that an impartial view of our remoteness be taken into consideration; that great inconveniency attending your seat of Government, and also the great difficulty in ruling well and giving protection to so remote a people, to say nothing of the almost impassable mountains Nature has placed between, which renders it impracticable for us to furnish ourselves with a bare load of the necessaries of life, except we in the first instance travel from one to two hundred and more miles through another State ere we can reach your Government.

Every tax paid you from this country would render us that sum the poorer, as it is impossible, from the nature of our situation, that any part could return into circulation, having nothing that could bear the carriage, or encourage purchasers to come so great a distance; for which reasons were we to continue under your Government a few years, the people here must pay a greater sum than the whole of the medium now in circulation for the exigencies and support of your Government, which would be a sum impossible for us to secure, would we be willing to give you our all; and of course we must be beholden to other States for any part we could raise; and by these means our property would gradually diminish, and we at last be reduced to mere poverty and want by not being able equally to participate with the benefits and advantages of your Government. We hope that having settled West of the Appalachian Mountains ought not to deprive us of the natural advantages designed by the bountiful Providence for the convenience and comfort of all those who have spirit and sagacity enough to seek after them. When we reflect on our past and indefatigable struggles, both with savages and our other enemies during our late war, and the great difficulty we had to obtain and with-hold this Country from those enemies at the expense of the lives and fortunes of many of our dearest friends and relations; and the happy conclusion of peace having arrived, North Carolina has derived great advantages from our alertness in taking and securing a Country, from which she has been able to draw into her Treasury, immense sums of money, and thereby become enabled to pay off, if not wholly, yet a great part, and sink her national debt. We therefore humbly conceive you will liberally think that it will be nothing more than paying a debt in full to us for only to grant what God, Nature, and our locality entitles us to receive. Trusting that your magnanimity will not consider it a crime in any people to pray their rights and privileges, we call the world to testify our conduct and exertion in behalf of American Independence; and the same to judge whether we ask more than free people ought to claim, agreeable to Republican principles, the great foundation whereon our American fabric now stands. Impressed with the hope of your great goodness and benevolent disposition that you will utterly abhor and disclaim all ideas of involving into innumerable, disagreeable and irksome contentions, a people who have so faithfully aided and supported in the time of imminent and perilous dangers; that you will be graciously pleased to consent to a separation; that from your paternal tenderness and greatness of mind, you will let your stipulations and conditions be consistent with honour, equity and reason, all of which will be cheerfully submitted to; and we, your petitioners, shall always feel an interest in whatsoever may concern your honour and prosperity. Lastly, we hope to be enabled by the concurrence of your State to participate in the fruits of the Revolution; and to enjoy the essential benefits of Civil Society under a form of Government which ourselves alone can only calculate for such a purpose. It will be a subject of regret that so much blood and treasure have been lavished away for no purpose to us; that so many sufferings have been encountered without compensation, and that so many sacrifices have been made in vain. Many other considerations might be here adduced, but we hope what hath been mentioned will be sufficient for our purpose, adding only that Congress hath, from time to time, explained their ideas so fully and with so much dignity and energy that if their arguments and requisitions will not produce conviction, we know of nothing that will have a greater influence, especially when we recollect that the system referred to is the result of the collected wisdom of the United States, and, should it not be considered as perfect, must be esteemed as the least objectionable.

John Corson
James English
William Hannah
Peter McNamee
James Shanks
David Robinson
Robert Allison
Isaac Davis
James Mitchell
David Gewel
Thomas Bell
Thomas Rodgers
Anthony Kelly
Thos. McMackin
George Davies
Nathaniel Davies
Samuel Davies
John Lowe
Joseph Wilson
David Brown
William Brown
Jas. Henry
Alexr. Potter
William Reynolds
David Reynolds
Aaron Been
William Wilson
Thos. Thomson
David Rankin
John Lee
Sam'l Vance
Rd. Kerr
Samuel McPherson
Matthew Rue
Joseph Lusk
Andrew Jackson
Jos. Gest
Jos. Newberry
Joseph Blair

Thomas Williams
Henry Styers
     his
Thomas x Tadlock
    mark
William McPick
Botholmu Odeneal
     his
Shadrack x Hale, Jr.
    mark
Daniel Denny, Jr.
John Wear
Ashael Rawlings
Henry Earnest
James Patterson
Francis Hughes
Robert Hood
     his
Wm. x Francis
    mark
     his
Patrick x Kirkpatrick
    mark
John Tadlock
James Davis
Benn Brumley
Mary Webster (?)
George Kirkpatrick
Thomas Jones
William Jones
Reuben Simmon
Archibel Alexander
Moses Kelsay
Robert McCall
Joseph Alexander
Wm. Cocke
Archibald Roan
Elias Witt
Thomas Witt

APPENDIX 351

Alex. Lowry
Jno. McClelland
Solomon Reed
Uriah McClellennon
James Stinson
Alexander Street
James McPherson
John Prim
Jacob Smelser
Joshua Kidwell
Samuel Jameson
John Brumley
William Davidson
Wm. Boyd
Benja. Gist
Thos. Bromley
Hugh Beard
Samuel Beard
James Millikin
Robert Orr
Searling Bowman
Rich'd Woods
Robert McCall
John Galbreath
  (Illegible)
James Watson
  (Illegible)
William Goings
James Hays
David Carr
Joseph Garrison
William Gillehan
Stephen Strong
Michael Rawlings
Donnell Cremor
Nath. McMeno.
William La''' (?)
  (Illegible)
Wm. Morrow
Charles Ramsey
  (Illegible)
John R.''' (?)
Peter Nowels
James Millikan
Thomas Millikan
Thomas Dicson
Redman McDaniel
Nathaniel Witt

Rich'd Dunn
Wm. Dunn
Thomas Call
H. Call
Joseph N. Newport
Wm. W. Newport
John Greer
Absolem Greer
Thomas Springer
Levy Springer
Thomas Wolfe
Conrod Wolfe
Phillip Suibb
Henry Easter
William Eatster
Simeon Craine
Harmon Nowel
James Patton
Robert Patton
John Fout
Peter Fout
Harman Kennedy
Moses Long
Coonnas Miller
Thomas McKee
And. Wray
Wm. Wood
Gordon Potter
Wm. Peck
Thomas Mosely
Henry Mosely
Phillip Rudolph
Wm. Stubblefield
Thomas Baits
John Keller
Moses Keller
William Fergosen
Adam Fergosen
Ralph Hogan
William Hogan
Richard Webb
Josiah Epperson
Humph'y Montgomery
Carmack George
Charles Willson
John Johnston
Samuel Gilbertson
Samuel McMinn

Auborn'" (?)
Anson Rit
Nuness Potter
John Noman (?)
Peter Nuless
James W. Begses (?)
Dalton Ridgs
James Jack
John Adkins
Adword Adword
Henry Brumley
Simon Ridgs
Joseph Donn
Allen Bellew
Rows Potter
John Norton
Aaron Norton
Aaron Rider
John Jameson
Dan'l Rawlings
William Jinkins
Robert Smith
Wm. Howard
Joshua Tadlock
Robert Hayes
Thomas Johnson
Francis Johnson
  his
Js. x Huston
  mark
  his
John x Huston
  mark
Lanry Armstrong
William Hennidge
John Armstrong
Andrew English
Nathaniel Hayes
Daniel Leming
John Williams
  his
Robert x Miller
  mark
(Illegible)
  his
William x Hust.
  mark

Wm. Magill
Oton Clark
John Gibson
Reuben Gibson
William Adkins
Thomas Fryar
John Lyon
William Brownin
Rich'd Wood
James Pickins
Robert Bettey
George Black
Reuben Riggs
George Hayes
William Hill
Henry Richardson
Shiffell Goodlop
John Shane
Miller Doget
Christy Miers
John Miers
William Owins
Thomas Owins
John Jarrett
Thomas Pickny
James Stump
Leonard Hopkins
Martha Gahee
Patrick Gahee
Jeremiah Smith
Robert Sample
Anthony Moore
James McCammis
Thomas McCammis
William McCammis
Adam McCammis
Henry H. Hammer
Franses Castel
Jacob Meek
Thomas Miller
Robert Pain
Joseph Hamilton
Robert Kerr
John Sellars
Benj. Wray
Wm. Moore
Joseph Ray

APPENDIX

    his
Thomas x Baley
   mark
Moses Moore

Joseph Lachlen, Sen.
Joseph Lachlen, Jur.
Edward Crunt (?)
James Crunt

The following names are taken from the back of the petition:

Nicholas Hayes
Sam'l Hayes
Jno. Mitchell
James Hammer
Henry Hokimer
Geo. Martin
David Moore
Henry Winterberger
Jos. Winterberger
Sam'l Winterberger
Joseph Lusk
Thos. Wood
Joseph Gest
William Gest
Joshua Kidwell
Thomas Davie
John Kidwell
Charles Kidwell
Whaley Newby
Craven Dunear
Alexr. Lowrey
James Stinson
Adam Guthrey
Wm. Craige
Benjamen Henslee
Abel Morgan
Thomas Vincent
Jno. Chester
Patrick Morrison
Stephen Easley
Jackal Light
Robert Easley
Henry Sullivan
John Light
Moses Robinson
William Light
William Light, Sen.
Thomas Easley
William Goad
Jesey Holland
James Walb''' (?)
William Wilson

Moses Kennedy
Hermon King
Joseph Screat
Lewis Tadlock
Thomas Tadlock
Joshuaway Padfield
   his
Thomas x Bennet
   mark
Moses Kelsay
John Anderson
James Richardson
David Taylor
Benja. Gist
Joseph Huson
Mikill Borders
Alx. Pethrow
Oystan Hewtower
Wm. Davies
John Noris
Robert Hayes
James Hayes
William Sippard
Alexander Cavitt
Moses Cavitt
Jacob Jobe
Nathan Jobe
Joseph Birdwell
Geo. Birdwell
James Smith
Moses Russel
Conrad Shepley
John Comin
Walker Barren
John Bell
William Carson
Robert Christian
Abraham Tittsworth
Benjamin Walb''' (?)
Green Chote
John Goad, Jun.
George Vincent

Henry Heckey
Owen Atkin
Nicholas Mercer
Richard Mercer, Sen.
Arch'd McHaughan
Edward Mercer
John Black
John Hunt, Jr.
Basset Hunt
Reuben Hunt
Thomas Tipton
Jonathan Hunt
James Cooper
Isaiah Waldrew
Lewis Hunt
James Smart
James Smith
Joseph Smith
John Duncan
Wm. Berry
Isaac White
Samuel Cox
James Wheeler
John Cottrell
Hugh Gentry
Valentine Rose
Eli Shipley
Thomas Shipley
William Childress
Joshway Hampton
Christurphur Cross
Benjamin Aze
Reuben Hunt
Ellecander Moore
Martin Roller
John A. Caft
D. Wright
Adam Stake
William Shewmaker
Gabriel Goad
Peter Easley
Jacob Cox
William Bucknell
Haley Bucknell
Preley Bucknell
Shadrick Haile
Forrester Mercer
Bryce Russell, Sen.

Bryce Russell, Jr.
James Pickens
Phil. Grafford Pierce
William Gewil
Charles Parker
Antony Agee
John Sawyer
Joseph Moore
John Yancy
Richard Shipley
W. Cage
Timothy Huff
George Christian
Deness Murfee
Isaac Thomas
William Massengill
John Tulley
Thos. Easterlin
William Copeland
Rich'd Gamon
John Spurgin
Thos. King
Roger Gibson
James Adam
Geo. Gabriel (black)
John Yokley
John Woolsey
James Arbutton (?)
Martin Roller, Jr.
Joseph Blair
David Arwin
William''' (?)
Thos. Taylor
Adam Stoaks
Joseph Waldrep
Mattw. Caruthers
Gilbert Christian
John Pryor
Moses Looney
Macajah Adams
James McLern
Alexander Caright
Benj. Burdwell
John Dean
William Holland
William Morroson
John Morroson
James Morroson

Samuel Bofman	John Bilensy
David Merryon	William Combs
Richard Morell	William Combs, Jr.
Dudley Rutherford	Henry Combs
John Bradford	William Stacey
Peter Fin	Adam Coumb
John Hunt	Daniel Agee
William Bailey	John Comay
George Smith	James Peterson
Jacob Joab	Jeremiah Taylor
William Cooper	Joseph Taylor
Wm. Jackson	Stephen Taylor
Ephraim Joab	Isaac Taylor
William Mehallm	John Chisholm
Charles Bacon	Edward Tule
John French	Nathaniel Tule

Endorsement:

Petition of the Inhabitants of the Western Country, December, 1787.

In Senate, December, 1787. Read and referred to Court on Public Bills. (*N. C. St. Rec.*, XXII, 705-714.)

APPENDIX C

PROCEEDINGS

At a meeting of the subscribers, the 12th day of January, 1789, to consult on some plan to defend our frontiers from the common enemy, unanimously agreed that it is a voluntary plan, and not under the authority of any State, or name of State, nor in opposition to the laws of any State, or the United States, but purely to defend ourselves from the savage enemy.

Present: Mr. Outlaw, Mr. Roddy, Mr. McCay, Mr. Gest, Mr. Buckingham, Mr. Gibson, Mr. Crosby, Mr. Weir, Mr. Taylor, Mr. Smith, Mr. Henderson, Mr. Lee, Mr. Coulter, Mr. Adear, Mr. Gillaspie.

Unanimously agreed that Colonel Gest be chosen chairman. Agreed unanimously that Henry Rowan be chosen clerk for said committee.

On motion of Mr. Crosby, seconded by Mr. Adear, the house adjourned till to-morrow at 8 o'clock.

On the 13th of January, the council met agreeable to adjournment, and it appeared from the report of some members present the names of Mr. Buckingham and Mr. Gillaspie were not inserted in the list of members. On motion of Mr. Outlaw seconded by Mr. Smith, their names were entered on the list.

The members of the Assembly from Greene county, at the general request of the meeting, gave information that the General Assembly had made no provision to assist the frontiers in defending themselves from the savages, except a small station of 36 men, including officers, on the north side of Tennessee; that they declared the campaign ordered by General Martin in August last, was contrary to the orders of the Governor and Council, and, therefore, refused to pay any part of the expense incurred thereby, and resolved that the fines levied on any person for refusing to obey said Martin's orders should be restored. That an act was passed consigning to oblivion the supposed offenses and misconduct of certain persons among ourselves. That, agreeable to a requisition of Congress, and also from General Wynn, the Indian Commissioner for the Southern District, a commissioner was appointed to make peace and fix out a certain boundary between us and the Indians. That the treaty was to be held in May next, at the upper ford on French Broad, above the mouth of Swanano. That the committee was directed to purchase the land of French Broad, if possible, and that the people in that quarter were directed to continue in possession of said land until the treaty.

Wherefore, after maturely considering the said information, and our present distressed situation, we conceive that our lives and properties are in continual danger until peace is made, as the Indians still continue their depredations, unless we agree on some plan to defend and secure ourselves from their inroads. We conceive also that General Martin is a person unworthy our confidence as an officer from the partial representation he has given of us; witness, his conduct at the treaty of Hopewell, from his not residing in the district, and from the declaration of the Assembly that he has not acted agreeable to the orders of the Government. In order, therefore to secure our lives and properties from the present dangers that threaten from the frequent incursions of the savage enemy, we unanimously agree to adopt the following plan, viz:

1st. That we mutually lay aside all animosities and disputes that so much distract us, and unite against the common enemy, and make legal application for redress for grievances.

2nd. That we recommend it to the people to petition the next Assembly to divide the State at the Appalachian Mountains, or cede the territory west of said mountains to Congress, with such restrictions and reservations as will guarantee to us our just rights and privileges.

3rd. That, sensible of the disagreeable situation under which we labor by the rejection of the Federal Constitution by the State of North Carolina, we think it would be good policy, and of great advantage to this Western Country to raise a fund to defray the expense of sending some person to lay before the first meeting of Congress under the new Constitution, our present situation, and to express our earnest desire to be admitted into the Union as soon as possible.

4th. That the peculiar situation of the people of this country and laws of French Broad, require that the people should appoint a Council of Safety for the regulation of their affairs, and whose business it shall be to endeavor to hold talks with the Indians, to procure an exchange of prisoners and bring about peace whenever it is practicable; to make any contract or agreement with the Indians that they may think most advantageous for this country, and lay the same before the commissioners at the treaty of May, if they think proper. If the Indians do not agree to a peace or truce, they may keep out spies and call for assistance whenever it shall be necessary to defend the settlements, or pursue after any party of Indians who come in with a hostile intent.

5th. That John Sevier keep the command of the inhabitants on the frontiers, or any that may come to their assistance, when ordered to march for defense of the country; that we endeavor to raise by voluntary contribution a support for the commander and the spies and scouts that may be necessary until the peace.

6th. We also conceive that it would be good policy, and of essential service to this country if the Indians will agree to give up any of the country south of Tennessee river to our Council of Safety. That they agree to give them a compensation for the same in blankets and lindsey, and that the inhabitants pay the same by voluntary contributions, and lay the same before the Commissioners of Indian Affairs in May next.

7th. We are also of opinion that this plan, if justly carried into effect, will entitle our brave volunteers to a right of pre-emption in a legal and constitutional manner, proportioned agreeable to their services and expenses.

8th. They unanimously agree his Honor, John Sevier, by and with the advice of the Council of Safety, hold all the talks with the Indians.

9th. We also agree that every man in this Convention raise what cash he can by donations from the neighborhoods and deliver the same to the Committee of Safety in one month from this date, to raise a fund to defray the expense of a representative to Congress.

10th. Also recommend to the different Captains of companies in this country to divide themselves into three classes, in order to march with twenty days provisions, when called on by the Council of Safety, to the assistance of the frontiers.

11th. We also request John Sevier, Alexander Outlaw, Archibald Rowan [Roane] David Campbell, and Joseph Hamilton to draw a representation of our situation and our earnest desire to be in the Federal Union, and lay it before the Council of Safety for their revisal [so] as copies may be circulated as soon as possible, to be signed by all friends.

12th. We also agree to request William Nelson to wait on Congress with such instructions and powers in him invested as the Council of Safety think right to give him; and that he be furnished with two hundred silver dollars to defray expenses. And in case Mr. Nelson refuse to wait on Congress, we request Alexander Outlaw to attend the Honourable body.

13th. We also agree to request Joseph Hardin to wait on Cumberland Settlement with our plan of Safety and Redress of Grievances, and with such instructions and requisitions as the Council of Safety think it right to give him.

14th. We also agree to meet at Greene Court House on the first Tuesday in February next to consult with any number of gentlemen who shall attend from Washington and Sullivan Counties to consult on our voluntary plan of safety and that we send a request to the Inhabitants of said Counties to meet at the time and place above mentioned, and that each County, previously mentioned, elect five members on the twenty-third of this instant. Likewise, the settlements of Little Pigeon and South of French Broad elect three members to attend at the time and place above mentioned.

15th. We, the subscribers, agree to persevere in supporting the above plan and in recommending [it] to the people in general as the most likely method that we can devise at present for the safety and protection of our Country.

JOSHUA GIST, Chairman.
T. ROWAN, C. C.

BIBLIOGRAPHY

PERIODICALS AND PAMPHLETS

ALDEN, GEORGE H. The State of Franklin, *American Historical Review*, VIII, 271.
—— Forming and Admitting New States, *Annals American Academy*, XVIII, 476.
ALEXANDER, J. E. and MATHES, C. H. A Historical Sketch of Washington College (Tennessee).
ALLISON, JOHN. East Tennessee a Hundred Years Ago. An address. (1887).
ASHE, SAMUEL A. Forming of the State of Franklin; pointing out Injustice to North Carolina and North Carolinians of that Period. *North Carolina Review*, December 4, 1910, January 4.
—— The State of Franklin, *North Carolina Booklet*, XIV, 22.
BOWER, L. F. The State of Franklin, *Magazine of American History*, XXVI, 48.
BOYD, W. K. Early Relations of North Carolina and the West, *North Carolina Booklet*, VII, 193.
CALDWELL, JOHN H. A History of Presbyterianism in East Tennessee. An Address (1897).
CLEMENS, W. M. The State of Franklin, *New England Magazine*, XXVII, 772.
COCKE, WALTER M. William Cocke, *American Historical Magazine*, VI, 315.
FITCH, WILLIAM E. The Origin, Rise, and Downfall of the State of Franklin Under Her First and Only Governor, John Sevier. Address (1910).
GENTRY, SUSIE M. The Volunteer State (Tennessee) as a Seceder, *North Carolina Booklet*, III, No. 3, p. 4.
GOODRICH, WM. Life of William Cocke. *Journal of American History*, V.
—— Records Relating to the Cocke Family. *American Historical Magazine*, IV, 110.
—— The Cocke Family of Tennessee, *American Historical Magazine*, II, 152.
GRIGSBY, HUGH BLAIR. Founders of Washington College (Va.), *Washington and Lee Historical Papers*, (1890), II.
HENDERSON, ARCHIBALD. The Spanish Conspiracy in Tennessee, *Tennessee Historical Magazine* (November, 1917), III, 229.
HENDERSON, WM. A. "Nolachucky Jack" (Governor John Sevier); a Lecture.
KELLEY, DAVID C. The Scotch-Irish of Tennessee, *Proceedings Scotch-Irish Congress*, I, 132.
KINGSBURY, OLIVER A. Watauga and Franklin, *Transactions of the Oneida Historical Society* (1894), VI, 53.
LOSSING, B. J. Early Secessionists. *Harper's Magazine* (March, 1862), XXIV, 515.
MATHES, JOHN S. The State of Franklin; a series of articles in the *Chattanooga Times*.
McGILL, J. T. Franklin and Frankland, *Tenn. Hist. Magazine*, VIII, 248.
RAMSEY, J. G. M. The State of Franklin, in the *Land We Love*, V, 13-22, 109-116, 216-229.

——— The State of Franklin or Frankland. An article on the proper designation of the State. In *The Magnolia*, a Charleston magazine (1842), IV, 312.
REYNOLDS, LOUISE WILSON. The Commonwealth of Franklin, *D. A. R. Magazine* (January, 1918), III, 23.
SIOUSSAT, ST. GEORGE L. The North Carolina Cession of 1784 in its Federal Aspects; *Proceedings of Mississippi Valley Historical Association*, 1908, p. 35.
SNYDER, ANN E. On the Watauga and the Cumberland.
TEMPLE, OLIVER P. John Sevier (pamphlet).
——— The Scotch-Irish in Tennessee, *Proceedings Scotch-Irish Congress*, III, 160.
TODD, C. H. The Lost State of Franklin, *Register Kentucky Historical Society*, II, 84.
TURNER, FREDERICK J. Western State-Making in the Revolutionary Era, *American Historical Review*, I, 70, 251.
WARFIELD, E. D. The Constitutional Aspect of Kentucky's Struggle for Autonomy, *American Historical Association Papers*, IV, 23.
WAGENER, J. A. Frankland and Franklin, *Der Deutsche Pionier* (Feb., 1871), p. 364.
WEEKS, STEPHEN B. General Joseph Martin and the War of the Revolution in the West; *Annual Report American Historical Association*, 1893, 403-407. Also Reprint.

BOOKS

ALEXANDER, J. E. *History of the Synod of Tennessee.*
ALLEN, W. C. *Centennial of Haywood County, North Carolina* (1908).
ALLISON, JOHN. *Dropped Stitches in Tennessee History.*
ARMSTRONG, ZELLA. *Notable Southern Families.* (Two Volumes).
ARTHUR, JOHN P. *Western North Carolina; a History.*
ASBURY, FRANCIS. *Journal.*
BAILY, FRANCIS. *Journal of a Tour in Unsettled Parts of North America.*
BALLAGH, J. G. *Letters of Richard Henry Lee.*
BANCROFT, GEORGE. *History of the Formation of the Constitution.*
——— *History of the United States.*
BENEDICT, DAVID. *General History of the Baptist Denomination in America.*
BRAZELTON, B. G. *History of Hardin County, Tennessee.*
BREAZEALE, J. W. *Life As It Is.*
BROWN, JOHN MASON. *Political Beginnings of Kentucky.*
CALDWELL, JOSHUA W. *Constitutional History of Tennessee.*
——— *Bench and Bar of Tennessee.*
Calendar of Virginia State Papers.
CISCO, J. G. *Historic Sumner County.*
Documentary History of The Constitution of the United States.
DRAPER, LYMAN C. *King's Mountain and its Heroes.*
ELLET, ELIZABETH F. *Pioneer Women of the West.*
FAUST, A. B. *German Element in the United States.*
FOOTE, HENRY S. *The Bench and Bar of the South and Southwest.*
FOOTE, WM. H. *Sketches of Virginia.*
——— *Sketches of North Carolina.*
GARRET, W. R. and GOODPASTURE, A. V. *History of Tennessee.*
GILMORE, JAMES R. *John Sevier as a Commonwealth Builder.*

―――― *Rear Guard of the Revolution.*
―――― *Advance Guard of Western Civilization.*
GREEN, THOMAS M. *The Spanish Conspiracy.*
HAYWOOD, JOHN. *Civil and Political History of Tennessee.*
HENDERSON, ARCHIBALD. *The Conquest of the Old Southwest.*
HENRY, WILLIAM WIRT. *Life and Correspondence of Patrick Henry.*
HUMES, THOMAS W. *Loyal Mountaineers of Tennessee.*
McFERRIN, JOHN B. *History of Methodism in Tennessee.*
JAMES, JAS. A. *George Rogers Clark.*
JEFFERSON, THOMAS. *Writings.* Ford edition, and Washington edition.
MADISON, JAMES. *The Madison Papers.*
McREE, GILBERT J. *Life and Correspondence of James Iredell.*
MICHAUX, ANDRE. *Journal of,* in Thwaite's Early Western Travels, III.
―――― F. A. *Travels to the West of Alleghany Mountains. Ib.*
MONETTE, JOHN W. *Discovery and Settlement of the Mississippi Valley.*
MOONEY, JAMES. *Myths of the Cherokees.*
NEVINS, ALLEN. *The American States During and After the Revolution.*
North Carolina Colonial Records.
North Carolina State Records.
PARTON, JAMES. *Life of Andrew Jackson.*
PERKINS, JAMES H. *Annals of the West.*
PHELAN, JAMES. *History of Tennessee; the Making of a State.*
PRICE, RICHARD N. *History of Holston Methodism.*
PUTNAM, A. W. *History of Middle Tennessee.*
RAMSEY, J. G. M. *Annals of Tennessee.*
Revolutionary Records of Georgia.
ROOSEVELT, THEODORE. *The Winning of the West.*
ROYCE, CHARLES C. *The Cherokee Nations of Indians.* Annual of Bureau of Ethnology, V.
RULE, WILLIAM. *History of Knoxville.*
SCOTT, NANCY M. *Memoirs of Hugh Lawson White.*
SERRANO, Y SANZ. *Espana y Los Indios Cherokis y Chactas.*
SKINNER, CONSTANCE L. *Pioneers of the Old Southwest.*
STEVENS, W. B. *History of Georgia.*
SUMMERS, L. P. *History of Southwest Virginia.*
―――― *Annals of Southwest Virginia.*
TAYLOR, OLIVER. *Historic Sullivan.* [County].
TEMPLE, OLIVER P. *The Covenanter, the Cavalier and the Puritan.*
―――― *East Tennessee and the Civil War.*
―――― *Eminent Tennesseans.*
TURNER, FREDERICK J. *The Frontier in American History.*
TURNER, F. M. *Life of General John Sevier.*
VICTOR, O. J. *History of American Conspiracies. . . . The State of Franklin Insurrection.*
WARE, REVEREND THOMAS. *Sketches of the Life and Travels of Reverend Thomas Ware.*
WHITAKER, A. P. *Spanish-American Frontier.*
WHITE, KATE K. *The King's Mountain Men.*

WILLIAMS, S. C. *Early Travels in the Tennessee Country.*
WINSOR, JUSTIN. *The Westward Movement.*
WINTERBOTHAM, W. *Historical,* etc. *View of the United States and of the European Settlements,* III.

INDEX

INDEX

ABILITY OF FRANKS and descendants, 279
Abingdon, Va., 6, 259, 268
Abingdon Presbytery, 271, 321
Abraham, Cherokee chief, 77, 212
Acts of assembly lost, 58
Adair, John, 46, 356
Address of Wm. Graham, public burning of, 97
Adear, see *Adair*
Alden, G. H., quoted, 80, 219
Alexander, Adam R., 280
Alexander, Dr. Archibald, 270
Alexander, Eben., 78
Allen, Ethan, 235
Allison, John, corrected, 42, 49, 75
Allison, Robert, 96, 245
Altitude, 278
Amis, Thomas, sketch, 315, 153, 161, 246, 249
Ancoo, Cherokee chief, 78
Anderson, G. W., 281
Anderson, John, sketch, 315, 41, 46, 58
Anderson, Joseph, 284
Anderson, Josiah M., 280
Antiquity, remains of, 262
"Appallachia, State of," 287
Arkansas, first governor and senator from F., 281
Armstrong, John, entry office of, 22, *et seq.*, frauds in, 175, 196, 251
Armstrong, Lieut. John, in F., 237, 258
Armstrong, Martin, 259, *et seq.*
Arrest of Sevier, 231, *et seq.*
Articles of Association of French Broad, 226
Asbury, Bishop Francis, 209; travels in F., 267, 270, 273, 311, 316
Ashe, John B., 23
Atakullakulla, chief, 217
Avery treaty, 13
Avery, Waighstill, 76

BAKER, ELISHA, 30

Baker, Francis, 198
Bachman, N. L., 280
Balch, Rev. H., 80, 94, 96, *et seq.*, 270, *et seq.*
Balch-Graham controversy, 92 *et seq.*
Baldwin, Judge Simeon E., quoted, 220
Banbury, Thomas, 23
Baptists, 271, *et seq.*
Barrett, Capt. S. T., 278
Barton, David, 280
Barton, Col. J., 158
Barton, Rev. Isaac, 272
Barton, Robt. M., 280
Battle, at Tipton's, 198, *et seq.*; how conducted, 257; at Lookout Mountain, 216; last of F., 223
Bean, John, 30
Berry, Campbell P., 281
Berry, Francis, 217
Berry, James Henderson, 280
Bethabara church, 262
Big Bend of the Tennessee, see *Great Bend*
Bibliography, 359
Blair, John, 195, 245, 246, 280
Bland, of Va., 10
Bledsoe, Abraham, 313
Bledsoe, Anthony, 126, 144, 170, 172, 196
Bloodworth, Timothy, 124, 128
Blount College, 94, 312
Blount County in F., 80, 91, 161
Blount, Wm., in Great Bend Scheme, 14-15; on cession, 19, 23, *et seq.;* County in F. named, 91, 176; in federal convention, 183, 196, 246; governor of territory, 253, 302; see *sketches of Franklinites and Antis*
Boat Yard, The, see *Kingsport*
Boering, Vincent, 281
Bond, Phineas, 129
Boundaries of Franklin, 44, 49
Bowyer, Luke or Lew, 77
Brabson, Reese B., 280
Brissot de Warville, 275

Bristol, Tenn., 173, 330
Brown, Alexander, 217
Brown, Jacob, 59, 231
Brown, Mrs. Jacob, 231
Bryce, James, quoted, 271
Buckingham, Mr., 356
Buffalo Ridge church, 271
Bullard, Joseph, 30, 38, 216
Bunch, Samuel, 280
Burnett, Edmund C., quoted, 85, 127
Burning of Graham's address, 93; of his effigy, 97; of Tipton's effigy, 137
Burton, Robert, 196
Butler, Pierce, on new States, 185

CABARRUS, S., 23
Cage, Harry, 280, 281, 313
Cage, Wm., sketch, 313, 24, 39, 41; Speaker, 57; treasurer, 61, 65, 83; in debate 152
Caldwell, Andrew, 109, 163, 198
Caldwell, J. W., quoted, 95
Camden, Lord, on the West, 4
Campbell, Arthur, sketch, 291; leads in separation, 5, *et seq.*, 32, 41, 45; enthusiasm for, 48; meets opposition, 48; letter to Gov. P. Henry, 50; Henry's message names, 53; boundaries of his Frankland, 54; compelled to yield, 54; and Martin, 61; on Cherokee treaty, 88; works on F. constitution, 94, 128; to Cherokee, 141; called on for aid, 205, 209, 219; on West, 243; his F., 282, 285; County named for, 294
Campbell, Brookings, 280, 286
Campbell, Judge David, sketch, 298, 38, 42, 44, 57; 61, 94, 96, 109; commissioner to N. C., 114, 115, protest of, 131; elected N. C. Senator, 163; 189, 195; elected N. C. judge, 197, 232; to draft petition to Congress, 226, 358
Campbell, Capt. David, sketch, 316; 39, 41
Campbell, Mrs. Elizabeth, 8
Campbell, Thomas J., 280, 299
Campbell, Wm., 6, 8, 99, 293, 315, 331
Campbell, Wm. B., 280, 316

Candler, Col. Wm., 111
Capital of F., Jonesborough the first, 57; Greeneville the second, 57
Carmack, E. W., 280
Carrick, Rev. S., 94, 270
Carter, Col. John., 290
Carter, Landon, sketch, 299, 24, 26, 30; Speaker, 57; Secretary of state, 61, 65, 83; 108, 115, 136; Commissioner to N. C., 189, 248, 249; County named for, 301
Carter County, in Wayne, F., 60
Carter, Samuel P., 281
Carter, Wm. B., 280, 301
Carter, Wm. B., Jr., 301
Caruthers, Robert L., 280
Caruthers, Samuel, 281
Casey, Joseph, 217
Caswell County, F., created, 59, 161, 199
Caswell, Fort, 290, 307
Caswell, Richard, in Bend scheme, 13-18; lands on French Broad, 22; speaker 23; lands in Washington County 24; County named for, 59; governor, written by S., 73; popular in West, 73; reply to S., 76; on Cherokees, 77, 80; on Hopewell treaty, 101; Judge Campbell to, 115, 131, 132; to Campbell, 133; to Sevier, 133; to E. Shelby, 134; Shelby to, 145; from S., 146; his policy of conciliation, 146, 148, 171, 207; policy vindicated, 230; N. C. assembly, 246
Caswell, Winston, 135
Cavet, Alexander, 39, 41
Census, see *Population*
Cession by N. C., urged, 19, 23; Gov. Martin on, 10; Spaight on, 23; first, 23, *et seq*; repeal of, 35, *et seq.*; protest on repeal 36; irrepealability, 37; F. assembly on, 63; Gov. Martin, 67; S. on, 74; memorial of F. to Congress, 82; Cocke on, 117; N. C. on, 119; speculation following repeal, 175; requested, 195; act to repeal, 195; White on, 223; Willie Jones' bill to cede, 1788, 247; second cession, 249,

INDEX

et seq.; land problem the crux of, 250; deed's condition, 250; bad bargain for nation, 252
Chamberlain, Andrew, 136
Chambers, Rev. Alexander, 272
Chapman, Thomas, 57, 65, 83, 108, 115
Charleston, S. C., 2
Cherokee Indians, Transylvania purchase, 2; checked by Wataugans, 2; Long Island treaty, 13; boundary line, 13, 62; N. C. grants lands of, 65; Martin on, 68; S. on, 74; Caswell on, 76; treaty of Dumplin Creek, 77, 79; consolidation with F., 80; hostility, 82; Hopewell treaty, 99, *et seq.*; of Coyatee, 103; consider removal, 102, 104, 106, 116; Cocke on, 118; in confusion, 141; Benj. Franklin on, 167; 190, 207, 213, 218; battle of Flint creek, 223; 238; Brother Schneider among, 259, *et seq.*; hot-houses of, 263; forecast of fate, 282, 357, *et seq.*
Chickamauga campaign, 215, *et seq.*, 249, 252
Chickamauga Indians, 140, 170, 207, 210, 213, 214, 215, *et seq.*, 237, 259
Chickasaw Indians, 21, 26, 36, 106, 141, 168, 171, 191, 196, 238, 264, *et seq.*; domain of, proposed for a state, 284
Chickasaw Purchase, 284, 313
Chisholm, John, 30, 159
Choctaw Indians, 141, 238, 282
Christian, Gilbert, sketch, 303, 30, 39, 41; F. records, 58; Colonel, 58; Speaker, 114; S. to, 163, 206, 315; Chickamauga campaign, 217
Christian, George, to Draper, 58
Christian, Col. Wm., for separation, 12; letter to, 17
Churches, see *Religion*
Cincinnati, Society of, S. elected to membership, 178; 320
Cittico battle, 215
Clark, George Rogers, succored by Holston, 2; and Spain, 126
Clarke, Col. Elijah, 111, 178, 179
Clarkson, George M., first man legally executed in F., 138

Clendenning, James, 246
Climate, 265, 267, 278, 283
Cobb, W. R. W., 281
Cocke, John H., 280, 281
Cocke, Wm., sketch, 294, 39, 41, 44, 45; appeals to S., 56; brigadier 59, 61; delegate to Congress, 65, 76, 97, 104, 140; memorial carried by 82, 83; treaty 102; to B. Franklin, 104; from B. Franklin, 105; personal appearance, 117; speech before N. C. assembly, 117; declines compromise, 143; in debate, 149; uses force, 162, 164, 189; N. C. assembly, 246, 248
Cocke, W. M., 280
Coinage, 102
Colyar, A. S., 281
Compromise, efforts to, 140, 142, 159; defeat of, 161, *et seq.*, 207, *et seq.*
Congress, F. and, 49, 79, 80; disesteem of, 128, 130; bad bargain in second cession, 252; magnanimity of, 252
Connecticut, infected, 129
Conner, James, 302
Constitution of F., 43; Appendix A, protest against, 96
Constitution of "Frankland" proposed, 95; controversy over, 97
Constitution of U. S., supported by F., 64; N. C. fails to ratify, 245; ratifies, 250
Constitutional Convention of Tennessee, 284
Control of the West, 1; by N. C., 19
Conway, Elias N., 280, 311
Conway, George, sketch, 311
Conway, Henry, sketch, 310, 102, 114; in Sevier-Tipton battle, 200; treasurer, 223
Conway, Henry W., 230, 281, 311
Conway, James S., 280, 311
Conway, Joseph, 114, 311
Conway, Wm., 280
Cooper, James, 217
Cosby, James, 232, 356
Counties of F., representation, 92; population of, 276

Court raiding, 109, 163, 198
Cox, John I., 280
Cox, Wm., 30, 39, 41, 201, *et seq.*
Cozby, see *Cosby*
Crafford, John, 217
Craig, David, 231
Creek Indians, 106, 111, 141, 168, 170, 179, 189, 191, 209, 237
Crockett, David, 280
Crockett, John W., 280
Cross, E., 280, 281
Crozier, John H., 280
Cumberland Gap., 259; see Kentucky road
Cumberland region, settled by Wataugans, 1, 13; military reservation in, 20; on separation, 33; separate from F. by Ordinance, 1784, 48, 62; courts, 63; favored, 100; about to join F., 113, 121, 127, 137, 139; look to Kentucky for connection, 163, 175; cry for help from, 170; ireful towards N. C., 173; seek separation, 176; delegate to visit, 226, 236; D. Smith on, 242; urge separation, 248, 252; slaves in, 277; see *Middle Tennessee*
Cummings, Rev. Charles, 46, 50
Cunningham, S. B., 281
Cunningham, Wm., 216
Currency of F., 59, 219, *et seq.*
Customs of people, see *Modes of Life*

DANDRIDGE, TENN., 199
Davie, William R., 23, 24
Davis, William, 39, 120, 136, 183, 198
Deaderick, David, 231
Deaderick, James W., 280
Debate, a high, in F. convention, 150, *et seq.*
Deeds, validated, 254
Denominational rupture, 94, *et seq.*
Denton, Abraham, 30
De Renne Library, Savannah, 150
Descendants of Franks, 279, *et seq.*
Dickinson, John, on West, 3
Diseases, 278
Dixon, Robert, 106
Doak, Rev. John W., 281, 317

Doak, Rev. Samuel, sketch, 317; 30, 94, 270-71
Doak, Samuel, of Hawkins, 215
Doctors of medicine, 271
Doherty, George, sketch, 317; 59, 174; 217; in debate, 158; 216, 256; Natchez expedition, 318
Donelson, John, 14, 16, 22, 106, 313
Donelson, Stockley, sketch, 313, 14, 30; Surveyor-general, 61; Speaker, 90; ardor cools, 144; 161, 245
Downes, Wm., 16
Droomgoole, Alexander, 168, 169
Duel, challenge, Tipton-Roddy, 247
Dumplin Creek, treaty, 77, 79, 218, 228
Dungan's ford, 202
Dunkin, John, 245

EAST TENNESSEE, 282; proposes separation, 284, *et seq.*; emancipation of slaves and, 286; third agitation of separation, 286
Edmiston, Wm., 55
Effigy, burning of Graham's, 96; of John Tipton, 137
Elections in F. irregular, 91, 149, *et seq.*, 155
Elholm district, 140
Elholm, George, sketch, 309; 112, 121; district named for, 140; delegate to Congress, 140, 144; in debate, 150; mission to Ga., 177, *et seq.*, furnished plans for campaign, 182; to Moultrie, 191, 192; in Sevier-Tipton battle, 200; treasurer, 223; on population of F., 275
Emancipation movement, 285
English, E. H., 280
English, Thomas, 102
English, (Ingles) Wm., 215
English element in F., 276
Episcopalians, 273
Evans, Nathaniel, sketch, 319; 59, 199, 204, 214, 232, 241
Evans, Major Thomas, battalion of, 148, 170, 173, *et seq.*
Evans, Wm., 30, 39; slave of hung, 277
Execution, legal, first, 134; of negro, 277

INDEX

FAIN, CAPT. JOHN, 215
Farragut, Admiral David, 281
Federal Constitutional Convention, F. hopes for recognition from, 183, *et seq.*, debate on F. in, news of action of, on new States, in F., 189; N. C. refuses to ratify 237, 245; F's attitude towards, 238, 241; Cumberland Country and, 242; Innes on, 243
Fegan, John, 217
Fighting, customs of soldiers, 257
Fitzgerald, Garrett, 39, 41
Fitzgerald, Wm., 280
Flat-boats, 258
Floridablanca, 236
Flour (Flower) Gap, 259, 275
Forrest, Nathan B., fought like S., 257, 316
France and the West, 128
"Frankland," name proposed, 94; B. Franklin's understanding, 105; Constitution proposed, 94, *et. seq.*; Arthur Campbell uses as name of F., 62; and Houston, 94; proposed revival of, 285
Franklin, Benjamin, State named for, 86, 104; Cocke to, 104; reply, 105; S. to, 165; reply, 166; S. to, 168, 198
Franklin Commonwealth Society, 96
Franklin, the Greater, boundaries, 44, 49, 54, 55
Franklinites, sketches of, 289; offended by Carolinians in debate, 28; independence of, 28; for federal constitution, 64; cession, 63; buoyancy of, 66, 77, 92; proclamation to, 72; number of contrasted, 135; troublesome children of Uncle Sam, 139; aroused to action, 145, 155; protected N. C. records in Revolution, 158; two hundred in arms to rescue S., 163; cry for help from Cumberland, 170; enlistment of, 173; punished, 252; where from, 275; literacy, 278; healthy, 278; youthfulness, 279; descendants of, 279; spirit survives, 287
Franklin, State of, genesis 6; exodus threatened, 13; Virginians in, 28; first convention, 29; records of, 58; acts of, 58, cession act, 63; held in revolt, 68; administrative functioning, 77; treaty, 77; memorial to Congress, 82; Green's letter in, 127; first legal execution, 138; Sullivan's boast, 138; military districts, 140; deputies to Ky., 163; Benj. Franklin recommends compromise, 167; seeks alliance with Ga., 177, *et seq.*; Indian campaign to bolster, 180; hopes for recognition in federal constitutional convention, 183; vote seals fate of, 184, *et seq.*; tendency to dismemberment, 189; offers to assume N. C.'s war debt, 194; Lesser Franklin, 218, *et seq.*; end of, 230; agent of Secretary of War in, 236; Innes on, 243; Tennessee solves F. problems, 254; Chickasaws desire trade with, 265; population of, 275; slavery in, 277; women of, 277; literacy, 278; schools, 278; eminent men produced, 279; survival of concept, 282
Frazier, James B., 280
French Broad Country, 14, 22, 77, 78, 79, 91, 100, 116, 136, 199, 211, 213, 216, 218, 234, *et seq.*, convention of, 225; articles of Association, 226, 229, *et seq.*, 237, 261, *et seq.*, 261, 262, 328, 356 *et seq.*
French Lick, 2; see *Nashville*
Frost, Rev. John, 272
Fruits, 256
Fuller, Capt., 216

GAINES, GEN. EDMUND P., 281
Gammon, Richard, 39, 41
Gardoqui, Diego de, 123, 129, 219, *et seq.*; 235, 237, *et seq.*
Gardner, John A., 285
Garrett, A. E., 280
General Assemblies of F., first, 56, 59, reply of Martin, 63; second, 90; of 1786, 106, 114; of 1787, 136, 140, 189; of Lesser Franklin, 219
Gentlemen's Magazine, quoted, 87
Gentry, Jesse, 261

Georgia, Great Bend in, 14; cession, 25; example, 36; support of F. in Congress, 84; alliances sought, 106; refugees, 111; on Mississippi, 126, 127, 138; and F., 177, *et seq.*; described, 179; F. to aid, 180, 189, *et seq.*; S. to governor, 209; 249, 259, 309
German element, 276
Gerry, Elbridge, 185
Gest, see *Gist*
Gibson, Wm., 356
Gibson, Capt., 216
Gilbert, Rev. M., 273
Gillespie, George, 356
Gillespie, Thos., 217
Gillespie's Fort, attack on, 233
Gilliland, John, 96
Gilmore, J. R., Roosevelt on, 173, quoted, 241
Gist, Benjamin, 39, 41, 262, 314
Gist, Joseph, 30
Gist, Joshua, sketch, 314, 24, 39, 41, 58, 76, 262, 356, *et seq.*
Glasgow, James, 13, 314
Gluglu, Indian name of Joseph Martin, 260, 333
Goodpasture, A. V., quoted, 216
Gorham, Nath'l, on F., 184, 185
Graham, Rev. Wm., 94, 96, 97
Grayson, Wm., 85, 88, 129
Greasy Cove, 196, *et seq.*, 200, 201
Great Bend of Tennessee, not in N. C., 13; to be settled from F., 14, 43, 54, 90, 106, 110; P. Henry and, 89; plans for, 181
Greater Franklin, 5, *et. seq.*, 32, 45, 54, 94, 163, 282
Greater Britain, and West, 87, 128, 129, 282
Green, Jesse, 232
Green, Thomas, 126
Greene County, *passim.*
Greeneville, second capital of F., 57; first body held at, 94; rendezvous at, 199; 258, 307, 311, 356, *et seq.*
Greeneville College, 94; see *biographical sketches*

HALL, JOHN, 30
Hamilton, Alexander, on West, 244
Hamilton, Joseph, 61; on Sevier-Tipton battle, 204; 226, 358
Hammer, John, 119, 136
Handcrafts in F., 256
Handley, George, 190, 192
Handley, S., sketch, 319
Hanging Maw, Cherokee chief, 103
Hardiman, Thomas, 246
Hardin, Capt. John, 216, 217
Hardin, Col. Joseph, sketch, 304, 39, 41, 42; Speaker, 62, 72, 77, 78, 207, 208, 216, 226, 230; County named for, 306; Commissioner to Cumberland Country, 358
Hardin, Capt. Joseph, 202
Hardy, Samuel, 52
Harland, Ellis, 260
Harris, Nathaniel E., 280
Hawkins, Benj., 99, 101; County named for, 120, 195
Hawkins County, N. C., created, 120, 136, 144, 163, 205, 258
Hawkins, Joseph, 246
Hay, John, 23
Haynes, Landon C., 200, 280
Haywood, John, 34, 250, quoted, on Cocke, 115; *passim.*
Health, 278
Heard, Stephen, 16
Henderson, Archibald, quoted, 62, 219, 236, 239
Henderson, John B., 280
Henderson, Nathaniel, 195
Henderson, Richard, 2, 9, 62, 293, 295, 332
Henderson, Samuel, 62, 63, 65, 67, 72
Henderson, Thomas, 61, 205
Henry, Patrick, 8, 11; Great Bend, 14; Martin agent of, 14, 38, 50; proclamation Va. Franks, 51; opinion of the man, 88; to Martin, 134, favors Martin for governorship of Territory, 253; efforts in 1788 for new State, 89
Henry, Samuel, 77
Highways, 257, 275

INDEX

Hiwassee river, garrison on projected, 140, 217
Holland, Benjamin, 30
Holston Association, 271
Holston Country, see Watauga Settlements and French Broad Country, 2, 5, *et seq.*, 12, 13, 17, 28, 32, 34
Homes in F., 255
Hooper, Wm., 23, 35
Hopewell, treaty of, 99, *et seq.*, 130, 141, 218, 357
Horses, 256; pack, 268
Hospitality, 258
Hoss, E. E., 281; quoted, 258
Hothouses of Cherokees, 263
Houck, John C., 280
Houck, L. C., 280
Houston, James, 59, 322
Houston, Robert, 215n.
Houston, Rev. Samuel, sketch, 320, 30, 32, 39, 41; family in French Broad, 79, 94, 98
Houston, Sam, of Texas, 79, 281, 322
Houston Station, 214, 215, 319
Hubbard, David, 280
Hubbard, James, 63, 75, 212, 214, 261, 279, 314
Huguenot element, 276
Humphreys, Andrew, 281
Hunter, John, 217
Hunter's Station, 212
Hutchings, Thomas, sketch, 335, 61, 144, 145, 211, 216

IMLAY, GILBERT, quoted, 275, 282
Indian atrocities, 212, 266
Indian haters, 279
Indian hothouses, 263
Indians, see *Cherokees, Chickamaugas, Chickasaws, Choctaws, Creeks*
Indian mounds, 262
Indiana, first senator from F., 281
Ingles (English) Thomas, 102
Inman, Abednego, 206
Inman, Hugh and S. M., 281
Innes, Harry, 243
Irish element, 276
Iron, manufacture of, 255

Irwin, John, 30

JACKSON, ANDREW, for separation, 194, 350; State proposed to be named for, 285; and spirit of Franks, 287; lost Tennessee, 287, 290; commends Cocke, 297; mentioned, 316
Jackson-Shelby treaty with Chickasaws, 21, 284, 313
Jarnagin, Spencer, 280
Jay, John, treaty by, 123
Jefferson, Thomas, 3, 9, 11, 22, 25, 28, 86; on closure of the Mississippi, 124; estimates acreage sold by N. C., 251
Jefferson's Ordinance of 1784, 25, 28, 32, 34, 48, 87, 92, 184
Jett, Stephen, 106
Johnson, Andrew, 284
Johnson City, 120, 199, 200, 209, 269, 306
Johnson County, Tenn., 29, 60
Johnston, Samuel, 35, 219, 236; Gen. Smith to, 242
Jones, Allen, 36
Jones, Calvin, 22
Jones, Joseph, 5
Jones, Willie, 246, 247
Jonesborough, first capital of F., 57; academy near, 58; records at, 59, 77; last assembly at, 90; punished, 119; 136; first legal execution at, 138; raided by Tiptonites, 198; council of war at, 215, 231; arrest of S., near, 231; 258, 328
Judgments of F. Courts, status of, 254

KEEL, REV. JAMES, 272
Kelley, David C., 316
Kelly, Alexander, 59
Kelly, Wm., 280
Kennedy, Daniel, sketch, 307, 30, 39, 41, 43; brigadier, 59, 140; clerk, 61; council of state, 61, 66; in debate, 154; S. to, 161, 195, 198, 206; on Chickamauga campaign, 213, 216, 217, 234
Kentucky Gazette, quoted, 140

Kentucky, founding aided by Wataugans, 2; claimed by Va., 3; petitions for statehood, 9, 11, 12, 27, 62; separation in, 121; and Spain, 127; Gov. Henry on, 134, 138; deputies from Franklin to consult, 163; aid for Cumberland settlement, 170; Evans' battalion in, 174; Cumberland seeks political connection, 175; in constitutional convention, 184, *et seq.*; Spanish intrigue in, 180, 244; road to, 259; first governor from F., 281; and Cumberland, 284
Kentucky road, 275, 332
Key, D. M., 279, 280
King's Mountain, battle, 8, 70, 111, 165, 222, 290, 293, 303, 307, 318, 326, 328
King, Austin A., 280, 281
King, Rufus, on navigation of the Mississippi, 123; on the West, 184
King, Thomas, 217, 245, 248
Kingsport (Sullivan Court House), 213, 258; Christianville, 303, 322
Kirk family, 212
Kirk, John, Jr., 212, *et seq.*, 215n., 279
Knoxville (White's Fort), 216, 233, 291, 301, 322
Knoxville Convention, 1861, 287

Lambert, Rev. Jeremiah, 273
Land office of N. C., opened, 16-18
Lands, cleared, 256; value of, 277; conveyances validated, 254
Lane, Tidence, 271
Lead, supply, 257
Lee, Henry, on West and Spain, 123
Lee, John, in French Broad, 350, 356
Lee, Richard Henry, on A. Campbell, 51
Legality of repeal of cession act, 37
Legislative records, lost, 58
Lenoir, Wm., 23
Lenoirs, Tenn., 299
Lesser Franklin, 218, *et seq.*; end of, 230
Liberty Hall Academy, Va., 94, 270
Life, modes of in F., see *Modes*
Literacy, 278
Loid, Col., 224

Logan, Col. John, 140
Long, John, 39
Long Island, treaty at, 13; 17, 259, 264, 306, 323, 332
Lookout Mountain, skirmish at, 216
Looney, David, sketch, 322, 24, 39, 41, 46, 96, 245
Looney, Moses, sketch, 322, 39, 41
Louisiana, 235, see *New Orleans*
Love, Robert, sketch, 336, 96, 119, 136, 200, 216, 231, 328
Love, Thomas, 203, 336
Lovett, O. B., 280
Lowry, Robert, 281
Lutherans, 273

McAdoo, Wm. G., 280
McAlister, W. K., 280
McCarter, James, Gen., 224
McCay (McKee), E. D. H. P., III, 356
McClellan, W. M., 280
McDowell, Gen. C., 207, 232
McDowell, Joseph, 232
McDowell, Samuel, 175n.
McFarland, Robert, 280
McFarland, Wm., 280
McGayha, Samuel, 217
McGillivray, Alexander, 130, 242
McGhee, C. M., 281
McIntosh, Lachlan, 16, 99
McKee, John, 281
McLaughlin, quoted, 1
McMinn, Joseph, 194
McNab, John, 59

Maclaine, A., 23, 38
Macon, Nathaniel, 23
Madison, James, 5, 11, 88, 129, 184, 185
Mahon, John, 217
Maine, separation movement, 121, 184
Manifee, John, see *Menefee*
Manifesto, of Gov. Martin, 67, 74, 76; of Gov. Sevier, 72
Marriages, at early ages, 277; of F., validated, 254
Marshall, John; on new governments in West, 88

INDEX

Marshall, Wm., 195, 245
Martin's Academy, 58
Martin, Gov. Alexander, 20, 26, 42, 58, 62, 63, 67, 71, 72, 73, 75, 183
Martin, John, 280
Martin's Station, 259, 332
Martin, Joseph, sketch, 331; Great Bend, 14, 17; agent P. Henry, 14; in F. Convention, 30; to S., 42; to Henry, 45, 51, 99, 102, 108; lost Va. agency, 54, 56, 61, 62; Henry to on S., 88; to Caswell, 92, treaty of Hopewell, 101, 102; opposes Cocke, 121; from Henry, 134; on Cherokees, 141; in senate of N. C., 195; displeased with Tipton, 206; to Kennedy, 206; to Gov. Johnston, 207; from S., 207, 208; to Gov. Randolph, 209; and Chickamaugas, 210; and Cherokees, 211; projects Chickamauga campaign, 213; out of jurisdiction, 214; returns to lead Chickamauga Expedition, 215; defeated, 216; married daughter of Nancy Ward, 217; to Gov. Johnston, 226, 231, 233; and Spain 242; N. C. convention, 245, *et seq.*, 249; in disfavor, 252; fails in effort for governorship of Territory, 253; Schneider's references, 259, *et seq.*; Indian name, 260, 356
Martin, Joshua L., 280
Martin, Luther, on F., 185, *et seq.*
Martin, Wm., 217
Maryland attitude on West, 4
Maryville, 214
Massachusetts, 121, 129n.
Mason, George, 185
Mastin, Rev. J., 273
Mathews, Gov. George, 112, 173, 177, 180
Matlock, Wm., 232
Maughan, John, 30, 39, 41
Maxwell, George, sketch, 337, 39, 41, 96, 145, 195, 214, 246
Mebane, Alexander, 23, 35
Memorial, of Virginians to Congress, 46; of F. to Congress, 82; to N. C., Appendix B, 194

Menefee, John, sketch, 315, 30, 41, 189
Merchandize, where bought, 258
Mero district, see *Cumberland region*
Methodists, 265, 267, 268
Michaux, A., 316
Michaux, F., quoted, 256, 283
Middle Tennessee, 282, 283
Migration, current of, 92, 275–76
Military customs, 257
Military reservation of N. C., 19, 249, 275
Military districts of F., 140
Miller, John, 217
Milligan, Rev. Thomas, 58
Milligan, Samuel, 279, 280
Mint established, 102
Miro, don Estevan, 126, 235
Mississippi river, closure, 123, 139, 179, 180, 235, *et seq.*; Hamilton on, 244
Missouri, first senator from F., 281
Mitchell, George, 108
Mitchell, R., 90
Moccasin Gap, 259, see *Kentucky road*
Modes of Life, 255
Monroe, James, surprised at F's support in Congress, 85; on feeling between East and West, 128
Montgomery, James, 96, 136, 217
Montgomery, Col. John, 2
Moore, John, 16
Moore, Moses, 217
Moore, Rev. Nathaniel, 273
Moore, Wm., 119
Moravians, 259, 273
Morganton, N. C., S. at, 233
Morris, G., on western States, 184
Morrison, Wm., 232
Moultrie, Gen. Wm., 191
Mounted infantry, Franks fought as, 257
"Mount Pleasant," home of S., 199, 290; see *Sevier*
Muffet, Alex., 136
Mulky, Rev. Jonathan, 272
Murphey, John, 30
Murphey, Wm., sketch, 323; 30, 272
Muscle (Mussel) Shoals, 48, 107, 141, 260

NAMES, see "*Frankland*," *Franklin*; "West Carolina" proposed, 38; of those killed and wounded at Cittico, 215; "State of Jacksoniana," 285, 286; "State of Appalachia," 287; "Bonnie Kate," 290; attached to petition to N. C., 350, *et seq.*

Nashville, see French Lick, 2, 22, 92; Green at, 127; anti-Spanish letter from, 138; Evans' battalion reaches, 173, 287

Natchez Country, 126, 130, 138, 180, 318

Navarro, M., 235

Negroes, 277; see *Slavery*

Nelson, Rev. David, 281

Nelson, T. A. R., 280

Nelson, Henry, 136n.

Nelson, William, delegate to Congress, 140, 209, 226, 269, 358

Nelson, Valentine S., 281

Newell, Samuel, 323, 94, 96, 158

Newell's Station, 228

New Hampshire, infected, 87, 129

Newman, John, 217

New Orleans, coveted, 138, 180, 235; mentioned, 318

New States in West, 7, 10, 11, 27, 28, 45, *et seq.*, 125; national leaders on, 85, *et seq.*, 123; Patrick Henry's effort for, in 1788, 89; in Congress, 121, 183, *et seq.*

North, George, 232

North Carolina, see *Cession, Franklin;* conditions in (1784), 26; military reservation, 20; nation expecting cession, 21; land policy made Chickasaws hostile, 21; aroused over unrest, 139; treated with contempt, 144; delegation undeceived, 145; on military pressure, 148; sends relief to Cumberland, 148; records of sent into F., during Revolution, 158; treatment of Evans' battalion, 174, *et seq.;* position in convention of 1787, 184, *et seq.;* continental debt offered to be assumed by F., 195; Gov. Johnston holds estoppel, 219; on federal constitution, 245, *et seq.;* second Cession, 249, *et seq.;* called on for, 249; policy respecting, 250; issue with Tennessee over land control, 251; deprives Martin of brigadier's commission, 252; price of lands, 277

North Carolina element in F., 275; strong in Cumberland Country, 20, 251

O'FALLON, DR. JAMES, intrigues with Spain, 243

Officers' salaries, 60

Option of Congress to accept Cession irrevocable, 37

Otto, on the West, 125

Outlaw, Alexander, sketch, 324, 30, 36, *et seq.*, 42; Colonel, 59, 66, 77, 100, 102, 133, 213, 215, 226, 246, 284, 356, *et seq.*

PAINE, THOMAS, quoted on Virginia's claim to the West, 27

Parkinson, Peter, sketch, 337, 96, 159, 200

Patterson, David T., 280

Patterson, Robert, 281

Patterson, W. C., 281

Peck, J. H., 280

Peck, Jacob, 280

Person, Thomas, 23, 24; to Robertson, 120

People of F., 275, *et seq.*

Petitions, to N. C., 115, 226, *et seq.*, Appendix B, 348

Physicians, 278

Pickens, Andrew, 99, 213

Pinckney, Charles, on Mississippi closure, 123

Piomingo, Chickasaw Chief, 142, 264, *et seq.*

Point Pleasant, battle of, 1

Population, drift away from Ky., to Watauga country, 13, 94; composition, 275, *et seq.;* in 1788, 275; of counties, 276; of slaves, 277; of Tennessee, 1790–1800, 276

Powder, supply, 257

Prehistoric remains, 262

INDEX 375

Presbyterian Church, 94, 270, *et seq.*
Priestly, Wm., 119
Pritchard, Jeter C., 280
Proceedings of Western inhabitants, Appendix C
Proclamation of Gov. Henry, 51; of Gov. Martin, 67; of Gov. Caswell, 141, 218
Protest against Cession act, 36
Pugh, Jonathan, 109, 198, 202
Pursley, Wm., 136
Putnam's Middle Tennessee, quoted, *passim.*

QUAKERS, 273

RACES OF PEOPLE IN F., 276
Ramsey, Francis A., sketch, 311, 61, 90, 195, 248
Ramsey, J. McG., Annals of, quoted, *passim.*; 312
Ramsey Wm. B. A., 312
Randolph, Gov. Edmund, 54, 128n. 209
Rankin, Rev. John, 281
Rawlings, Asahel, 30, 39, 41, 245
Reagan, John H., 280, 281
Reelfoot Lake, 22
Repeal of Cession act, 35; illegal, 37
Reese, James, sketch, 325, 39, 41
Reese, Wm. B., 280
Religion in F., 94, 270, *et seq.*
Rennoe, John, 108
Rhea, John, 56, 61, 144, 280
Richardson, James, 217
Roane, Archibald, 194, 226, 350, 358
Robertson, Drury, 201
Robertson, Charles, of Greene, sketch, 325, 30
Robertson, Charles, of Washington, sketch, 306; for Cession, 24, 30, 39, 41; Colonel, 59; in charge of mint, 102; Speaker, 189; in Sevier-Tipton battle, 200, 231, 260
Robertson, Elijah, 24, 26, 246
Robertson, James, 2, 22, 34; Person to, 120, 170, 176, 195; Spanish intrigue, 230, *et seq.*, 246
Robertson, Julius C., 281

Roberston, Mark, 171
Robinson, see *Robertson*
Roddy, James, sketch, 326, 39, 59, 245, 246, 356
Rogersville, 213, 258, 260, 316
Ross, David, 89
Ross, Rev. F., 89
Roosevelt, Theodore, quoted, 128, 213; corrected, 52, 162, 165, 212, 219, 241, 245, 278; strictures on Gilmore justified, 173
Rowan, Henry, 356
Russell, Col. Wm., 8, 45, 50, 54, 144, 199, 268
Rutherford, Gen. Griffith, 15; bill to settle dispute, 119; county named for, 119, 131, 260, 304
Rutledge, John, on the West, 184

SALARIES OF OFFICERS, 60
Salem, N. C., 259, 263
Savannah, Ga., Siege of, 309
Schneider, Bro. Martin, travels, 259, *et seq.*, 273
Scotch-Irish element, 94, 271, 276
Scott, John, 217, 245, 246
Seaboard, people of on Westerners, 139n.
Seal of State, 59
Second Cession, see *Cession*
Seehorn, John, 199
Separation, see *New States*
Servant class, 277
Sevier County, F., 59, 161, 228, 276, 324
Sevier's Island, 262
Sevier, Ambrose H., 280, 281
Sevier, Rev. E. F., 281
Sevier, James, 199, 202, 240
Sevier, Gov. John, sketch, 289; on Campbell expedition, 9; in Great Bend Scheme, 15; in N. C. Provincial Congress, 29, 157; first F. Convention, 30; brigadier-general, 38; F. Constitutional Convention, 39; on repeal of Cession act, 41, 56; from Martin, 43; elected governor, 57; county named for, 59; from Gov. Martin, 62; reply, 65; defeat reported, 67; to Gov. Caswell, 73; Indian treaty, 77, 89; first

message, 90; denominational dispute, 97; to Gov. Telfair, 106; fight with Tipton, 109; Green's letter, 127, 130; resentment of Tipton, 135; to E. Shelby, 135; visited by Indian delegation, 141; Conference with Shelby, 142; changes to boldness, 145; speech in F. Convention, 151, 156; to Shelby, 159; to Kennedy, 161; stands for N. C. legislature, 162; rumor of arrest, 163; correspondence with B. Franklin, 165, *et seq.*; on aid to Cumberland, 173; and Georgia, 177, *et seq.*; to Mathews, 180; continues efforts in behalf F., 190; from Telfair, 190; calls for volunteers against Creeks, 191; distraught, 197; battle at Tipton's, 198; as president of Greeneville council to Tipton, 205: to Martin, 207–08; to governor of Ga., 209; headquarters at Greeneville, 210; goes against Cherokees, 211, 214; *et seq.*; in French Broad Country, 219, *et seq.*; last battle under F., 223; efforts behalf people of French Broad, 229, *et seq.*; arrest of, 231, *et seq.*; to N. C. assembly, 233; oath of allegiance to N. C., 230; Spanish intrigue, 235, *et seq.*; on navigation of Mississippi, 241; on federal constitution, 245, *et seq.*; provision excluding from office, 246, *et seq.*; no longer an outlaw, 248; elected N. C. senator, 249; in convention votes ratification U. S. Constitution, 250; for Cession act, 250; favored by N. C., 253, *et seq.*; first member Congress, 253; first governor of Tennessee, 254; mode of warfare adopted by Forrest, 257; Chickamaugas visit, 259; Chickasaws visit, 264; mentioned, 311, 316, 327, 357

Sevier, Geo. W., 204
Sevier, John, Jr., 202, 203, 232, 311
Sevier, John, nephew, 203, 311
Sevier, Joseph, 232
Sevier, Valentine, Sr., 289
Sevier, Valentine, Jr., 16, 17, 39, 59, 289; sketch, 326

Sevier-Tipton Skirmish, 198, *et seq.*, 237, 267
Seymour Sta., 228
Shaler, N. S., quoted, 163
Sharkey, Wm. L., 280
Sharpe, John, 245
Shelby, Anthony Bledsoe, 280
Shelby, D. D., 280
Shelby, Evan, sketch, 330, 72, 134, 135, 137; conference of S. and, 138; sends call for aid, 142; attitude of F., communicated to, 159; elected governor of F., 164; S. to, 164; resigns as brigadier and recommends S., 164, 206, 241; N. C.'s treatment of, 253, 260; mention of, 289, 290
Shelby, Isaac, 21, 165, 280
Shelby, J. O., 281
Shelby, Wm. R., 281
Sherrill, Kate, married to S., 290
Skirmish at Tiptons, 198, *et seq.*
Slavery, see Cession acts perpetuating, 25, 277, 286
Slim Tom, 212
Smith, Anderson, 108
Smith, Gen. Daniel, 242
Smith, James, Sr. and Jr., 260, 356
Smith, John, 203
Smith, Samuel, 142
Smith, Samuel A., 280
Smith, Wm., 232n.
Snodgrass, C. E., 280
Snodgrass, D. L., 280
Snodgrass, H. C., 280
Southwest Territory, 253, 276; population by counties, 276
Spaight, R. D., 85, 183
Spain, 17, 21, 123, 126, 138, 171, 179, 193, 235, *et seq.*
Spanish Intrigue, 235, *et seq.*
Speech of Sevier, only one preserved, 151, 156
Spencer County, F., 59, 205
Springston, trader, 263
St. John, James P., place of, 202
Standifer, James, 280
"State of Appalachia," 287

INDEX

Statehood, first movement for, 5; granted to Tennessee, 254
Stewart, James, see *Stuart*
Stewart, Alex. P., 281
Stewart, Thomas, 39, 91, 214
Stone, Archibald, 30
Stone, Wm., 280
Strain, John, 96, 136
Strawberry Plains, name, 256
Stuart, James, sketch, 337, 96, 107, 115, 133, 195, 245, 246
Sugar-making, 255, 266
Sullivan County, 61, 144, 162, 213
Sullivan, John, letter against Spain, 138, 237
Swift, Rev. Richard, 273

TALBOT, THOMAS, 39, 41, 57, 65, 83, 347
Talbot, Matthew, 280
Tallahassee Town, 211
Tassel, Chief, 79, 212
Tate, Samuel, 281
Tatham, William, 196
Taverns and rates, 258
Taylor, Alfred A., 280, 327
Taylor, Andrew, sketch, 327, 39
Taylor, Christopher, 30, 39, 61, 199n.
Taylor, Isaac, 114, 327, 355
Taylor, Nathaniel, 280, 281, 327
Taylor, N. G., 327
Taylor, Robt. L., 280, 327
Telfair, Gov. E., 106; S. to, 111; Elholm to, 112, 114, 177, 190
Tennessee, State of, comes into existence, 254; issue with N. C. over lands in West, 251; S. first governor, 254; solution of F. problems, 254; as independent state, 284; secession of, 287; intense democracy, 288; spirit that of F., 287, *et seq.*
Tennessee river, see *Great Bend*, Valley of, 20n., 33, 90, 138; French and Spaniards on, 171, 265
Territory S. of O., see *Southwest Territory*
Thornburg, J. M., 280
Thomas, Isaac, 280
Tipton, Jacob, 281
Tipton, Jonathan, Jr., 203
Tipton, Col. John, sketch, 334; 39; Gov. Martin to, 72; reply, 72; 94, 96; leads dissenters, 107, 109; fight with S., 110; seeks to punish Jonesborough, 119; presses issue, 136, 137, 154; effigy of burned, 137; raid into Spencer County, 163; denied seat in No. Car. Assembly, 163; on pay of Evans battalion, 174; senate of N. C., denied seat, 195; battle at house of, 198, *et seq.*; arrests S., 231, *et seq.*; Kennedy to, 234; in N. C. Convention, 245; assembly, 246; altercations with Amis and Roddy, 246; would bold F. territory in N. C., 247; isolation of, 247; in territorial government, 253
Tipton, John, of Indiana, 280
Tipton, Joseph, 39, 96, 245
Toboka, Choctaw Chief, 141
Totten, A. O. W., 280
Tracey, Micajah, 266
Trans-Alleghania, 125
Transportation, 258
Transylvania, founding aided by Wataugans, 2, 293, 332
Traveling, 258, 259, *et seq.*; see *Asbury, Schneider and Ware*
Treaty, see *Dumplin creek, Coyatee and Hopewell*
Trimble, John, 280
Trimble, Wm., 30, 41
Tunnel, John, 266
Turner, F. J., quoted, 11, 48, 66, 271
Turner, F. M., corrected, 248
Turney, Hopkins, L., 280, 328
Turney, Peter, sketch, 328; 162, 280
Turney, Gov. Peter, 162, 328
Tusculum College, 317

UNION, GOVERNMENT OF THE, see *Congress and Constitution*
University of Tennessee, see *Blount College*, 312, 325

VERGENNES, 125
Vermont, separation of, 87, 121, 129; intrigue in, 235

Village, principal, 258
Vincent, George, sketch, 328, 39, 216
Vincent, Thos., 217
Vincent, Wm. D., 281
Virginia, attitude on West, 27, genesis of F., 5; element in F., 28; F. movement in, 45; memorial to Congress, 46; Southwestern Counties, 49; S. on, 51; Henry to legislature, 52; opposes F. in Congress, 84; suppresses separation movement, 53, *et seq.*; P. Henry, advocated New State, 89
Virginian element in F., 28, 275

WAKHOVEE, 217
Wallace, Wm., 30
Ward, Benjamin, 119
Ward, John, 96
Ward, Nancy, 217
Ware, Rev. Thomas, quoted, 199; travels in F., 265, 273
Warfare, how waged, 257
Washington College (Tenn.), 58, 308, 317
Washington County, *passim*
Washington district of F., 140
Washington, George, favored new States, 88; on the Mississippi river, 123; on separation, 186
Watauga Association, 1, 29, 226
Watauga Fort, see *Fort Caswell*
Watauga Settlement, volunteers in Dunmore's War; 1; aids founding Transylvania, 2; at siege of Charleston, 1776, 2; petitions N. C., 2, 157; loses people to Cumberland, 13; both gain in population, 13; efforts of Great Britain to seduce, 157; slavery in, 277
Watts, John, chief, 213, 233
Wayne, Gen. Anthony, county named for, 60
Wayne County, F., 60
Wear, Hugh, 230
Wear, John, 136
Wear, Samuel, sketch, 328, 30, 39, 61, 102; in debate, 150, 356
Webb, Moses, 217
Webster, Daniel, on F., currency, 220, *et seq.*

Weir, see *Wear*
Welsh element in F., 276
West, control of, 1; Jefferson on, 3; by N. C., 10, 19; movement for separation, 27; Washington on, 28; Jefferson on, 28; feeling between East and West, 128; unrest in, 139; in constitutional convention of 1787, 183; equities of, 187; Spain and, 236, *et seq.*; Gov. Clinton on 244; Hamilton on, 244
"West Carolina," name proposed, 38
Western Country of N. C., Washington district formed, 38; conditions in, 63; manifesto to people of, 67; N. C. holds to, 119, 120; and the Mississippi, 123; Great Britain, 128; subdued by Franks, 157; won by Westerners, 187
West Tennessee, 21, *et seq.*, 34, 36, 196, 284, *et seq.*; proposes separation, 285; "Jacksoniana," 285
West Virginia, example, 287
White's Fort (Knoxville), 216
White, Col. James, sketch, 301, 24; Speaker, 90, 96; on D. Campbell, 197, 221; brigadier-general, 302
White, Dr. James, 235
White, Hugh Lawson, on F., 221, 280, 303
White, Richard, 107, 115, 133
White, Robert, 119
Wilkinson, James, 243
Williams, Edmond, 136
Williams, Edward, 119
Williams, James, 280
Williams, Samuel, 30, 108
Williamson, Hugh, 19, 35, 36, 85, 137, 183, *et seq.*, quoted, 256
Wills, Rev. Henry, 273
Wilson, James, 3, 39, 41, 245
Wilson, Samuel, 30
Women, 266, 277, 278
Wood, Capt. John, 161, 142, 166
Wyer, see *Wear*

YANCEY, AMBROSE, 198
Young, Robert, Jr., 204

ZAHAUN, see *Seehorn*

www.ingramcontent.com/pod-product-compliance
Lightning Source LLC
Chambersburg PA
CBHW051625230426
43669CB00013B/2181